2017 SQA Past Papers with Answers

Higher
HISTORY

2015, 2016 & 2017 Exams

HODDER
GIBSON
AN HACHETTE UK COMPANY

This book contains the official SQA 2015, 2016 and 2017 Exams for Higher History, with associated SQA-approved answers modified from the official marking instructions that accompany the paper.

In addition the book contains study skills advice. This advice has been specially commissioned by Hodder Gibson, and has been written by experienced senior teachers and examiners in line with the Higher for CfE syllabus and assessment outlines. This is not SQA material but has been devised to provide further guidance for Higher examinations.

Hodder Gibson is grateful to the copyright holders, as credited on the final page of the Answer section, for permission to use their material. Every effort has been made to trace the copyright holders and to obtain their permission for the use of copyright material. Hodder Gibson will be happy to receive information allowing us to rectify any error or omission in future editions.

Hachette UK's policy is to use papers that are natural, renewable and recyclable products and made from wood grown in sustainable forests. The logging and manufacturing processes are expected to conform to the environmental regulations of the country of origin.

Orders: please contact Bookpoint Ltd, 130 Park Drive, Milton Park, Abingdon, Oxon OX14 4SE. Telephone: (44) 01235 827720. Fax: (44) 01235 400454. Lines are open 9.00–5.00, Monday to Saturday, with a 24-hour message answering service. Visit our website at www.hoddereducation.co.uk. Hodder Gibson can be contacted direct on: Tel: 0141 333 4650; Fax: 0141 404 8188; email: hoddergibson@hodder.co.uk

This collection first published in 2017 by
Hodder Gibson, an imprint of Hodder Education,
An Hachette UK Company
211 St Vincent Street
Glasgow G2 5QY

Typeset by Aptara, Inc.

Printed in the UK

A catalogue record for this title is available from the British Library

ISBN: 978-1-5104-2151-6

2 1

2018 2017

Introduction

Study Skills – what you need to know to pass exams!

Pause for thought

Many students might skip quickly through a page like this. After all, we all know how to revise. Do you really though?

Think about this:

"IF YOU ALWAYS DO WHAT YOU ALWAYS DO, YOU WILL ALWAYS GET WHAT YOU HAVE ALWAYS GOT."

Do you like the grades you get? Do you want to do better? If you get full marks in your assessment, then that's great! Change nothing! This section is just to help you get that little bit better than you already are.

There are two main parts to the advice on offer here. The first part highlights fairly obvious things but which are also very important. The second part makes suggestions about revision that you might not have thought about but which WILL help you.

Part 1

DOH! It's so obvious but …

Start revising in good time

Don't leave it until the last minute – this will make you panic.

Make a revision timetable that sets out work time AND play time.

Sleep and eat!

Obvious really, and very helpful. Avoid arguments or stressful things too – even games that wind you up. You need to be fit, awake and focused!

Know your place!

Make sure you know exactly **WHEN and WHERE** your exams are.

Know your enemy!

Make sure you know what to expect in the exam.

How is the paper structured?

How much time is there for each question?

What types of question are involved?

Which topics seem to come up time and time again?

Which topics are your strongest and which are your weakest?

Are all topics compulsory or are there choices?

Learn by DOING!

There is no substitute for past papers and practice papers – they are simply essential! Tackling this collection of papers and answers is exactly the right thing to be doing as your exams approach.

Part 2

People learn in different ways. Some like low light, some bright. Some like early morning, some like evening / night. Some prefer warm, some prefer cold. But everyone uses their BRAIN and the brain works when it is active. Passive learning – sitting gazing at notes – is the most INEFFICIENT way to learn anything. Below you will find tips and ideas for making your revision more effective and maybe even more enjoyable. What follows gets your brain active, and active learning works!

Activity 1 – Stop and review

Step 1

When you have done no more than 5 minutes of revision reading STOP!

Step 2

Write a heading in your own words which sums up the topic you have been revising.

Step 3

Write a summary of what you have revised in no more than two sentences. Don't fool yourself by saying, "I know it, but I cannot put it into words". That just means you don't know it well enough. If you cannot write your summary, revise that section again, knowing that you must write a summary at the end of it. Many of you will have notebooks full of blue/black ink writing. Many of the pages will not be especially attractive or memorable so try to liven them up a bit with colour as you are reviewing and rewriting. **This is a great memory aid, and memory is the most important thing.**

Activity 2 – Use technology!

Why should everything be written down? Have you thought about "mental" maps, diagrams, cartoons and colour to help you learn? And rather than write down notes, why not record your revision material?

What about having a text message revision session with friends? Keep in touch with them to find out how and what they are revising and share ideas and questions.

Why not make a video diary where you tell the camera what you are doing, what you think you have learned and what you still have to do? No one has to see or hear it, but the process of having to organise your thoughts in a formal way to explain something is a very important learning practice.

Be sure to make use of electronic files. You could begin to summarise your class notes. Your typing might be slow, but it will get faster and the typed notes will be easier to read than the scribbles in your class notes. Try to add different fonts and colours to make your work stand out. You can easily Google relevant pictures, cartoons and diagrams which you can copy and paste to make your work more attractive and **MEMORABLE**.

Activity 3 – This is it. Do this and you will know lots!

Step 1

In this task you must be very honest with yourself! Find the SQA syllabus for your subject (www.sqa.org.uk). Look at how it is broken down into main topics called MANDATORY knowledge. That means stuff you MUST know.

Step 2

BEFORE you do ANY revision on this topic, write a list of everything that you already know about the subject. It might be quite a long list but you only need to write it once. It shows you all the information that is already in your long-term memory so you know what parts you do not need to revise!

Step 3

Pick a chapter or section from your book or revision notes. Choose a fairly large section or a whole chapter to get the most out of this activity.

With a buddy, use Skype, Facetime, Twitter or any other communication you have, to play the game "If this is the answer, what is the question?". For example, if you are revising Geography and the answer you provide is "meander", your buddy would have to make up a question like "What is the word that describes a feature of a river where it flows slowly and bends often from side to side?".

Make up 10 "answers" based on the content of the chapter or section you are using. Give this to your buddy to solve while you solve theirs.

Step 4

Construct a wordsearch of at least 10 × 10 squares. You can make it as big as you like but keep it realistic. Work together with a group of friends. Many apps allow you to make wordsearch puzzles online. The words and phrases can go in any direction and phrases can be split. Your puzzle must only contain facts linked to the topic you are revising. Your task is to find 10 bits of information to hide in your puzzle, but you must not repeat information that you used in Step 3. DO NOT show where the words are. Fill up empty squares with random letters. Remember to keep a note of where your answers are hidden but do not show your friends. When you have a complete puzzle, exchange it with a friend to solve each other's puzzle.

Step 5

Now make up 10 questions (not "answers" this time) based on the same chapter used in the previous two tasks. Again, you must find NEW information that you have not yet used. Now it's getting hard to find that new information! Again, give your questions to a friend to answer.

Step 6

As you have been doing the puzzles, your brain has been actively searching for new information. Now write a NEW LIST that contains only the new information you have discovered when doing the puzzles. Your new list is the one to look at repeatedly for short bursts over the next few days. Try to remember more and more of it without looking at it. After a few days, you should be able to add words from your second list to your first list as you increase the information in your long-term memory.

FINALLY! Be inspired...

Make a list of different revision ideas and beside each one write **THINGS I HAVE** tried, **THINGS I WILL** try and **THINGS I MIGHT** try. Don't be scared of trying something new.

And remember – "FAIL TO PREPARE AND PREPARE TO FAIL!"

Higher History

The course

The Higher History course gives you the opportunity to study the subject in a variety of time periods and places. You will be given an understanding of one important part of Scottish history as well as British and European and World history. You will gain skills in understanding of key historical areas as well as being able to structure writing, support argument with knowledge, analyse presented information and draw conclusions based on presented and recalled information. You will also learn how to research and present your findings.

How the course is graded

The grade you are finally awarded for Higher History depends on three things:

- The unit assessments you do in school or college – these don't count towards the final grade, but you must have passed them before you can achieve a final grade.
- Your Assignment – this is an independent piece of research carried out by you on a question you agree with your teacher/lecturer. You will complete the assignment in a 90-minute supervised write-up. It is then submitted in April for marking by the SQA, is marked out of 30, and counts for 33% of your overall grade.
- The exam you sit in May or June is marked out of 60 and counts for 66% of your overall grade – that's what this book is all about!

The exam

The Higher History examination is 2 hours and 20 minutes long. The examination paper is divided up into three sections. Each section is about a different area of history. Section 1 is about Scottish History, Section 2 is about British History and Section 3 is about European and World History. Each section is worth 20 marks giving an overall mark out of 60.

Section 1 – Scottish History

Section 1 is about a period of Scottish History. You will have a choice from five periods of Scottish History. You only have to study one and your learning centre will have chosen which topic you will study.

The exam paper is based around four sources. These sources will be a variety of primary and secondary sources. You will have to answer three questions about these sources.

- There is one question that tests your ability to evaluate a primary source. This question is worth 6 marks.
- There is one question that tests your ability to compare two sources. This question is worth 5 marks.
- There is one question that tests your ability to contextualise the presented source information. This question is worth 9 marks.

In total, this section of the paper is worth 20 marks.

Source analysis

Section 1 of your Higher History exam is based entirely on source analysis and will be divided into five topics. You must answer one Scottish topic in this section of the exam. Make sure you select the topic you have been taught in school and therefore know. You must answer all of the questions set on the topic you have studied. There are three things you must do to succeed.

1. You must do what you are asked to do with each question.
2. You must use some of the information contained in the sources.
3. You must also include your own relevant recalled information when asked to do so.

You get a mark for each specific point you make. For the *"evaluate the usefulness"* and *"how fully"* questions, a point means a piece of information from the source OR from recalled information *that has been used relevantly* when answering the question. For the comparison question, a point means that an individual point of similarity or difference has been identified, explained and backed up by using the content of the source.

There are no marks for just copying out sections of the presented source or sources.

WATCH YOUR TIME

With this section it is important to keep an eye on time. You will need to build in reading time and thinking time before you start to write. It is also important to look at the number of marks that are on offer. The *"evaluate the usefulness"* question is worth six marks and *"comparison"* question is worth five marks. The *"how fully"* question is worth nine marks. You also need to think about the essays that you are going to have to complete after you do this section. This part of the exam should take no more than one hour to complete. This then leaves you with 40 minutes for each of the essays.

The "evaluate the usefulness" question

This question asks you to judge a primary source. It will ask you to *"Evaluate the usefulness of Source X in describing/explaining/illustrating a historical event/ development."* You are given instructions to use the source's origin, purpose and content as well as relevant recall that has not been mentioned in the presented source.

Four marks are available for evaluations that make use of who the author was, the type of source, its purpose and when it was written as part of your judgement.

Two marks are available for relevant evaluations of the source content.

Two marks are available for identifying information that has been missed out but would have made the source more reliable. Remember, you only need to make six points to gain full marks.

The biggest problem with this sort of question is when people do not read the question carefully. As a result, the source is simply described when what the marker is looking for is some link with the 'usefulness' of the source in answering the question. So the trick is to identify information that is relevant to the answer and then comment on it. You need to do both things to be sure of the mark.

The "comparison" question

This question will ask you to compare two sources. It will ask you to, *"Compare the views of Sources X and Y about an event/issue, etc"*. You are given instructions to comment on the sources overall and then in detail.

The two sources contain four different points that agree or disagree with each other. You have to identify the area they agree or disagree about and then illustrate this difference by selecting relevant phrases from the sources that show this. The overall comparison refers to the general areas of agreement and disagreement that are mentioned and explained in your answer. You do not need specific detail from the sources to make an overall comparison, but you do need to mention in general

ways what the two sources are about and in what ways they agree or disagree.

Each individual point of comparison gains one mark and the overall comparison gains up to two marks. A single comparison is when the area of similarity or difference is mentioned and then illustrated using relevant compared content from the two sources. Overall comparison marks are awarded when the specific areas of similarity/ difference are summarised.

The biggest problem with this sort of question is when people make what are known as "ghost comparisons". You will get NO MARKS for "ghost comparisons". In other words, no marks for writing *"Source B says … but Source C makes no mention of this"*.

The "how fully" question

This question tests your knowledge on one specific area of mandatory content listed as part of the course. You can see what these areas are in the Higher History Course support notes.

The question will be worded as follows, *"How fully does Source X describe/explain/illustrate a historical event/ development"*. The source will contain four points that are relevant to the question asked and three marks are available for finding three of those points, then explaining what these points mean in your own words and why the point is relevant to the question. You then need to include information not covered in the source, but would help give a fuller understanding of the issue in the question. This part of the question is worth up to seven marks.

The biggest problem with this sort of question is, again, people not reading the question carefully then writing irrelevant information in their answer. You will get no marks for just listing factual information even if it is "correct" information. You will need at least six relevant points of recalled information if you want to get full marks. Like the evaluation question, you need to identify relevant information then link it to the question with relevant comment. This shows that you have interpreted the information rather than just copied it.

Section 2 and 3 – British History and European and World History

Sections 2 and 3 are assessed by extended responses, often referred to as essays. These extended responses are worth 20 marks each.

In the British section, there are five periods of history to choose from. You only have to study one of them and your learning centre will have chosen which topic you will study. You only have to write ONE EXTENDED RESPONSE from a choice of three questions in the British section.

In the European and World section, there are nine topics to choose from. You only have to study one topic, but some learning centres choose to teach more than that.

You only have to write ONE EXTENDED RESPONSE from a choice of three questions. If you have studied more than one topic, you still only write one extended response but from a wider choice of questions.

The SQA gives detailed advice on the course content in their Higher History Course Support Notes: http://www.sqa.org.uk/files_ccc/CfE_CourseUnitSupportNotes_Higher_SocialStudies_History.pdf

Extended responses

The SQA uses the term 'extended responses' rather than essays but this book will use the word 'essays' because that is the word most teachers and learners use. To be successful you must:

- **structure** your answer correctly
- **use relevant knowledge** in your answer
- **analyse and evaluate** this information in order to answer the question effectively.

Structure – the introduction

The introduction is awarded up to two marks. To ensure you get two marks you need to do three things.

1. Your introduction must include context. That means you must set the scene by describing the "back story" of the question. In a couple of sentences, describe the historical situation that the question is based on.

2. You need to give a line of argument. Now, this will depend upon the question asked. The easiest way to do this is to use the words of the question directly in the argument. So, if a question asks, *"How important were the reports of Booth and Rowntree in causing the Liberal reforms of 1906–14?"*, a relevant line of argument might be, *"the reports of Booth and Rowntree were important to an extent in causing the Liberal reforms of 1904–14, but they were not the only reason"*. This is a basic line of argument.

3. You will also need to identify the main headings or factors that you are going to explain in the main body of your essay. These can be done in a list or, more effectively, treated separately. This shows that you understand the topic and are showing the marker what you are going to develop as part of your answer.

A good introduction is well worth taking time over. It shows the direction that the essay is going to take and will help settle you and give you confidence before you develop the main part of the essay. It will also give you a guide to refer back to if you get half way through the essay and wonder what comes next.

Structure – the conclusion

The conclusion is worth up to two marks. In order to gain two marks you will need to do the following three things.

1. Your conclusion must be based on the information you have mentioned in the main part of the essay. Do not introduce new information in the conclusion.

2. In the conclusion, you summarise the arguments that you have created in the main part of your essay. This should show balance which means you should try to look at both sides of the argument – for example, how much the idea in the question was responsible for something and how far other things were responsible.

3. You then need to come to an overall judgement which directly answers the main question. The last sentence must refer back to the specific question asked as well as provide a judgement on that question if you are to get a good mark.

Knowledge

There are six marks given for the use of accurate and relevant knowledge in the main part of the essay. Your knowledge has to be relevant to the question asked and you must USE the information to help answer the question. For example, if a question asked how democratic Britain was by 1918, relevant knowledge on the franchise would be to say that by 1918 women aged over 30 who were graduates or married to a householder had gained the vote in national elections, but women under this age could not vote.

Reading the question carefully is important here as irrelevant information is not awarded any marks. Good essays will contain much more than six marks of accurate and relevant knowledge because detailed knowledge is essential for success in developing analysis and evaluation.

Analysis and evaluation

In total, there are ten marks for analysis and evaluation and there are three different things to do to build up your marks.

1. Basic analysis

    You will get a mark each time you make a simple comment that makes a basic judgement about your information. In a question about the reasons why unification was achieved in Germany, a comment may be made such as *"The Zollverein was very important to German unification because it made people realise the advantages of states joining together"*. You have mentioned the Zollverein, which is knowledge, and you have made a simple judgement about its importance. Make this sort of comment four times in your essay and you will get four marks.

2. Getting more marks

    If you can develop your simple comment a bit more to link it to the factor you are writing about, then that is worth an extra mark. For example, in a question about the Liberal reforms, a simple comment about old-age pensions would be, *"Old-age pensions were an attempt to help people too old to work. It shows how the Liberals tried to help people who were poor through no fault of their own"*. To develop it further you must link to the factor you are writing about – in this case the factor is helping the old. Here is how you could do it – *"In fact the pensions were below the poverty line created by Rowntree and only given to people of good character aged over 70, therefore, the Liberals only partly eased the problem of poverty in old age"*. If you make that sort of developed comment twice, that will gain you an extra two marks.

3. Evaluation

    There are up to four marks awarded for the way in which you evaluate the knowledge to answer the question posed. Evaluation is where you make judgements on the factors that are relevant when answering an essay question.

    For example, for an essay on the unification of Germany, a number of factors will be looked at, including the development of nationalism, the rise of Prussian economic and military power, the weakness of Austria and the role of Bismarck.

Each factor can be evaluated by saying that it is important in some way. Better answers may put in some judgement as to the relative importance of a factor and even try to link them with each other. For example, *"without the growth of nationalist feeling that Germans should live together, Bismarck's job would have been much harder to complete"*. This is evaluation.

Beware!

The biggest problem with essay writing happens when people write descriptive essays or try to repeat an essay they did well in class. You must react to the wording of the question asked. The quality of evaluation and analysis is what makes an essay. If this is carefully linked to the question asked, then the mark will be good.

Timing again

It is very important to keep an eye on time in the examination. You should aim to have at least 40 minutes put aside to answer each essay. You are expected to do a lot in these 40 minutes. It is far better to write two essays of the same length rather than one long essay and one short essay. Two consistent essays will always score more marks than one good and one poor essay.

Good luck!

In the exam, THINK before you put pen to paper. You will have worked hard to get to this stage. Don't panic! Keep calm, read the questions carefully and decide what the question wants you to do. Then just follow the process described above.

HIGHER

2015

**National
Qualifications
2015**

X737/76/11

History

FRIDAY, 1 MAY
1:00 PM – 3:20 PM

Total marks — 60

SECTION 1 — SCOTTISH — 20 marks

Attempt ONE Part

SECTION 2 — BRITISH — 20 marks

Attempt ONE question from the Part you have chosen

SECTION 3 — EUROPEAN AND WORLD — 20 marks

Attempt ONE question from the Part you have chosen

Write your answers clearly in the answer booklet provided. In the answer booklet you must clearly identify the question number you are attempting.

Use **blue** or **black** ink.

Before leaving the examination room you must give your answer booklet to the Invigilator; if you do not, you may lose all the marks for this paper.

[BLANK PAGE]

DO NOT WRITE ON THIS PAGE

SECTION 1 — SCOTTISH

Attempt ONE Part

PARTS

SECTION 2 — BRITISH

Attempt one question from the Part you have chosen

PARTS

SECTION 3 — EUROPEAN AND WORLD

Attempt one question from the Part you have chosen

PARTS

SECTION 1 — SCOTTISH — 20 marks

Part A — The Wars of Independence, 1249–1328

Study the sources below and attempt the questions which follow.

Source A: from Michael Brown, *The Wars of Scotland 1214–1371* (2004)

> In March 1286 Scotland's leaders gathered for the funeral of Alexander III. There would be no crowning of a new king to balance the burial of the old. Alexander III's sudden death had brought the male line of the royal dynasty to an end. A measure of the problems now facing the Scottish leaders was the desire for "advice and protection" from Edward I, which would later lead to demands for recognition of Edward's authority over the Scottish realm. Six Guardians were appointed in response to the vital need to carry on the day-to-day running of the government in the absence of a royal leader. The belief that the queen, Yolande of Dreux, was carrying the dead king's child turned out to be mistaken. The young child Margaret of Norway was now the only descendant of King Alexander III.

Source B: from Fiona Watson, *Under the Hammer* (1998)

> John Balliol was enthroned at Scone on St Andrew's Day, 1292. Within another month King John had sworn homage for the kingdom of Scotland for a second time. However, it would be foolish to ignore the fact that John's reign was overshadowed by Edward I's determination, right from the start, to enforce the widest possible interpretation of his rights as overlord of Scotland. English influence was noticeable at a number of levels. King John was left in no doubt that he personally could, and would, be called to answer for the actions of the Scottish courts, in the presence of Edward I and the English parliament. For example, only one week after King John's enthronement, Edward I had heard a court appeal on behalf of a Scottish merchant, Roger Bartholomew who complained against a decision taken by the Scottish courts.

Source C: from Michael Prestwich, *Edward I* (1988)

> Any doubts about John Balliol's position must have been resolved on 26 December 1292 when King John did homage to the King of England which clearly recognised Edward I's overlordship of the realm of Scotland. Edward I was not however content with a mere recognition of his overlordship: he was determined to exercise his authority to the full. It was the question of appeals to Edward I's court that was the first test of Edward I's strength and King John's weakness. Edward I made it clear that he intended to hear any appeal cases brought to him as overlord of Scotland, when and where he chose. Furthermore, if need be, Edward I would even summon King John to appear before him in England to answer legal claims and complaints in person.

MARKS

SECTION 1 — SCOTTISH (continued)

Source D: from The Chronicle of Lanercost, August 1314

> In August 1314, Edward Bruce, James Douglas, John Soules and other nobles of Scotland, under the authority of Robert Bruce, invaded England by way of Berwick with cavalry and a large army. They devastated almost all Northumberland with fire and they burned the towns of Brough, Appelby and Kirkoswald in Cumberland and other towns here and there on their route through Durham and into Yorkshire as far south as Richmond. But the people of Coupland, fearing their return and invasion, sent messengers and paid much money to the Scottish King to escape being burned by them in the same way as they had destroyed other towns. Passing near the priory of Lanercost, the Scottish forces then re-entered Scotland.

Attempt all of the following questions.

1. How fully does **Source A** describe the succession problem in Scotland 1286—1296?   9

    Use the source and your own knowledge.

2. Compare the views of **Sources B** and **C** about the relationship between John Balliol and Edward I.   5

    Compare the sources overall and in detail.

3. Evaluate the usefulness of **Source D** as evidence of the reasons for the ultimate success of Robert Bruce in maintaining Scotland's independence.   6

    In making a judgement you should refer to:
    - *the origin and possible purpose of the source*
    - *the content of the source*
    - *your own knowledge*

[Now go on to SECTION 2 starting on *Page fourteen*]

SECTION 1 — SCOTTISH — 20 marks

Part B — The Age of the Reformation, 1542–1603

Study the sources below and attempt the questions which follow.

Source A: from M. Lynch, *Scotland a New History* (1991)

The Reformation of 1560 was sparked off by a riot in Perth in which the town's Catholic religious houses were sacked. By July groups of nobles, lairds and burgesses, which made up a cross-section of society, had attacked a series of towns in central Scotland, including St Andrews and Dundee, and had entered Edinburgh.

After returning to the capital from France and Geneva, Knox was installed as its first Protestant minister on the seventh of the month. There had been a change of Regent in October 1559 and a provisional government had also been established. This pleased Knox and his followers as they were unhappy with Mary of Guise's heavy taxation and her pro-French policies. Also pleasing was the support of England and the arrival of an English army in March 1560 which proved to be a decisive factor.

Source B: from T. Booher, *The life and impact of Scottish Reformer John Knox* (2012)

Mary Queen of Scots returned from France after her husband had died. She returned on the condition that she would not take part in the forbidden Catholic mass. She agreed not to, but went back on her word upon arrival attending mass at Holyrood Chapel. She also upset many of the Scots nobility by surrounding herself with French servants. However, it was events in her personal life that were to cause her the most harm. Most notable was her secret marriage to the Earl of Bothwell, who was suspected of murdering her previous husband Lord Darnley. This led to further distrust towards Mary. Knox had five meetings with Mary Queen of Scots, criticising her marriages. From this time on, Knox was able to teach and preach in relative safety, until his death in 1572.

Source C: from J.E.A. Dawson, *Scotland Re-formed 1488–1587* (2009)

On her return Mary's half-brother James Stewart, Earl of Moray, advised she settle into her natural place at the head of the kingdom without rocking the religious boat. Mary surrounding herself with French servants did not go down well with the Scottish nobility. Her choice of husbands also caused shock waves, particularly her marriage to Bothwell. She ignored advice and attended mass at Holyrood on her arrival, to many Protestants' disgust. Problems and distrust were also caused by many other errors of judgment. Such events did not go unnoticed by Knox who held five meetings with the queen to show his disapproval of the goings-on in her personal and public life.

MARKS

SECTION 1 — SCOTTISH (continued)

Source D: from the Second Book of Discipline (1578)

> We must have respect to the poor members of Jesus Christ's kingdom, who sadly multiply amongst us. The Kirk belongs to the poor as much as it does everyone else and our duty is to help them. We also call for the liberty of the election of persons called to the ministry to be in the hands of the congregation. As for the Kirk rents, we desire the order to be admitted and maintained with the sincerity of God's word and practice of the purity of the Kirk of Christ. Doctors will be appointed in universities, colleges, and schools to open up the meaning of the scriptures in every parish, and teach the basics of religion.

Attempt all of the following questions.

4. How fully does **Source A** explain the reasons for the Reformation of 1560?   **9**

    Use the source and your own knowledge.

5. Compare the views of **Sources B** and **C** about Mary's difficulties in ruling Scotland.   **5**

    Compare the sources overall and in detail.

6. Evaluate the usefulness of **Source D** as evidence of the impact of the Reformation on Scotland.   **6**

    In making a judgement you should refer to:
    *   *the origin and possible purpose of the source*
    *   *the content of the source*
    *   *your own knowledge*

[Now go on to Section 2 starting on *Page fourteen*]

MARKS

SECTION 1 — SCOTTISH — 20 marks

Part C — The Treaty of Union, 1689–1740

Study the sources below and attempt the questions which follow.

Source A: from The History Today Companion to British History (1995).

> The Darien Scheme was a plan for the foundation of a Scottish colony, to be called New Caledonia, on the Darien area of Panama, Central America. The colony was to be managed by the Company of Scotland, founded in 1695. The chief object was to promote Scottish trade. It was hoped that the colony might provide a market for Scottish goods. There was English political opposition because of the threat to the English-owned East India Company. English sabotage was blamed for underfunding and mismanagement of the scheme. King William was held responsible for encouraging Spanish opposition in Central America, which led to the scheme's failure. Anglo-Scottish relations were strained and this was shown by anti-English riots in Edinburgh.

Source B: from a pamphlet by Seton of Pitmedden, *Scotland's great advantages by a Union in England*, (1706).

> With union, England will secure its old and dangerous Scots enemy to be its friend, and this ensures peace for the English. Scotland will no longer be threatened by its powerful neighbour, nor conquered by foreign enemies. Our brave and courageous Scotsmen will join a British fleet and army and we will be secured by their protection. Our burgh merchants will take our manufactures to England and return with profits. English merchants will have free access to all our seas and ports and will have the same privileges as citizens of Scotland. We Scots will be the same among them, and can travel to plantations in the colonies with greater assurance than ever before. We will see our craftsmen's lives improve as a result of union. Our land will be better cultivated and manured.

Source C: from a speech by Lord Belhaven in Parliament, November 1706

> When I think about union, my mind is crowded with sad thoughts:
>
> I think I see a free kingdom losing power to manage its affairs. I think I see the royal burghs losing all the branches of their old commerce and trades in the face of English competition. I think I see our valiant and brave Scottish soldiers at home asking for a small pension, or left to beg, once their old regiments are broken, while young English soldiers form part of the standing British army. I think I see the honest industrious craftsman loaded with new taxes, drinking water instead of ale. I think I see the backbroken farmer, with his corn wasted upon his hands, because his land is worthless.
>
> Are these not very affecting thoughts?

MARKS

SECTION 1 — SCOTTISH (continued)

Source D: from a Jacobite leaflet, *The Miserable State of Scotland* (1723)

> Before the union we had to pay no taxes other than those raised by the Scots parliament, and these were not high, and were spent by the government in Scotland. Now we have not only a Land Tax, but a Salt Tax, Malt Tax, Window Tax, Leather Tax, a Candle Tax, a Soap Tax, a Starch Tax, and Paper Tax. In addition, our import custom duties are now set at English rates which are three times what we used to pay before union, and these have been set by parliament in London to be raised for the next 99 years! There are many reasons for bringing back the old Scots parliament whose incorporation into the English parliament the Scots were bullied and bribed into accepting.

Attempt all of the following questions.

7. How fully does **Source A** explain worsening relations between Scotland and England?   **9**
    Use the source and your own knowledge.

8. Compare the views of **Sources B** and **C** about attitudes towards union with England.   **5**
    Compare the sources overall and in detail.

9. Evaluate the usefulness of **Source D** as evidence of the effects of union to 1740.   **6**
    In making a judgement you should refer to:
    - *the origin and possible purpose of the source*
    - *the content of the source*
    - *your own knowledge*

[Now go on to Section 2 starting on *Page fourteen*]

SECTION 1 — SCOTTISH — 20 marks

Part D — Migration and Empire, 1830–1939

Study the sources below and attempt the questions which follow.

Source A: from James Hunter, *The Last of the Free* (1999)

> It is unarguable that following the collapse of the kelp trade landlords were looking for change. Many landlords were of the view, by the 1840s, that it could only be of benefit to them to rid their land and properties of people. They attempted to do this following the hardship of the famine period, perhaps the most far-reaching occurred on Barra, South Uist and Benbecula. Those islands belonged to John Gordon of Cluny. Gordon chartered a fleet of five ships in order to transport 1,700 people from his Hebridean properties to Canada. Similarly, other landlords contributed to the cost of fares to encourage families to emigrate. More than 16,000 people were helped to emigrate from the Highlands and Islands between 1847 and 1857.

Source B: from a speech by Mr R. Smillie, who was President of the Scottish Miners' Federation in May 1903.

> The Scottish Miners' Federation represents about 85–90% of miners in Scotland. Figures show that 1,320 aliens (foreign workers) are working underground in Lanarkshire out of a total employment figure of 31,000. Some of these aliens may never have seen a coalmine before their arrival in Scotland. The Federation has complained about the employment of aliens in the mines on the grounds of safety. Their lack of English language is a hazard to themselves and fellow workers. There has been action over the past months as many British miners are idle, while aliens are employed. Preference, it seems, has been given to the foreigner. There is also a widespread belief that the foreigners are being used to bring wages down. Although aliens in the mining industry are described as Poles about 90% are Lithuanian.

Source C: from Robert Duncan, *The Mineworkers* (2005)

> The Lithuanians first came to work in North Lanarkshire coalmines in the early 1890s. They were the focus of considerable concern largely because of their ignorance of coal mining. Until the early 1900s at least there is evidence that Lithuanian labour was used to cut wages. As one would expect, the expressed view of the mining employers was usually complimentary about the hardworking and reliable foreign workers. Contrary to the evidence from the miners' union, the employers were also adamant that the foreign workers did not present additional dangers to safety. They claimed adequate provision was made to instruct them in their duties, including translations of mining regulations into their own language. It is difficult to work out just what proportion of foreign mine workers were involved in accidents as many Lithuanians adopted Scots names so records are unclear.

MARKS

SECTION 1 — SCOTTISH (continued)

Source D: from a letter by a Scottish politician to the editor of *The Scotsman* newspaper on 4th July 1938.

> Dear Sir — The upcoming Empire Exhibition will be a welcome opportunity to showcase the industrial might of Glasgow and the west of Scotland created by the Empire. A meeting of the Empire Development Conference is to be held during the exhibition. The intention of the meeting is to encourage emigration from Britain "to populate the empty spaces of the Empire". Many Scots feel that renewed emigration would be entirely contrary to Scotland's interests. The primary need for Scotland is reconstruction at home so that Scotland's "empty spaces" can be populated once more. It is more than time that a firm check was put on the drain from Scotland of her best types. For far too long Scotland's best have been drawn away by the opportunities that the Empire has presented.

Attempt all of the following questions.

10. How fully does **Source A** explain the reasons for Scottish migration?

    Use the source and your own knowledge.

    9

11. Compare the views of **Sources B** and **C** about the reactions of Scots to immigrants.

    Compare the sources overall and in detail.

    5

12. Evaluate the usefulness of **Source D** as evidence of the impact which the Empire had on Scotland.

    In making a judgement you should refer to:
    - *the origin and possible purpose of the source*
    - *the content of the source*
    - *your own knowledge*

    6

[Now go on to Section 2 starting on *Page fourteen*]

SECTION 1 — SCOTTISH — 20 marks

Part E — The Impact of the Great War, 1914–1928

Study the sources below and attempt the questions which follow.

Source A: from a letter by Private Howard, a soldier in the 7th Cameron Highlanders.

> On the morning of the 25th we had given the Germans gas but it came back on us. I got a dose but it didn't knock me out. On we went. German shells were falling amongst us and time and time again I was knocked off my feet but I wasn't struck. A pal of mine, a fellow Cameron Highlander from Paisley, was lying alongside me when he gave a groan. He pointed to his left arm. I cut off his tunic and shirt sleeves. A bullet had got him on the arm and blood gulped out and the smell of it was sickening. I got out my field dressing to help him but before I had finished I was drenched in his blood. My pal I am glad to say managed alright.

Source B: from T. Royle, *The Flowers of the Forest: Scotland and the First World War* (2006).

> In the streets women carried placards stating: "We are fighting the Prussians in Partick". Unusually, the strikers were supported by their employers who did not want productivity slowed down by factors outside their control. Matters came to a head when a mass meeting was held in Glasgow's George Square on 17 November to protest against the prosecution of 18 tenants due to appear in court for refusing to pay rent increases. By then the rent strikes had escalated, with men taking their own wildcat strike action at Fairfield's and Beardmore's. Rebellion was in the air but the strikes ended the following month when the government rushed through the Rent Restriction Act. It was a victory for what would later be known as "people power".

Source C: from a pamphlet by Councillor A. McBride of the Glasgow Labour Party Housing Association (1921).

> Our committee organised demonstrations with banners demanding the Government to take action. We informed the Secretary for Scotland Mr McKinnon-Wood that the people desired that the rents should not be increased above the pre-war standard. Rents were still soaring and events were rapidly approaching a crisis. With the summoning of a number of munitions workers to attend court the most dramatic incident of the struggle happened. Men engaged in work on the Clyde stopped working and marched in their thousands with those summoned to the court. As a result of this daring innovation in Rent Eviction trials, the cases were dismissed and the Rent Strikers won a fight which justified the wisdom of the Glasgow Labour Party Housing Committee. A few days after this an Act to limit rent increases was introduced by the Government.

MARKS

SECTION 1 — SCOTTISH (continued)

Source D: from an editorial comment made in the *Glasgow Herald* newspaper, 1st February 1919.

It is impossible not to be upset by the disgraceful proceedings of yesterday in George Square and other parts of the city. In the scenes of violence and bloodshed there have been no fatalities to report but 53 people were injured by the throwing of missiles or the use of the baton. David Kirkwood, one of the strike leaders, and a member of the ILP, is under arrest on the charge of inciting the mob. It has been known from the first that the strike movement is controlled by a small section of the Clyde Workers' Committee who are pressing for a 40 hour week. Many works on Clydeside have been closed due to picketing by crowds numbering several hundreds of strikers that can only be called organised intimidation. The revolutionary activities of these Bolshevists have damaged Glasgow's reputation.

Attempt all of the following questions.

13. How fully does **Source A** describe the experience of Scots on the Western Front?   9

    Use the source and your own knowledge.

14. Compare the views of **Sources B** and **C** about the events of the Rent Strikes.   5

    Compare the sources overall and in detail.

15. Evaluate the usefulness of **Source D** as evidence of political developments in Scotland after the war.   6

    In making a judgement you should refer to:
    • the origin and possible purpose of the source
    • the content of the source
    • your own knowledge

[Now go on to Section 2 starting on *Page fourteen*]

MARKS

SECTION 2 — BRITISH — 20 marks
Attempt ONE question

Part A — Church, State and Feudal Society, 1066–1406

16. To what extent was religion the main role of the Church in medieval society?

20

17. *King John of England successfully increased royal authority.*
How valid is this view?

20

18. *The Peasants' Revolt was the main reason for the decline of feudal society.*
How valid is this view?

20

Part B — The Century of Revolutions, 1603–1702

19. *The policies of Charles I led to problems ruling Scotland.*
How valid is this view?

20

20. To what extent were James II's attempts at absolutism the main cause of the Revolution of 1688–89?

20

21. To what extent did the Revolution Settlement of 1688–1702 alter the balance of power between the monarchy and parliament?

20

Part C — The Atlantic Slave Trade

22. How important was the slave trade in the development of the British economy in the eighteenth century?

20

23. *The power of vested interests was the most important obstacle to the abolition of the slave trade.*
How valid is this view?

20

24. To what extent was the decline in the economic importance of slavery the main reason for the abolition of the slave trade?

20

MARKS

SECTION 2 — BRITISH (continued)

Part D — Britain, 1851–1951

25. *Britain was a fully democratic country by 1918.*

    How valid is this view?   20

26. *The Liberal reforms of 1906 to 1914 failed to improve the lives of the British people.*

    How valid is this view?   20

27. To what extent did the reforms of the Labour Government of 1945–1951 meet the needs of the British people?   20

Part E — Britain and Ireland, 1900–1985

28. *The First World War totally changed the political situation in Ireland.*

    How valid is this view?   20

29. *Economic issues were the reason for the crisis that developed in Northern Ireland by 1968.*

    How valid is this view?   20

30. How important were economic differences as an obstacle to peace, 1968–1985?   20

[Now go on to Section 3 starting on *Page sixteen*]

MARKS

SECTION 3 — EUROPEAN AND WORLD — 20 marks
Attempt ONE question

Part A — The Crusades, 1071–1204

31. To what extent do religious motives explain why many Christians from different classes went on Crusade to the Holy Land?   **20**

32. *Richard and Saladin were both great military and diplomatic leaders during the Third Crusade.*

    How valid is this view?   **20**

33. To what extent had the crusading ideal declined by the time of the Fourth Crusade in 1204?   **20**

Part B — The American Revolution, 1763–1787

34. To what extent did the punishment of Massachusetts contribute to the colonists' moves towards independence by 1776?   **20**

35. How important was the role of George Washington in the colonists' victory in the War of Independence?   **20**

36. *The American Constitution addressed the key political issues in the new United States.*

    How valid is this view?   **20**

Part C — The French Revolution, to 1799

37. How important was the influence of the Enlightenment as a reason for the French Revolution in 1789?   **20**

38. *The role of Sieyes was the reason for the establishment of the Consulate.*

    How valid is this view?   **20**

39. *The Clergy gained most from the French Revolution.*

    How valid is this view?   **20**

MARKS

SECTION 3 — EUROPEAN AND WORLD (continued)

Part D — Germany, 1815–1939

40. *By 1850 supporters of nationalism had made significant progress in their aims.*
    How valid is this view?   20

41. How important was resentment towards the Treaty of Versailles as a reason why the Nazis had achieved power by 1933?   20

42. How important was the use of fear and terror as a reason why the Nazis were able to stay in power, 1933–39?   20

Part E — Italy, 1815–1939

43. *Between 1815 and 1850, there was a real growth in nationalist feeling in Italy.*
    How valid is this view?   20

44. To what extent were economic difficulties the reason why the Fascists achieved power in Italy by 1925?   20

45. How important were Mussolini's economic and social policies in maintaining Fascist power in Italy between 1922 and 1939?   20

Part F — Russia, 1881–1921

46. How important was military defeat in the war against Japan in causing the 1905 Revolution in Russia?   20

47. How important was the appeal of the Bolsheviks in the success of the October Revolution of 1917?   20

48. How important was the role of Trotsky in the victory of the Reds in the Civil War?   20

MARKS

SECTION 3 — EUROPEAN AND WORLD (continued)

Part G — USA, 1918–1968

49. To what extent was a lack of political influence the main obstacle to the achievement of Civil Rights for black people up to 1941?

20

50. How important was the role of Martin Luther King in the development of the Civil Rights campaign, after 1945?

20

51. To what extent did the Civil Rights Movement meet the needs of black Americans, up to 1968?

20

Part H — Appeasement and the Road to War, to 1939

52. *Military agreements, pacts and alliances were the most important method used by Germany and Italy to pursue their foreign policies from 1933.*

How valid is this view?

20

53. *The Munich Agreement of 1938 was a reasonable settlement under the circumstances.*

How valid is this view?

20

54. How important was the Nazi-Soviet Pact in causing the outbreak of war in 1939?

20

Part I — The Cold War, 1945–1989

55. *Soviet policy towards Eastern Europe up to 1961 was very effective.*

How valid is this view?

20

56. To what extent was the economic cost of the arms race the reason why the superpowers attempted to manage the Cold War, 1962–1985?

20

57. To what extent did the actions of President Reagan lead to the end of the Cold War?

20

[END OF QUESTION PAPER]

HIGHER

2016

National
Qualifications
2016

X737/76/11   History

FRIDAY, 20 MAY
9:00 AM — 11:20 AM

Total marks — 60

SECTION 1 — SCOTTISH — 20 marks
Attempt ONE Part

SECTION 2 — BRITISH — 20 marks
Attempt ONE question from the Part you have chosen

SECTION 3 — EUROPEAN AND WORLD — 20 marks
Attempt ONE question from the Part you have chosen

Write your answers clearly in the answer booklet provided. In the answer booklet you must clearly identify the question number you are attempting.

Use **blue** or **black** ink.

Before leaving the examination room you must give your answer booklet to the Invigilator; if you do not, you may lose all the marks for this paper.

[BLANK PAGE]

DO NOT WRITE ON THIS PAGE

SECTION 1 – SCOTTISH

Attempt ONE Part

PARTS

SECTION 2 – BRITISH

Attempt one question from the Part you have chosen

PARTS

SECTION 3 – EUROPEAN AND WORLD

Attempt one question from the Part you have chosen

PARTS

SECTION 1 — SCOTTISH — 20 marks

Part A — The Wars of Independence, 1249–1328

Study the sources below and attempt the questions which follow.

Source A: from the statement by the Scottish nobles in reply to Edward I's demand made at Norham, May 1291.

> Greetings. We, the representatives of the Scottish political community, give thanks to His Highness, King Edward I for his great kindness towards the Scottish nation. In response to Edward I's demand at Norham that he is recognised as overlord of Scotland before he can judge between the claimants to the Scottish succession, the Scottish people have sent us here to answer that, they know nothing of this right of overlordship of Scotland nor have they ever seen it claimed by Edward I or his ancestors. Therefore we have no power to reply to Edward I's claim as we lack a king to whom the demand ought to be addressed and only a king has the power to answer. King Edward I has himself guaranteed the kingdom of Scotland's independence in the Treaty of Birgham-Northampton.

Source B: from Michael Brown, *The Wars of Scotland 1214–1371* (2004)

> In the weeks which followed Wallace and Murray's victory at Stirling Bridge, English garrisons across central and southern Scotland surrendered leaving only Edinburgh, Roxburgh and Berwick in English hands. During the winter of 1297 Wallace was knighted and named guardian of the realm, thus reviving the office used between 1286 and 1292. Tensions amongst the Scottish leadership lingered from previous years and resurfaced when Wallace appointed William Lamberton, a supporter of Scottish independence, as the new bishop of St Andrews. Despite the reluctance on the part of some of the nobility to accept Wallace's leadership, many of the nobles, clergy and others who opposed Edward's rule accepted Wallace as the best hope for the defence of the kingdom.

Source C: from G.W.S. Barrow, *Kingship and Unity, Scotland 1000–1306* (1981)

> Tragically, Murray had been mortally wounded at Stirling Bridge and died in November 1297. However Wallace and Murray and their infantry army's startling defeat of the largely cavalry force brought against them by Surrey and Cressingham at Stirling in September 1297 led to the near collapse of the English military control in Scotland. Wallace, the hero of the hour, whose victory had electrified Western Europe, was knighted and afterwards elected as guardian, still in the name of King John but also of the Community of the Realm. Wallace issued commands and appointed new bishops—most importantly his friend William Lamberton to succeed William Fraser as bishop of St Andrews. Scotland's traditional leaders fought under Wallace's command and a few even escaped from English custody in Flanders in order to give him their support.

MARKS

SECTION 1 — SCOTTISH (continued)

Source D: from Fiona Watson, *Scotland from Prehistory to the Present* (2003)

> The power of the Comyn family combined with their close bond with their relation, the deposed King John presented Bruce with a formidable problem. Fortunately for Bruce, the Comyns never displayed any outstanding talent in military matters. Bruce himself had quickly matured into a cunning and effective guerrilla leader, qualities that mattered far more to Scotland's interests than playing by the established rules. The new King was also blessed with an ability to attract and sustain a close-knit team of military commanders who were as effective in military terms as Bruce himself. As a result, Bruce could maintain a war on more than one front, sending his only surviving brother, Edward, and the enthusiastic James Douglas, down into Galloway to deal with Balliol supporters there, while he himself tackled the Comyn heartland in Lochaber, Badenoch and Buchan.

Attempt all of the following questions.

1. Evaluate the usefulness of **Source A** as evidence of the succession problem.   6

   In making a judgement you should refer to:
   - *the origin and possible purpose of the source*
   - *the content of the source*
   - *your own knowledge.*

2. Compare the views of **Sources B** and **C** about the role of William Wallace and Scottish resistance.   5

   Compare the sources overall and in detail.

3. How fully does **Source D** explain the reasons for the rise and triumph of Robert Bruce?   9

   Use the source and your own knowledge.

[Now go on to SECTION 2 starting on *Page fourteen*]

MARKS

SECTION 1 — SCOTTISH — 20 marks

Part B — The Age of the Reformation, 1542–1603

Study the sources below and attempt the questions which follow.

Source A: from the *"Beggars' Summons"* written to the friars: 1st January 1559.

We the blind, crooked, bedridden widows, orphans and all other poor have grievances with all friars within the realm. We wish to amend past wrongs and seek reformation in times coming.

Seeing our number is so great, so poverty-stricken, and so heavily oppressed by your false ways, we believe that we must oppose you rather than allow you to steal from us our lodgings, and then leave us to perish and die from the effects of poverty. We have thought it wise to warn you by this public writing fixed to your gates, that between now and the Feast of Whitsunday next, you must remove yourselves from the friaries so that we can enjoy that which belongs to the Kirk. If you fail to leave we will enter and take possession of your houses and throw you out.

Source B: from http://www.marie-stuart.co.uk

James VI was brought up under the strict Presbyterianism of his senior tutor, George Buchanan, in the stern atmosphere of the Mars, his guardians. James had inherited a poor country divided by religious factions which viewed the monarch with mistrust. James's main claim was that the Sovereign's right came straight from God. He favoured the model of the English Protestant Church with bishops and the King at its Head. Presbyterians however claimed that power over the Kirk came directly from God. While James's views were questioned by extremist Presbyterians, his resolve to exercise authority over the Kirk strengthened and in 1597, Andrew Melville was deposed as rector of St Andrew's. Thereafter, the King attended all General Assemblies between 1597 and 1603, cementing his influence. On the whole, and despite the tensions, both sides co-existed in relative harmony during his reign.

Source C: from Alan MacDonald, "James VI and the General Assembly", in Goodare and Lynch, *The Reign of James VI* (2000)

James VI was viewed with a degree of distrust by his Kirk. Throughout his reign, there were moments of peace, but true agreement did not last. This was in part due to his relentless view that Kings were in charge of the church by divine rule. As a result of the riots demonstrating opposition to this view in December 1596, the initiative passed to the king, and with the dismissal of Melville many ministers who had previously been happy to criticise him were more willing to accept. By 1603, James had exerted his influence with attendance at every General Assembly since 1597. This was an opportunity for the establishment of royal control over the Kirk, however, after James left Scotland the opportunity was lost.

MARKS

SECTION 1 — SCOTTISH (continued)

Source D: from A.M. Renwick, *The Story of the Scottish Reformation* (2006)

In 1560 only a few ministers in all Scotland taught the reformed Protestant faith. However, by 1573 there were over 500 such men preaching to the people showing the growing influence of the Kirk, in many parishes the people were being served by ministers who were well informed on religious matters. The Kirk also remained committed to improving education throughout the land. Above all, the people now heard the Word of God in their own language, a matter of indescribable worth. Following its guidance men were now able to come freely to the Lord Jesus for salvation. However, Kirk services became more serious as the sound of music, and the playing of the organ in particular, were associated with the Catholic faith and became a thing of the past. Life for ordinary people was harsh.

Attempt all of the following questions.

4. Evaluate the usefulness of **Source A** as evidence of the reasons for the Reformation of 1560.

   In making a judgement you should refer to:
   - *the origin and possible purpose of the source*
   - *the content of the source*
   - *your own knowledge.*

   6

5. Compare the views of **Sources B** and **C** about the relationship between monarch and Kirk in the reign of James VI.

   Compare the sources overall and in detail.

   5

6. How fully does **Source D** explain the impact of the Reformation on Scotland, to 1603?

   Use the source and your own knowledge.

   9

[Now go on to SECTION 2 starting on *Page fourteen*]

MARKS

SECTION 1 — SCOTTISH — 20 marks

Part C — The Treaty of Union, 1689–1740

Study the sources below and attempt the questions which follow.

Source A: from a speech by John Dalrymple, Earl of Stair, during the union debates (1706)

> We followed the example of other nations and formed the Company of Scotland to trade with the West Indies. We built ships and planned a colony on the isthmus of Darien. What we lacked were not men or arms, or courage, but the one thing most needful: we lacked the friendly co-operation of England. The pitiful outcome of that enterprise is too sad a story to be told again. Let us just say that the English did not treat us as partners or friends or fellow subjects of a British king. They treated us as pirates and enemy aliens. The union of crowns gave us no security. We were exposed to the hostile rivalry of Spain, encouraged by England. Our colony was sacked. We suffered every cruelty an enemy can inflict.

Source B: from Simon Schama, *A History of Britain* (2001)

> Defoe was a paid secret agent of the English government, and published essays in 1706 which argued that the history of Britain was a history of happy relations between the English and the Scots. These sentiments, and any Court party arguments in favour of union, however well meaning, persuaded only a few despite winning their votes. Sums of money were certainly distributed to various MPs in order to secure the necessary votes for the passage of the Act of Union through the Scottish Parliament. Promises of English landed estates were dangled before members of the Scottish nobility who supported the Treaty. As far as Defoe was concerned, the biggest sweetener was £398,085.10s—the precise "Equivalent" of all the losses of the Darien expedition. In 1706–07 it needed just ten weeks for the Act of Union to go through parliament in Edinburgh.

Source C: from Paul Henderson Scott, *The Union of 1707, Why and How* (2006)

> The Scottish parliament met in October 1706. There were inducements in the Treaty itself. The Court party won all the votes, without making much effort to argue in reply to the Country party or troubling themselves with reasoning. Although a cruel deception, the Equivalent seemed to offer repayment to the many Scots, including members of the Scottish Parliament, who had lost their savings through the collapse of Darien. The English government was determined to secure the Treaty by offering Scottish nobles large and prosperous estates as a means of making money after union. A sum of £20,000 advanced from the Queen to ease the passage of the Treaty was distributed to various members of the Scottish Parliament by the Earl of Glasgow.

MARKS

SECTION 1 — SCOTTISH (continued)

Source D: from Paul Henderson Scott, *The Union of 1707, Why and How* (2006)

Debate exists as to whether the Union had any social, political and economic effects after it was passed by both Scottish and English parliaments in 1707. One irony of the Union is that it did not in the end extinguish Scotland as a nation; it retained its own distinctive identity, attitudes and ideas, and its traditions were so strong that they were not easily removed. The consequences of the Treaty in this respect were not as harmful as they might have been, although it did exert a strong Anglicising influence. Nevertheless, the guarantees to the Scottish legal system in the Treaty and to the Church in the Act of Security for the Kirk had more influence on Scotland than the distant British parliament. English and Scottish historians have concluded that the continuation of the Scottish systems of education and local government were a significant achievement of Union.

Attempt all of the following questions.

7. Evaluate the usefulness of **Source A** as evidence of worsening relations between Scotland and England.   6

    In making a judgement you should refer to:
    - *the origin and possible purpose of the source*
    - *the content of the source*
    - *your own knowledge.*

8. Compare the views of **Sources B** and **C** about the reasons for the passing of the Union by the Scottish Parliament.   5

    Compare the sources overall and in detail.

9. How fully does **Source D** explain the effects of the Union to 1740?   9

    Use the source and your own knowledge.

[Now go on to SECTION 2 starting on *Page fourteen*]

MARKS

SECTION 1 — SCOTTISH — 20 marks

Part D — Migration and Empire, 1830–1939

Study the sources below and attempt the questions which follow.

Source A: from an article about emigration written by the editor of Chambers' Journal, a popular weekly Scottish magazine, from 1872.

> Canada continues to be a popular destination for Scots emigrants. Many Scots from the Highlands to the Lowlands have already taken up the opportunity of living abroad in places such as Ontario and Nova Scotia. Experienced farmers and skilled agricultural workers can earn far more overseas than they can here at home. The attraction of emigration to Canada is not simply this, but the familiarity and neighbourliness of living among fellow Scots who had already emigrated in the past. By far the biggest attraction is the confident prospect that the poorest may become landowners thereby earning sufficient to make a living and to comfortably settle one's children.

Source B: from Malcolm Prentis, *The Scots in Australia* (2008)

> In the nineteenth and early twentieth century, there was a strong Scottish presence in the pastoral (sheep and cattle) industry, especially in eastern Australia. The Scots were able to apply their farming traditions and skills in developing their new land but were also adaptable and willing to experiment with new crops such as sugar or with new techniques such as irrigation. Miners were also among the Scottish emigrants to Australia and were mainly to be found in coal mining rather than in copper and tin. The Scots remained predominantly Presbyterian thus the Presbyterian Church was by far the most important Scottish institution brought to Australia which was to influence many areas of Australian life. Scots and Presbyterians were prominent in the teaching profession with Presbyterian secondary schools established in great numbers in Victoria.

Source C: from Gordon Donaldson, *The Scots Overseas* (1966)

> An indication of the distribution of the Scots in Australia is given by the establishment of Presbyterian churches, especially as there were very few highland Roman Catholics among the emigrants to Australia. In areas where the Scots were strong, they were usually also associated with educational effort; for example, the support of the Church of Scotland for Melbourne Academy was so significant that it became known as "the Scotch College". The Scots made valuable contributions in other respects. All over eastern Australia Scots played a large part in covering the land with homesteads and sheep stations. In the coal mining industry, particularly influential were James and Alexander Brown, originally from Lanarkshire whose mining business employed many fellow Scots and produced most of the coal in New South Wales by 1868.

MARKS

SECTION 1 — SCOTTISH (continued)

Source D: from T.M. Devine, *To the Ends of the Earth: Scotland's Global Diaspora, 1750-2010* (2012)

> On the eve of the Great War, Scotland was at the pinnacle of global prominence. The shipbuilding industry still possessed a world reach and remained pre-eminent as in 1914 the Clyde yards built almost a fifth of the world's total output. Then there was the interlinked coal, steel, iron and engineering industries, employing over a quarter of the Scottish labour force all dependent upon access to overseas markets in the Empire. Nor was the global dependency unique to the heavy industries of the west. Other manufacturing sectors—carpets, thread and woollens—covering the country from the Borders to the north-east Lowlands—were also dependent on overseas trade. The role of the Scots as key junior partners in Empire was maintained after 1918 with the careers of numerous professional and middle class Scots continuing to be pursued within the Empire.

Attempt all of the following questions.

10. Evaluate the usefulness of **Source A** as evidence of the reasons for the migration of Scots.

    In making a judgement you should refer to:
    - *the origin and possible purpose of the source*
    - *the content of the source*
    - *your own knowledge.*

    6

11. Compare the views of **Sources B** and **C** about the impact of Scots emigrants on the Empire.

    Compare the sources overall and in detail.

    5

12. How fully does **Source D** explain the effects of migration and empire on Scotland, to 1939?

    Use the source and your own knowledge.

    9

[Now go on to SECTION 2 starting on *Page fourteen*]

SECTION 1 — SCOTTISH — 20 marks

Part E — The Impact of the Great War, 1914–1928

Study the sources below and attempt the questions which follow.

Source A: from the diary of Private MacPherson, 9th Royal Scots, 21st July 1916.

> We passed through the ruined village of Mametz, where lay the 6th Argylls and Forth Garrison Artillery. We got a whiff of tear gas still lingering after German bombardment, which made our eyes sore and watery. On the hillside we passed a large wooden cross erected by the Germans on the grave of some of their dead. We plunged into a hail of shells. The air was full of the roar of their approach and the drawn out shattering detonations of their explosions. We continued our rapid advance and with a sigh of relief found ourselves beyond the barrage in comparative safety. We were then sent to relieve the survivors of the Division which had suffered terrible losses in the unsuccessful attempt to occupy High Wood.

Source B: from Leah Leneman, *Fit for Heroes? Land Settlement in Scotland after World War I* (1989)

> The reaction from ex-servicemen might not have been so violent had the propaganda during and after the war not been so effective. As one Highlander put it, "During the war agents appointed by the government flooded Sutherland with literature containing guarantees to all of land." In the Highlands and Islands trouble erupted after the war, as demobilized men used the only weapon that had proved successful since the late nineteenth century which was land seizure. The owners' response was to take out legal action against those illegally occupying the land. When this was ignored, as it almost invariably was, the landlord could have them arrested for breaking the law. In 1919 the Land Settlement (Scotland) Act came into operation, the stage now seemed to be set for rapid settlement, but it did not work out that way.

Source C: from Ewan A Cameron and Iain J M Robertson, *Fighting and Bleeding for the Land* (1999)

> War did not solve the Highland land problem. In the short term it intensified it. Highlanders wanted more access to land. For crofters this usually took the form of enlargements to their existing croft. The illegal occupation of land in the Highlands led to the arrest and imprisonment of many. However the war removed much of this fear and altered the sympathies to the landless. The promise of land for men who served in the war was a central part of government policy. The Land Settlement (Scotland) Act was unable to redistribute land according to the precise nature of the demand put by crofters. When the government was unable to meet demand for land, expectation turned to frustration and generated land seizures on a scale not seen in the Highlands for forty years.

MARKS

SECTION 1 — SCOTTISH (continued)

Source D: from Neil Oliver, *A History of Scotland* (2010)

> For as long as anyone could remember, Scotland had been a country dominated by the Liberal Party. After the war, however, more people were listening to the Labour Party. Since 1912 the Scottish Conservatives and the Scottish Liberal Unionists had joined forces as the Scottish Unionist Party. These were Conservatives by any other name and in the aftermath of the Great War they emerged as a major force. For an increasing number of Scots the atmosphere of discontent during the 1920's persuaded them that none of the existing political parties were focused enough on Scotland's needs. Voices were raised in calls for a separation of powers and the Scottish Home Rule Association re-established itself in 1918. From the time of the "Red Clydeside" rising of 1919 Scots had found much in common with firebrands such as John Maclean.

Attempt all of the following questions.

13. Evaluate the usefulness of **Source A** as evidence of the experience of Scots on the Western Front.   **6**

    In making a judgement you should refer to:
    - *the origin and possible purpose of the source*
    - *the content of the source*
    - *your own knowledge.*

14. Compare the views of **Sources B** and **C** about the domestic impact of war on the land issues in the Highlands and Islands.   **5**

    Compare the sources overall and in detail.

15. How fully does **Source D** explain the impact of the war on politics in Scotland?   **9**

    Use the source and your own knowledge.

[Now go on to SECTION 2 starting on *Page fourteen*]

MARKS

SECTION 2 — BRITISH — 20 marks

Attempt ONE question

Part A — Church, State and Feudal Society, 1066–1406

16. To what extent were the peasant classes the most important part of feudal society?   20

17. *David I was successful in increasing royal power in Scotland.*
    How valid is this view?   20

18. To what extent was King John successful in increasing royal authority in England?   20

Part B — The Century of Revolutions, 1603–1702

19. *Political issues were the main cause of the problems faced by King James after the Union of the Crowns in 1603.*
    How valid is this view?   20

20. To what extent were economic issues the most important reason for the outbreak of civil war in England?   20

21. To what extent were religious issues the main reason for the Revolution Settlement of 1688-89?   20

Part C — The Atlantic Slave Trade

22. To what extent was the failure of alternative sources of labour the main reason for the development of the slave trade?   20

23. *The fear of revolt was the most important factor governing relations between slaves and their owners.*
    How valid is this view?   20

24. How important were the effects of the French Revolution as an obstacle to abolition?   20

MARKS

SECTION 2 — BRITISH (continued)

Part D — Britain, 1851–1951

25. To what extent were changing political attitudes the most important reason why Britain became more democratic, 1851–1928?   **20**

26. *The part played by women in the war effort was the main reason why some women received the vote in 1918.*

    How valid is this view?   **20**

27. To what extent did the social reforms of the Liberal government, 1906–1914, meet the needs of the British people?   **20**

Part E — Britain and Ireland, 1900–1985

28. To what extent was the Nationalist response to the Home Rule Bill responsible for the growth of tension in Ireland to 1914?   **20**

29. *The policies and actions of the British government were the main obstacle to peace in Ireland, 1918–1921.*

    How valid is this view?   **20**

30. To what extent was the Unionist ascendancy the main reason for the developing crisis in Northern Ireland by 1968?   **20**

[Now go on to SECTION 3 starting on *Page sixteen*]

MARKS

SECTION 3 — EUROPEAN AND WORLD — 20 marks
Attempt ONE question

Part A — The Crusades, 1071–1204

31. To what extent were attempts to assert Papal authority the main reason for the calling of the First Crusade?

20

32. To what extent were divisions among the Islamic states the main reason for the success of the First Crusade?

20

33. *During the Third Crusade Richard was more successful than Saladin both as a military leader and as a diplomat.*

How valid is this view?

20

Part B — The American Revolution, 1763–1787

34. To what extent was George III the main reason for colonial resentment towards Britain by 1763?

20

35. To what extent did the views of Thomas Paine represent British opinion towards the conflict in the colonies?

20

36. How important was British military inefficiency in the colonists' victory in the War of Independence?

20

Part C — The French Revolution, to 1799

37. *Taxation was the main cause of the threats to the security of the Ancien Régime before 1789.*

How valid is this view?

20

38. To what extent was the character of Louis XVI the main reason for the failure of constitutional monarchy, 1789–92?

20

39. To what extent was political instability the most important reason for the establishment of the Consulate?

20

MARKS

SECTION 3 — EUROPEAN AND WORLD (continued)

Part D — Germany, 1815–1939

40. How important were cultural factors as a reason for the growth of nationalism in Germany, 1815–50? **20**

41. To what extent was Austrian strength the main obstacle to German unification, 1815–50? **20**

42. To what extent were weaknesses of the Weimar Republic the main reason why the Nazis achieved power in 1933? **20**

Part E — Italy, 1815–1939

43. To what extent were cultural factors the main reason for the growth of nationalism in Italy, 1815–50? **20**

44. How important was the dominant position of Austria and her dependent duchies as an obstacle to Italian unification, 1815–50? **20**

45. To what extent was the role of Mussolini the main reason why the Fascists achieved power in Italy, 1919–1925? **20**

Part F — Russia, 1881–1921

46. *Opposition groups were unable to effectively challenge the security of the Tsarist state before 1905.*

    How valid is this view? **20**

47. *The Tsar was successful in strengthening his authority between 1905 and 1914.*

    How valid is this view? **20**

48. To what extent were the weaknesses of the Provisional Government the main reason for the success of the October Revolution, 1917? **20**

SECTION 3 — EUROPEAN AND WORLD (continued)

Part G — USA, 1918–1968

49. To what extent were the effects of the First World War the main reason for changing attitudes towards immigration in the 1920s?

20

50. *The weaknesses of the US banking system was the main reason for the economic crisis of 1929–33.*

How valid is this view?

20

51. How important was the continuation of prejudice and discrimination in the development of the Civil Rights campaign, after 1945?

20

Part H — Appeasement and the Road to War, to 1939

52. How important was Fascist ideology as a reason for the aggressive nature of the foreign policies of Germany and Italy in the 1930s?

20

53. *Military weakness was the most important reason for the British policy of appeasement, 1936–38.*

How valid is this view?

20

54. To what extent was the Munich agreement a success?

20

Part I — The Cold War, 1945–1989

55. To what extent were tensions within the wartime alliance the most important reason for the emergence of the Cold War, up to 1955?

20

56. To what extent was US foreign policy the main reason for the Cuban Crisis of 1962?

20

57. *The danger of Mutually Assured Destruction was the main reason why the superpowers attempted to manage the Cold War, 1962–1985.*

How valid is this view?

20

[END OF QUESTION PAPER]

HIGHER

2017

National
Qualifications
2017

X737/76/11   History

TUESDAY, 9 MAY
9:00 AM – 11:20 AM

Total marks — 60

SECTION 1 — SCOTTISH — 20 marks

Attempt ONE Part

SECTION 2 — BRITISH — 20 marks

Attempt ONE question from the Part you have chosen

SECTION 3 — EUROPEAN AND WORLD — 20 marks

Attempt ONE question from the Part you have chosen

Write your answers clearly in the answer booklet provided. In the answer booklet you must clearly identify the question number you are attempting.

Use **blue** or **black** ink.

Before leaving the examination room you must give your answer booklet to the Invigilator; if you do not, you may lose all the marks for this paper.

[BLANK PAGE]

DO NOT WRITE ON THIS PAGE

SECTION 1 — SCOTTISH

Attempt ONE Part

PARTS

SECTION 2 — BRITISH

Attempt ONE question from the Part you have chosen

PARTS

SECTION 3 — EUROPEAN AND WORLD

Attempt ONE question from the Part you have chosen

PARTS

MARKS

SECTION 1 — SCOTTISH — 20 marks

Part A — The Wars of Independence, 1249–1328

Study the sources below and attempt the questions which follow.

Source A: from Geoffrey W.S. Barrow, *Robert Bruce and the Community of The Realm of Scotland* (1988).

> The atmosphere in the summer of 1290 was hopeful, even joyful. Then tragic events in late September 1290 set in motion a struggle for the throne between a number of claimants, of whom two were of outstanding importance: Robert Bruce of Annandale and John Balliol, Lord of Galloway. While the nobles were gathering at Perth, Robert Bruce, in his seventieth year, had arrived unexpectedly with a strong body of armed men. It looked as though the question of the succession would be settled by open war between the two claimants and their supporters. Bishop Fraser went so far as to write to the English king in October 1290, suggesting that if John Balliol was to come to Edward, the king would be well advised to reach an understanding with him, as the likely king of Scots.

Source B: from Michael Penman, *The Scottish Civil War* (2002).

> It was a second royal death which heralded the eruption of the rival campaigns of the Bruce and Balliol families to secure the Scottish throne. At a meeting between the Scots and English ambassadors at Perth, Robert Bruce of Annandale arrived with a great following. Bruce had undeniably revived his efforts of 1286 and was canvassing military support to press his claim to the throne. He was not without hope of success. At the same time, one of the Guardians, William Fraser, the bishop of St Andrews wrote to Edward recommending Edward "deal" with John Balliol, whom he believed to be the best claimant to the throne. He was also concerned at the terrible prospect of "the shedding of blood" between the rival candidates and their allies.

Source C: from Caroline Bingham, *Robert the Bruce* (1999).

> After his inauguration as King of Scots on 30 November 1292 John Balliol travelled south to Newcastle where King Edward was holding his Christmas Court, and there on 26 December 1292 he paid homage to Edward I for his kingdom. Well advised by his kinsmen, the Comyns, John indicated in his first parliament of February 1293 that he intended to build upon Alexander III's achievements. But even as he began to assert his authority it was undermined by Edward's intention to accept appeals from King John's Court. When the case of Macduff of Fife came before the Court of King Edward at the November parliament, John was subjected to the most public humiliation. In the summer of 1294 King John was again in England, and was made to promise Scottish participation in Edward's proposed expedition against Philip IV of France.

MARKS

SECTION 1 — SCOTTISH (continued)

Source D: from a medieval chronicle written by the monks of Westminster Abbey, 1305.

> A certain Scot, by the name of William Wallace, collected an army of Scots in 1298 at the battle of Falkirk against the King of England. Seeing that he could not defeat such a powerful army, Wallace said to the Scots, "Behold I have brought you into a ring, now dance as well as you can," then fled from the battle. In 1305 Wallace was taken prisoner by servants of Edward and brought to London, where on the eve of St. Bartholomew, 23 August, he was condemned to a justly deserved death. For acts of treason against the English king, Wallace was dragged to a gallows where he was hanged. For his sacrilege, the burning of churches in England, his heart, liver, and entrails were cast upon a fire. Wallace's divided body was then sent to the four quarters of Scotland.

Attempt all of the following questions.

1. Compare the views of **Sources A** and **B** about the succession problem.   5

   Compare the sources overall and in detail.

2. How fully does **Source C** explain the relationship between John Balliol and Edward I?   9

   Use the source and your own knowledge.

3. Evaluate the usefulness of **Source D** as evidence of the role of William Wallace and Scottish resistance.   6

   In *reaching a conclusion you should refer to:*

   - *the origin and possible purpose of the source*
   - *the content of the source*
   - *recalled knowledge.*

[Now go to SECTION 2 starting on *Page fourteen*]

SECTION 1 — SCOTTISH — 20 marks

Part B — The Age of the Reformation, 1542–1603

Study the sources below and attempt the questions which follow.

Source A: from Alec Ryrie, *The Age of Reformation: 1485–1603* (2009).

On 11 May 1559, Knox preached an inflammatory sermon at Perth which triggered a riot. Mary of Guise regarded this as an act of rebellion. The Protestant Lords now styling themselves "the Congregation" mobilised to defend themselves against her forces. In January 1560, Queen Elizabeth granted the Lords help: a naval blockade of Leith, followed by an army. It was not a huge force but the English treated their Scottish allies with courtesy, and made clear their wish to withdraw as quickly as possible. Guise's forces were besieged in Leith from April till July 1560 and while they were able to repel assaults, their hopes of reinforcement were melting away. Worse, Guise herself was gravely ill with dropsy, and died on 11 June by which time France sent not an army but ambassadors to negotiate peace with the English.

Source B: from Gordon Donaldson, *The Scottish Reformation* (1960).

Military operations by the Lords of the Congregation against Mary of Guise began in the summer of 1559. By October 1559 they suspended her from the regency and transferred authority to a "great council of the realm". However, Mary of Guise's French troops were based on a strongly fortified position at Leith, well placed to maintain communications with France and they fiercely resisted the Lords. While the arrival of an English fleet and army to assist the Lords between January and March 1560 was helpful, the fortress of Leith still held out. It was Mary of Guise's death, on the night of 10–11 June which opened the way for peace arranged between the English and French commissioners. On 6 July the Treaty of Edinburgh was concluded by which foreign troops were withdrawn from Scotland and a new parliament summoned.

Source C: from Jenny Wormald, *Court, Kirk and Community, Scotland 1470–1625* (1981).

As consort to the King of France, Mary's refusal to recognise the Reformation Parliament in Scotland made her position difficult. In August 1561 following the death of her husband she returned to Scotland. The Catholics of Europe, the pope, the kings of France and Spain, and the Earl of Huntly saw her return as the beginning of a Scottish Counter-Reformation. Instead, Mary made a deal with her half-brother Lord James Stewart, raising concerns when she became the only Catholic in Scotland entitled to hear Mass. She then settled down to write a series of polite and friendly letters to leaders of the Catholic Church. More than anything though, Mary was driven by her ambition to sit on the English throne and England fearing a revival of French influence in Scotland remained cautious of her.

SECTION 1 — SCOTTISH (continued)

Source D: from *The Black Acts*, passed by the Scottish Parliament, 1584.

> Our sovereign lord and his parliament proclaim that Patrick, Archbishop of St Andrews, and the bishops, shall direct and put order to all matters ecclesiastical by visiting the kirks and the ministers. Where they shall find persons worthy and qualified they should appoint them to parishes, and where those appointed fail in their duties, they will be tried by their bishops and lose their livings. Treasonous crimes have been committed against his highness and those involved in the plot at Ruthven have been prosecuted. Following these troubling times, it is ordered by our sovereign lord that none of his highness's subjects should gather together for holding of councils, conventions or assemblies, where any matter civil or religious is to be discussed, without his majesty's special commandment, and licence obtained to that effect.

Attempt all of the following questions.

4. Compare the views of **Sources A** and **B** on the relationships Scotland had with France and England.

   Compare the sources overall and in detail.

   5

5. How fully does **Source C** explain the difficulties arising during the reign of Mary 1561–1567?

   Use the source and recalled knowledge.

   9

6. Evaluate the usefulness of **Source D** as evidence of the relationship between monarch and Kirk in the reign of James VI.

   In reaching a conclusion you should refer to:

   - *the origin and possible purpose of the source*
   - *the content of the source*
   - *recalled knowledge.*

   6

[Now go to SECTION 2 starting on *Page fourteen*]

MARKS

SECTION 1 — SCOTTISH — 20 marks

Part C — The Treaty of Union, 1689–1740

Study the sources below and attempt the questions which follow.

Source A: from *The History Today Companion to British History* (1995).

> The scheme was a plan devised by Scottish bankers and businessmen in 1695 for the foundation of a Scottish settlement, to be called New Caledonia, in Panama, Central America. It was hoped that the colony might achieve the chief object of providing a market for Scottish goods, and lead to Scotland competing with its European economic rivals. However, there was significant English political opposition to the scheme. Because of the perceived threat to the English-owned East India Company, English sabotage was blamed for underfunding and mismanagement. King William, who viewed the Scots settlers as aliens, was held responsible for the scheme's failure. He had done little to prevent Spanish military opposition to the Scots settlers in Central America. Anglo-Scottish relations were strained even further and this was shown by anti-English riots in Edinburgh.

Source B: from a speech by John Dalrymple, Earl of Stair, during the union debates, 1706.

> We followed the example of other nations and formed the Company of Scotland to trade with the West Indies. We built ships and planned a colony on the isthmus of Darien. What we lacked were not men or arms, or courage, but the one thing most needful: we lacked the political co-operation of England. The pitiful outcome of that enterprise is too sad a story to be told again. The British king treated us as pirates and enemies, as if we were aliens. Suffice it to say that because the English wanted to protect their East India Company they did not treat us as partners or friends or fellow subjects. The union of crowns gave us no security, as the English did not prevent us being exposed to the hostile rivalry of Spain. Our colony was attacked. We suffered every cruelty an enemy can inflict.

Source C: from *History of the Union* by Daniel Defoe (1709).

> Many MPs knew that the standing of Scotland in the British Parliament would not be that of a kingdom, but of a province of England. Also, they knew that Cornwall would send almost as many members to Parliament as the whole of Scotland. The people cried out that they were Scotsmen and they would remain Scotsmen. They condemned the word "British" as fit only for the Welsh, who had already been made the subjects of the English. Scotland had always had a famous name in foreign courts, and had enjoyed privileges and honours there for many years, bought with the blood of their ancestors. They would never give away their birth right, though some in the nation had been negotiating such a bargain for themselves, at the price of selling their country.

MARKS

SECTION 1 — SCOTTISH (continued)

Source D: from *The Act of Union*, Scottish Parliament (1707).

> Article 3. The United Kingdom of Great Britain will be represented by one parliament to be called the parliament of Great Britain.
>
> Article 4. There shall be full freedom of trade from the United Kingdom to the colonies belonging to the United Kingdom, and from the colonies to the United Kingdom.
>
> Article 8. Scotland shall be free from paying the Salt Tax for 7 years after the union.
>
> Article 15. Three hundred and ninety eight thousand and eighty-five pounds and ten shillings shall be granted by the English parliament to Scotland before union, the Equivalent of debts owed to Scotland by England.
>
> Article 17. The same weights and measures shall be used throughout the United Kingdom.

Attempt all of the following questions.

7. Compare the views of **Sources A** and **B** about worsening relations between Scotland and England.

   Compare the sources overall and in detail.   5

8. How fully does **Source C** explain the arguments for and against Union with England?   9

   Use the source and recalled knowledge.

9. Evaluate the usefulness of **Source D** as evidence of the reasons for the passing of the Act of Union by the Scottish parliament.   6

   In reaching a conclusion you should refer to:

   - *the origin and possible purpose of the source*
   - *the content of the source*
   - *recalled knowledge.*

[**Now go to SECTION 2 starting on** *Page fourteen*]

MARKS

SECTION 1 — SCOTTISH — 20 marks

Part D — Migration and Empire, 1830–1939

Study the sources below and attempt the questions which follow.

Source A: from Marjory Harper, *Crossing borders: Scottish emigration to Canada* (2006).

> In 1923, 600 Hebrideans took advantage of the year-old Empire Settlement Act to secure passage to Canada. They embarked on two Canadian Pacific liners at Lochboisdale and Stornoway. The unprecedented subsidised state funding also encouraged lowland workers to emigrate. This provided opportunity to escape from the depression and unemployment that blighted the heavy industries of the Central Belt after the First World War. Rural lowlanders had been attracted to Canada precisely because it offered the prospect of changing from tenancy to independent ownership, as for the price of a year's rent, a farm of good quality could be purchased, in direct contrast to the erosion of farming opportunities at home. The land could then be passed on to their children. They anticipated that such a step would bring economic betterment.

Source B: from an article by Alan Harrow, in the *Kintyre Antiquarian Magazine* (2011).

> Rural populations of Canada and other parts of the British Empire were increased by the Empire Settlement Act of 1922. For Scots across the land it provided a welcomed opportunity to break their mundane existence and gave an opportunity for travel. Travel was possible as subsidies were paid to the immigrants who agreed to work the land for a certain amount of time. Both town and country workers also seized this opportunity to escape from the grip of depression and the lack of employment opportunities that existed in Scotland. Many went to Canada where they were offered the chance to become independent landowners, something that there was little opportunity to achieve in Scotland. However, for many it was not the land of "milk and honey" that they had hoped for, but a land of broken promises.

Source C: from Tom Devine, *The Scottish Nation: 1700–2000* (2000).

> Initially the reaction of the native workers to the swelling tide of alien immigration from Lithuania was hostile as it was believed that foreigners had been brought into the Ayrshire coalfields to break strikes and dilute the power of the Unions. Friction further intensified after 1900 as depression in the coal trade caused successive reductions in miners' wages while Lithuanian immigration into the labour market continued. However, over the next two decades things changed. To enhance their own economic advantage Lithuanians gave a convincing display of loyalty to the Trade Union which improved relations with Scots. Nonetheless, assimilation was initially confined to industrial relations, as in all other spheres they were still separate and distinct, yet due to their smaller numbers the Lithuanians were not viewed as a threat to the Scottish way of life.

MARKS

SECTION 1 — SCOTTISH (continued)

Source D: is a diary entry by Sir Charles Dilke in 1868 talking about Scots in India.

> The history of British industry in India is one where, again, the Scots are of paramount importance. The stories of the tea and jute industries begin with the Scots and their impact on these industries. While visiting Bombay in the 1860s, I was struck by the importance of Scots within the business classes of one of India's largest cities, as Bombay merchants were all Scotch. In British settlements, from Canada to Ceylon, from Dunedin to Bombay, for every Englishman that you meet who has worked himself to wealth from small beginnings without external aid, you find ten Scotchmen. It is strange indeed that Scotland has not become the popular name for the United Kingdom, particularly with their impact on education, not only in India but across the Empire.

Attempt all of the following questions.

10. Compare the views of **Sources A** and **B** on the reasons for the migration of Scots.   5

    Compare the sources overall and in detail.

11. How fully does **Source C** explain the experiences of immigrants in Scotland?   9

    Use the source and recalled knowledge.

12. Evaluate the usefulness of **Source D** as evidence of the impact of Scottish emigrants on the Empire.   6

    In reaching a conclusion you should refer to:

    • *the origin and possible purpose of the source*
    • *the content of the source*
    • *recalled knowledge.*

[**Now go to SECTION 2** starting on *Page fourteen*]

MARKS

SECTION 1 — SCOTTISH — 20 marks

Part E — The Impact of the Great War, 1914—1928

Study the sources below and attempt the questions which follow.

Source A: from Trevor Royle, *The Flowers of the Forest* (2007).

> Amongst those attacking the German defensive system called the Frankfurt Trench on 18 November 1916 in what was the last act of the Battle of the Somme were the Glasgow Boys Brigade Battalion — officially the 16th Highland Light Infantry, who fought their way into the Frankfurt Trench where they were stranded. Finding themselves cut off with no hope of escape, they set about barricading a section of the trench to repel the expected German counter attack. It soon became painfully clear that the men of the 16th Highland Light Infantry were in no position to offer prolonged resistance — of their number only half were uninjured and they only had four Lewis guns with limited ammunition. Against the odds they managed to hold out until 25 November, over a week after the original attack.

Source B: from Lyn MacDonald, *Somme* (2013).

> An urgent signal from Divisional Headquarters brought Colonel Kyle of the 16th Highland Light Infantry, the astonishing news that ninety of his men were not "missing" at all. They had been trapped by the German counter-attack and were lying low in the Frankfurt Trench some distance behind the recaptured German line. The small armed party of German soldiers sent to take the Scots prisoner, returned reporting that half of their number had been killed or captured by the Scots who had blocked a stretch of the Frankfurt Trench. It was now Tuesday, 21 November and three days had passed but still the Scots soldiers had the fixed intention of defending their position: they held out until Sunday. Far from being armed to the teeth however, all the Scots had, were four Lewis-guns and a small amount of ammunition.

Source C: from Ewen A. Cameron, *Impaled Upon a Thistle: Scotland Since 1880* (2010).

> During the Great War, Scottish society had to reacquaint itself with mass mortality with the census of 1921 suggesting a figure of 74,000 for war related mortality, nearly 11 per cent of the Scots who enlisted. Prior to 1914, the loss of a relative in battle was not a common experience for most Scottish families, but mounting losses now brought this to the forefront of Scottish life. Nineteenth century conflicts had been fought in an age when the profession of arms was held in low esteem. The dead of the Great War however were glorified and idealised by the culture of remembrance which grew up around the symbols upon which they were counted. The Scottish landscape is littered with war memorials, in towns and villages and in places where the number of names on the memorial outnumbers the current population.

MARKS

SECTION 1 — SCOTTISH (continued)

Source D: from a report on Scotland's heavy industries by the Ministry of Munitions 1916.

By way of showing how existing works have been affected reference might be made to the large steel works, at Motherwell, of Mr David Colville and Sons and the engineering works of Mr William Beardmore and Company Limited at Parkhead (Glasgow). The increase in the number of workers employed by these great establishments is suggestive of a substantial expansion in business with practically the whole of the output — which includes shell bars, special aircraft steel and bullet-proof plates — being for the purposes of the war. Mr Beardmore and Company, in addition to all they had to do in connection with their large engineering works, undertook the management of various National Projectile (shell) factories for the government. These developments were not enough in themselves. Existing works have been supplemented by entirely new factories established for the express purpose of supplying munitions.

Attempt all of the following questions.

13. Compare the views of **Sources A** and **B** about the experience of Scots on the Western Front.   5

    Compare the sources overall and in detail.

14. How fully does **Source C** explain the domestic impact of war on society and culture?   9

    Use the source and recalled knowledge.

15. Evaluate the usefulness of **Source D** as evidence of the impact of war on industry and the economy.   6

    In reaching a conclusion you should refer to:

    • *the origin and possible purpose of the source*
    • *the content of the source*
    • *recalled knowledge.*

[Now go to SECTION 2 starting on *Page fourteen*]

MARKS

SECTION 2 — BRITISH — 20 marks

Attempt ONE question

Part A — Church, State and Feudal Society, 1066–1406

16. *The landed classes played the most important role in feudal society.*

How valid is this view?   20

17. To what extent was the increase of central royal power in the reign of Henry II in England due to the need to develop the economy?   20

18. How important was the Black Death as a reason for the decline of feudal society?   20

Part B — The Century of Revolutions, 1603–1702

19. *Religious issues were the main reason for the problems faced by King James after the Union of the Crowns in 1603.*

How valid is this view?   20

20. How important were foreign matters as a reason for the failure to find an alternative form of government, 1649–1658?   20

21. To what extent did the Revolution Settlement significantly alter the authority of the monarch, 1688–1702?   20

Part C — The Atlantic Slave Trade

22. How important were racist attitudes as a reason for the development of the slave trade?   20

23. To what extent did the slave trade have negative implications for African societies?   20

24. *The role of William Wilberforce was the most important reason for the success of the abolitionist campaign in 1807.*

How valid is this view?   20

MARKS

SECTION 2 — BRITISH (continued)

Part D — Britain, 1851—1951

25. *Britain became more democratic between 1851 and 1928 due to the effects of industrialisation and urbanisation.*

    How valid is this view?   20

26. How important were the fears over national security as a reason why the Liberals introduced social reforms, 1906—1914?   20

27. To what extent did the Labour welfare reforms, 1945—1951, deal effectively with the social problems of Britain?   20

Part E — Britain and Ireland, 1900—1985

28. How important was the British position, as seen by the results of the 1910 elections, as a reason for the growth of tension in Ireland by 1914?   20

29. To what extent were divisions in the republican movement a reason for the outbreak of the Irish Civil War?   20

30. *Economic differences were the main obstacle to peace in Ireland between 1968 and 1985.*

    How valid is this view?   20

[Now go to SECTION 3 starting on *Page sixteen*]

MARKS

SECTION 3 — EUROPEAN AND WORLD — 20 marks
Attempt ONE question

Part A — The Crusades, 1071–1204

31. How important was the Papal desire to channel the aggressive nature of feudal society as a reason for the calling of the First Crusade?

20

32. To what extent was the Christian states' lack of resources the main reason for the fall of Jerusalem in 1187?

20

33. *The crusading ideal had declined by the time of the Fourth Crusade in 1204.*

How valid is this view?

20

Part B — The American Revolution, 1763–1787

34. How important were the Navigation Acts as a cause of colonial resentment towards Britain by 1763?

20

35. To what extent was the American War of Independence a conflict which was global in nature?

20

36. *The American Constitution addressed the key political issues in the new United States.*

How valid is this view?

20

Part C — The French Revolution, to 1799

37. To what extent was corruption the most important threat to the security of the Ancien Régime before 1789?

20

38. How important was the threat of counter-revolution as a reason for the Terror, 1792–1795?

20

39. *The peasantry gained the most from the French Revolution.*

How valid is this view?

20

MARKS

SECTION 3 — EUROPEAN AND WORLD (continued)

Part D — Germany, 1815–1939

40. *Economic factors were the main reason for the growth of nationalism in Germany, 1815–1850.*

    How valid is this view?   20

41. How important was Prussian economic strength in the achievement of German unification by 1871?   20

42. To what extent was propaganda the main reason why the Nazis were able to stay in power 1933–1939?   20

Part E — Italy, 1815–1939

43. *The secret societies played the most important role in the growth of nationalism in Italy, 1815–1850.*

    How valid is this view?   20

44. To what extent was the decline of Austria the main reason why unification was achieved in Italy, by 1870?   20

45. How important was foreign policy as a reason why the Fascists in Italy were able to stay in power, 1922–1939?   20

Part F — Russia, 1881–1921

46. *The authority of the Tsarist state was never seriously challenged in the years before 1905.*

    How valid is this view?   20

47. How important were military defeats in the First World War in bringing about the February Revolution, 1917?   20

48. To what extent was disunity among the Whites the main reason for the victory of the Reds in the Civil War?   20

MARKS

SECTION 3 — EUROPEAN AND WORLD (continued)

Part G — USA, 1918–1968

49. How important was prejudice and racism as a reason for changing attitudes towards immigration in the 1920s?   **20**

50. To what extent was the New Deal effective in solving America's problems in the 1930s?   **20**

51. *The Civil Rights movement was effective in meeting the needs of black Americans, up to 1968.*

    How valid is this view?   **20**

Part H — Appeasement and the Road to War, to 1939

52. To what extent does the British policy of appeasement explain the aggressive nature of the foreign policies of Germany and Italy in the 1930s?   **20**

53. *British foreign policy was successful in containing fascist aggression between 1935 and March 1938.*

    How valid is this view?   **20**

54. How important was the invasion of Poland in causing the outbreak of war in 1939?   **20**

Part I — The Cold War, 1945–1989

55. To what extent were ideological differences the main reason for the emergence of the Cold War, up to 1955?   **20**

56. *The Americans lost the war in Vietnam due to the relative strengths of North and South Vietnam.*

    How valid is this view?   **20**

57. How important was Western economic strength in explaining the end of the Cold War?   **20**

[END OF QUESTION PAPER]

HIGHER

Answers

GENERAL MARKING PRINCIPLES FOR HIGHER HISTORY

The specific Marking Instructions are not an exhaustive list. Other relevant points should be credited.

(i) For credit to be given, points must relate to the question asked. Where candidates give points of knowledge without specifying the context, up to **1 mark** should be awarded unless it is clear that they do not refer to the context of the question.

eg *Some soldiers on the Western Front suffered from trench foot as they were unable to keep their feet dry.* (**1 mark for knowledge**, even though this does not specify that it relates to the Scottish soldiers)

(ii) Where marks are awarded for the use of knowledge, each point of knowledge must be developed, eg by providing additional detail, examples or evidence.

(iii) There are four types of question used in this Paper, namely:
   A. Evaluate the usefulness of Source . . .
   B. Compare the views of Sources . . .
   C. How fully does Source . . .
   D. Extended response questions using a range of stems, including 'how important', 'how successful', 'how valid', 'to what extent'. These require candidates to demonstrate knowledge and understanding and to apply their skills of analysis and evaluation in order to answer the question asked.

(iv) For each of the question types (in iii above), the following provides an overview of marking principles and an example of their application for each question type.

A Questions that ask candidates to *Evaluate the usefulness of a given source as evidence of* . . . (6 marks)

Candidates must evaluate the extent to which a source is useful by commenting on evidence such as the author, type of source, purpose, timing, content and omission.

Up to the total mark allocation for this question of 6 marks:
- a maximum of **4 marks** can be given for evaluative comments relating to author, type of source, purpose and timing
- a maximum of **2 marks** may be given for evaluative comments relating to the content of the source
- a maximum of **2 marks** may be given for evaluative comments relating to points of significant omission

Example:

Source A is useful as evidence of Scottish involvement on the Western Front because it is from a diary of an officer from the Black Watch who will be well informed about the Scots military involvement at the Battle of Loos. (**1 mark for origin: authorship**) *As it is a diary it is also useful as it will give an eyewitness view of the battle.* (**1 mark for origin: purpose**) *The source was written at the end of October 1915 which makes it useful because it was in the immediate aftermath of the battle.* (**1 mark for origin: timing**)

The content is about the men his battalion lost in the attack. This is useful as the deaths of 19 officers and 230 men shows the losses Scots took. (**1 mark for content**) *It is also useful as the Black Watch were part of 30,000 Scots who attacked at Loos, showing a lot of Scottish involvement.* (**1 mark for a point of context**)

However, the source does not give other ways in which Scots were involved on the Western Front. General Douglas Haig who was Scottish made a large contribution to the war as he was Commander in Chief of British Forces after 1915. (**1 mark for a point of significant omission**)

B Questions that ask candidates to *Compare the views of two sources* (5 marks)

Candidates must interpret evidence and make direct comparisons between sources. Candidates are expected to compare content directly on a point-by-point basis. They should also make an overall comparison of the viewpoints of the sources.

Up to the total mark allocation for this question of 5 marks:

Each point of comparison will be supported by specific references to each source and should be awarded **1 mark**.

An overall comparison which is supported by specific references to the viewpoint of each source should be awarded **1 mark. A second mark** should be awarded for a development of the overall comparison.

Examples:

Sources A and B agree that Cressingham was killed and skinned by the Scots after the battle. Source A says Cressingham, a leader amongst the English knights, was killed during the battle and later skinned. Source B agrees when it says 'the treacherer Cressingham was skinned following his death during the battle'. (**1 mark for a point of comparison supported by specific reference to each source**)

Sources A and B agree that William Wallace and Andrew Murray were leaders of the Scottish army at Stirling and that the Scots were victorious. (**1 mark for overall comparison**) *However, they disagree about the importance of the English mistakes made by Warrenne.* (**a second mark for developing the overall comparison**)

C Questions that ask *How fully does a given source explain/describe* . . . (9 marks)

Candidates must make a judgement about the extent to which the source provides a full description/explanation of a given event or development.

Up to the total mark allocation for this question of 9 marks:
- candidates should be given **up to 3 marks** for their identification of points from the source that support their judgement; each point from the source needs to be interpreted rather than simply copied from the source
- candidates should be given **up to 7 marks** for their identification of points of significant omission, based on their own knowledge, that support their judgement
- a maximum of **2 marks** may be given for answers in which no judgement has been made

Example:

Source B gives a fairly good explanation of the reasons why people left Scotland. The source mentions the potato famine in the Highlands in 1846 which led to large numbers of people leaving rather than starving. (**1 mark for interpreting the source**) *It mentions specifically how landlords evicted crofters to make way for sheep farming in order to make their land profitable.* (**1 mark for interpreting the source**) *It also talks about the terrible living conditions which drove people to look for a better life abroad.* (**1 mark for interpreting the source**)

However, the source does not mention all the reasons why people left Scotland. It fails to mention the decline of the kelp industry which forced many Scots to look for work elsewhere. (**1 mark for a point of significant omission**) *The problems of the fishing industry led to hardships for many Scots. When the herring industry declined due to loss of markets after the war, people left Scotland.* (**1 mark for a point of significant omission**) *Others, such as handloom weavers from the Western Isles, left as they couldn't compete with the new factories in the towns and cities of the Central Belt.* (**1 mark for a point of significant omission**)

D Extended response questions (20 marks)

Historical context

Marks can be awarded for answers which describe the background to the issue and which identify relevant factors. These should be connected to the line of argument.

Conclusion(s)

Marks can be awarded for answers which provide a relative overall judgement of the factors, which are connected to the evidence presented, and which provide reasons for their overall judgement.

Eg *This factor was clearly more significant in bringing about the event than any other factor because ….*

While conclusions are likely to be at the end of the essay, they can also be made at any point in the response.

Use of evidence

Marks can be awarded for evidence which is detailed and which is used in support of a viewpoint, factor or area of impact.

For knowledge/understanding marks to be awarded, points must be:

- *relevant to the issue in the question*
- *developed (by providing additional detail, exemplification, reasons or evidence)*
- *used to respond to the demands of the question (ie explain, analyse, etc)*

Analysis

Analysis involves identifying parts, the relationship between them, and their relationships with the whole. It can also involve drawing out and relating implications.

An analysis mark should be awarded where a candidate uses their knowledge & understanding, to identify relevant factors such as political, social, economic, religious, etc (although they do not need to use this terminology), or which explore aspects within these, such as success vs failure; different groups, such as elderly vs youth; or different social classes **and** clearly show at least one of the following:

- links between different components
- links between component(s) and the whole
- links between component(s) and related concepts
- similarities and consistency
- contradictions and inconsistency
- different views/interpretations
- the relative importance of components
- understanding of underlying order or structure

Examples of relationships between identified factors could include:

- Establishing contradiction or inconsistencies within factors
  Eg *While they were successful in that way, they were limited in this way.*
- Establishing contradiction or inconsistencies between factors
  Eg *While there were political motives for doing this, the economic factors were against doing this.*
- Establishing similarities and consistencies between factors
  Eg *In much the same way as this group were affected by this development, this group were also affected in this way.*
- Establishing links between factors
  Eg *This factor led to that factor.* OR *At the same time there was also …*
- Exploring different interpretations of these factors
  Eg *While some people have viewed the evidence as showing this, others have seen it as showing …* OR *While we used to think that this was the case, we now think that it was really …*

Evaluation

Evaluation involves making a judgement based on criteria. Candidates will make reasoned evaluative comments relating to, for example:

- The extent to which the factor is supported by the evidence
  Eg *This evidence shows that X was a very significant area of impact.*
- The relative importance of factors
  Eg *This evidence shows that X was a more significant area of impact than Y.*
- Counter-arguments including possible alternative interpretations
  Eg *One factor was … However, this may not be the case because …* OR *However, more recent research tends to show that …*
- The overall impact/significance of the factors when taken together
  Eg *While each factor may have had little effect on its own, when we take them together they became hugely important.*
- The importance of factors in relation to the context
  Eg *Given the situation which they inherited, these actions were more successful than they might appear.*

Marks can be awarded for developing a line of argument which makes a judgement on the issue, explaining the basis on which the judgement is made. The argument should be presented in a balanced way making evaluative comments which show their judgement on the individual factors and may use counter-arguments or alternative interpretations to build their case.

	Mark	0 marks	1 mark	2 marks		
Historical context	2	Candidate makes one or two factual points but these are not relevant.	Candidate establishes two out of three from the background to the issue or identifies relevant factors or a line of argument.	Candidate establishes the background to the issue, identifies relevant factors and connects these to the line of argument.		
Conclusion	2	No overall judgement is made on the issue.	Candidate makes a summary of points made.	Candidate makes an overall judgement between the different factors in relation to the issue.		
Use of knowledge	6	No evidence is used to support the conclusion.	**Up to a maximum of 6 marks**, 1 mark will be awarded for each developed point of knowledge used to support a factor or area of impact. For a knowledge mark to be awarded, points must be: • relevant to the issue in the question • developed (by providing additional detail, exemplification, reasons or evidence) • used to respond to the demands of the question (ie explain, analyse, etc)			
Analysis	6	There is a narrative response.	**Up to a maximum of 6 marks**, 1 mark will be awarded for each comment which analyses the factors in terms of the question. **A maximum of 3 marks** will be awarded for comments which address different aspects of individual factors.			
Evaluation	4	No evidence of an overall judgement being made.	**1 mark** should be awarded where the candidate makes an isolated evaluative comment on an individual factor that recognises the topic of the question.	**2 marks** should be awarded where the candidate makes isolated evaluative comments on different factors that recognise the topic of the question.	**3 marks** should be awarded where the candidate connects their evaluative comments to build a line of argument that recognises the issue.	**4 marks** should be awarded where the candidate connects their evaluative comments to build a line of argument focused on the terms of the question.

Detailed Marking Instructions for each question

SECTION 1: SCOTTISH

Question	General marking principles for this type of question	Max mark	Specific Marking Instructions for this question
1	Candidates must make a judgement about the extent to which the source provides a full description/ explanation of a given event or development.	9	*Candidates can be credited in a number of ways **up to a maximum of 9 marks**.* • candidates should be given **up to 3 marks** for their identification of points from the source that support their judgement; each point from the source needs to be interpreted rather than simply copied from the source • candidates should be given **up to 7 marks** for their identification of points of significant omission, based on their own knowledge, that support their judgement • a maximum of **2 marks** may be given for answers in which no judgement has been made
2	Candidates must evaluate the extent to which a source is useful by commenting on evidence such as the author, type of source, purpose, timing, content and omission.	6	*Candidates can be credited in a number of ways **up to a maximum of 6 marks**.* • a maximum of **4 marks** can be given for evaluative comments relating to author, type of source, purpose and timing • a maximum of **2 marks** may be given for evaluative comments relating to the content of the source • a maximum of **2 marks** may be given for evaluative comments relating to points of significant omission
3	Candidates must interpret evidence and make direct comparisons between sources. Candidates are expected to compare content directly on a point-by-point basis. **Up to the total mark allocation for this question of 5 marks:** A developed comparison will be supported by specific references to each source and should be given **1 mark**. An overall comparison will be supported by specific references to the viewpoint of each source and should be given **1 mark**.	5	*Candidates can be credited in a number of ways **up to a maximum of 5 marks**.* **Up to a maximum of 4 marks**, each developed comparison which is supported by specific references to each source should be given **1 mark**. An overall comparison will be supported by specific references to the viewpoint of each source and should be given **1 mark**.

SECTION 2: BRITISH

Question			General marking principles for this type of question	Max mark	Specific Marking Instructions for this question
1	A		**Historical context** Up to 2 marks can be awarded for answers which describe the background to the issue and which identify relevant factors.	2	*Candidates can be credited in a number of ways up to a maximum of 2 marks.* **2 marks** Candidate establishes the background to the issue, identifies relevant factors and connects these to the line of argument. **1 mark** Candidate establishes two out of three from the background to the issue or identifies relevant factors or a line of argument. **No marks** Candidate makes one or two factual points but these are not relevant.
	B		**Conclusion(s)** Up to 2 marks can be awarded for answers which provide a relative overall judgement of the factors, connected to the evidence presented and which provide reasons for their overall judgement. While conclusions are likely to be at the end of the essay they can also be made at the start or throughout the essay.	2	*Candidates can be credited in a number of ways up to a maximum of 2 marks.* **2 marks** Candidate makes an overall judgement between the different factors in relation to the issue. **1 mark** Candidate makes a summary of points made. **No marks** No overall judgement is made on the issue
1	C		**Use of evidence** Up to 6 marks can be awarded for evidence which is detailed and which is used in support of a viewpoint, factor or area of impact.	6	*Candidates can be credited in a number of ways up to a maximum of 6 marks.* **1 mark** should be awarded for each point of knowledge used to support a factor. *For knowledge/understanding marks to be awarded, points must be:* • *relevant to the issue in the question* • *developed (by providing additional detail, exemplification, reasons or evidence)* • *used to respond to the demands of the question (ie explain, analyse, etc)*
	D		**Analysis** Up to 6 marks can be awarded for answers which move beyond description and explanation of relevant detail to comment on the factors. This can include, for example: • establishing links between factors • establishing contradiction or inconsistencies within factors • establishing contradiction or inconsistencies between factors • establishing similarities and consistencies between factors • exploring different interpretations of these factors	6	*Candidates can be credited in a number of ways up to a maximum of 6 marks.* **Up to a maximum of 6 marks, 1 mark** will be awarded for comments which analyse the factors in terms of the question. **A maximum of 3 marks** will be awarded for comments which address different aspects of individual factors.

Question	General marking principles for this type of question	Max mark	Specific Marking Instructions for this question
E	**Evaluation** **Up to 4 marks** can be awarded for evaluative comments which show a judgement on the factors such as: • the extent to which the factor is supported by the evidence • the relative importance of factors • counter-arguments including possible alternative interpretations • the overall impact/ significance of the factors when taken together • the importance of factors in relation to the context	4	*Candidates can be credited in a number of ways **up to a maximum of 4 marks**.*

4 marks	**4 marks** should be awarded where the candidate connects their evaluative comments to build a line of argument focused on the terms of the question.
3 marks	**3 marks** should be awarded where the candidate connects their evaluative comments to build a line of argument that recognises the issue.
2 marks	**2 marks** should be awarded where the candidate makes isolated evaluative comments on different factors that recognise the topic of the question.
1 mark	**1 mark** should be awarded where the candidate makes an isolated evaluative comment on an individual factor that recognises the topic of the question.
No marks	No evidence of an overall judgement being made.

SECTION 3: EUROPEAN AND WORLD

Question			General marking principles for this type of question	Max mark	Specific Marking Instructions for this question
1	A		**Historical context** Up to **2 marks** can be awarded for answers which describe the background to the issue and which identify relevant factors.	2	*Candidates can be credited in a number of ways up to a maximum of 2 marks.* **2 marks** Candidate establishes the background to the issue, identifies relevant factors and connects these to the line of argument. **1 mark** Candidate establishes two out of three from the background to the issue or identifies relevant factors or a line of argument. **No marks** Candidate makes one or two factual points but these are not relevant.
	B		**Conclusion(s)** Up to **2 marks** can be awarded for answers which provide a relative overall judgement of the factors, connected to the evidence presented and which provide reasons for their overall judgement. While conclusions are likely to be at the end of the essay they can also be made at the start or throughout the essay.	2	*Candidates can be credited in a number of ways up to a maximum of 2 marks.* **2 marks** Candidate makes an overall judgement between the different factors in relation to the issue. **1 mark** Candidate makes a summary of points made. **No marks** No overall judgement is made on the issue
1	C		**Use of evidence** Up to **6 marks** can be awarded for evidence which is detailed and which is used in support of a viewpoint, factor or area of impact.	6	*Candidates can be credited in a number of ways up to a maximum of 6 marks.* **1 mark** should be awarded for each point of knowledge used to support a factor. *For knowledge/understanding marks to be awarded, points must be:* • *relevant to the issue in the question* • *developed (by providing additional detail, exemplification, reasons or evidence)* • *used to respond to the demands of the question (ie explain, analyse, etc)*
	D		**Analysis** Up to **6 marks** can be awarded for answers which move beyond description and explanation of relevant detail to comment on the factors. This can include, for example: • establishing links between factors • establishing contradiction or inconsistencies within factors • establishing contradiction or inconsistencies between factors • establishing similarities and consistencies between factors • exploring different interpretations of these factors	6	*Candidates can be credited in a number of ways up to a maximum of 6 marks.* **Up to a maximum of 6 marks, 1 mark** will be awarded for comments which analyse the factors in terms of the question. **A maximum of 3 marks** will be awarded for comments which address different aspects of individual factors.

Question	General marking principles for this type of question	Max mark	Specific Marking Instructions for this question
E	**Evaluation** **Up to 4 marks** can be awarded for evaluative comments which show a judgement on the factors such as: • the extent to which the factor is supported by the evidence • the relative importance of factors • counter-arguments including possible alternative interpretations • the overall impact/ significance of the factors when taken together • the importance of factors in relation to the context	4	*Candidates can be credited in a number of ways up to a maximum of 4 marks.*

4 marks	**4 marks** should be awarded where the candidate connects their evaluative comments to build a line of argument focused on the terms of the question.
3 marks	**3 marks** should be awarded where the candidate connects their evaluative comments to build a line of argument that recognises the issue.
2 marks	**2 marks** should be awarded where the candidate makes isolated evaluative comments on different factors that recognise the topic of the question.
1 mark	**1 mark** should be awarded where the candidate makes an isolated evaluative comment on an individual factor that recognises the topic of the question.
No marks	No evidence of an overall judgement being made.

2015
SECTION 1: SCOTTISH

Part A: The Wars of Independence, 1249–1328

1. *Candidates can be credited in a number of ways **up to a maximum of 9 marks**.*

A maximum of 2 marks may be given for answers which refer only to the source.

Possible points which may be identified in the source include:

- Alexander III's sudden death had brought the male line of the royal dynasty to an end.
- A measure of the problems now facing the Scottish leaders was the desire for 'advice and protection' from Edward I which would later lead to demands for recognition of his authority over the Scottish realm.
- Six Guardians were appointed in response to the vital need to carry on the day to day running of the government in the absence of a royal leader.
- The young child Margaret of Norway was now the only descendant of King Alexander.

Possible points of significant omission may include:

- Scotland faced potential difficulties with the succession of a young female, Alexander's three year old granddaughter.
- The seriousness of the situation after the death of Alexander III required the Scottish nobles to carry on the government of the country.
- Alexander's death presented a problem over the succession as there was no male heir.
- The Scottish leaders compromised the independence of Scotland by asking Edward for help and advice.
- Alexander's children had all died before him; Alexander (1284), David (1281) & Margaret (1283).
- There was fear of civil war. Bishop Fraser of St Andrews was afraid of violent disorder when Robert Bruce the elder arrived in Perth with an army. Bishop Fraser asked Edward to come to the Scottish border in order to maintain peace.
- A potential problem was the prospect of war amongst the nobility. In order to avoid civil war, Bishop Fraser asked Edward to help chose the next ruler of Scotland.
- Six Guardians were elected (two bishops, two earls, two barons) in a parliament in Scone.
- There was uncertainty during the winter of 1286–1287 after a rebellion in the South West by the Bruce faction. Robert Bruce seized the Balliol castle of Buittle and the royal castles of Wigtown and Dumfries. Although order was restored by the Guardians, the threat from the Bruce faction created the need to settle securely the question of the succession.
- There were concerns to maintain the independence of Scotland. The Treaty of Birgham, the marriage of Margaret, Maid of Norway and King Edward's son, Edward, Prince of Wales, appeared to solve the potential threat of civil war and to establish a secure relationship with England through marriage. The Guardians however, were concerned to keep Scotland's separate customs and laws.
- Although Edward made concessions to the separate identity of Scotland in the Treaty of Birgham, Edward's actions, such as his seizure of the Isle of Man and the appointment of the Bishop of Durham, suggested that Edward wanted to increase his influence over the kingdom of Scotland.

- A problem arose over the succession after Margaret's death on her way to Scotland in 1290. Her death left no obvious heir to the kingdom of Scotland.
- There was a renewed threat to stability after the death of the Maid of Norway. Tension grew between the two factions, ie Bruce V Balliol/Comyn. Bishop Fraser's letter to Edward favoured Balliol's claim to the throne while Bruce's claim was put forward in the Letter of the Seven Earls.
- Following the invitation to be arbiter in the issue of Scottish succession, Edward showed his authority by inviting the Scottish leaders to meet him at his parliament at Norham rather than Edward travelling over the border into Scotland. Edward also showed his strength by ordering his northern armies to assemble at Norham. In addition, Edward organised his navy for a blockade of Scotland and raised taxes to prepare for a possible war.
- Edward took advantage of Scotland's weakness. When the Scots leaders travelled to Norham, Roger Brabazon gave a speech on behalf of Edward requiring the Scots to recognise Edward as overlord. Pressure was also brought to bear on the competitors at Norham to recognise Edward's overlordship of Scotland in order for him to make a judgement.
- The task of choosing a new king, known as the Great Cause was a long drawn out process, lasting over 15 months from August 1291 until November 1292. Thirteen claimants presented themselves although only three, John Balliol, Robert Bruce and John Hastings, had a strong legal claim.
- Problems arose at the Great Cause at Berwick due to the self-interest of the nobles. For example, John of Hastings' argument that Scotland should be divided showed little regard for the kingdom.
- Edward continued to exercise his overlordship over Scotland even after deciding in favour of John Balliol in November 1292. Balliol had the strongest legal claim, based on primogeniture, being a descendant of the eldest daughter of Earl David. Balliol however had to swear fealty to Edward. Balliol also did homage to Edward in December 1292 at Newcastle. Edward exercised such authority which created problems for King John's reign.

Any other valid point of explanation that meets the criteria described in the general marking instructions for this kind of question.

2. *Candidates can be credited in a number of ways **up to a maximum of 5 marks**.*

Possible points of comparison may include:

Source B	Source C
Overall: Both sources agree that as overlord of Scotland, Edward intended to interfere fully in Scottish affairs.	
Both sources agree that Edward used the issue of appeals to test his relationship with John Balliol and to demonstrate that John, although Scotland's ruler, possessed only the shadow of real power.	

Source B	Source C
King John had sworn homage for the kingdom of Scotland for a second time.	King John did homage to the King of England which clearly recognised Edward I's overlordship of the realm of Scotland.

John's reign was overshadowed by Edward I's determination, right from the start, to enforce the widest possible interpretation of his rights as overlord of Scotland.	Edward was not however content with a mere recognition of his overlordship: he was determined to exercise his authority to the full.
King John was left in no doubt that he personally could, and would, be called to answer for the actions of the Scottish courts in the presence of Edward I and the English parliament.	Edward I would even summon King John to appear before him in England to answer legal claims and complaints in person.
Only one week after King John's enthronement, Edward I had heard a court appeal on behalf of a Scottish merchant, Roger Bartholomew who complained against a decision taken by the Scottish courts.	Edward I made it clear that he intended to hear any appeal cases brought to him as overlord of Scotland, when and where he chose.

3. *Candidates can be credited in a number of ways up to a maximum of 6 marks.*

Examples of aspects of the source and relevant comments:

Aspect of the source	Possible comment
Author: A chronicler of Lanercost Priory in northern England. An English source.	• The source is useful as the author is a monk, educated and well informed as Lanercost Priory was a favourite stopping place for both King Edward I and King Edward II. The source is less useful as it is biased against the Scots.
Type of source: A Chronicle	• Useful as the chronicle records the key events of the Scottish Wars.
Purpose: To keep a record of local, national and international affairs	• It is useful as it describes the effects of the Scottish invasions of northern England after the Battle of Bannockburn.
Timing: August 1314	• The source is more useful as it dates from the time of the Scottish attacks on the north of England and reflects the viewpoint of the English at the time of the raids and the Priory was attacked during Bruce's campaigns in Northern England.
Content	**Possible comment**
• In August 1314, Edward Bruce, James Douglas, John Soules and other nobles of Scotland, under the authority of Robert Bruce, invaded England by way of Berwick with cavalry and a large army.	• Useful as it tells us that raids into northern England were part of Bruce's royal policy in maintaining Scotland's independence. Despite victory at Bannockburn, the war between Scotland and England was not over. Bannockburn won Bruce support in Scotland but not recognition from Edward.

• They devastated almost all Northumberland with fire.	• Useful as it provides a detailed insight into the nature of the warfare Robert Bruce unleashed upon the north of England. Bruce's forces burned and devastated villages. Bruce hoped that such destruction would spread terror and force Edward II to negotiate and recognise Bruce's right to the kingship of Scotland.
• The people of Coupland, fearing their return and invasion, sent messengers and paid money to the Scottish king to escape being burned by them in the same way as they had destroyed other towns.	• Useful as it provides a detailed insight into a short term aim of the raids which was economic. That English shires were prepared to pay tribute tells us that Bruce was prepared to be bought off. Deals were struck with terrified inhabitants. Bruce's forces were willing to grant truces which ensured that his war effort became self-financing. If ransoms were not paid however, Bruce's troops returned to burn and loot.

Possible points of significant omission may include:

• Other common features of the raids into northern England were plundering, the stealing of cattle and the taking of prisoners as hostages.

• For Bruce, a short term aim of the raids was to supplement revenue and to reward and enrich loyal and successful lieutenants.

• The source describes one raid shortly after the Battle of Bannockburn in 1314. Raids were made on the north of England after 1311 and Bruce and his lieutenants led regular raids into England after 1314 to force Edward II to the negotiating table. Bruce attacked England in 1315, 1316, 1318, 1322, 1323 and 1328.

• The raids on England did not succeed in bringing Edward II to the negotiating table. The centre of government and the wealth of England lay in the south and were largely unaffected. The raids into England only seriously affected the nobles and inhabitants of the northern counties. An example being the Earl of Carlisle who rebelled against Edward II and entered into a local truce with Bruce in 1323 to prevent his lands being destroyed.

• The raids into northern England did result in war weariness which contributed to a series of truces in the 1320s. Berwick, England's last major outpost in Scotland was captured by the Scots in 1318 and Bruce inflicted a major defeat on the English at Old Byland in 1322 which almost resulted in the capture of Edward II.

• In addition to the wars in the north of England, other reasons for the triumph of Bruce in maintaining Scotland's independence include

• Bruce recovered his power in Scotland by fighting a highly successful campaign of guerrilla warfare between 1307 and 1309 aimed at harassing English occupation forces and defeating his Scottish enemies led by the Comyns.

• The death of King Edward I in 1307 while leading an army against Bruce removed Bruce's main military adversary. Edward's death also weakened English resolve to prosecute the war in Scotland. King Edward II did not lead a major campaign into Scotland for several years which allowed Bruce to concentrate on fighting his Scottish enemies. Edward's failure to commit to a major campaign in Scotland was also crucial in leaving the major English held Scottish castles vulnerable to attack.

- Bruce defeated his enemies in Scotland. Bruce's campaign in the north east of Scotland, the centre of Comyn power, his decisive victory over the Earl of Buchan in the battle of Inverurie and the destruction of Comyn lands in the 'Herschip of Buchan' removed the threat from the powerful Comyn family. In addition, Bruce's control of the north not only provided a refuge from English attacks but provided manpower and essential supplies from the Continent via Aberdeen.
- Bruce reconquered Scotland from 1310–14 by conducting a successful campaign against English held castles in Scotland. Lacking siege equipment, castles were taken by stealth and their defences dismantled or razed to prevent them being recaptured and used against Bruce in the future. By 1314, most of Scotland's major castles had been recovered including Dundee, Perth, Dumfries, Linlithgow, Roxburgh and Edinburgh.
- The support of the Scottish Church was also significant in Bruce's maintaining Scottish independence. Not only did the Church avoid excommunicating Bruce for the sacrilegious murder of John Comyn in a church in 1306 but Bruce had the active support of the bishops of St Andrews and Glasgow. In the Declaration of the Clergy in 1310 Scotland's bishops declared their support for Bruce as the legitimate king of Scotland.
- Bruce's triumph over a huge English army at the Battle of Bannockburn (23–24 June 1314) completed Bruce's military control of Scotland and gains him increased support thereby securing his position as king of Scots.
- Bruce also weakened English power by sending Scottish armies under his brother Edward to campaign in Ireland. Despite the failure of the Scots to conquer Ireland and the defeat and death of Edward Bruce in 1318, the possibility of a Celtic fringe alliance diverted English attention and forces from Scotland. The opening of a second front in Ireland also stopped the English use of Irish troops and resources against Scotland.
- Diplomacy also contributed to Bruce maintaining Scottish independence. Bruce's position was strengthened by King Philip of France's recognition of Bruce in 1310 which helped to raise Scottish morale. A powerful case for Scottish Independence was presented to the pope, in the letter known as the Declaration of Arbroath in 1320 and in the Treaty of Edinburgh Bruce made major concessions to gain recognition of his kingship and of Scotland's independence.
- Bruce's position was also strengthened by his brutal crushing of the 1320 'Soulis Conspiracy'. However Bruce also showed leniency towards former enemies. Bruce gathered support and ensured loyalty by rewarding his followers. At a parliament held at Cambuskenneth Abbey in 1314, Bruce gave the nobles the opportunity to pledge their allegiance and keep their Scottish lands whilst disinheriting those who chose to side with England.
- Bruce triumphed when he finally secured peace between Scotland and England. Bruce exploited the weakness of the English government after the deposition of Edward II by once more launching attacks into northern England and into Ireland which succeeded in forcing the insecure government of Isabella and Mortimer to negotiate. The Treaty of Edinburgh (1328) formally recognised Bruce as king of an independent Scotland.

Any other valid point that meets the criteria described in the general marking instructions for this kind of question.

Part B: The Age of the Reformation, 1542–1603

4. *Candidates can be credited in a number of ways up to a maximum of 9 marks.*

A maximum of 2 marks may be given for answers which refer only to the source.

Possible points which may be identified in the source include:
- The Reformation of 1560 was sparked off by a riot in Perth in which the town's Catholic religious houses were sacked.
- Knox was installed as its first Protestant minister on the seventh of the month in the capital.
- The change of Regent pleased Knox and his followers as they were unhappy with Mary of Guise's heavy taxation and her pro-French policies.
- Support of England and the arrival of an English army in March 1560 which proved to be a decisive factor.

Possible points of significant omission may include:
- Increase in popular support of Protestant sentiment between 1547 and 1559 despite the absence of the figurehead Knox. Displayed in Perth riot 11th May 1559 and stealing of the image of St Giles on the day of the saints celebration (1st September) 1558 in Edinburgh.
- Return of Knox as a figurehead. Hugely influential in gathering support for the movement through his preaching.
- Unhappiness under Mary of Guise due to heavy taxation. Attempts at engineering a war with England and suspicions of her pro-French policies.
- Increase in support of the poor. Shown by Beggars' Summons copies of which were nailed to the doors of many friaries in Scotland on 1st Jan 1559 declaring that the needs of the poor were greater than that of the friars who were rich and ungodly.
- Evolution of the Protestant Congregation.
- Increase of Protestant literature.
- Presence of Protestant martyrs such as George Wishart (1546) and Walter Myln (1558) helped garner popular support.
- Socio-economic reasons relating to standards of living and over taxation.
- Wish for Scots to create their own national cultural identity. Wish for no interference from England or France.
- Lack of strong leadership from the Catholic Church in Scotland. Particularly following the murder of Cardinal Beaton.
- Scotland disliked being ruled by a woman, Mary of Guise, because she was French and a Catholic.
- Protestant religious commitment. Hard-line and unwavering commitment to the cause.
- The Lords of the Congregation were encouraged by the prospect of support from the English after Elizabeth, a fellow Protestant, became Queen in 1558.
- Protestant ideas had been coming into Scotland for some time.
- English Bibles and books critical of the Catholic Church were distributed in Scotland following the Reformation in England.
- The Catholic Church failed to make sufficient reform to satisfy its critics.
- Increased numbers of the nobility opted for the new faith.
- The Lords of the Congregation had increasing support and took up arms against Mary of Guise.

- The weaknesses of the Catholic Church — decline and corruption; pluralism had not been addressed. Minors being given top positions in church — crown and nobility taking much of churches' revenues; Monarchs placed their offspring in important positions in the Church.
- Mary of Guise's religious attitude and pro-French stance meant she asked the French for help. It pushed many Scots into supporting the Lords of the Congregation.
- Mary of Guise's prosecution of reformers was unpopular.

Any other valid point of explanation that meets the criteria described in the general marking instructions for this kind of question.

5. *Candidates can be credited in a number of ways **up to a maximum of 5 marks**.*

Possible points of comparison may include:

Source B	Source C
Overall: Sources B and **C** agree Mary continued to practise her Catholic faith causing concern. They also agree that Mary having French servants caused problems as the Scots did not like this.	
Source B mentions Mary's marriage to Bothwell and how he was suspected of murdering Darnley. Source C places greater emphasis on the problem of marrying Bothwell.	

Source B	Source C
Went back on her word upon arrival attending mass at Holyrood Chapel.	She ignored advice and attended mass at Holyrood on her arrival, to many Protestants' disgust.
Also upset many of the Scots nobility by surrounding herself with French servants.	Mary surrounding herself with French servants did not go down well with the Scottish nobility.
Most notable was her secret marriage to the Earl of Bothwell, who was suspected of murdering her previous husband Lord Darnley.	Choice of husbands also caused shock waves, particularly her marriage to Bothwell.
Knox had five meetings with Mary Queen of Scots, criticising her marriages.	Knox who held five meetings with the queen to show his disapproval of the goings on in her personal and public life.

6. *Candidates can be credited in a number of ways **up to a maximum of 6 marks**.*

Examples of aspects of the source and relevant comments:

Aspect of the source	Possible comment
Author: The text was produced by a committee of over 30 members.	Useful as the source, articles from The *Second Book of Discipline* was central to the development of Presbyteries through which the Kirk would be virtually independent of secular government.
Type of source: Book on the role of the church in Scottish society.	Useful as it gives a clear explanation of the position of the church in society.
Purpose: To set out views of Presbyterian Kirk.	Useful in helping to establish the relationship between the church and state.

Timing: 1578	Useful as written at a time when the role of the Monarch in the Kirk was being discussed.

Content	Possible comment
- The Kirk belongs to the poor as much as it does everyone else and our duty is to help them.	- Useful as it tells us that the Kirk had a duty to help the poor. Although the reformed church had great intentions to help the poor it faced difficulties.
- We also call for the liberty of the election of persons called to the ministry to be in the hands of the congregation.	- Useful as it tells us that the congregation was given the freedom to pick their own minister.
- Doctors will be appointed in universities, colleges, and schools to open up the meaning of the scriptures in every parish, and teach the basics of religion.	- This is useful as the reformed church believed in education. However, the aim of a school in every parish was not achieved but there was some advancement in central Scotland.

Possible points of significant omission may include:

- Emphasis was placed upon attendance at daily and Sunday services.
- The Second Book of Discipline led indirectly to a regular meeting of ministers from 10 to 20 parishes for discussion of doctrine, which became the presbytery.
- The Kirk removed all organs from places of worship.
- It proved impractical to dispossess the Catholic clergy of their benefices so they were allowed to retain two-thirds of their revenues for life.
- Concessions made to Catholic clergy, on the grounds of old age or ill-health.
- At the beginning of 1560, Scotland was a Catholic country with a Protestant minority. By 1603, it was a Protestant country with a small Catholic minority.
- The Reformation did not lead to a significant transfer of wealth from the Church and much of the lands of the Catholic Church remained in the hands of the nobility.
- The new church still had the problem of not having enough revenue for the parishes.
- James VI was reluctant to enforce anti-Catholic laws.
- Kirk sessions were instruments of moral and religious control.
- The elaborate interiors of Catholic churches were replaced with plain, whitewashed parish kirks.
- Observance of Catholic festivals and saints' days and festivals were discouraged.
- Literary works and Kirk sermons were conducted in English rather than Latin. (The only Protestant Bibles available to lowland Scots were in English).
- Assistance given to the poor from the friaries ended. New plans to help the poor by literacy rates improved during this period.
- Many of the issues prevalent within the Catholic Church prior to the Reformation remained, such as: attendance; poverty of some parishes; and poor quality of preaching.
- Scots merchants continued to trade with England and trading ports across the North Sea.
- Scots focused on trade with the Protestant Dutch.

- Trade with France continued despite the change in religion — although pro-French foreign policy was replaced with pro-English under James.
- The Presbyterian church faced difficulty.

Any other valid point that meets the criteria described in the general marking instructions for this kind of question.

Part C: The Treaty of Union, 1689–1740

7. *Candidates can be credited in a number of ways **up to a maximum of 9 marks**.*

A maximum of 2 marks may be given for answers which refer only to the source.

Possible points which may be identified in the source include:

- There was English political opposition because of threat to the English-owned East India Company.
- English sabotage was blamed for underfunding and mismanagement of the scheme.
- King William was held responsible for encouraging Spanish opposition in Central America.
- Anglo-Scottish relations were strained and this was shown by anti-English riots in Edinburgh.

Possible points of significant omission may include:

- The "Ill" Years, famine, poor harvests.
- Favour shown by King William to England.
- Navigation Acts protecting English trade.
- Lack of an empire for Scotland to trade with.
- Effect of English wars on Scottish trade.
- English military intervention in Scots trade with mainland Europe.
- Dutch withdrawal from Darien scheme.
- The cost of Darien, c. £400,000.
- Act of Settlement, Scots did not want Hanoverian Succession imposed on Scotland.
- Act of Security asserting Scots' independence.
- Anne's delay in assenting to the Act of Security.
- Act Anent Peace and War.
- Wool Act defying English military strategy.
- Wine Act defying English military strategy.
- Alien Act threatening sanctions against Scots.
- Jacobite opposition to William.
- Scottish parliamentary opposition to the perceived threat of the Anglican church.
- Revolution of 1688–9.
- Failure to unite in the 1690s.
- Scottish parliament acting independently of William and Mary.
- English Bill of Rights asserting monarchical authority.
- Claim of Right in Scotland proclaiming parliamentary authority.
- Opposition to William in the Highlands.
- Glencoe Massacre.
- Jacobite plot to assassinate William.
- William and the Darien scheme.
- Covenanters' objections to monarchical interference in church affairs.
- The Worcester Affair.
- Scottish disaffection with William's governmental advisors.

Any other valid point of explanation that meets the criteria described in the general marking instructions for this kind of question.

8. *Candidates can be credited in a number of ways **up to a maximum of 5 marks**.*

Source B	Source C
Overall: the sources are in total disagreement in their attitude to union, in particular in relation to the potential military, manufacturing, and land benefits.	
Source C lays greater emphasis upon the emotional argument.	

Source B	Source C
Our brave and courageous Scotsmen will join a British fleet and army and we will be secured by their protection.	Our valiant and brave Scottish soldiers at home asking for a small pension, or left to beg, once their old regiments are broken.
Our burgh merchants will take our manufactures to England and return with profits.	The royal burghs losing all the branches of their old commerce and trades in the face of English competition.
We will see our craftsmen's lives improve as a result of union.	I see the honest industrious craftsman loaded with new taxes, drinking water instead of ale.
Our land will be better cultivated and manured.	The backbroken farmer, with his corn wasted upon his hands, because his land is worthless.

9. *Candidates can be credited in a number of ways **up to a maximum of 6 marks**.*

Examples of aspects of the source and relevant comments:

Aspect of the source	Possible comment
Author: Jacobite	Useful as the Jacobites were leaders of national sentiment after union, and were known to support repeal. Could argue less useful as author could be biased.
Type of source: Leaflet	This is less useful as this is propaganda so the Jacobites would be justifying their views at the time.
Purpose: To explain the reasons for bringing back the Scottish parliament.	Useful as it expresses an opinion to a reverse union.
Timing: 1723	Useful as it is written 16 years after union when its effects, both positive and negative would be felt across Scotland.

Content	Possible comment
Before union taxes raised by the Scots parliament were not high.	Useful as it informs of the Jacobites desire to return to pre-union government.
Taxes on land, salt, malt, windows, leather, candles, soap, starch, and paper.	Useful as it explains why some Scots would be financially worse off under union.
Custom duties now set at English rates, three times what was paid before union.	Useful as it suggests English influence has been negative for Scots merchants and importers.

Possible points of significant omission may include:

Either economic effects of union:

- Textile and paper industries suffered.
- Smuggling increased.
- Scottish linen lost out to English wool.
- Poverty in some parts of Scotland.
- Opposition from poor farmers to enclosures.
- Merchant shipping increased.
- Caribbean trade increased.
- Scots promotions in East India Company.
- Black cattle trade prospered.
- Improvements in agriculture were made.
- Enclosures benefitted wealthier farmers.
- Development of towns on market routes.
- Government investment in Scotland.
- Royal Bank of Scotland founded.
- Improved industrial practice.
- Growing professional classes.
- Scottish tobacco merchants prospered.

Or political effects of union:

- Opposition to union in the Highlands.
- Some Scottish and English politicians quickly adopted an anti-union stance.
- Motion to repeal union failed in 1713.
- British government wary of Scottish feelings so adopted cautious approach.
- Dominance of Whig party in Scotland.
- Abolition of office of Secretary of State.

Or causes of Jacobite rising of 1715:

- Desire for restoration of Stuart dynasty.
- Desire for return of Episcopalianism.
- Failure of French-sponsored 1708 rebellion.
- Resentment towards George I after 1714.

Any other valid point that meets the criteria described in the general marking instructions for this kind of question.

Part D: Migration and Empire, 1830—1939

10. *Candidates can be credited in a number of ways up to a maximum of 9 marks.*

A maximum of 2 marks may be given for answers which refer only to the source.

Possible points which may be identified in the source include:

- Following the collapse of the kelp trade landlords were looking for change.

- Many landlords were of the view, by the 1840s, that it could only be of benefit to them to rid their land and properties of people.
- They attempted to do this following the hardship of the famine period.
- Gordon chartered a fleet of five ships in order to transport 1,700/landlords contributed to the cost of fares to encourage families to emigrate.

Possible points of significant omission may include:

- In the Lowlands farm consolidation (Enclosures) meant that there was less chance of land ownership.
- Agricultural Revolution — changes in farming methods and new technology (eg mechanical reapers/binders and later tractors) meant there were fewer jobs available.
- In the Highlands the population was growing. Sub-division of land into crofts. Precarious nature of subsistence farming.
- Forced evictions during the Highland Clearances.
- There was poor quality housing in the countryside. Young farm labourers may have lived in bothies — shared accommodation.
- Farm work — long hours, low pay, out in all weathers, few days off.
- Highlanders migrated to the Lowlands to earn money to pay their rents/Rents were increasing.
- Decline of herring fishing industries (especially after Russian Revolution of 1917 brought an end to the Eastern European export trade — trawlermen/gutters lost their jobs).
- Attractions of "big city" employment — easier working life (factory work = indoors, set hours, possibly higher wages). Other jobs attractive, eg railway porter/ticket clerk = steady job, steady wage, possibly a uniform. For females — domestic service often better conditions than farmwork. Shop work offered a half day holiday.
- Social attractions of the towns, eg cinemas, theatres, football matches, pubs and dance halls.
- Emigration — Assisted passage schemes, Emigration agents, posters and advertisements.
- Opportunities to own land overseas, better climate, availability of jobs, possibly better wages.
- Friends and family already overseas encouraged emigration with letters home.
- Economic slump at end of WW1, decline in heavy industries.

Any other valid point of explanation that meets the criteria described in the general marking instructions for this kind of question.

11. *Candidates can be credited in a number of ways up to a maximum of 5 marks.*

Possible points of comparison may include:

Source B	Source C
Overall: Sources B and **C** agree that Scots miners were concerned because of the lack of experience of coal mining which the Lithuanians had. The Scots workers also worried that the foreign miners presented a safety risk. The sources also both mention that sometimes the Lithuanians spoke little English and finally the sources also agree that the foreign workers were accused of lowering wages.	
There was a point of disagreement over the translation of mining regulations.	

Source B	Source C
Some of these aliens may never have seen a coal mine before their arrival in Scotland.	They were the focus of considerable concern largely because of their ignorance of coal mining.
Complained about the employment of aliens in the mines on the grounds of safety.	The employers were adamant that the foreigners did not present additional dangers to safety.
Their lack of English language is a hazard to themselves and fellow workers.	There is adequate provision to instruct them in their duties, including translations of mining regulations into their own language.
There is widespread belief that the foreigners are being used to bring wages down.	Until the early 1900s at least there is evidence that Lithuanian labour was used to cut wages.

12. *Candidates can be credited in a number of ways up to a maximum of 6 marks.*

Examples of aspects of the source and relevant comments:

Aspect of the source	Possible comment
Author: Scottish politician	Useful as he was a contemporary commentator/eyewitness. As a politician he would have expertise on local and Scottish issues.
Type of source: Letter to newspaper	Useful as a letter to the public articulating a political viewpoint.
Purpose: To comment on emigration to the newspaper's readership.	Less useful as it might be biased. He believes further emigration to the Empire will have a negative impact on Scotland.
Timing: 1938	Useful as from a time when Scotland's links with the Empire were of great importance to Scotland's economy.

Content	Possible comment
• to showcase the industrial might of Glasgow and the west of Scotland created by the Empire.	• Useful as Glasgow's industry supplied markets all over the Empire.
• It is more than time that a firm check was put on the drain from Scotland of her best types.	• Useful as it was felt that there was a "brain drain".
• Scotland's best have been drawn away by the opportunities that the Empire has presented.	• Useful as Scots were attracted to jobs and careers in the Empire.

Possible points of significant omission may include:
- The Empire enabled some firms and individuals to make great commercial fortunes, eg Clyde shipbuilders, Napiers, John Browns and Beardmores.
- Scotland exported to the Empire in great quantities, eg Springburn produced ¼ of the world's locomotives.
- Empire provides raw material,s eg Jute from Indian province of Bengal. The textile manufactures in Dundee from this resource was subsequently exported all over the world.

- Heavy industry in Scotland exported a high proportion of products, eg American grain might be bagged into sacks made in Dundee, carried in locomotives manufactured in Springburn and then loaded onto ships built on the Clyde.
- Glasgow becomes known as the "workshop of the world". Glasgow's businesses grow which creates jobs.
- People from the countryside/Highlands move to Glasgow in search of employment.
- Employment opportunities offered by the Empire, eg Scottish middle-class boys had successful careers, especially in India, as civil servants, doctors and as soldiers.
- Scots who made their money in the Empire often returned to Scotland and built large mansions near the cities, eg Broughty Ferry.
- Scottish investors pioneer the use of "investment trusts". Cities like Edinburgh, Dundee and Aberdeen hold substantial investments abroad.
- Scottish capital was being used to finance projects abroad and not at home in Scotland.
- Scottish reliance on trade and commerce with the Empire left her vulnerable to trade slumps, eg the economic slump following World War 1.
- The low-wage economy in Scotland led to considerable poverty amongst many of the working people.
- Glasgow 2nd city of Empire.

Any other valid point that meets the criteria described in the general marking instructions for this kind of question.

Part E: The Impact of The Great War, 1914–1928

13. *Candidates can be credited in a number of ways up to a maximum of 9 marks.*

A maximum of 2 marks may be given for answers which refer only to the source.

Possible points which may be identified in the source include:
- We had given the Germans gas but it came back on us.
- German shells were falling amongst us and time and time again I was knocked off my feet.
- A pal of mine, a fellow Cameron Highlander from Paisley was alongside me.
- A bullet had got him on the arm and blood gulped out/I got out my field dressing to help him.

Possible points of significant omission may include:

Gas:
- First used by the British (Scots) at Loos 1915.
- Gas cylinders were replaced by gas-filled shells — wind could change direction.
- Different types of gas, chlorine, phosgene, mustard and their effects.

Shelling:
- Dangers of trench warfare, eg soldiers suffered from shell shock.
- Many Scots soldiers killed on the Western Front by artillery fire.

Wounded:
- Bloody minded attitude of the survivors who used it to stimulate them for future battles.
- Losses were replaced and the Scottish units carried on though grousing and criticisms became more common.

Western Front:

- Experience of trench warfare, eg rats, lice, trench foot, snipers, boredom, fear of death, lack of sanitation, food rations and shell shock.
- By the end of the first week in September 1914, Glasgow was able to boast that it had recruited more than 22,000 men.
- By December 1914, 25% of the male labour force of western Scotland had already signed up.
- 13% of those who volunteered in 1914–15 were Scots.
- Young Scots urged to join the army through a mixture of peer pressure, feelings of guilt, appeals to patriotism, hopes for escapism and adventure, heroism, self-sacrifice and honour. For the unemployed, the army offered a steady wage.
- Kitchener's campaign was a huge success: examples such as by the end of August 20,000 men from the Glasgow area had joined up.
- In Scotland there were no official 'Pals Battalions' but in reality – the Highland Light Infantry/Tramway Battalion; the 16th Battalion/the Boys Brigade.
- In Edinburgh, Cranston's battalion and McCrae's battalions became part the Royal Scots. McCrae's Battalion was the most famous because of its connection with Hearts football club.
- Loos: for many of Scotland's soldiers in Kitchener's New Army the initial taste of action for the volunteers came at Loos in September 1915.
- The 9th and 15th Scottish Divisions were involved in the attack; 9th lost almost 3,000 men killed and missing from 25 to 28 September; 15th lost over 3,000 in a single day.
- Loos was part of a series of British battles of Neuve Chapelle, Aubers Ridge, Festubert and Loos. Scottish losses were huge and all parts of Scotland were affected; of the 20,598 names of the missing at Loos a third of them are Scottish.
- Bravery and fighting spirit of Scottish units: 5 Victoria Crosses given to Scots after the Battle of Loos in recognition of their extraordinary bravery; The Somme: Three Scottish divisions 9th, 15th [Scottish] and 51st [Highland] took part in the Battle of the Somme, as well as numerous Scottish battalions in other units, ie the Scots Guards in the Household Division. 51 Scottish infantry battalions took part in the Battle of Somme offensive at some time.
- Piper Daniel Laidlaw of the KOSB played the pipes during an attack at Loos to encourage Scottish troops to charge. Laidlaw was awarded the VC for his bravery.
- Huge Scottish sacrifice: 15th (Cranston's) Royal Scots lost 18 officers and 610 soldiers wounded, killed or missing. 16th (McCrae's) Royal Scots lost 12 officers and 573 soldiers; 16th HLI lost 20 officers and 534 men – examples of Scottish losses on the first day. The 9th (Scottish) Division performed well during the five months of fighting. Casualties were high: 314 officers and 7,203 other ranks, yet morale remained high.
- Battle of Arras in 1917, saw concentration of 44 Scottish battalions and seven Scottish named Canadian battalions, attacking on the first day, making it the largest concentration of Scots to have fought together. One third of the 159,000 British casualties were Scottish.
- High numbers of Scottish deaths at Loos, Somme, Arras
- The official figure given at the end of the war calculated that Scotland had suffered 74,000 dead.

- Huge sacrifice of Scots during the war: of 557,000 Scots who enlisted in the services, 26.4% lost their lives. One in five British casualties were Scottish.
- Experience of Scottish women on Western Front.
- Scottish leadership: role of Douglas Haig; strong Presbyterian background; believed in his mission to win; stubborn and stoical; famous for order in 1918 not to give ground and to fight to the end.
- Debate over Haig's role: considered to be one of the soldiers of his generation, he had a reputation as an innovative commander. In a balanced judgment the historian John Terrain calls him 'The Educated Soldier'. He had to deal with a military situation which was unique and no other general had had to deal with.
- That he did so with a vision of what was needed – he embraced the use of tanks for example – is to his great credit. He could be distant and was touchy, but he did visit the front and was aware of the sacrifices made; he was the architect of eventual victory.

Any other valid point of explanation that meets the criteria described in the general marking instructions for this kind of question.

14. *Candidates can be credited in a number of ways up to a maximum of 5 marks.*

Possible points of comparison may include:

Source B	Source C
Overall: Sources B and **C** broadly agree about the events of the Rent Strikes. The sources agree about the carrying of placards and the summoning of tenants to court. Sources also note the involvement of men and the introduction of the Rent Restriction Act. **Source B** highlights the actions as a victory of people power whereas **Source C** highlights the role of the Glasgow Labour Party Housing Committee.	

Source B	Source C
In the streets women carried placards.	Our committee organised demonstrations with banners.
Prosecution of 18 tenants due to appear in court for refusing to pay rent increases.	With the summoning of a number of munitions workers to attend court the most dramatic incident of the struggle happened.
By then the rent strikes had escalated, with men taking their own wildcat strike action at Fairfield's and Beardmore's.	Men engaged in work on the Clyde stopped working and marched in their thousands with those summoned to the court.
The government rushed through the Rent Restriction Act.	A few days after this an Act to limit rent increases was introduced by the Government.

15. *Candidates can be credited in a number of ways up to a maximum of 6 marks.*

Examples of aspects of the source and relevant comments:

Aspect of the source	Possible comment
Author: Editor, Glasgow Herald newspaper	Useful as it is an informed view of the events. Sensationalist language highlighted a genuine fear, although brief, of a potential revolution.
Type of source: Newspaper	Useful as it explains some of the events of the 40 hours a week strike. It is less useful as it is limited to events of the 40 hours a week strike and not the wider impact of the war on Scottish politics.
Purpose: To express shock at the political events of 'Red Clydeside'	Useful as it highlights the view that the ILP and strikers had a negative impact on Glasgow.
Timing: 1st February 1919	Useful as it is a contemporary source written at the time of the 40 hour a week strike.

Content	Possible comment
David Kirkwood, one of the strike leaders, and a member of the ILP.	Useful as it shows the involvement of the important leaders such as Kirkwood.
It has been known from the first that the strike movement is controlled by a small section of the Clyde Workers Committee who are pressing for a 40 hour week.	Useful as it shows the involvement of the ILP in orchestrating and organising the strike.
The revolutionary activities of these Bolshevists has damaged Glasgow's reputation.	Useful as it highlights the fear of a Bolshevist led revolution in Glasgow.

Points from recall which support and develop those from the source:

- ILP members' activities — involved in resisting the Munitions Act of 1915; in opposing the introduction of the dilution of labour; anti-conscription...
- In Scotland the ILP was to the fore, campaigning on major issues. ILP supported workers' grievances over prices and rents.
- Both the ILP and the Labour party campaigned for reforms in housing and health after the war and their focus on local issues was a big reason for Labour's success in the 1920s.
- Clydeside ILP MPs confronted Conservatives and Liberals, even leadership of PLP MPs on issues of poverty and unemployment.
- ILP in Scotland had many women prominent in the party such as Mary Barbour, Agnes Dollan and Helen Crawfurd.
- The Clyde Workers' Committee (CWC) was formed to control and organise action for an extension of workers' control over industry.

- Forty Hours Strike and demonstration at George Square, waving of red flag, riot, troops and tanks appeared on streets of Glasgow. Riot Act was read. The Cabinet agreed with the Scottish Secretary Robert Munro, that the confrontation was not strike action but a 'Bolshevist rising.'
- After the war the Labour Party emerged as an important political force with seven seats in Scotland, winning as many votes as the Conservatives.
- In the 1922 election Labour made the breakthrough as the second political party.
- In 1922 Labour won 29 seats in Scotland (10 in Glasgow) and then in 1924 they won 34 seats but saw this fall to 26 seats in the second election in 1924.
- The role of Manny Shinwell, Willie Gallacher, John MacLean.
- Labour sought gradual reform as the leadership of people like Tom Johnstone, Maxton and Kirkwood took precedence over the more radical leaders like John McLean.
- The Conservative Party was strengthened as they worked hard to gain middle class support, helped by Presbyterian churches. Scottish legal system also had strong links with the Conservatives.
- Events in Ireland — growing fears in Scotland of extremism.
- They won 30% of the vote in 1918, increasingly associated with the growing middle-class.
- Conservatives also benefited from being seen as the party of law and order, especially in the aftermath of the George Square riots.
- In the second election of 1924 the Conservatives won 38 seats in Scotland compared to Labour's 26.
- Changes in newspaper ownership led to pro-Union press which was supported by institutions like the universities and legal profession.
- The rise of 'Red Clydeside' prompted a reaction amongst the Scottish elite (industrialists, bankers and politicians like James Lithgow, Eric Geddes and Andrew Bonar Law) to both restore Scotland's industrial and trading pre-eminence and break the power of the shop stewards' movement; this was done by a (near) doubling of the Treasury bill rate, which raised unemployment and led to cuts in public spending.
- Class conflict — breaking of shop stewards, engineers and miners by 1926.
- Splits and decline of the Liberal Party: Coalition Liberals supported Lloyd George and the coalition with the Conservatives at the end of the war. The supporters of Herbert Asquith, the old party leader, stood as Liberals.
- Old Liberal causes died in the aftermath of the war.
- The Liberal Party, which had claimed guardianship of workers' interests on the pre-war era, was increasingly perceived as defending the well-being of employers and capital.
- In the second 1924 election the Liberals won only 9 seats in Scotland.
- Growth of the Labour Party, in alliance with the Catholic Church, made the middle class feel isolated, but attempts to court the working class Protestant/Orange vote foundered on the Conservatives' support for the 1918 Act giving state support to Catholic secondary schools; separate Orange and Protestant party established in 1922, splitting 'Moderate' (Conservative) vote.

- The transformation of the Labour Party reflected a crisis in confidence; at the end of the war the party in Scotland was dominated by the ILP and appeared strong enough to impose its own radical solutions on society, but the defeats of the early 1920s led to the expulsion of the Communists (1925—27) and the defection of the Home Rule wing of the ILP in 1928.
- It was difficult for Home Rule to make progress in Westminster parliament.
- Private Members' Home Rule bills failed.
- Support for Home Rule waned within the Labour Party.
- Glasgow University Scottish National Association formed 1926.
- 1927 John MacCormack and Roland Muirhead, formed the National Party of Scotland.
- It distanced itself from the Labour Party. Drew support from intellectuals like Hugh McDiarmid.
- Some Liberals and Conservatives formed the Scottish Party at the end of the 1920s and proposed some form of devolution in an effort to attract Liberal and Unionist supporters.
- The latter formed the National Party of Scotland but it had little electoral impact. (MacCormack and Muirhead each got less than 3,000 votes in the 1929 election.)
- 'Scottish Renaissance' of the 1920s had strong leanings towards Home Rule and Independence — they challenged both the cultural and political relationship between Scotland and England.
- Beginnings of change in Scottish attitudes to the Empire — linked with the 'profound crisis which overwhelmed the nation between the wars' (Devine).
- Scots' faith in their role as the economic power-house of the Empire had been shattered.
- Extension of the franchise to women. Many working class women had become politicised by their war work and the rent strikes. Women, such as Mary Barbour, Agnes Dollan and Helen Crawfurd became role models for women keen to make their voice heard politically for the first time.

Any other valid point that meets the criteria described in the general marking instructions for this kind of question.

2015
SECTION 2: BRITISH

Part A: Church, State and Feudal Society, 1066—1406

16. The Roman Catholic Church emerged after the fall of Rome to play a central role in daily life in medieval Scotland and England. Although the Church was there to ensure people's salvation it served a broader role as well. Through its religious sacraments it marked the important stages of life. It fulfilled a social, economic and even a political role.

Arguments that the Church's role was religious

Belief in Christianity

- This was dominant within society; it provided people with an understanding of the world and how it worked. People were concerned about the fate of their souls after death. The Church taught that salvation, or the saving of a one's soul, would come to those who followed the Church's teachings.
- Those who failed were damned to a life of torment in hell. To many believers hell was a real place. It was depicted in lurid detail by many medieval painters.

Church services and rituals

- The importance of marriage, funerals and christenings brought people closer to attaining their passage to heaven.
- People were taught that the sacred acts of worship, or sacraments, brought special blessing from God.
- Therefore the ceremonies that marked the passage of life had power and importance to people.
- These could include baptism, confirmation, marriage and penance.

Relics and saints

- Significance of relics and saints as a means to communicate with God and beg divine favour or protection.

Importance of the pilgrimage

- Pilgrimage to holy centres was an important part of medieval life.
- People would travel long distances to places of religious importance, such as Jerusalem and Rome as well as places that had important religious relics like Canterbury.
- Pilgrimages would show devotion to God with such acts as travel was dangerous.
- Crusade was also part of this. The motivation of recovery of the Holy Land from Muslim rule for religious reasons was a powerful one for many Crusaders.

The role of the Regular Church

- Monasteries were seen as 'Prayer Factories' and used to intercede with God for the ordinary lay population.
- Monastic life of dedication to God and a simple life following the rule of St Benedict: poverty, chastity and obedience, was considered important.
- Many rulers clearly thought they were important and spent time and money resourcing the founding of monasteries. David I of Scotland is one example. His dedication to supporting different orders, such as the Cistercians, was undoubtedly pious as well as practical.

Arguments that the church's role was not religious

Economic

- Education provided wealth for the Church. The rich would pay to have their eldest son educated.
- Economic wealth was created through wool gathering eg Melrose Abbey. Additionally, wealth was created through iron foundry, wine making etc.
- The Church as landowners provided significant employment within the community.

Political

Investiture contest

- Political argument between the Church and State as to who had the right to appoint senior clergy members. Such offices came with large grants of land in England and often held considerable political and military significance.
- Monarchs did not wish the papacy to choose political undesirables for such an important position eg William the Lion and the argument over the Bishop of St Andrews in 1180.

Position within Feudal Structure

- Within the feudal system bishops and abbots were seen as other large landowners with the rights to raise troops in time of need eg Bishop of Durham led the English forces that defeated David I at the Battle of the Standard in 1138.

Administrative role

- The Church provided the majority of clerks for the state government. They were needed to keep records, write charters, laws, keep accounts etc.

Divine authority

- The development of canon law during this period was a direct threat to the growth of the monarchies. The papacy argued that all power of kings was invested through them during their coronation by God through the church.
- Monarchs argued that the power was given directly to them by God. As such, the papal position was that kings were subservient to monarchs. The papacy continued to argue their position and used papal sanctions such as excommunication and the interdict to bring monarchs to heel.

Social

- Gathering for religious festivals and services provided social function.
- The Church provided leprosy hospitals and inns for travellers.

Any other relevant factors.

17. **King John was the youngest son of Henry II and Eleanor of Aquitaine. On the death of his elder brother Richard, he became King of England despite the claims of his nephew Arthur. He struggled to hold the widespread Angevin Empire together in the face of the challenges of the Capetian monarch of France and his own barons.**

Impact of the loss of Normandy

- Had an impact on the royal finances as it reduced John's income.
- The recovery of the royal lands north of the Loire became the focus of John's foreign policy and led to policies which eventually led to challenges to his authority.
- The need to fund warfare to recover Normandy led to the frequent use of Scutage to raise cash. It was used much more frequently than under Henry II and Richard, (levied 11 times in 17 years).

Royal Finances

- John was more efficient in collecting taxes.
- Used wardships to raise cash.
- Introduced new taxes: eg 1207 tax on income and moveable goods.
- Improved quality of silver coinage.

Administration of government

- John filled many of the roles in the royal household with new men; especially from Poitou. This was not popular with the English barons.

Military Power

- Established the Royal Navy.
- Extensive use of mercenaries rather than feudal service.
- Able to exert his military strength against the nobility and the French.
- John an able military commander ie when conflict started with France and his nephew Arthur, he defeated them and captured Arthur.
- His forces and his allies were decisively beaten at the Battle of Bouvines in 1214.

Law and justice

- Increasingly partial judgements were resented.
- John increased professionalism of local sergeants and bailiffs.
- Extended the system of coroners.

Relations with the Church

- John fell out with Pope Innocent III over the appointment of the Archbishop of Canterbury. Innocent insisted on the appointment of Langton which John opposed.
- Papel interdict laid on England and Wales for 6 years.
- In 1213 John made England a fief of the papacy.
- Noble uprising led by Archbishop of Canterbury.

Relations with the Nobility

- Nobles refused to fight in France. This was especially true of the northern Barons who had little stake in France.
- Nobles felt their status was reduced by use of mercenaries.
- John became increasingly suspicious of the nobles.
- High cost of titles led to nobles becoming overly indebted.
- John took hostages to ensure nobles behaved. He showed he was prepared to execute children if the father opposed him.
- Relations worsened over the course of the reign, ending with Magna Carta and rebellion of many Barons.

John's personality

- He could be generous, had a coarse sense of humour and was intelligent.
- However, could also be suspicious and cruel: vicious in his treatment of prisoners and nobles.
- Arthur, his nephew, died in mysterious circumstances.
- Powerful lords like William de Braose fell from favour and were persecuted. William's wife and son were imprisoned and died. He died in exile in France.

Any other relevant factors.

18. The decline of feudalism happened as the previous order of society where land was exchanged for economic or military service was challenged. The Peasants' Revolt played a part in the decline as did economic developments, which changed the relationship between peasants and lord, as well as the development of new ways to trade and pay for labour/service led to its decline.

The Peasants' Revolt

- In England, the attempts of the Statute of Labourers Act in 1351 to force peasants back into serfdom were widely and strongly resisted. The extent of the revolt and the impressive way in which it was organised shows that the old feudal consensus had broken down.
- There is an argument that the Peasants' Revolt was a reaction to the attempts to force peasants to return to the old ideas of labour services.
- The use of the Poll Tax was a trigger to the revolt by secular leaders, John Ball and Wat Tyler.

Other factors

The Black Death

- The population decreased between 33% and 50% during the Black Death.
- The decline in the population meant that the survivors, particularly of the lower classes, could demand and often received better wages for their labour. Wage levels in England roughly doubled. Indeed, the shortage of labourers is often seen as causing the decline of serfdom.
- Landowners for the first time needed to negotiate for their serfs' services, leading to higher wages and better living conditions for those that survived.

The growth of towns

- Many found the freedom of burgh life allowed them to develop trade without the burden of labour services or restrictions in movement.
- There was a movement from the countryside to towns which saw a growth.
- Economy in towns did not depend on the ownership of land, rather on the production and selling of goods.

The growth of trade/mercantilism

- With markets for their goods fluctuating considerably, many nobles came to understand their weak economic position. For some it was better to let their peasants become tenants who rented their land than to continue as their feudal protector.
- Others discovered that sheep were a far more profitable resource than peasants could ever be. The monasteries in particular turned over large areas to sheep pasture to capitalise on the strong demand for wool.
- Peasants who could afford to purchase or rent extra land could propel themselves upwards on the social ladder.

Changing social attitudes

- Social mobility was increasing for a number of reasons, including the move to an economy based more on cash than service. In England the wars against France had brought riches to some, and enabled them to climb the social ladder.

Any other relevant factors.

Part B: The Century of Revolutions, 1603–1702

19. Charles I succeeded his father James I in 1625 and ruled over both England and Scotland until 1642. He continued to reign in Scotland until his death in 1649 at the hands of the English Parliament. During this time there were considerable challenges facing the king in his attempts to enforce his policies in Scotland.

Religious policy

- 1629 the king issued a Royal Demand that Scottish religious practice should conform to English models, and in 1633 the king's coronation at St. Giles in Edinburgh included many Anglican rituals such as candles and crucifixes. In the same year, Charles I introduced William Laud, the Archbishop of Canterbury, to Scotland, and he proceeded to oversee Anglican practice in Scottish churches. This meant that many Presbyterians resented the influence of Laud, whose position as the king's representative on spiritual matters led to resentment of royal authority.
- Acting on advice from Laud, Charles I agreed to the unification of the Churches of Scotland and England in 1625 without consulting the Privy Council. Despite Presbyterians' refusals to ratify this decision, in 1635 Laud issued the Book of Canons, which declared that the monarch had authority over the Church of Scotland, and he subsequently approved a new Service Book, a variation of the English Prayer Book, drawn up by the Scottish bishops. Scottish Presbyterian opposition grew in response to these developments.
- On 23 July 1637, a Prayer Book for Scotland modelled on the English Prayer Book was read at St. Giles Cathedral by the Bishop of Brechin who had two loaded pistols sitting in front of him in case of unrest. The Dean, John Hanna, subsequently had a stool thrown at him by a serving woman, Jenny Geddes, and in the chaos that ensued, the Bishop of Edinburgh was shouted down by the crowd in support of Geddes. This incident demonstrates the violent opposition to Charles I's policies in Scotland.
- Across Scotland people declared opposition to the new Prayer Book, placing the king's Scottish Privy Council in a difficult position, caught between Charles I and his rivals. A committee called the Tables was formed in Edinburgh in late 1637 by nobles, middle-class lawyers, Privy Councillors and ministers, all pledged to oppose the king's religious tyranny. This development represented a strengthening of the organised opposition to Charles I.

The Covenanters

- The Tables drew up the National Covenant and publically unveiled it at Greyfriars Kirk on 28 February 1638, and in the 3 days which followed many flocked to Edinburgh to sign it. Amongst its many undertakings, the Covenant pledged to preserve Presbyterianism in Scotland and promote a church free from monarchical meddling. The ensuing months when copies of the Covenant were carried by messengers around the country to be signed by thousands of new Covenanters symbolised the rejection in Scotland of the Divine Right of Kings, a significant political as well as religious development.
- In November 1638 the General Assembly met and deposed all bishops and excommunicated some, thereby abolishing Episcopalianism. These proceedings were, however, dismissed as invalid by Charles I because his representative, the Duke of Hamilton, had not been present. This highlights the open breach that was widening between the Kirk and the king.

- The Covenanting movement was growing, with the Campbells of Argyll prominent in promoting committed opposition to the king's influence in the west. Throughout Scotland, Covenanters were being equipped with arms coming into the country from overseas, and General Leslie assumed command of their army. This placed the
- movement at an advantage over Charles I who had no standing army and a floundering government in Edinburgh
- Charles I failed to suppress Covenanters, and this failure contributed to outbreak of the "Wars of the Three Kingdoms" which lasted from 1639 to 1651, were spread across Scotland, England and Ireland, and included the English Civil War. During this war, the English Parliament's treaty of alliance with Scottish Covenanters — called the Solemn League and Covenant of 1643 — was a key feature of positive change in fortunes of king's enemies. Therefore the Covenanters proved to be a major issue in a British context for the king.

First Bishops' War

- Charles I could not raise enough money to fight effectively as the English Parliament had not been called since 1629, so he could only put together a poorly trained force of 20,000 men at Berwick-on-Tweed, 12 miles from General Leslie's 12,000-strong force camped at Duns. Meanwhile there were several minor engagements in the north east of Scotland between Covenanters and Scottish Royalists, but as the king was unwilling to send his troops into open battle he was forced to agree to a truce in June. This demonstrates Charles I's inability to impose his authority on Scotland with military force.
- The king signed the Pacification of Berwick on 18 June 1639, agreeing to the General Assembly being the highest religious authority in Scotland. The treaty also acknowledged the freedom of the Scottish Parliament in legislative matters. It is clear that the Covenanters were, for the moment, succeeding in their action against Anglicanism.
- Charles I's inability to put down the Scots brought an end to his "Eleven Years' Tyranny" in England, as he recalled Parliament in 1640 to request revenue to continue war with Scotland. This "Short Parliament" lasted one month as the king dissolved it again rather than concede powers to Parliament as a condition of their granting him funds. Scotland, therefore, was proving a constant frustration to Charles I.

Second Bishops' War

- General Leslie crossed the English border with his troops and they successfully captured Newcastle and Durham. Charles I, having dismissed the Short Parliament before obtaining funds, was once more unable to wage war. This put the king in the weak position of having to negotiate a peace with Scotland in order to avoid defeat by the Covenanters.
- Charles I was forced to sign the Treaty of Ripon on 26 October 1640, the terms of which were dictated by the Scots. Aside from the Covenanters maintaining a military presence in Northumberland, the treaty cost England the price that the Scottish Parliament had to pay for its forces, which amounted to roughly £850 per day. The Treaty of Ripon meant that the Second Bishops' War ended in humiliation for the king at the hands of the Covenanters.

Political challenge

- In 1625 he introduced the Act of Revocation which restored those lands to the Church which had been transferred to the nobility at the time of the Reformation in 1560. This development also saw the proceeds from the tithe also passed back to the church, and the king continued to give increasing power to bishops. This behaviour undermined the status of the Scottish nobility, which they in turn deeply resented.
- Charles I's policy was to appoint bishops rather than nobles to the Scottish Privy Council, his chief advisory body in Scotland. In 1635 Archbishop John Spottiswoode was appointed as the king's Chancellor for Scotland, the first non-secular official in this position since the Reformation. Spottiswoode's position led to growing fears that the king would impose Anglicanism on the country.
- Charles I did not visit Scotland until 1633 when he was crowned there by Spottiswoode. His ignorance of the country's political customs and traditions led to a lack of understanding of Scottish affairs. Scots opposition to Charles I meant that the Stuart notion of the Divine Right of Kings was brought to an end by the king's own subjects.

Any other relevant factors.

20. After the Interregnum, the monarchy was restored in 1660. Charles II reigned until 1685, although he used loopholes in the Restoration Settlement to rule without Parliament from 1681 onwards. His brother James II ruled from 1685, but his attempts at absolutism led to the Revolution of 1688–9, when his daughter Mary and her husband William of Orange were asked by Parliament to become joint monarchs, under terms known as the Revolution Settlement.

James II

- The king, a Roman Catholic, ruled absolutely by dismissing Parliament in November 1685 before it could condemn Louis XIV's persecution of Huguenots, French Protestants. He then stationed a 16,000-strong army, including Roman Catholic officers, outside London. Parliament opposed absolutism as well as any monarch's control of a standing army.
- James II imposed his will on the judicial system, re-establishing Prerogative Courts in 1686. In 1687, he used the monarch's Suspending Powers to suspend laws against Roman Catholics, and used the Dispensing Powers later that year to dismiss these laws from the statute books. For Parliament, this demonstrated the old Stuart interventionist attitude towards legislation.
- James II replaced Anglican advisors and office-holders with Roman Catholic ones, including making the Earl of Tyrconnel the Lord Lieutenant of Ireland and Sir Roger Strickland the Admiral of the Royal Navy. He appointed Roman Catholics to important posts at Oxford and Cambridge Universities. Parliament resented these abuses of his power.
- In late 1688 as MPs made clear their determination to invite the king's Protestant daughter Mary to become queen, he tried to use the Stuarts' links with Louis XIV to appeal for military and financial assistance. However, the French king offered little more than vocal support. This actually harmed James II's cause more as Parliament had always disapproved of any monarch's attempt to promote an Anglo-French alliance.

Legacy of Charles II

- The king, exiled in France for the Interregnum, had accepted limitations on his power when the monarchy was restored in 1660. However, loopholes in the Restoration Settlement allowed him to make policy without Parliament. This caused indignation among MPs who had felt that one of the results of the Civil War would be monarchical recognition of the rights of the House of Commons.

- The legal terms of the 1660 Restoration had upheld the Triennial Act and the abolition of prerogative law courts, and prohibited non-parliamentary taxation. It also stated that Charles II should live off his own finances and not receive money from Parliament, although in return, Parliament granted the king taxation on alcohol. This was an indication that greater formalisation of the relationship between Crown and Parliament had to take place.
- In 1677 the king's Lord Treasurer, the Earl of Danby, who was anti-French, was persuaded by some MPs to arrange the marriage of the king's niece, Mary, to William of Orange, a Dutch prince. This was a response to Charles II's foreign policy which broke the 1668 Triple Alliance with Holland and Sweden against France, by allying himself with Louis XIV. This did not reduce Parliament's alarm at the king's pro-French and Roman Catholic leanings, which reflected the fear of many in the country.
- Nevertheless, towards end of reign Charles II ruled alone for 4 years after dissolving Parliament in March 1681 and ignoring the Triennial Act in 1684. In 1683 he imposed a new Charter for the City of London which said that all appointments to civil office, including Lord Mayor, should be subject to royal approval. The loss of power experienced by the House of Commons made MPs fear that the old Stuart combative approach to rule was re-asserting itself.

Political issues

- James II's use of the suspending and dispensing powers in 1687, although not illegal, was seen by Parliament as a misuse of royal privilege. Questions had also been raised by MPs over monarchical control of the army after the king called troops to London in 1685, which was perceived as another abuse of power. Therefore, throughout his short reign, James II provoked political controversy.
- As in the pre-Civil War era, both post-Restoration Stuart monarchs advocated Divine Right and practised absolutism. Charles II's dismissal of Parliament in 1681 and James II's dissolution in 1685 resembled Charles I's conduct at the start of his "Eleven Year Tyranny" in 1629. These actions meant that the status of monarchy was questioned by a resentful Parliament.
- Charles II's Lord Chancellor, the Earl of Clarendon, had been unpopular due to his mishandling of the Second Dutch War between 1665 and 1667, and was even blamed for the Great Plague of 1665 and the Fire of London in 1666. MPs opposed his influence at court and impeached him in 1667, forcing him into exile. This demonstrates differences between monarchical and parliamentary power which spanned both Charles II's and James II's reigns.
- So, in June 1688 as crisis approached, James II hastily promised to recall Parliament by November and announced that Roman Catholics would be ineligible to sit in it. He also replaced Roman Catholic advisors, as well as those in the high ranks of the army and navy, with Protestant ones. This suggests that James II was aware of the unpopularity of his political approach up until that point.

Religious issues

- James II issued the First Declaration of Indulgence in April 1687 which suspended the Test Act, which stated that all holders of civil office, both military and political, should be Anglican and should swear an oath against Roman Catholic doctrine. The king also issued the Second Declaration of Indulgence in May 1688, which stated that toleration towards Roman Catholics should be preached in every church in England on two successive Sundays. MPs, unable to meet in Parliament, expressed discontent at this and especially at the imprisonment of seven bishops for refusing to comply with the Declaration.
- Charles II had been an Anglican, but had secretly signed the Treaty of Dover in 1670, a deal agreeing with Louis XIV that he would declare himself Roman Catholic when his relations with Parliament improved. He entered the Third Dutch War in alliance with France in 1673, and eventually declared himself a Roman Catholic on his deathbed. Parliament reacted to the king's pro-French stance by passing the Test Act the same year.
- James II promoted Roman Catholics to key posts in government and the army. The new heir to the throne, born in 1685, was to be raised as a Roman Catholic. This religious crisis thus created in the minds of MPs drove the momentum for Parliamentarians to send for William and Mary.
- The Restoration Settlement in 1660 had stated that the Church of England would carry on using the Prayer Book approved by the Stuarts. There were hostile divisions between Episcopalians and Presbyterians. Many MPs, therefore, continued to be fearful of continued Stuart dominance of Anglican Church policy.

The role of Parliament

- Parliament resented James II's abuses of power but took comfort from the thought that he would be succeeded by his Protestant daughter Mary. However, the king's wife had a son, James Edward, in June 1688; he was to be raised as Roman Catholic. This led to Parliament writing to Mary, by now married to the Dutch Prince William of Orange, offering her the Crown.
- William and Mary arrived at Torbay in November with an army of 15,000, and after many in the House of Lords declared their support for William, on Christmas Day James II fled to France. Parliament had also persuaded the king's younger daughter Anne, as well as leading generals, to declare their support for Mary. Subsequent to these events, William and Mary became joint sovereigns on February 13th 1689.

Absence of a Bill of Rights between Crown and Parliament

- With no document resembling a Bill of Rights that would formalise the powers held by monarch and Parliament, some MPs felt that a settlement involving William and Mary would have to include one. Without one, future monarchs, including William and Mary, could preach notions of Divine Right, absolutism and passive obedience. This meant that Parliament wanted limitations on the power of the monarchy to be written into law.
- In March 1689, therefore, Parliament drew up a Declaration of Right, which legalised a new relationship between Crown and Parliament in matters such as finance, law, the succession and religion. This became the Bill of Rights in December that year, and had to be signed by William and Mary as a condition of their remaining on the throne. The importance of the Bill of Rights confirms the view that the blurred lines between monarchs and Parliament had been a problem in the past.

Any other relevant factors.

21. After the reign of Charles II, James II ruled between 1685 and 1688. His attempts at absolutism led to the Revolution of 1688–9. Parliament invited the king's daughter Mary and her husband William to become joint monarchs. A series of agreements made between 1689 and 1701, legalising the division of power between Parliament and the Crown, became known as the Revolution Settlement. This included the Bill of Rights, limiting the power of the monarch.

Finance

- Parliament granted William III and Mary II £1,200,000 for court expenses in 1689, including £700,000 to pay civilians working for the state, and these annual awards became fixed amount in the Civil List Act of 1697. A strict Procedure of Audit was established for MPs to check royal expenditure. This meant that financial independence of the crown was no longer possible.
- The 1689 Bill of Rights stated that the monarch could no longer levy taxes without Parliamentary consent. The House of Commons would now agree an annual Budget as proposed by the Chancellor of the Exchequer, who between 1690 and 1695 was Richard Hampden, son of John Hampden. Fiscal power now lay in the hands of Parliament rather than the Crown.
- It could be argued that the monarch benefited from no longer having to resort to unpopular or anachronistic methods of raising revenue, and from now on it would be Parliament that incurred the wrath of ordinary citizens for increasing taxation. However, financial authority had passed to the House of Commons in 1689, and future kings and queens would not be able to reverse this.

Religion

- Parliament passed the Toleration Act of 1689, which provided for toleration of all Protestants except Unitarians, those who did not acknowledge the Holy Trinity. Roman Catholics were also excluded from toleration in the legislation. This meant that Parliament was ensuring that Roman Catholicism could no longer be accepted as it had been under the Stuart dynasty.
- Although Non-Conformist Protestants could now worship freely, the new law maintained an Exclusion from Public Office clause, so they could not obtain teaching positions at universities or elected posts in towns or the House of Commons. The Toleration Act also insisted that Non-Conformists take the Oath of Allegiance and Supremacy as a condition of their religious freedom. It appeared that MPs were having a greater influence on the issue of toleration than they had been allowed during the rest of the 1600s.
- The Toleration Act stated that William III was the supreme head of the Church of England. In opposition to this, there were over 400 Non-Jurors, who were High Anglican priests and bishops refusing to acknowledge William III, and who maintained loyalty to James II, and who were expelled from their posts by Parliament. Parliament, it seemed, could now use its political power to interfere in religious affairs.
- One compromise in the Religious Settlement for the Crown, however, was that the king, as head of the church, now had the power to appoint bishops and archbishops. Nevertheless, the Revolution of 1688–9 established religion firmly within Parliamentary authority.

Legislation

- The 1689 Bill of Rights stated that monarchs could no longer require excessive bail to be demanded from defendants, nor ask judges to impose cruel and unusual punishments on anyone convicted of crimes against the Crown. In addition, ministers impeached by the House of Commons could not be pardoned by the Crown. William III, therefore, could not have the same sway over the justice system as the Stuart kings had.
- In 1695, the Treason Act was altered to give defendants the rights to be given copy of the indictment against them, to be defended by Counsel, to call witnesses in their defence, and to demand that there be two witnesses against them to prove a case instead of the previous one. The Legal Settlement was, therefore, making it harder for a monarch to use the law to enforce policy.
- Later, the Act of Settlement of 1701 stated that judges could only be removed from their positions if Parliament demanded this. The House of Commons alone would approve of judges' commissions being "quamdiu se bene gesserint" – during good behaviour. For judges now, Parliament was ensuring full judicial independence from the Crown, something which had never existed before in England.
- However, by way a compromise, monarchs could still appoint judges, and could be careful to select those who might be favourable to them, which could be a considerable advantage. Overall though, Parliament now enforced its own control over judicial procedure in England.

Parliament

- William and Mary had to agree to the Bill of Rights in December 1689, which legalised the new relationship between Crown and Parliament, before they were given the throne. The Bill of Rights made it clear that monarchs could no longer use royal prerogative to suspend or dispense with laws passed by Parliament, and also could not interfere in Parliamentary elections. This meant that Parliament could exercise independence in its normal business.
- The Bill of Rights also stated that, from now on, MPs and peers could not be punished for exercising Parliamentary freedom of speech during debates in the House of Commons or House of Lords. In addition, the Licensing Act was later repealed in 1695, which removed restrictions on the freedom of the press to report Parliamentary criticism of Crown. It would, therefore, now be impossible for William and Mary to curtail Parliamentary freedom of speech in the manner of Stuart kings earlier in the century.
- The Revolution Settlement provided for another Triennial Act which was passed in 1694. This was intended to keep MPs more closely in touch with public opinion. Parliament was now more relevant to voters than ever before, although voters were still the landed classes.
- It could be argued that the Revolution Settlement still allowed monarchs executive power, so they could dismiss Parliament at will and also rule alone for up to three years, leaving future kings and queens with a significant amount of constitutional power, and as well as this the monarch could still appoint peers and, therefore, wield considerable influence in the House of Lords. Despite this, Parliament was now in a better position in relation to its own rights than it had been at any time since the reigns of Elizabeth I or Henry VIII.

The succession

- The Bill of Rights of December 1689 had declared that no Roman Catholic could become king or queen in the future. More specifically, it stated that all future monarchs should be members of Church of England. Parliament was, therefore, permanently linking the monarchy with the Religious Settlement.
- Furthermore, the eventual Act of Settlement of 1701 stated that, if William and Mary had no heirs, the throne

would pass to Sophia of Hanover, Protestant daughter of Elizabeth of Bohemia, sister of Charles I. MPs wanted to prevent the crown falling back into the hands of the Stuart dynasty. It was now clear that Parliament now held the upper hand in relation to the question of the succession.

- Some historians would argue that the Hanoverian Succession was desired by William anyway, and so the Crown was getting its own way. It cannot be denied, however, that Parliament now governed the subject of who ascended the throne.

Scotland

- In April 1689, the Scottish Parliament, known as the Convention of the Scottish Estate, passed the Claim of Right which was accepted by William and Mary in May. This involved a vote to remove James VII (James II of England) from the throne and approve of William II (William III of England) and Mary II as his successors. The new monarchs' acceptance of the Claim of Right suggests that in Scotland there was now a contractual agreement between the Crown and the people.
- Under the Settlement as it related to Scotland, Scotland was to be allowed to have its own church, the Presbyterian Kirk. In addition, the Scottish Parliament would have a greater share in the government of Scotland and more say in the passing and enforcement of Scots law. These aspects of the Settlement indicate that the Crown had less power in Scotland after 1689 than before.
- There would be disputes in the late 1690s between the English and Scottish Parliaments as the English Parliament said that the monarchy had not approved of the Scots' declarations against Episcopalianism in the Claim of Right. Nevertheless, the Settlement had definitely established Parliamentary authority over the monarchy in Scotland.

Ireland

- The 1691 Treaty of Limerick brought an uprising led by James II's French and Irish volunteers to an end, and was signed by leading generals in James II's and William III's armies. The Treaty stated that, in Ireland, Roman Catholics would enjoy the same freedoms as they had done under Charles II, and the Irish Parliament could allow land confiscated from Roman Catholics by Oliver Cromwell to be given back to its original owners. This suggests that Roman Catholics would be treated with more toleration than they had been before the Revolution of 1688–9.
- The Treaty of Limerick also stated that, in the wake of James II's defeat by William III's troops at the Battle of the Boyne in July 1690, Jacobite soldiers were allowed to flee to France rather than face prosecution. 14,000 soldiers and their families left in a migration which became known as the Flight of the Wild Geese. Again, this freedom awarded by William's government represents an increase in rights for Irish Roman Catholics.
- It is debated by many, however, that promises to treat Roman Catholics better were broken by the Penal Laws of 1693–94, passed by Parliament and excluding Roman Catholics from the learned professions and elected public office. Overall, the Revolution Settlement was not as harsh on Roman Catholics in Ireland as many had feared during a time of cruel and violent persecution of religious minorities across Europe.

The status of the army

- The Bill of Rights in December of 1689 had stated that the monarch could not maintain a standing army during peacetime. The Mutiny Act of 1689 legalised the army, and this act had to be passed annually by Parliament, which forced the king to summon Parliament in order to do so. This meant that Parliament would be sitting on a more permanent basis than ever before.
- However, a significant compromise was the fact that the king still retained control over foreign policy, had the final say on the decision to send the army to war or to sign peace treaties, and used his patronage to appoint officers in both the army and navy. Nevertheless, the Revolution Settlement meant that Parliament had gained at least partial control of the military.

Any other relevant factors.

Part C: The Atlantic Slave Trade

22. The Atlantic slave trade was important in the development of the British economy in the eighteenth century. British manufacturing and industry was stimulated by the supply of factory made goods in exchange for Africans and profits from the slave trade provided the capital for investment in British industry and agriculture.

Evidence that the slave trade was important

The importance of tropical crops

- The climate and land in the West Indies were suited to the growing of luxury crops such as sugar, coffee and tobacco. Britain made large profits from the trade in fashionable products such as sugar and tobacco which became very popular with British people.

The role of the trade in terms of navigation

- The slave trade contributed to the growth of the Royal Navy. The slave trade was an important training ground for British seamen, providing experienced crews for the Merchant Marine and the Royal Navy.
- However, the high death rate, particularly from disease, meant that the slave trade could also be considered a graveyard for seamen.

The role of the trade in terms of manufacturing

- Goods manufactured in Britain were used to buy enslaved Africans. These goods included textiles, metals such as iron, copper and brass and metal goods such as pots, pans and cutlery.
- Cloth manufacturing grew. Manchester exported a large percentage of cotton goods to Africa.
- The slave trade was important to the economic prosperity and well-being of the colonies.

The procurement of raw materials and trading patterns

- The slave trade was important in providing British industries with raw materials which were turned into manufactured goods in Britain and then sold for large profits in Europe
- Liverpool grew wealthy from plantation grown cotton while Bristol's wealth was partly based on slave produced sugar.
- Plantation grown goods such as rum, tobacco, coffee, sugar, molasses and cotton was bought from the profits of selling African slaves to the plantation owners and sold for a profit in Britain and Europe.

Industrial development

- There was a growth in industries supplying the slave traders with goods such as guns, alcohol, pots and pans and textiles to exchange for captured Africans on the Outward Passage.
- Profits from the slave trade were invested in the development of British industries.

- Investment from the slave trade went into the Welsh Slate Industry. Canals and railways were also built as a result of investment of profits from the slave trade.
- The argument that the slave trade was the vital factor in Britain's industrialisation was put forward in Williams' Capitalism and Slavery thesis.
- Wealth generated by the slave trade meant that domestic taxes could be kept low which further stimulated investment.
- There was an expansion of the service industries such as banks and insurance companies which offered financial services to slave merchants.
- By the end of the eighteenth century the slave trade had become less important in economic terms. It has been argued that only a small percentage of the profits from the slave trade were directly invested as capital in the Industrial Revolution.

Wealth of ports and merchants

- Ports such as London, Bristol and Liverpool prospered as a direct result of their involvement in the slave trade. In the early eighteenth century London and Bristol dominated the British end of the slave trade. Liverpool also grew into a powerful city, directly through the shipping of slaves. By the end of the eighteenth century Liverpool controlled over 60% of the entire British slave trade. Liverpool's cotton and linen mills and other subsidiary industries such as rope making created thousands of jobs supplying goods to slave traders. Other ports such as Glasgow profited from trade with the colonies.
- Liverpool became a major centre for shipbuilding largely as a result of the slave trade. By the 1780s Liverpool had become the largest slave ship building site in Britain.
- The emergence of financial, commercial, legal and insurance institutions to support the activities of the slave traders also led to the development of the British economy. Huge fortunes were made by slave merchants who bought large country estates or built large town houses. Some merchants used their wealth from the slave trade to invest in banks and new businesses.

Evidence that other factors were important

- Changes in agriculture such as enclosure, mechanisation, four-field crop rotation and selective breeding helped create an agricultural surplus which fed an expanding population, produced a labour force in the towns for use in factories and created a financial surplus for investment in industry and infrastructure.
- The British economy also benefited from technological innovations. New machinery such as the Spinning Jenny in the textile industry played an important part in the growing industrialisation of Britain. Water and steam power were used to power machines for both spinning and weaving and led to the rapid spread of factories and transport changes in the form of the canals allowed heavy goods to be carried easily and cheaply.
- The British economy also benefited from the increased production of coal and iron.
- The relative political stability of the eighteenth century created the conditions through which trade and the British economy could flourish.
- Much of the profits of slavery was spent on individual acquisition and dissipated in conspicuous consumption, for example landed estates and large town houses built as status symbols.

Any other relevant factors.

23. **Despite a tireless abolitionist campaign inside and outside Parliament, it took many years before the slave trade was finally abolished in 1807. An important obstacle was the delaying tactics and opposition of well organised and powerful groups who had vested interests in the slave trade.**

The power of vested interests

- Successive British Governments were influenced by powerful vested interests in Parliament and industry that had the wealth and power to buy votes and exert pressure on others in support of the slave trade.
- Many absentee plantation owners and merchants involved in the slave trade rose to high office as mayors or served in Parliament. William Beckford, the owner of a 22,000 acre estate in Jamaica, was twice Lord Mayor of London. In the mid to late 1700s over 50 MPs in Parliament represented the slave plantations.
- Many MPs themselves had become wealthy as a result of the slave trade which made it difficult to get a law abolishing the slave trade through Parliament. These MPs were wealthy and powerful enough to bribe other MPs to oppose abolition. Liverpool MPs Banastre Tarleton and Richard Pennant used the House of Commons to protect their families' business interests.
- Members of Parliament who supported the slave trade made speeches in Parliament opposing abolition. They argued that millions of pounds worth of property would be threatened by the abolition of the slave trade. They also argued that the slave trade was necessary to provide essential labour on the plantations and that abolition of the slave trade would ruin the colonies.
- MPs with business interests which made money from the slave trade used delaying tactics to slow down any moves towards abolition or supported compromise solutions. In 1792, in a response to Wilberforce's Bill to end the slave trade, Henry Dundas proposed a compromise of gradual abolition over a number of years. Henry Dundas, termed the 'uncrowned king of Scotland' was Secretary of State for War and First Lord of the Admiralty and as such, protected the interests of Scottish and British merchants in the Caribbean.
- Wealthy merchants from London, Liverpool and Bristol also exerted pressure on governments to oppose the abolition of the slave trade. In 1775 a petition was sent to Parliament by the mayor, merchants and people of Bristol in support of maintaining the slave trade.
- The House of Commons was dominated by various interest groups, of which the West India Lobby was for long the most powerful. Tactics included producing pro-slave trade witnesses to testify in Parliamentary inquiries into the slave trade. The West India Lobby included the Duke of Clarence, one of the sons of George III, and proved tough opposition to the abolitionists. Governments were often coalitions of interests, and often relied on patronage, either through the distribution of posts or the appeasement of such interests.

Other factors

Slave rebellion in St Domingue

- Abolition was associated with this symbol of violence; it exaggerated the general fear of slave revolts. There was high loss of life, perhaps as high as 200,000. Slave violence played into the hands of the slave lobby, confirming their warnings of anarchy.
- Britain suffered humiliation when it attempted to take the rebel French Colony, beaten by disease and the ex-slave army.

- When the revolutionary government of France attempted to regain control, however, support for abolition grew as a means of striking at the French once war was declared.

The events of the French Revolution

- These encouraged the belief among many MPs that the abolitionist cause was associated with revolutionary ideas eg Clarkson openly supported the French Revolution. Radicals used the same tactics as abolitionists to win public support — associations, petitions, cheap publications, public lectures, public meetings, pressure on Parliament. Some abolitionists were linked to radicals and therefore they had to be resisted because of fear that events in France may be repeated in Britain.

The importance of the slave trade to the British economy

- The slave trade generated finance — it was an important source of tax revenue and West Indian colonies were an important source of valuable exports to European neighbours. Taxes would have to be raised to compensate for the loss of trade and revenue. Abolition would help foreign rivals such as France as other nations would fill the gap left by Britain.
- British cotton mills depended on cheap slave produced cotton.
- Africa provided an additional market for British manufactured goods.
- Individuals, businesses and ports in Britain prospered on the back of the slave trade.
- Shipbuilding benefited as did maritime employment.
- It was also argued that the slave trade was vital in Britain being able to sustain an expensive war effort against France.

Fears over national security

- Abolition could destroy an important source of experienced seamen; there was a possibility that Britain would lose its advantage over its maritime rivals. On the other hand, the triangular trade was as much a graveyard as a nursery of seamen.

Anti-abolition propaganda

- Vested interests conducted a powerful propaganda campaign to counter that of the abolitionists, though some of the arguments and evidence were specious.
- Slave owners and their supporters argued that millions of pounds worth of property would be threatened by the abolition of the slave trade. The slave trade was necessary to provide essential labour on the plantations. Abolition of the slave trade would ruin the colonies.

The attitudes of British governments

- Initially British governments were anxious to protect the rights of property, which attacks on slavery seemed to threaten. The tactical decision to concentrate on the abolition of the slave trade circumvented this to an extent.

Any other relevant factors.

24. **By the late eighteenth century, the economic importance of the slave trade had begun to decline. The increased price of slaves and the unpredictability of the triangular slave trade meant that the slave trade was no longer as profitable as it once had been. This was a powerful argument in the case for abolition.**

The decline in the economic importance of slavery

- Effects of wars with France — slave trade declined by two-thirds as it was seen as harming the national interest in time of war.

- The slave trade had become less important in economic terms — there was no longer a need for large numbers of slaves to be imported to the British colonies.
- There was a world over-supply of sugar and British merchants had difficulties re-exporting it.
- Sugar could be sourced at a lower cost and without the use of slavery from Britain's other colonies eg India.
- Industrial Revolution: technological advances and improvements in agriculture were benefiting the British economy.

Other factors

The religious revival

- Many of the first Christian opponents of the slave trade came from non-conformist congregations such as Quakers, Presbyterians, Methodists and Baptists.
- Many of the early leaders were Quakers (the Society of Friends), who opposed slavery on the grounds that Christianity taught that everyone was equal. When the Society for the Abolition of the Slave Trade was formed in 1787, 9 of its 12 original members were Quakers.
- The main thrust of Christian abolitionism emerged from the Evangelical Revival of the eighteenth century based on its beliefs on morality and sin.
- The Methodist founder John Wesley questioned the morality of slavery which influenced many Christian abolitionists including the former slave trader turned clergyman, John Newton.
- Evangelical Christians included Thomas Clarkson, William Wilberforce and Granville Sharp, who fought for the freedom of a young African, Jonathan Strong.
- Clergymen such as James Ramsay who had worked in the Caribbean were influential in exposing the facts of plantation slavery and in pointing out that many Africans died without hearing the Gospel.
- However some Quakers continued to have links with the slave trade eg David and Alexander Barclay set up Barclays Bank, Francis Baring set up Barings Bank.
- The Church of England had links to the slave trade through the United Society for the Propagation of the Gospel (USPG) missionary organisations which owned slave plantations in Barbados.
- Scottish churches were amongst the key drivers in the abolitionist movement, although the Church of Scotland did not petition Parliament to end the slave trade.

The effects of slave resistance

- Successful slave rebellion in Saint-Domingue led to an exaggerated, general fear of slave revolts. There was an argument that if conditions were not ameliorated by, for example, the abolition of the slave trade, further revolts would follow. It was argued that Britain began to plan for an exit from the slave trade as a result of this revolt which shook the whole system to its foundations. Already on Jamaica a substantial number of runaways lived outside the control of the authorities.

Military factors

- Napoleon's efforts to restore slavery in the French islands meant that the abolitionist campaign would help to undermine Napoleon's plans for the Caribbean. The Act banning any slave trade between British merchants and foreign colonies in 1806 was intended to attack French interests.

Campaign of the Society for the Abolition of the Slave Trade

- Thomas Clarkson obtained witnesses for the Parliamentary investigations of the slave trade which provided Wilberforce with convincing evidence for his speeches.
- Books and pamphlets published eg eyewitness accounts from former slaves such as Olaudah Equiano.
- Campaigns to boycott goods produced by slaves in the West Indies such as sugar and rum.
- Petitions and subscription lists, public meetings and lecture tours involving those with experience of slave trade eg John Newton, churches and theatres used for abolitionist propaganda, artefacts and illustrations eg Wedgwood pottery.
- Lobbying of Parliament by abolitionists to extract promises from MPs that they would oppose the slave trade. Effective moderate political and religious leadership among the abolitionists influenced major figures such as Pitt and Fox; abolitionists gave evidence to Parliamentary Commissions.

The role of Wilberforce

- Wilberforce put forward the arguments of the Society for the Abolition of the Slave Trade in Parliament for eighteen years.
- Wilberforce's speeches in Parliament against the slave trade were graphic and appealing and were influential in persuading many others to support the abolitionist cause.
- Wilberforce's Christian faith had led him to become interested in social reform and link the issues of factory reform in Britain and the need to abolish slavery and the slave trade within the British Empire.
- Wilberforce was prepared to work with other abolitionists to achieve his aims, including the Quakers, Thomas Clarkson and Olaudah Equiano.
- Despite campaigning inside Parliament over the course of two decades, his attempts to introduce bills against the slave trade were unsuccessful due to powerful opposition to abolition in Parliament.

Any other relevant factors.

Part D: Britain 1851–1951

25. **Political change in Britain was an evolutionary, rather than revolutionary, process. These slow changes tended to see people given access to the political system in the 19th century because they had proven themselves worthy of the vote. By the 20th century, developments tended to be about rights of citizens and their equality in the political system.**

The widening of the franchise

- In 1867 most skilled working class men in towns got the vote. In 1884 many more men in the countryside were given the vote. In 1918 most men over 21 and some women over 30 gained the vote. It was not until 1928 that all men and women over 21 were given the vote.

Corruption and intimidation

- Secret Ballot 1872, Corrupt and Illegal Practices Act 1883

Distribution of seats

- The re-distribution of seats in 1867, 1885 and 1918 all helped created a fairer system of voting. The effectiveness of these varied; they were less effective in areas where the electorate was small, or where a landowner or employer was dominant in an area eg Norwich.

Choice

- Although the working class electorate increased by 1880s there was no national party to express their interests. The Liberals and Conservatives were perceived as promoting middle, and upper-class capitalist values. The spread of socialist ideas and trade unionism led to the creation of the prototype Labour Party – the LRC – by 1900 thereby offering a wider choice to the electorate.

National Party Organisation

- As the size of the electorate grew individual political parties had to make sure their 'message' got across to electorate eg development of National Liberal Federation, Conservative Central Office, Primrose League.

The role of the House of Lords

- From 1911 Lords could only delay bills from the House of Commons for two years rather than veto them. They had no control over money bills.

Widening opportunity to become an MP

- The property qualification to be an MP was abolished 1858. Payment for MPs began in 1911 enabling working class men to sit.
- However, by 1918 Parliament was more representative of the British people but points still to be resolved included:
  - undemocratic anomalies – plural votes and the university constituencies – were not abolished until 1948
  - in 1949 the two year delaying power of the House of Lords was reduced to only one year but the power of House of Lords (not reformed until 1990s) in law making still continues
- voting system still first past the post in UK.

Any other relevant factors.

26. **A number of reforms were introduced by the Liberal Government between 1906 and 1914 to help improve the lives of the British people. Although some people benefited, overall they had a limited impact.**

The young

- The Provision of School Meals Act (1906) allowed local authorities to raise money to pay for school meals but the law did not force local authorities to provide school meals.
- Medical inspections after 1907 for children were made compulsory but no treatment of illnesses or infections found was provided until 1911.
- The Children's Charter of 1908 banned children under 16 from smoking, drinking alcohol, or begging. New juvenile courts were set up for children accused of committing crimes, as were borstals for children convicted of breaking the law. Probation officers were employed to help former offenders in an attempt to avoid re-offending.
- The time taken to enforce all the legislation meant the Children's Charter only helped improve conditions for some children during the period.

The old

- Old Age Pensions Act (1908) gave people over 70 up to 5 shillings a week. Once a person over 70 had income above 12 shillings a week, their entitlement to a pension stopped. Married couples were given 7 shillings and 6 pence.
- The level of benefits was low. Few of the elderly poor would live till their 70th birthday. Many of the old were excluded from claiming pensions because they failed to meet the qualification rules.

The sick

- The National Insurance Scheme of 1911 applied to workers earning less than £160 a year. Each insured worker got 9 pence in contributions from an outlay of only 4 pence – 'ninepence for fourpence'.
- Only the insured worker got free medical treatment from a doctor. Other family members did not benefit from the scheme. The weekly contribution was in effect a wage cut which might simply have made poverty worse in many families.

The unemployed

- The National Insurance Act (Part 2) only covered unemployment for some workers in some industries and like Part 1 of the Act, required contributions from workers, employers and the government. For most workers, no unemployment insurance scheme existed.
- Some workers who were covered by the Act benefited, but only for a limited period of time.
- Labour Exchanges were introduced to help people back into work but largely in urban areas.

Other reforms

- In 1906 a Workman's Compensation Act covered a further six million workers who could now claim compensation for injuries and diseases which were the result of working conditions.
- In 1909, the Trade Boards Act tried to protect workers in the sweated trades like tailoring and lace making by setting up trade boards to fix minimum wages.
- The Mines Act and the Shop Act improved conditions.

Any other relevant factors.

27. **Between 1945 and 1951, the Labour Government introduced a number of social welfare reforms aiming to meet the needs of the British people 'from the cradle to the grave'. These reforms dealt with the 5 Giants of Poverty: Want, Disease, Ignorance, Squalor and Idleness as identified in the 1942 Beveridge Report. These reforms dealt successfully with the needs of many but not all of the people.**

Want

- 1946 the first step was made: the National Insurance Act: consisted of comprehensive insurance sickness and unemployment benefits and cover for most eventualities.
- It was said to support people from the 'cradle to the grave' which was significant as it meant people had protection against falling into poverty throughout their lives.
- This was very effective as it meant that if the breadwinner of the family was injured then the family was less likely to fall further into the poverty trap, as was common before. However, this act can be criticised for its failure to go far enough.
- Benefits were only granted to those who made 156 weekly contributions.
- In 1948 the National Assistance Board was set up in order to cover those for whom insurance did not do enough.
- This was important as it acted as a safety net to protect these people.
- This was vital as the problem of people not being aided by the insurance benefits was becoming a severe issue as time passed. Yet, some criticised this as many citizens still remained below subsistence level showing the problem of want had not completely been addressed.

Disease

- Establishment of the NHS in 1948 dealt effectively with the spread of disease.
- The NHS was the first comprehensive universal system of health in Britain.
- Offered vaccination and immunisation against disease, almost totally eradicating some of Britain's most deadly illnesses.
- It also offered helpful services to Britain's public, such as childcare, the introduction of prescriptions, health visiting and provision for the elderly, providing a safety net across the whole country: the fact that the public did not have to pay for their health meant that everyone, regardless of their financial situation, was entitled to equal opportunities of health care they had previously not experienced.
- NHS could be regarded as almost too successful. The demand from the public was overwhelming, as the estimated amount of patients treated by them almost doubled. Introduction of charges for prescriptions, etc.

Education

- Reform started by the wartime government: The 1944 Education Act was implemented by the Labour Government. This act raised the age at which people could leave school to 15 as part of a drive to create more skilled workers which Britain lacked at the time. Introduction of school milk, etc.
- Labour introduced a two-tiered secondary schooling whereby pupils were split at the age of 11 (12 in Scotland) depending on their ability. The smarter pupils who passed the "11+ exam" went to grammar and the rest to secondary moderns.
- Those who went to grammar schools were expected to stay on past the age of 15 and this created a group of people who would take senior jobs in the country thus solving the skills shortages. Whilst this separation of ability in theory meant that children of even poor background could get equal opportunities in life, in practice the system actually created a bigger division between the poor and the rich. In many cases, the already existing inequalities between the classes were exacerbated rather than narrowed.
- Labour expanded university education: introduction of grants so all could attend in theory.

Housing

- After the war there was a great shortage of housing as the war had destroyed and damaged thousands of homes; and the slum cleaning programmes of the 1930's had done little to rectify the situation which was leading to a number of other problems for the government.
- Tackling the housing shortage and amending the disastrous results of the war fell upon Bevan's Ministry of Health.
- Labours' target for housing was to build 200,000 new homes a year. 157,000 pre-fabricated homes were built to a good standard, however this number would not suffice and the target was never met.
- Bevan encouraged the building of council houses rather than privately funded construction.
- The New Towns Act of 1946, aimed to target overcrowding in the increasingly built up older cities. By 1950, the government had designed 12 new communities.
- In an attempt to eradicate slums the Town and Country Planning Act provided local communities more power in regards to building developments and new housing.

- By the time Labour left government office in 1951 there was still a huge shortfall in British housing.

Idleness

- Unemployment was basically non-existent so the government had little to do to tackle idleness.
- The few changes they did make were effective in increasing the likelihood of being able to find work, because they increased direct government funding for the universities which led to a 60% increase in student numbers between 1945–46 and 1950–51, which helped to meet the manpower requirements of post-war society. This provided more skilled workers and allowed people from less advantaged backgrounds to pursue a higher education, aiming to keep unemployment rates down.
- Labour government also nationalised 20 percent of industry — the railways, mines, gas and electricity. This therefore meant that the government were directly involved with people employed in these huge industries which were increasing in size dramatically.
- This tackled idleness by the government having control which meant that employees were less likely to lose their job through industries going bankrupt and people were working directly to benefit society.

Any other relevant factors.

Part E: Britain and Ireland, 1900–1985

28. Initially the First World War brought prosperity to Ireland. The demands on manufacturing and farming brought low unemployment thus improving relations between Britain and Ireland. However, Sinn Fein, the Easter Rising and the Protestant reaction were to change this along increasingly sectarian lines.

Irish Attitudes to World War I

- Propaganda — powerful Germany invading helpless and small Catholic Belgium so Ireland supported Britain.
- Ulster very supportive of Britain to ensure favourable treatment at the end of the war.
- Nationalists and Redmond backed war to get Home Rule, urging Irish men to enlist.
- Press gave support to the war effort.
- Irish Volunteers gave support to help Home Rule be passed after the war.
- Recruitment was successful in the south as almost ¼ million men join up.

The Nationalist Movement

- Opposition to war very much a minority in 1914 but supported by Sinn Fein and Arthur Griffith (not powerful at this time), as well as Pearse, Connolly and their supporters and also a section of the Irish Volunteers. This damaged relations with Britain.

Easter Rising

- Rebels saw war as chance to rid Ireland of British by force.
- Felt it was opportunity to gain independence by force as Britain had their troops away fighting the Germans in World War I. This greatly strained relations between Britain and Ireland.
- Britain had to use force to suppress rebellion, such as using the Gunboat, 'Helga' to sail up the River Liffey and fire on the rebels in the GPO, thus distracting Britain's attention and resources away from War effort, thus straining relations.
- Strong criticism of Rising initially from the public, politicians, churchmen, as well as press for unnecessary

death and destruction. 450 dead, 2500 wounded, cost £2½ million, showing that majority still sided with Britain therefore indicating that there was not too much damage to relations between the two countries.
- Initial hostility by majority of Irish people to Rising by small group of rebels, majority of people supported Redmond and the Nationalists Party.
- Strong hostility and criticism by Dubliners to rebels for destruction of city centre.

Changing Attitudes towards British Rule after 1916

- The secret court martial, execution of leaders over 10 days as well as imprisonment without trial and at least one execution without a trial saw the rebels gain a lot of sympathy from the Irish public, turning them against British rule.
- These political developments meant a growth of sympathy and compassion for rebels who were seen as martyrs and replaced the initial condemnation of the Rising.
- Sinn Fein initially blamed for the Rising saw a subsequent rise in support for them.
- Catholic Church and business community became more sympathetic to the cause of independence

Anti-Conscription Campaign

- Irish opposed conscription and pushed people in protest to Sinn Fein who openly opposed it.
- Caused the Nationalists to withdraw from Westminster.
- Sinn Fein and Nationalists organised campaign eg general strike April 23rd.
- Catholic Church, Mayor of Dublin drew up the National Pledge opposing conscription.
- Conscription was not extended to Ireland which Sinn Fein was given credit for.
- Conscription campaign drove Sinn Fein underground which improved their organization.

Decline of Nationalist Party

- Irish Convention failed to reach agreement, which weakened position of Nationalists.
- Led to feeling British could not be trusted and Nationalists could not deliver.
- Three by-elections wins for Sinn Fein gave impression they spoke for people not Nationalists which increased tension between Ireland and Britain politically.
- March 1918 Redmond died which accelerated the decline of the Nationalists. Sinn Fein gained influence and popularity as a result.
- Many moved from the Nationalist Party as they felt Sinn Fein was doing more for Ireland.

Rise of Sinn Fein

- Release of rebel prisoners from Frongoch meant Sinn Fein's struggle against British Rule in Ireland gained momentum.
- Michael Collins was building up IRB and Irish Volunteers when in prison.
- Collins ready to encourage anti-British activity in Ireland on release.
- Collins and De Valera improved Sinn Fein's leadership.
- Opposition to Britain due to martial law, house searches, raids, control of press, arrest of "suspects" without trial, and vigorous implementation of the Defence of the Realm Act.
- Hunger striker Thomas Ashe died in 1917. His funeral became a propaganda tool for Sinn Fein.

Entrenchment of Unionism in the North

- Unionists' 'blood sacrifice' on the Western Front — expectation that this would be recognised in any post-war settlement. The rise of Sinn Fein was viewed with increasing alarm, as was the participation of the Catholic Church in wartime politics eg the National Pledge.

Any other relevant factors.

29. **In 1964 a peaceful civil rights campaign started to end the discrimination against Catholics in Northern Ireland. This led to a Protestant reaction and the crisis that developed was in part caused by economic issues.**

Economic issues

- Northern Ireland was left relatively prosperous by World War Two, with the boom continuing into the 1950s. But by the 1960s, as elsewhere in Britain, these industries were in decline eg Harland and Wolff profitable until early '60s, but government help in 1966. Largely Protestant workforce protected as a result.
- Catholic areas received less government investment than their Protestant neighbours. Catholics were more likely to be unemployed or in low-paid jobs than Protestants in N. Ireland. Catholic applicants also routinely excluded from public service appointments.
- The incomes of mainly Protestant landowners were supported by the British system of 'deficiency payments' which gave Northern Ireland farmers an advantage over farmers from the Irish Republic.
- Brookeborough's failure to address the worsening economic situation saw him forced to resign as Prime Minister. His successor, Terence O'Neill set out to reform the economy. His social and economic policies saw growing discontent and divisions within his unionist party.

Other factors

The Unionist ascendancy in Northern Ireland and challenges to it

- Population of Northern Ireland divided: two-thirds Protestant and one-third Catholic: it was the minority who were discriminated against in employment and housing.
- In 1963, the Prime Minister of N.Ireland, Viscount Brookeborough, stepped down after 20 years in office. His long tenure was a product of the Ulster Unionist domination of politics in Northern Ireland since partition in 1921.
- Unionist ascendancy: Before 1969 elections not held on a "one person, one vote" basis: gerrymandering used to secure unionist majorities on local councils. Local government electoral boundaries favoured unionist candidates, even in mainly Catholic areas like Derry/Londonderry. Also, right to vote in local elections restricted to ratepayers, favouring Protestants, with those holding or renting properties in more than one ward receiving more than one vote, up to a maximum of six. This bias preserved by unequal allocation of council houses to Protestant families.
- Challenges as Prime Minister O'Neill expressed desire to improve community relations in Northern Ireland and create a better relationship with the government in Dublin, hoping that this would address the sense of alienation felt by Catholics towards the political system in Northern Ireland.
- Post-war Britain's Labour government introduced the welfare state to Northern Ireland, and it was implemented with few concessions to traditional sectarian divisions.

Catholic children in the 1950s and 1960s shared in the benefits of further and higher education for the first time. This exposed them to a world of new ideas and created a generation unwilling to tolerate the status quo.

- Many Catholics impatient with pace of reform and remained unconvinced of Prime Minister O'Neill's sincerity. Founding of the Northern Ireland Civil Rights Association (NICRA) in 1967. NICRA did not challenge partition, though membership mainly Catholic. Instead, it called for the end to seven "injustices", ranging from council house allocations to the "weighted" voting system.

Role of the IRA

- Rioting and disorder in 1966 was followed by the murders of two Catholics and a Protestant by a 'loyalist' terror group called the Ulster Volunteer Force, who were immediately banned by O'Neill.
- Peaceful civil rights marches descended into violence in October 1968 when marchers in Derry defied the Royal Ulster Constabulary and were dispersed with heavy-handed tactics. The RUC response only served to inflame further the Catholic community and foster the establishment of the Provisional IRA by 1970 as the IRA split into Official and Provisional factions.
- The Provisional IRA's strategy was to use force to cause the collapse of the Northern Ireland administration and to inflict casualties on the British forces such that the British government be forced by public opinion to withdraw from Ireland.
- PIRA were seen to defend Catholic areas from Loyalist attacks in the summer of 1970.

Cultural and political differences

- The Catholic minority politically marginalised since the 1920s, but retained its distinct identity through its own institutions such as the Catholic Church, separate Catholic schools, and various cultural associations, as well as the hostility of the Protestant majority.
- Catholic political representatives in parliament refused to recognise partition and this only increased the community's sense of alienation and difference from the Unionist majority in Northern Ireland.
- Nationalists on average 10–12 in NI Parliament compared to average 40 Unionists. In Westminster 10–12 Unionists to 2 Nationalists
- As the Republic's constitution laid claim to the whole island of Ireland, O'Neill's meeting with his Dublin counterpart, Seán Lemass, in 1965, provoked attacks from within unionism, eg the Rev. Ian Paisley.
- Violence erupted between the two communities, in 1966 following the twin 50th anniversaries of the Battle of the Somme and the Easter Rising. Both events were key cultural touchstones for the Protestant and Catholic communities.

The issue of Civil Rights

- From the autumn of 1968 onwards, a wide range of activists marched behind the civil rights banner, adopting civil disobedience in an attempt to secure their goals. Housing activists, socialists, nationalists, unionists, republicans, students, trade unionists and political representatives came together across Northern Ireland to demand civil rights for Catholics in Northern Ireland.
- The demand for basic civil rights from the Northern Ireland government was an effort to move the traditional fault-lines away from the familiar Catholic-Protestant, Nationalist-Unionist divides by demanding basic rights for all citizens of Britain.
- Civil rights encouraged by television coverage of civil rights protest in USA and student protests in Europe. Also

by widening TV ownership: 1954, 10,000 licences, by 1962 there were 200,000 leading to increased Catholic awareness of the issues that affected them.

- As the civil rights campaign gained momentum, so too did Unionist opposition. Sectarian tension rose: was difficult to control, and civil disobedience descended into occasions of civil disorder.

Any other relevant factors.

30. **Nationalists and Unionists were polarised throughout the period. The two communities were increasingly divided along sectarian lines and economic differences were in part an obstacle to peace. The deployment of British troops in Northern Ireland and imposition of Direct Rule saw the conflict widen.**

Economic differences

- From 1973, the Common Agricultural Policy changed the decision making environment for food prices and farm economics, and employment in the farming sector continued to decline. Traditionally this sector had been dominated by the Unionist community.
- Discrimination against Catholic applicants for employment declined steadily during this period as Catholics in the province began to enjoy the same civil rights enjoyed by the population of the rest of the UK.

Other factors

Religious and communal differences

- The Protestant majority in Northern Ireland belonged to churches that represented the full range of reformed Christianity, while the Catholic minority was united in its membership of a Church that dominated life in the Republic and much of Europe. These religious divisions made it very difficult for both communities to come together.
- These divisions further enhanced by traditions embraced by both communities, such as the 'marching season', which became a flashpoint for sectarian violence. Also differences in sport, language.
- Many Catholic political representatives refused to recognise partition and their views only heightened the nationalist community's sense of alienation and fostered unionist hostility towards the Catholic minority.
- The speeches and actions of Unionist and Nationalist leaders such as Reverend Ian Paisley and Gerry Adams polarised views in the province, and emphasised the divisions between both communities.

The role of the British Army

- The so-called 'Battle of Bogside' in 1969 only ended with the arrival of a small force of British troops at the request of Chichester Clark. An acknowledgement that the govt. of Northern Ireland had lost its grip on the province's security.
- By 1971 policing the province was fast becoming an impossible task, and the British Army adopted increasingly aggressive policies on the ground.
- On 30 January 1972, the army deployed the Parachute Regiment to suppress rioting at a civil rights march in Derry. Thirteen demonstrators were shot and killed by troops, with another victim dying later of wounds. Appalling images of 'Bloody Sunday' led to increased recruitment by Provisional IRA.
- The British Army's various attempts to control the PIRA, such as house-to-house searches and the imposition of a limited curfew, only served to drive more recruits into the ranks of the paramilitaries.

Hardening attitudes – the role of terrorism

- Paramilitary groups began to operate on both sides of the sectarian divide, while civil rights marches became increasingly prone to confrontation.
- In late 1969, the more militant 'Provisional' IRA (PIRA) broke away from the so-called 'Official' IRA. PIRA was prepared to pursue unification in defiance of Britain and would use violence to achieve its aims.
- Unionist paramilitaries also organised. The UVF was joined by the Ulster Defence Association, created in 1971.
- Examples of terrorist activity: by the end of 1972 sectarian violence had escalated to such an extent that nearly 500 lives were lost in a single year. PIRA prisoners protest at loss of special status prisoners leading to hunger strikes. Second hunger strike in 1981, led by Bobby Sands. Sands was put forward for a vacant Westminster seat and won. Sands and nine other hunger strikers died before the hunger strikes were called off in October 1981.
- Sinn Fein won the by-election following Sands' death in June 1983. These electoral successes raised the possibility that Sinn Fein could replace the more moderate SDLP as the political voice of the Catholic minority in Northern Ireland.
- Indiscriminate terrorism meant Eire public opinion turned against PIRA.
- In 1985 the violence of Northern Ireland's paramilitary groups still had more than a decade to run and the sectarian divide remained as wide as it had ever been.

British government policies – Internment

- New Prime Minister Brian Faulkner reintroduced internment ie detention of suspects without trial, in 1971 in response to unrest. The policy was a disaster, both in its failure to capture any significant members of the PIRA and in its sectarian focus on Nationalist rather than Loyalist suspects.
- Reaction was predictable, even if the ferocity of the violence wasn't. Deaths in the final months of 1971, over 150.

Direct Rule

- A number of reforms had followed on from the Downing Street Declaration, ie on allocation of council housing, investigate the recent cycle of violence and review policing, such as the disbanding of the hated 'B Specials' auxiliaries.
- The British government, now led by Prime Minister Edward Heath, decided to remove control of security from the government of Northern Ireland and appointing a secretary of state for the province leading to resignation of Stormont government. Direct rule imposed.
- Despite attempts to introduce some sort of self-rule, such as the Sunningdale agreement of 1973, which failed in the face of implacable Unionist opposition and led to the reintroduction of direct rule. It would last for another 25 years.

The role of the Irish government.

- Irish government's role in The Anglo-Irish Agreement, signed in November 1985, confirmed that Northern Ireland would remain independent of the Republic as long as that was the will of the majority in the north. Also gave the Republic a say in the running of the province for the first time.
- The agreement also stated that power could not be devolved back to Northern Ireland unless it enshrined the principle of power sharing.

Any other relevant factors.

2015
SECTION 3: EUROPEAN AND WORLD

Part A: The Crusades, 1071–1204

31. It was religious passion which swept across Europe that motivated people first and foremost, overwhelming Pope Urban and the Emperor Alexius. The tradition of pilgrimage, combined with full remissions of sins and entry to Heaven, explains why so many Christians went on Crusade to the Holy Lands.

Religious motives

- A key factor driving the largest range of people to take the cross was spirituality, the belief that the Crusade was a spiritual war which would purify their souls of sin. This was a powerful motive in a world deeply concerned with matters of religion, where everything in life was potentially sinful. Many responded to Urban's promise of spiritual rewards for those who fought for the Church. Urban took an unprecedented step at Clermont and offered entry to heaven to those who pledged their soul to the Crusade.

- All Christians, rich and poor were being promised by God's representative on earth, the Pope that fighting in a war against the enemies of the Church would bring what so many deeply wanted: a full indulgence — the highest of prizes — a direct path to heaven and eternal salvation from the moment of death.

- It was generally believed that the Remission of Sins offered by Pope Urban was an attractive solution to the dilemma of knights. At Clermont, Urban assured nobles and knights that they could slaughter the 'infidel' in the name of Christ and not have to complete penance for such action. The very act of crusading itself would form the penance.

- Urban successfully resolved the need to protect Christianity from the Muslim threat and the general desire to re-establish the pilgrimage routes to the Holy Lands. Many believed it was their Christian duty to help fellow Christians under threat by Muslims. Many felt the Crusade would be a spiritually rewarding pilgrimage. Urban drew on the ancient tradition of pilgrimage. For centuries people had journeyed to Jerusalem and the holy sites as well as Rome as a form of penance and to gain remission for their sins.

- Of the leaders of the Princes' Crusade, Raymond of Toulouse, is often held up as an example of a knight riding to the defence of the Holy Lands. Deeply religious, Raymond was the first Prince to agree to join the Crusade. He sold all his lands and wanted to die in the Holy Land. However, his decision to take Tripoli in 1100 casts a shadow over this interpretation of his motives.

- The appeal of the People's Crusade shows the power of the belief that they were doing good and helping God.

- In the First Crusade recruitment was strongest in areas which had supported Pope Gregory VII's reform movement and among families with a tradition of pilgrimage and from areas of France that Pope Urban had visited in person.

- Such omens as showers of meteorites and heavy rains after years of drought were regarded as prophesies, signs of intervention by the Hand of God. Witnesses to these signs believed they were predestined to join the soldiers of Christ and journey to the Holy City.

- Evidence from the charters reveal Crusaders did indeed want to free Jerusalem and win forgiveness for their sins although it should be noted that most charters were written by clergy who may have recorded the Church's official view.

Other factors
Seeking of fame and riches

- It is recognised that not all Crusaders were motivated purely by religion and that many had mixed motives and agendas which included the prospect of financial gain and glory seeking.

- Some knights did go seeking glory and to prove their bravery. The Crusade had provided the solution to the problem of knights and their need for salvation. Young knights like Tancred may have been partly motivated by the desire to use their military skills in the East.

- The idea of crusading was popular with Norman knights who saw the chance of becoming rich and powerful.

- The lure of unimaginable wealth may have motivated some. It was known that there was a lot of wealth in the East. It was the centre of trade.

- Some were attracted by the prospect of booty and plunder.

- The desire for financial gain motivated the Italian city of Pisa, Genoa and Venice who supported the Crusades in the hope of gaining bases for their trading ships.

- The seeking of riches per se was relatively uncommon. For many lesser knights, going on Crusade meant risking financial ruin. They were more likely to lose money than make money since many had to sell or mortgage their lands on poor terms. In addition, land was the real source of wealth and power.

The desire to acquire territory in the Holy Land

- Urban promised that those who went on Crusade would keep possession of any lands they conquered. The traditional view is that this especially appealed to the younger sons of noble families, because of the system of primogeniture.

- Many of the great magnates on this expedition had intentions to acquire new estates for themselves. The motives of many of the leaders of the Princes' Crusade have been put down to this.

- The prospect of gaining land said to 'flow with milk and honey' was tempting for a younger son who would not inherit his father's lands.

- Territory was important to some of the knights and princes who had nothing in Europe;

- Examples of Crusaders who set off for the Holy Land in search of the 'land of milk and honey' which Urban had offered, were Bohemond and Baldwin who showed little zeal in carrying on with the Crusade once they had acquired Antioch and Edessa respectively. Bohemond of Taranto had not inherited his father's lands in Italy and was eager to gain land elsewhere.

- Some of the leaders of the First Crusade personified the desire for land. Notable examples were Robert Duke of Normandy (son of William the Conqueror) and the Normans from southern Italy, Bohemond of Taranto and his nephew Tancred, one of eleven brothers, a classic example of younger sons of the nobility striving for a living. Robert Guiscard's eldest son, Bohemond saw the Crusade as an opportunity to extend his territory.

- The promise of land was an incentive to some although the traditional historians' view of land hunger being a motivation is questioned by the huge financial cost of going on Crusade. The cost of chain mail, armour, horses and weapons amounted to several years' income for most knights.

Peer pressure

- The pressure put on knights by their families to take the cross was at times severe. Noblemen's wives tended to be keenly aware of the politics at court and had a role in influencing the decisions of some.
- Stephen of Blois had married Adela, daughter of William I of England. It would have been unthinkable for such a notable knight not to go on the Crusade. Stephen of Blois was the son-in-law of William the Conqueror and was devoted to his very religious wife Adela. He may have joined the Crusade to please her but it would have been unthinkable for such a notable knight not to go on the Crusade. Overpopulation and famine
- A motive of many may have been a desire to escape the hardships of life at the time. Northern Europe was experiencing rising population, constant food shortages and petty wars and lawlessness. Many craved a better life, in this world as well as the next.
- Several years of drought and poor harvests in the 1090s led to a widespread outbreak of a deadly disease called ergotism, caused by eating bread made from fungus infected cereal. Against this background, a long and dangerous journey to a distant land in the east from which they might never return must have seemed a risk worth taking.
- Many were forced to leave because of the lack of available farmland in an already overcrowded Europe.
- Several famines have also been suggested as a possible motive. It was popularly believed that the Holy Land was a land of plenty.
- Northern Europe was experiencing rising population and constant food shortages.

The sense of adventure

- Going on Crusade was exciting and engendered a sense of adventure.
- Pilgrimages had always been seen as important, and the idea of this as an armed pilgrimage was very appealing. It offered a way out for many serfs from their lives in bondage, or perhaps a chance to see the Holy Land.

Any other relevant factors.

32. The military skills and leadership of both Richard the Lionheart and Saladin were much in evidence during the Third Crusade. However away from the battlefield, the relationship between Richard and Saladin demonstrated that both men were also skilled in diplomacy.

Richard's military strengths

- Despite Muslims and Christians having fought an on and off battle over Acre over two years, Richard's leadership and expertise broke the deadlock and forced the surrender of Acre after 5 weeks of bombardment, mining and repeated assaults.
- Richard's arrival in June 1191 with money and with the cutting edge of western military technology in the form of enormous siege engines struck the fear of God into opponents. This enabled Richard to seize control of the battle and to intensify the bombardment.
- Richard switched tactics at Acre after the destruction of his great war machines. He offered his soldiers four gold coins for every stone they could remove from the base of one of the towers, putting so much effort on the one point that a breach in the wall was created.
- Further evidence of Richard's leadership skills at Acre, were shown when, despite falling ill with 'arnaldia' he ordered himself to be carried to the walls in a silken quilt and there, protected by a screen, fired his crossbow at the city which further inspired his troops.
- The capture of Acre was a major boost for the Crusaders and brought the unimpeded rise of Saladin to a halt.
- Richard demonstrated firm, if brutal, leadership in August 1191 when he took the drastic decision to massacre the 2,700 Muslim prisoners taken at Acre when Saladin failed to meet the ransom payment. Richard knew feeding and guarding the prisoners would be a considerable burden and suspecting that Saladin was deliberately using delaying tactics to pin Richard down, Richard resolved the situation quickly and effectively in order to carry on his momentum and capitalise on his victory at Acre.
- Richard demonstrated that he was a great military strategist on the march from Acre down the coast to Jaffa. Under Richard's leadership, the Crusader army of 12,000 men set out along the coast in immaculate formation. Inland were the foot soldiers with their vital role of protecting the heavy cavalry, the cavalry themselves were lined up with the Templars at the front and the Hospitallers at the back, the strongest men to protect the most vulnerable parts of the march. Between the cavalry and the sea was the baggage train, the weakest, slowest and most difficult part to defend. Finally out to sea was the crusader fleet to provide the well-defended columns with essential supplies.
- Richard's military leadership was crucial to the survival of the Crusaders on the march to Jaffa. Forced to face terrible conditions, Richard allowed the soldiers rest days and prevented fights over the meat of dead horses. Despite the constant attacks, Richard showed enormous discipline as he kept his troops marching even as they were being peppered by arrows. Richard was insistent that no Crusader should respond and break formation denying Saladin an opportunity to inflict a crushing defeat on the Crusader forces. Richard wanted to charge on his own terms. Such discipline showed Richard to be a true military genius.
- At the battle of Arsuf, Richard reacted immediately to the breaking of the Crusader ranks and personally led the attack which eventually swept the Muslims from the battlefield. Richard turned his whole army on the Muslims and fought off two fierce Muslim counter attacks. Led by Richard, the Crusader charge smashed into Saladin's army forcing them to retreat. Richard's planning and meticulous attention to detail created the circumstances in which his personal bravery could shine through. The victory of Richard's army over Saladin's forces at the Battle of Arsuf and the success of the Crusaders in reaching Jaffa were important turning points in the Third Crusade. Saladin's aura of success had been breached.
- Richard displayed inspired military leadership and immense personal bravery at Jaffa. When Richard heard that Saladin had stormed the port of Jaffa in July 1192, Richard responded with characteristic brilliance. Richard rushed south from Acre with a tiny force of only 55 knights and crossbowmen at the head of a sea borne counter attack. Despite being heavily outnumbered Richard ordered his men to attack and was one of the first to wade ashore at the head of his small army. The surprise of his attack turned the battle around and gave the Crusaders an improbable and dramatic victory. The Muslim troops themselves were overawed by Richard's courage and nerve. Richard's highly disciplined and organised army had again proved too much for Saladin's men and they retreated.

- Richard's ability as a military tactician was shown by his caution on the march to Jerusalem. To ensure his advance on Jerusalem could be properly sustained, Richard carefully rebuilt several fortresses along the route.
- Richard also demonstrated his strategic competence when he withdrew twice from Jerusalem, realising that once recaptured, Jerusalem would be impossible to defend due to insufficient manpower and the possibility that their supply lines to the coast could be cut off by the Muslims. Despite his personal desire to march on Jerusalem, Richard was a general and knew that military sense told him that his depleted force of 12,000 men and lack of resources couldn't hold Jerusalem against Saladin's vast army drawn from across the Muslim world.
- That Richard was a military strategist of the highest order was also demonstrated on his journey to the Holy Land when he captured Cyprus and sold part of it to the Templars. Richard recognised the long term importance of Cyprus as a base for crusading armies to use when supplying and reinforcing expeditions to the Holy Land.
- Richard also realised that Egypt was the key to Saladin's wealth and resources. Ever the military strategist Richard wanted to take the mighty fortress of Ascalon which would threaten Saladin's communications with Egypt. Richard was aware that in order to keep Jerusalem after it was captured; Egypt would need to be conquered first. Richard wrote to the Genoese asking for a fleet to support a campaign in the summer of 1192 but the Crusader army was not interested in Jerusalem and wanted to proceed to Jerusalem. Richard reluctantly agreed to march on Jerusalem before campaigning in Egypt.
- Although the Third Crusade failed in its ultimate aim of the recovery of Jerusalem, Richard's leadership played a crucial role in providing the Crusaders with a firm hold on the coastline which would provide a series of bridgeheads for future crusades. Compared to the situation in 1187, the position of the Crusaders had been transformed.

Richard's military weaknesses

- Richard was ultimately unable to recapture Jerusalem, the main objective of the Third Crusade.
- Richard also failed to draw Saladin into battle and inflict a decisive defeat. He failed to comprehensively defeat Saladin.

Saladin's military strengths

- Saladin counter attacked at Acre. Saladin's troops launched fierce attacks on the Crusaders at given signals from the Muslim defenders and launched volley after volley of Greek fire putting Richard on the defensive as all three of his giant siege towers went up in flames. Saladin also sent a huge supply ship with 650 fighting men in an attempt to break into Acre's harbour. After destroying a number of English vessels, it was scuttled to prevent its cargo falling into Christian hands.
- On the march south to Jaffa, Saladin's army unleashed a relentless series of forays and inflicted constant bombardment, tempting the Christians to break ranks. Saladin's skilled horsemen made lightning strikes on the Crusaders showering the men and their horses with arrows and cross-bow bolts. The Crusaders lost a large number of horses and the Crusaders themselves resembled pincushions with as many as ten arrows or crossbow bolts protruding from their chain mail.
- Saladin massed his forces from Egypt and all across Syria and launched an intense bombardment on the Crusaders which tested the Crusader knights' discipline and patience, not to react, to the absolute limits.

- At the Battle of Arsuf, despite the devastating impact of the Crusader charge, Saladin's own elite Mamluk units rallied and offered fierce resistance.
- To prevent the Crusaders taking Ascalon, Saladin made the decision to pull down Ascalon's walls and sacrifice the city.
- While the Crusaders remained in Jaffa and strengthened its fortifications Saladin took the opportunity to destroy the networks of Crusader castles and fortifications between Jaffa and Jerusalem.
- In October 1191 as the Crusaders set out from Jaffa and began the work of rebuilding the Crusader forts along the route to Jerusalem, they were repeatedly attacked by Saladin's troops.
- At the end of July Saladin decided to take advantage of the Crusaders' retreat from Jerusalem by launching a lightening attack on Jaffa in an attempt to break the Christian stranglehold on the coast. In just four days the Muslim sappers and stone throwers destroyed sections of Jaffa's walls which left only a small Christian garrison trapped in the citadel. Saladin's forces blocked help coming from overland which meant that relief could only arrive by sea.
- Arguably Saladin's greatest military achievement was to gather and hold together (despite divisions) a broad coalition of Muslims in the face of setbacks at Acre, Arsuf and Jaffa. Although the consensus is that Saladin was not a great battlefield general (it could be argued that his triumph at Hattin was down more to the mistakes of the Crusaders than his own skill), Saladin was still able to inspire his troops and fight back. Saladin's continued resistance had ensured that Jerusalem remained in Muslim hands.

Saladin's military weaknesses

- Saladin found it increasingly difficult to keep his large army in the field for the whole year round. In contrast to the Crusading army, many of his men were needed back on their farms or were only expected to provide a certain number of days' service.
- Saladin's authority was ignored when the garrison at Acre struck a deal with Conrad of Montferrat to surrender. Saladin lost control of his men at Jaffa.
- The stalemate at Jaffa showed that Saladin was incapable of driving the Crusaders out of southern Palestine.

Richard's diplomatic strengths

- During the siege of Acre and despite his illness Richard opened negotiations with Saladin showed his willingness to use diplomacy.
- That Richard was skilled in the art of diplomacy was shown in his negotiations with Saladin's brother, Al-Adil. A bond was forged between them and Richard even offered his sister Joan to be one of al-Adil's wives as part of a deal to divide Palestine between the Crusaders and the Muslims. Richard's connection with Al-Adill was enough of an incentive for Saladin to agree to a truce with Richard.
- Richard negotiated a five year truce over Jerusalem.

Richard's diplomatic weaknesses

- Richard showed poor diplomacy towards his allies. After the victory at Acre, Richard's men pulled down the banner of Count Leopold of Austria, claiming his status did not entitle him to fly his colours alongside the king of England, even though Leopold had been fighting at Acre for almost two years. This resulted in Leopold leaving Outremer in a rage, taking his German knights with him (Eighteen months later he imprisoned Richard after the king was captured returning through Austria).

- Richard also failed to show subtlety in his dealings with King Philip. Richard's inability to share the spoils taken during his attack on Cyprus with Philip helped persuade the ill king of France that he was needed at home. The one thing Richard had wished to do was keep Philip with him on the Crusade; now he had to worry about French incursions into his Angevin Empire.
- Against advice Richard backed Guy de Lusignan to become King of Jerusalem, against the popular Conrad of Montferrat, perhaps because he was the favourite of Philip. This continued support of Guy resulted in a compromise that no one liked. The assassination of Conrad was even whispered by some to be Richard's fault. The end result was the withdrawal of the support of Conrad's forces and those of the Duke of Burgundy's remaining French knights.

Saladin's diplomatic strengths

- During the siege of Acre and alongside the military skirmishes as the Crusaders set out on their march to Jerusalem, Saladin and Richard were engaged in diplomacy. Both sides were willing to find areas of agreement at the same time as engaging in brutal combat.
- Following Richard's victory at Jaffa, Saladin knew he could not maintain such a level of military struggle indefinitely. He recognised the need to make a truce with Richard. On 2 September 1192, the Treaty of Jaffa was agreed which partitioned Palestine in return for a three year truce. While Saladin was to retain control of Jerusalem, the Crusaders were allowed to keep the conquests of Acre and Jaffa and the coastal strip between the two towns. Christian pilgrims were also allowed access to the Church of the Holy Sepulchre in Jerusalem.

Saladin diplomatic weaknesses

- Saladin faced increasing discontent from his Muslim allies.
- Saladin negotiated a five year truce over Jerusalem despite his strong position.

Any other relevant factors.

33. **The outcome of the Fourth Crusade was the sacking of Constantinople, the Christian capital city of the Byzantine Empire leading to the claim that by 1204 enthusiasm for reclaiming the Holy Land had begun to wane. The self interest of many of the nobles on the Fourth Crusade was also far removed from the religious ideals of the early crusaders.**

Co-existence of Muslim and Crusading states

- There were many attempts at peace between Muslim and the Crusading states during the reign of Baldwin IV, before his death and the fall of Jerusalem.
- Other examples include the treaty of mutual protection signed between King Alric of Jerusalem and the Emir of Damascus prior to the Second Crusade.

The corruption of the crusading movement by the Church and nobles

- There are many examples of nobles using the Crusade for their own ends. Examples include Bohemond and Baldwin in the First Crusade and arguably Richard in the Third Crusade. The greed of many nobles on the Fourth Crusade was a far cry from the religious ideals of the early crusaders.
- At the end of the Fourth Crusade, the Pope accepted half of the spoils from the Crusaders despite his earlier excommunication of them.

Effects of trade

- Trade links directly into the Fourth Crusade and the influence of Venice.
- The Italian city-states (Genoa, Pisa and Venice) continued to trade with various Muslim powers throughout the crusading period.
- Pisa and Genoa both had a lot of influence in events during the Third Crusade; they both had favoured candidates for the vacant throne of Jerusalem for example and used trade rights as a bargaining chip to get what they wanted.

The Fourth Crusade

- The initial inspiration of the Fourth Crusade had a strong crusading ideology behind it. Pope Innocent III was a highly effective pope. He had managed to settle the problem of the Investiture Contest with Germany, and hoped to sort out the issue of the Holy Lands as well. Innocent believed that the inclusion of medieval monarchs had caused the previous two Crusades to fail, unlike the First Crusade that was nominally under the command of Bishop Adhemar. This Crusade would fall under the command of six papal legates. These men would hold true to the ideal of the Crusade and not be bound by earthy greed of politics.
- However, the Fourth Crusade has also been described as the low point of the crusading ideal. Hijacked by the Venetians, the Crusade instead became a tool for their growing political and economic ambitions.
- While attacking Zara, Alexius, son of the deposed emperor of Byzantium, arrived with a new proposal for the Crusaders. He asked them to reinstate his father, who had been imprisoned by his brother, and if they agreed they would be handsomely rewarded. He also promised to return control of the Byzantine Church to Rome. The Church was against such an attack on another Christian city, but the prospect of wealth and fame led the Crusade to Constantinople.
- When the Crusaders discovered that Alexius and his father could not, or would not, meet the payment as agreed, the Crusaders stormed the city. The murder, looting and rape continued for three days, after which the Crusading army had a great thanksgiving ceremony.
- The amount of booty taken from Constantinople was huge: gold, silver, works of art and holy relics were taken back to Europe, mostly to Venice. Most crusaders returned home with their newly acquired wealth. Those that stayed dividing up the land amongst themselves, effectively creating several Latin Crusader States where Byzantium had once stood.

Role of Venice

- By 1123 the city of Venice had come to dominate maritime trade in the Middle East. They made several secret trade agreements with Egypt and North African emirs, as well as enjoying concessions and trade agreements within the Kingdom of Jerusalem. Byzantium however, remained a constant rival for this dominance of trade and in 1183 Venice was cut off from the lucrative trading centres of the empire.
- Venice's participation in the Crusade was only secured when the Pope agreed to pay huge sums of money to Venice for the use of its ships, and supplies as well as half of everything captured during the Crusade on land and sea.
- Venice's leader, the Doge Enrico Dandolo, had sold the Crusaders three times as much supplies and equipment as required for the Crusade. The crusading leader, Boniface

of Montferrat, found that he was unable to raise enough money to pay, and the Crusaders were all but imprisoned on an island near Venice. Dandolo's proposal to pay off the Crusaders' debt involved attacking Zara, a Christian city that had once belonged to Venice but was now under the control of the King of Hungary, a Christian monarch. Thus the Crusade had become a tool of the Venetians.

- The Fourth Crusade's intended target, Egypt, was totally unsuitable from a Venetian perspective. Thus when the Pope's representative approached the Venetians in 1201 they agreed to help transport the Crusaders, hoping to divert the Crusade to a less friendly target. The final target for the Fourth Crusade was therefore determined by politics and economics.

Any other relevant factors.

Part B: The American Revolution, 1763–1787

34. **Since the 1600s, the thirteen colonies of North America had been part of the British Empire. However, on 4 July 1776 the Continental Congress met in Freedom Hall, Philadelphia and issued the Declaration of Independence. This historic event, the turning point in the American Revolution, came after over ten years of opposition by colonists to British rule. The action by the delegates in Philadelphia led to the American War of Independence.**

Punishment of Massachusetts and Quebec Act

- The British response to the Boston Tea Party, was a series of measures between March and June 1774, known to colonists as the Intolerable Acts and the British as the Coercive Acts — the Port of Boston Act closed the port, denying valuable revenue to the city, the constitution of the Massachusetts Assembly was altered reducing its powers, the Quartering Act billeted British troops in colonial homes, and trial by jury was suspended. In addition, the Quebec Act, passed in June, allowed French-speaking Catholics to settle in the Ohio valley with local law-making powers that were now being denied to Massachusetts. These legislative measures enraged colonists such as Thomas Jefferson of Virginia who proclaimed that "the British have a deliberate plan of reducing us to slavery".

- The Virginia Assembly was now motivated to call for unity amongst the thirteen colonies to discuss the current crisis and the 1st Continental Congress, with delegates from all colonies except Georgia, met on 5 September in Philadelphia. There it issued the Declaration of Rights and Grievances which, although proclaiming loyalty to George III, dismissed the Coercive Acts as null and void and rejected the supremacy of the British Parliament.

Taxation and the Stamp Act

- Indirect taxation appeared in 1764 with the Sugar Act which controlled the export of sugar and other items which could now only be sold to Britain. This was to be enforced through greater smuggling controls. Colonist merchants protested on the grounds of their reduced income and the idea that there should be no taxation of colonists who had no representation in the British Parliament.

- Also, the Stamp Act, passed by Grenville's administration in 1765, was the first direct taxation on colonists. It stated that an official stamp had to be bought to go on printed matter such as letters, legal documents, newspapers, licences pamphlets and leases. Many colonists subsequently refused to pay the tax, with James Otis of Boston arguing that "taxation without representation is tyranny".

- While the British argued that taxation would contribute to the costs of Seven Years War and pay for the continued presence of British Army in America, colonists claimed that they already paid financial dues to British through the Navigation Acts and other trading restrictions, and also that they had their own militia and did not need the British Army to protect them.

- The slogan "No Taxation without Representation" was a familiar protest during this time, and due to inability to enforce the Stamp Act, Prime Minister Rockingham oversaw its repeal in March 1766. At the same time he passed the Declaratory Act, supporting any future taxation of the colonies. To underline opposition to any taxation by Britain, the secret organisation Sons of Liberty was founded in February 1766 by colonist like John Adams and Patrick Henry, who proclaimed loyalty to the king but opposition to Parliament.

- In 1767, new Prime Minister William Pitt proposed indirect taxation in the form of duties against imports into the colonies. Chancellor of the Exchequer Lord Townshend introduced taxes on glass, tea, paper and lead. These were opposed by those such as Boston merchant John Hancock whose ships, including the "Liberty", were regularly raided by Customs Board officials acting on behalf of new Prime Minister Grafton, and there were riots across Massachusetts.

Boston Massacre

- On 5 March 1770, during a riot in Boston in opposition to the Townshend Duties, forces sent by General Gage, the British Commander-in-Chief in North America, to quell resistance opened fire on a crowd on the orders of Captain Preston, killing three people instantly, injuring eleven others, and fatally wounding two more. Preston and four soldiers were charged with murder. Many Bostonians were horrified at what they perceived as the brutal actions of the British Army.

- Committees of Correspondence, which had been established during the 1760s, quickly spread news of the massacre around the thirteen colonies, and Paul Revere, a Boston silversmith, depicted the event in an engraving which shocked colonists viewing prints of it. The soldiers were represented at the trial in October by John Adams after he volunteered to ensure there was a fair hearing, and the result was the acquittal of all defendants. This outcome outraged colonists as it suggested that British soldiers had a free hand to kill Americans.

- Committees of Correspondence would later prove effective after the Gaspee Incident in the summer of 1772, when a Royal Navy schooner was captured off Rhode Island and burned by smugglers who resented its enforcement of the Navigation Acts. Britain resolved to transport any culprits to England for trial. Subsequently, all the thirteen colonies' Committees worked together to investigate the legality of all British actions towards them from now onwards.

Proclamation of 1763

- The Proclamation, made by George III, forbade anyone from settling beyond the Frontier, which was a line drawn in the map along the Appalachian Mountains. When it passed through Parliament and became the Proclamation Act, it caused anger amongst colonists of a bold and adventurous nature who were now to be kept within the jurisdiction of British authorities.

- In addition, the Proclamation enforced the re-imposition of the Navigation Acts, restricting colonist trade with European merchants. This meant Royal Navy cutters patrolling the east coast for smugglers collaborating with the French, Dutch or Spanish. Colonist traders greatly resented this curtailment of their economic activities which had gone unhindered for over 40 years during the Whig Ascendancy of the mid-1700s.

The Tea Act

- In 1773, tea duties in the colonies were reduced by the Tea Act, designed by the Lord North's government to give the British East India Company a monopoly in North America to help ease it out of financial difficulty. Although this also benefited colonist tea merchants, many felt not only that Britain may extend this monopoly to other commodities. The key effect of the act was to lead many to suggest that accepting the cheap tea symbolised acceptance of Britain's right to tax America.
- In Boston, crowds of colonists organised blockages of loading bays to prevent the unloading of tea cargoes. On 16 December 1773, in what became known as the Boston Tea Party, hundreds of people, co-ordinated by Samuel Adams, boarded three British East India Company ships and threw £10,000 worth of tea into the harbour. This destruction of British government property was an expression of colonist frustration at policies.

Events at Lexington and Bunker Hill

- On 19 April 1775 British troops encountered colonial militia at Lexington Green in Massachusetts after General Gage sent a force of 700 men to Concord to seize a store of military supplies held by local militia, and were intercepted on the way by Lexington's "minutemen". Eight colonists were killed, and reports of the skirmish raised issues about the conduct of British officers, as there were questions about warnings not being given before firing. This incident was significant because it was the first blood spilled in a military engagement between colonist and British in the developing conflict in America, and led to a series of attacks by various New England militia groups on British forts.
- The Battle of Bunker Hill over 16–17 June 1775 saw the British defeat 1,200 militia on high ground overlooking Boston, but although the colonists suffered over 400 casualties, the British sustained over 1,000, including 200 dead. This was an important development as colonists took heart and attacked more British posts in New England and even Canada, and the 2nd Continental Congress, which had met on 10 May, decided in June to form the Continental Army in June with George Washington of Virginia appointed as its Commander.

Rejection of Olive Branch Petition

- The 2nd Continental Congress had written an appeal to the King in June 1775, known as the Olive Branch Petition, which pledged colonists' allegiance to the crown but expressed bitterness towards Parliament, Lord North and the King's ministers. Congress requested Constitutional Union, which would allow the colonies to legislate for themselves and raise their own taxes but remain within the British Empire under royal authority, yet this last hope of compromise fell on deaf ears as George III rejected the petition in October, declaring the colonists to be in rebellion.

Events of 1775–6

- Congress's Trade Declaration stated that the colonies would no longer obey the Navigation Acts. In response, General Gage requested further military support in the colonies, including the hiring of foreign troops, but thousands of German mercenaries in place of regular soldiers offended colonist sensibilities as Britain was underestimating the Continental Army.
- In November 1775, Governor Dunmore of Virginia formed a regiment of black soldiers in the South, promising freedom to slaves, and this brought many indignant Southerners, previously reluctant to become involved in the conflict, on board the movement towards independence.
- In January 1776 the British republican writer Thomas Paine produced his pamphlet 'Common Sense' which advocated war in order for the colonies to free themselves from British rule. This sold 100,000 copies and influenced many middle-class, educated colonists.
- British intransigence and uncompromising attitudes in the face of continued colonist protest and pleas for compromise, as well as a perception in America of Parliamentary ignorance of the spirit and determination of the colonists, irked many in the colonies.
- On 4th July 1776 Congress met to sign the Declaration of Independence, which had been drafted by Jefferson and Franklin to state that "all men are created equal", and they have "inalienable rights" amongst which are "life, liberty and the pursuit of happiness". It expressed the "right of the people" to abolish their own government if they so desire. Lord North immediately ordered more troops to America in preparation for war.

Any other relevant factor.

35. **The American War of Independence took place between 1776 and 1781, between Britain and its thirteen colonies of North America. For many colonists, this was a revolutionary conflict fought by people fighting for freedom against tyranny, monarchy and the threat of enslavement. The war was fought not only on American soil, but on the high seas and across the world once other European Powers became involved.**

Washington's military capability

- Washington was aware that the British forces would hold the advantage in open battle, so he fought using guerrilla warfare effectively, for example at the significant crossing of the Delaware River in December 1776. This was part of a surprise raid on British posts which resulted in Washington's small bands of men crossing the river back to their positions in Pennsylvania with captured supplies and arms. Guerrilla warfare, therefore, was an effective weapon in Washington's armoury.
- In addition, Washington taught his troops to fire accurately from a distance on those occasions when they were engaged in open battle, particularly in the fight to control the New Jersey area in the first half of the war. During the attack on Princeton in January 1777 and the Battle of Monmouth in June 1778, Washington's forces successfully drove the British from the battlefield.
- Washington's "scorched earth" campaign during the summer of 1779 was aimed at Iroquois settlements in New York in revenge for their co-operation with the British early in the war. This policy deterred further collaboration between Native Americans and the British Army. Although brutal, this strategy increased colonists' chances of winning the war on land.
- Moreover, Washington had experience of serving with the British Army during the Seven Years War, and had been a leading figure in the British capture of Pittsburgh in 1758. He was aware of British military practice and the weaknesses in the chains of communication between

London and North America. This meant he was well-placed to second-guess British manoeuvres during the War of Independence.

Washington's leadership

- He was a self-made Virginian who had become a successful tobacco planter in the 1760s and involved himself in local politics as a member of the Virginia legislature. As a military hero from the Seven Years War, his choice as Commander of the Continental Army in 1775 gave heart to many. So Washington's business and political reputation were key features of his authority during the war.

- His personal qualities included the ability to give speeches to his troops, emphasising the incentive of independence if they won the war. Washington was aware of the political aspect of the conflict, and turned military defeats, of which he suffered many, into opportunities to inspire his forces to fight on. Therefore, this motivational aspect of his nature, an asset which the British did not possess, was an important advantage to the colonists.

- Washington's leadership at Valley Forge during the winter of 1777—8 saw him preserve the morale of his 10,000-strong army in terrible conditions, particularly by his allowing soldiers' families, known as Camp Followers, to remain with the troops. His appointment of celebrated Prussian drill sergeant Baron Friedrich von Steuben to maintain discipline meant firearms skills stayed of a high quality; his promotion of Nathaniel Greene through the ranks from Private to Quartermaster-General meant regular food for the soldiers as well as adequate supplies of ammunition and uniforms, including boots; and the trust he showed in the French General Lafayette led to Congress commissioning Lafayette into the Continental Army before the French entered the war, allowing him an important role in strategic planning. These astute decisions were vital to the colonists' war efforts, both practically and militarily.

French entry into the war

- The Franco-American Treaty of Alliance was signed by Franklin and Louis XVI at Versailles in February 1778. This formalised French recognition of the United States, the first international acknowledgement of American independence. The agreement cemented the colonists' autonomy and provided much-needed help in the fight against the British.

- From this period onward, the French guaranteed the colonists abundant military support in the form of troops sent to fight on land and a naval contribution on the Eastern seaboard, around Britain and across the world. In addition, France provided the Continental Army with ammunition, uniforms, expertise, training and supplies. This meant that the colonists were better equipped to tackle the British successfully in America.

- Importantly, the forces under the command of Count Rochambeau who landed at Rhode Island in 1780 hampered the British army's attempts to dislodge colonist strongholds in Virginia throughout 1780 and 1781. Rochambeau's co-operation with the colonist General Lafayette and the clear lines of communication he established between himself and de Grasse led to the trapping of Cornwallis at Yorktown and the French navy's arrival in Chesapeake Bay. Thus, the French army significantly contributed to the ending of the war on land.

French contribution worldwide

- The strength of the French navy meant Britain had to spread its forces worldwide, particularly as France attacked British colonies in the Caribbean Sea and

Indian Ocean. In addition, there were attempts to raid Portsmouth and Plymouth in order to land soldiers on the British mainland. Although these failed, French naval activity worldwide reduced the efforts which Britain could make to defend its North American possessions.

- Admiral d'Orvilliers defeated the Royal Navy in the Battle of Ushant in the English Channel in July 1778, weakening British defences in preparation for further attacks on the south-coast of England. Admiral de Grasse successfully deceived British fleets in the Atlantic to arrive at Chesapeake Bay in September 1781 prior to the Yorktown surrender. It is clear, therefore, that leading French naval figures planned a strategy to divide British maritime forces, thus exposing their hold on the colonies to greater threat from the Continental Army and American Navy.

- The entry of France into the conflict encouraged Spain and Holland to follow suit within next two years, declaring war against Britain in June 1779 and December 1780 respectively. French action against the Royal Navy gave these European Powers confidence to attack British interests in India and the southern colonies.

British military inefficiency

- On several occasions British generals did not act appropriately to instructions, such as when Lord George Germain, the British Secretary of State for America, hatched a plan to separate the New England colonies from the others in mid-1777. This involved General Howe moving his forces north from New York, but Howe misinterpreted his orders and moved south during August, rendering the plan futile. This demonstrates a costly incompetence on the part of the leading British military figure in North America.

- Meanwhile, General Burgoyne, commander of British forces in Canada, had received orders to march south into the Hudson Valley towards Ticonderoga in early 1777. Burgoyne, however, was left isolated in the Hudson Valley after capturing Ticonderoga because Howe had gone south and General Clinton was too slow to move north in place of Howe, and so, confronted by large American forces, Burgoyne was forced to surrender his 3,500 men and equipment at Saratoga in October 1777.

- Furthermore, changes in personnel hindered operations, as politicians such as Lord North and Lord Germain promoted or appointed officers frequently, causing inconsistency and lack of stability at command level. Petty jealousies amongst military leaders also obstructed progress, so that even after military campaigns had been waged successfully or battles had been won, there was no co-operation, leading to the British losing land gained, particularly after French entry in 1778.

Local knowledge

- The main theatre of the land war was on American soil, with the main battles being fought out in Massachusetts, the Middle Colonies and Virginia. Even if the British gained ground, the revolutionary forces knew the terrain well enough to find ways of re-occupying lost territory. This gave the Continental Army an obvious advantage over their British enemies.

- Key colonist victories such as the Battle of Princeton on 3 January 1777, the Battle of King Mountain on 7 October 1780, and the Battle of Yorktown between September and October 1781 were in no small part due to colonist forces' ability to utilise local geography to advantage. British forces constantly found themselves having to react to the movement of the Continental Army. This meant that the British found it hard to go on the attack in the field.

- Furthermore, as witnessed in British victories such as the Battle of New York City between August and October 1776, the Battle of Fort Ticonderoga on 6 July 1777, and the Battle of Brandywine on 25 August 1777, colonist troops had intimate knowledge of the surrounding areas and were able to avoid capture, and so withdrew to safety in order to fight another day. This meant it was difficult for the British to reduce the size of their enemy's numbers.
- On occasions, such as during the Saratoga campaign, local people burned their crops rather than let them fall into British hands. The distance between Britain and the colonies already meant that supplies were slow in arriving at the front. Therefore, the behaviour of locals further reduced the potential supplies for the British army.

Other worldwide factors

- Spain entered into the war in June 1779, intent on mounting an attack on the British mainland. Dutch entry into war came in December 1780, providing another threat of invasion. These European Powers stretched British resources even further and made the British less effective in their overall military effort.
- The Armed League of Neutrality was formed in December 1780. The involvement of Russia, Denmark and Sweden in an agreement to fire on the Royal Navy, if provoked, placed extra pressure on Britain.
- The war at sea was a vital feature of Britain's weaknesses. British concentration was diverted from maintaining control of the colonies on land towards keeping control of maritime access to its wider Empire. Ultimately, with the surrender at Yorktown, it was loss of control of the sea which led to the eventual British defeat.

Any other relevant factors.

36. **The American War of Independence took place between 1776 and 1781, between Britain and its thirteen colonies of North America. When the colonists drew up their constitution they built in a separation of powers that would be essential to the government of the new United States.**

Separation of power

- When the colonists drew up their Constitution, they built in a separation of powers providing checks and balances within the political system, influenced by the thinking of the French philosopher Montesquieu. This was driven through by Alexander Hamilton and James Madison who had disapproved of the too-powerful Continental Congress. The separation of powers, in its division of authority between branches of government in a modern industrialising nation, is, therefore, considered to be the most revolutionary aspect of the Constitution.
- The Constitution stated that no branch of government should ever be subordinate to any other. The Executive, Legislature and Judiciary had to remain apart, with no one person allowed to participate in more than one branch at any one time. This prevented, for example, the administration of justice being subject to outside influence from anyone with political interest.
- This separation of power would be essential to the government of the United States. The President could not take a seat in Congress, Congressmen could not be part of the Supreme Court, and members of the Supreme Court could only be appointed by an agreed confirmation between President and Congress. This secured the separation of powers as a vital component of the Constitution.
- The separation of powers had a built-in system of checks and balances, whereby each branch of government could be kept in line by the other two. The Philadelphia Convention had arranged this to ensure that no single branch could establish tyrannical authority. This meant that the Legislature and Judiciary could check the power of the Executive if necessary.
- The President and his Cabinet, Congressmen and Supreme Court judges could all lose their jobs if they acted improperly. Each strand of government acted independently of each other. This system thus ensured that no one person could rule tyrannically.

Executive

- Executive power was vested in the elected President, and his Vice-President and Cabinet. The first President, George Washington, was elected in February 1789, and could make all key decisions and establish policy. This gave Washington and future Presidents clearly defined powers within the American political system.
- Members of the Executive, including the President, or Thomas Jefferson, who became the USA's first Secretary of State, could be removed from office by the electorate in four-yearly elections. Other branches of government could also remove Executive members from office if it was felt they were not doing their job appropriately. This meant that even the most powerful were kept in check by others in government.

Legislature

- Legislative power lay in the hands of an elected Congress which was divided into two Houses, the Senate and Representatives. The Senate was set up with each state equally represented and the House of Representatives was set up with states represented proportionately to size and population. This was an attempt to divide power equally amongst those representing the electorate.
- The job of Congress was to pass laws and raise taxes. In addition, Congress was given responsibility for international trade, war and foreign relations. This presented Senators and Representatives with significant powers within the country as well as influence around the world.
- No-one in the legislature could serve in the judiciary or executive without first resigning from the legislature. In addition, Congressional elections were held regularly to ensure that Congressmen remained in touch with the people they served. Therefore, the views of the American people would be represented as faithfully as possible amongst those setting taxes and enacting laws.

Judiciary

- The newly formed Supreme Court of Justice, consisting of nine judges, would hold judicial power in the United States. The Supreme Court was formed in order to prevent legal matters becoming entwined with political ones. Therefore, this Judiciary also had a plain role to act out in the country.
- The Supreme Court could be called upon to debate the legality of new laws enacted by Congress. It also acted as the highest court of appeal in the United States. It can be seen, therefore, that one of the key functions of the Supreme Court was to protect individual citizens from unconstitutional behaviour on the part of law-makers and law-enforcers.
- Supreme Court judges were nominated by the President upon advice from his Cabinet and political staff. New appointments had to be ratified by Congress after a rigorous vetting process. This design led to the Supreme Court representing a mix of views on various legal issues.

Bill of Rights

- The Bill of Rights was drawn up in 1791 as the first ten amendments to the Constitution, after several states refused to ratify the Constitution as it stood. These states' delegates at Philadelphia wanted greater protections for citizens against the federal government. Therefore, the Bill of Rights became an important document that set out the limitations of the power of Congress.
- The Bill of Rights established liberty for individual citizens in states within a federal union of all states, and set out clear lines of authority between federal government and individual states. Central government controlled matters of national importance, and state assemblies were to be responsible for local government and administration. This meant that the Constitution would prevent central government from exerting a controlling power over people's lives.
- In addition, the Bill of Rights stated that neither Congress nor the government could pass laws which established religion as a part of state institutions, for example within the education system. School prayer was, therefore, prohibited. This meant that religion was disestablished in the United States.
- Moreover, the Bill of Rights protected the freedom of the press, freedom of speech, and the right to peaceable assembly. Also it set out the rights of citizens who were under investigation or being tried for criminal offences; for example, no-one could be compelled to give evidence which might incriminate them. This was designed to prevent the government from assuming too much power over individuals.
- Furthermore, any powers which had not been written into the Constitution as being delegated to the federal government would be delegated to state governments. This meant that any future disputes over certain powers, for example, the power to abolish slavery, which had not been envisaged at the time of the Revolution, would be ceded to states automatically and, therefore, taken out of the hands of Congress and central government.

Democratic ideals

- The hierarchy of colonial government which had existed under rule by Britain was altered drastically by the Constitution. The Constitution stated that "all men are created equal" and that everyone was entitled to "life, liberty and the pursuit of happiness". This established, therefore, a new approach to the rights and position of ordinary citizens within the processes of government.
- From now on, people would be asked to ratify many of the stages within democratic processes at state and national level. This meant ordinary citizens were involved in the election of various offices from local education boards to state governors. The Constitution was thus ensuring government by the people.
- However, women and blacks were excluded from the franchise, and in reality only one-fifth of eligible voters turned out for national elections. Forces of vested interest were too strong. This suggests that democracy was more of an ideal than an actuality.
- Moreover, the Philadelphia Convention introduced an elitist system of electors in Presidential elections voting for an electoral college. The electoral college consisted of educated men who would vote for the President, a system which still exists today. The electoral college system implies an institutional distrust of ordinary citizens, which is an undemocratic practice.

The experience of rule by Britain

- As part of the British Empire, colonists had been ruled by the King and the British Parliament, who together made key policy decisions, set laws and taxes, and enforced the law. As a result there had been no checks and balances on executive, legislative and judicial processes. This created a need for a Constitution which had built in safety mechanisms to prevent tyrannical behaviour on any ruler's part.
- The notion of "No Taxation without Representation" had been a source of much of the original resentment towards British colonial policy. After 1787, representation would be a key feature of the new system of politics. This meant that the new branches of government were to be predominantly elective, to ensure participation of the people.
- During their experience of being ruled by Britain, colonists had learned to be suspicious of all forms of government, and they feared the potentially tyrannical power of a monarch. They designed the Constitution to thwart any future attempts of American heads of state to act in a similar manner as George III. Therefore, the separation of powers was devised.

Other features

- The Articles of Confederation had been written in 1776, signed in 1781, and acknowledged in 1787, to declare that states would retain individual sovereignty and provided for state representatives to Continental Congress. This led to states rights being fiercely guarded by states in the future.
- In relation to religion, the church was separated from the state in order to ensure equality was extended to include freedom of belief for everyone. The church was thus disestablished.
- Regarding the question of slavery, in northern states measures were taken for the practice, already declining, to be gradually abolished, although pro-slavery sentiment in the South intensified simultaneously.

Any other relevant factors.

Part C: The French Revolution, to 1799

37. By 1789 the problems of the Ancien Regime were coming to a head. A series of foreign wars had led the state into debt. The demands for more cash, attempts to reform the taxation system, demands for political change, the influence of the Enlightenment and an ineffectual monarch all led to pressures on the Ancien Regime, which was put into stark relief by the economic crisis of 1788/9.

Influence of the Enlightenment

- The Enlightenment encouraged criticism, and freedom of thought, speech and religion, and was seen as the end of man's self-imposed irrationality at the hands of the Church in particular.
- Ideas of Philosophes like Voltaire who attacked God, Montesquieu who favoured a British system of government and Rousseau who put forward the idea of direct democracy.
- Very much appealed to the middle-classes, who led the revolution.

Other factors

The economic crisis of 1788/9

- Bad harvests and grain shortages inspired unrest among the peasantry and the urban workers in Paris and in provincial cities throughout France, exerting critical pressures on the Ancien Regime.

- There was less demand for manufactured goods, which led to unemployment increasing amongst the urban workers.
- The nobility were increasingly blamed as peasants started to take political action.
- The economic crisis clearly created an environment in which the Ancien Regime was struggling to survive.

Financial problems of the Ancien Regime

- Because of exemptions the crown was denied adequate income. The privileged orders were an untapped source of revenue but it would require reforms to access it.
- This created resentment amongst the Third Estate
- Exacerbated divisions that already existed between the Estates.
- Tax-farming meant not all revenues were reaching the government.
- By the 1780s France faced bankruptcy due to heavy expenditure and borrowing to pay for wars.
- Government failed to gain agreement on tax reform.
- This was arguably the biggest threat facing the Ancien Regime. The opposition which this generated not only led to Calonne's dismissal in 1787 but more importantly to the convocation of the Estates General in 1788. When it met in May 1789 the long-standing divisions between the three Estates unleashed forces which culminated in the overthrow of the Ancien Regime.

The American Revolution

- This war contributed to the financial crisis which came to a head in France post-1786 as the French had to finance both their navy and army fighting America.
- For many in France at the time they also represented the practical expression of the enlightened views of the Philosophes in terms of the rights of the individual, no taxation without representation and freedom from tyrannical government.
- The wars inspired many of the lesser nobility and the bourgeoisie to seek the same freedoms.

The political crisis of 1788/9

- The convocation of the Estates General in August 1788 sharpened divisions between the three Estates which came to a head between May and August 1789.
- The Cahiers des Doleances revealed the depth of dissatisfaction with the existing order, especially among the bourgeoisie and the peasantry.
- The creation of the National Assembly, the abolition of feudalism and the Declaration of the Rights of Man and the Citizen all contributed to a revolutionary change in French government, society and economy.

Actions of Louis XVI

- Louis was largely under the influence of his wife, Marie Antoinette who, although strong minded, failed to grasp the serious nature of the situation and was also unpopular as she was Austrian.
- Louis XVI's handling of the Estates-General contributed towards the start of the Revolution. He wanted to make reform difficult by making the three Estates meet separately, in the hope that the First and Second Estates would vote the Third down.
- This backfired: opposition to the King grew, the Third Estate refused to act separately, and many of the clergy changed sides, changing the balance of power.
- Louis allegedly closed the meeting halls, which led to the Tennis Court Oath from members of the Third Estate.

He later agreed to a constitution when the Third Estate representatives occupied the royal tennis courts.

- The King had lost more political ground than if he had just listened to the grievances of the middle classes and the Third Estate from the start.

Role of Bourgeoisie

- As part of the Third Estate resented paying the taxation.
- Dominated the Third Estate representatives in the Estates-General.
- Were outside the political process unless they bought a noble title: wanted access to power.
- Very attracted to ideas of a constitutional monarchy as advocated by people like Montesquieu.
- Provided the leadership for the Revolution.

Any other relevant factors.

38. **French military performance in 1798 and 1799 led to the eventual collapse of the Directory. The British encouraged Royalist insurrection in the south of France, further complicating matters. Subsequent political intrigue by Sieyes backed by the military reputation of Bonaparte led to the coup that established the Consulate.**

Role of Sieyes

- Afraid that France would descend into anarchy as a result of the on-going political conflict and deeming the 1795 constitution unworkable, Sieyes enlisted the aid of Bonaparte in mounting a coup against it.
- The Convention, the Directory and the legislative councils had run their course and few, if any, mourned their passing.

Other factors

Increasing intervention of the army in politics

- Even before the 1795 constitution was ratified the army had been used to quell sans-culottes insurgents who sought to invade the Convention and to repel an émigré invasion at Quiberon.
- Napoleon's use of a 'whiff of grapeshot' to put down the disturbances in October merely underlined the parlous nature of politics at the time.
- The deployment of the army in May 1796 to put down the left-wing Babeuf Conspiracy was followed by the Coup of Fructidor in September 1797 when the first 'free' Convention elections returned a royalist majority.

Political instability

- In the late summer of 1794 France was emerging from two years of increasing radicalisation and resulting bitterness between opposing factions.
- The Jacobins under Robespierre had been overthrown and a 'White Terror' was soon to sweep the country in revenge for the excesses of the radical left during the Terror.
- France had been torn apart by civil war, threatened by foreign armies egged on by émigré nobles seeking to overthrow the Revolution and riven by religious conflict occasioned by the State's opposition to the primacy of the Catholic Church.

The Constitution of 1795

- Policy-makers framed a new constitution which sought to reconcile the bitterness of the preceding years by imposing checks and balances against the emergence of one dominant individual, group or faction. In so doing, many historians argue that the new constitution was a recipe for instability in the years which followed.
- A bi-cameral legislature was established wherein each chamber counter-balanced the power of the other. By so doing it inhibited strong and decisive government.

- To ensure continuity, the new Convention was to include two-thirds of the outgoing deputies from the old. This enraged sections of the right who felt that the forces of left-wing radicalism still prevailed in government.
- The resulting mass protests in October 1795 were put down by the army under Bonaparte. The principle of using extra-parliamentary forces to control the State had been established with Bonaparte right at the heart of it. It was to prove a dangerous precedent.
- Annual elections worked against consistent and continuous policy-making.
- So did the appointment of an Executive — the Directory — one of whose members rotated on an annual basis.
- Again, the counter-balance between the legislature and the executive may have been commendable but it was to prove inherently unstable in practice.

Role of Bonaparte

- A supreme self-propagandist, he seemed to offer the strength and charisma which the Directory and the legislative councils singularly lacked.
- Afraid that his spectacular victories in Italy during 1795 might be jeopardised by the election of a right-wing government less sympathetic to conducting a war against monarchical states, Bonaparte threw his support behind the Directory who effectively annulled the election results by purging right-wing deputies.
- The 1788 and 1799 elections were similarly 'adjusted'.
- The Consulate — with Bonaparte as First Consul — came into being. A notably more authoritarian constitution was promulgated by referendum, supported by a populace tired of weak and ineffectual government and the instability it had brought between 1795 and 1799.

Any other relevant factors.

39. **The effects of the French Revolution were profound and lasting. In particular the impact was felt by the French Aristocracy and Clergy. However, there was also an impact on the peasantry, the middle class and urban workers.**

The impact of the Revolution on the First Estate

- The Catholic Church was a key pillar of the Ancien Regime. The Upper Clergy (usually drawn from the ranks of the traditional nobility) enjoyed considerable wealth and status based on a raft of privileges and tax exemptions. These privileges and exemptions were swept away by the Revolution and the position of the Catholic Church within France by 1799 was far less assured than it had been under the Ancien Regime.
- The Civil Constitution of the Clergy (July 1790) polarised attitudes towards the place of the Catholic Church within French society and promoted conflict between opposing factions through the rest of the period to 1799. In November 1789 Church lands were nationalised, stripping the Church of much of its wealth. The net result of all of this was that the Church never regained its primacy within the French state and can be seen to have lost far more than it gained.

The impact of the Revolution on the Second Estate

- The aristocracy had enjoyed similar privileges and tax exemptions to those of the Catholic Church under the Ancien Regime. Advancement in the key positions of the State, the Army and, indeed the Church, depended more often on birth than merit. The traditional nobility monopolised these key positions and sought at all times to defend its favoured position. Again, the Revolution swept away aristocratic privilege even more completely than that of the clergy.

- The ending of feudalism in August 1789 marked the prelude to a decade when the status of the nobility in France effectively collapsed. In 1790 outward displays of 'nobility' such as titles and coats of arms were forbidden by law and in 1797, after election results suggested a pro-royalist resurgence, the Convention imposed alien status on nobles and stripped them of French citizenship.
- The Revolution brought in a regime where careers were open to talent regardless of birth or inheritance and the traditional aristocracy simply ceased to exist. Having said that, some nobles simply transformed themselves into untitled landlords in the countryside and continued to exercise significant economic and political power.

The impact of the Revolution on the Third Estate

The peasantry

- In contrast to the Catholic Church and the nobility the position of the peasantry was in many ways strengthened by the Revolution. The ending of feudalism in August 1789 removed many of the legal and financial burdens which had formed the basis of peasant grievances in the Cahiers des Doleances presented to the Estates-General in 1789.
- The revolutionary land settlement, instigated by the nationalisation of church lands in November 1789, had transferred land from the nobility and the clergy to the peasantry to their obvious advantage.
- Not all peasants benefited equally from the land settlement. Only the well-off peasants could afford to purchase the Church lands which had been seized by the National Assembly.

The bourgeoisie

- The Revolution instigated a fundamental shift in political and economic power from the First and Second Estates to the bourgeoisie.

  The ending of feudalism in August 1789 heralded profound social and economic change (eg facilitating the development of capitalism) whilst the Declaration of the Rights of Man and the Citizen later in the month did the same for political life. In both cases the main beneficiaries were the bourgeoisie.
- Successive constitutions and legislative reforms throughout the1790s favoured the bourgeoisie above all other social groups by emphasising the notion of a property-owning democracy with voting rights framed within property qualifications, whilst the ending of trade restrictions and monopolies favoured an expanding business and merchant class.
- France had moved from a position of privileged estates to one where increasingly merit was what counted. It was the educated bourgeoisie who were best placed to benefit from this change in French society.

The urban workers

- At key points throughout the Revolution overt demonstrations of discontent by the urban masses- particularly in Paris — impacted on key events as successive regimes framed policy with an eye to appeasing the mob.
- The modest gains by the urban poor were short-lived. A decade of almost continuous wars in the 1790s had created shortages and inflation which hit the urban poor particularly hard.
- The passing of the Chapelier Law in May 1791, by a bourgeois-dominated National Assembly protecting the interests of industrialists, effectively banned the formation of trade unions and thereafter the Revolution brought few tangible economic or political gains for urban workers.

Any other relevant factors.

Part D: Germany, 1851–1939

40. German nationalism, the desire for a united Germany, was already in existence in 1815 as a response to the ideas of the French Revolution and due to resentment of French domination under Napoleon. However, the lack of popular support for nationalism — especially amongst the peasants — and the political repression coordinated by Metternich meant there were still many factors unfavourable to German nationalism.

Evidence that nationalism had made significant progress in their aims:

- Cultural nationalism — work of poets, musicians, writers and their effects on Germans. Impact largely on educated Germans and not everyone was interested in such ideas. Not considered vital to the everyday lives of the ordinary people.
- *Vormarz* period — evidence suggests that workers were starting to take a real interest in politics and philosophy, but only in relatively small numbers.
- Nationalism remained largely middle-class before 1848.
- In 1815 there were tens of thousands of people, especially among the young, the educated and the middle and upper classes, who felt passionately that the Germans deserved to have a fatherland.
- 1840 — French scare to German states. Ordinary Germans were now roused to the defence of the fatherland. This was not confined to the educated classes — spread of nationalist philosophy to large numbers of ordinary Germans. Enhanced reputation of Prussia among German nationalists.
- Economic nationalism — middle class businessmen pushed the case for a more united Germany in order to be able to compete with foreign countries. Benefits evidenced by the Zollverein to German states. Arguments that 'economic' nationalism was the forerunner to political nationalism.

Evidence that nationalists had not made significant progress

- Growth of the *Burschenschaften* — dedicated to seeing the French driven from German soil. Nationalist enthusiasm tended to be of the romantic type, with no clear idea of how their aim could be achieved. Much of the debate in these societies was theoretical in nature and probably above the comprehension of the mass of ordinary Germans.
- Political nationalism — virtually non-existent between 1820 and 1848. Suppressed by the Karlsbad Decrees and the Six Acts. Work/success of Metternich in suppressing such a philosophy.
- Work of the German Confederation and the rulers of the autonomous German states to suppress nationalism.
- Troppau Congress — decision taken by the representatives of Austria, Prussia and Russia to suppress any liberal or nationalist uprisings that would threaten the absolute power of monarchs. This was a huge blow to nationalists within the German states.
- German *Bund* remained little more than a talking shop. Austrian domination of the *Confederation* and the *Bund* stifled political change. 'The French spread liberalism by intention but created nationalism by inadvertence' (Thomson). The French united these German states in a common feeling of resentment against them.
- 1848 Revolutions and the Frankfurt Parliament.

No agreement was reached on a grossdeutsch or a kleindeutsch solution. German rulers regained authority. Divided aims of revolutionaries. Self-interest of the rulers of the German states led to their opposition to Frankfurt Parliament. Frederick William of Prussia backed down in face of Austrian pressure at Olmutz and the humiliation of Prussia. German nationalism was arguably a spent force.

Any other relevant factors.

41. In 1933 Hitler became Chancellor of Germany. His ability to tap into German resentment towards the Treaty of Versailles aided his rise to power.

Resentment towards the Treaty of Versailles

- The Treaty of Versailles: acceptance by Republic of hated terms.
- Land loss and accepting blame for the War especially hated.
- Led to growth of criticism; 'November Criminals', 'Stab in the back' myth.

Other factors

Weaknesses of the Weimar Republic

- A Republic without Republicans/a Republic nobody wanted — lack of popular support for the new form of government after 1918.
- Peasants in a palace — commentary on Weimar politicians.
- Divisions among those groups/individuals who purported to be supporters of the new form of government eg the socialists.
- Alliance of the new government and the old imperial army against the Spartacists — lack of cooperation between socialist groups — petty squabbling rife.
- The Constitution/Article 48 ('suicide clause') — arguably Germany was too democratic.
- Proportional representation led to weak coalition governments.
- Lack of real, outstanding Weimar politicians who could strengthen the Republic, Stresemann excepted.
- Inability (or unwillingness) of the Republic to deal effectively with problems in German society.
- Lukewarm support from the German Army and the Civil Service.

Social and Economic difficulties

- Over-reliance on foreign investment left the Weimar economy subject to the fluctuations of the international economy.
- 1922/23 (hyperinflation) — severe effects on the middle classes, the natural supporters of the Republic; outrage and despair at their ruination.
- The Great Depression of the 1930s — arguably without this the Republic might have survived. Germany's dependence on American loans showed how fragile the recovery of the late 1920s was. The pauperisation of millions again reduced Germans to despair.
- The Depression also polarised politics in Germany — the drift to extremes led to a fear of Communism, which grew apace with the growth of support for the Nazis.

Appeal of the Nazis after 1928

- Nazi Party attracted the increasingly disillusioned voting population: They were anti-Versailles, anti-Communist [the SA took on the Red Front in the streets], promised to restore German pride, give the people jobs etc.
- The Nazis put their message across well with the skilful use of propaganda under the leadership of Josef Goebbels.
- Propaganda posters with legends such as "Hitler — our only hope" struck a chord with many.

- The SA was used to break up opponents' meetings and give the appearance of discipline and order.
- Gave scapegoats for the population to blame from the Jews to the Communists.

The role of Hitler

- Hitler was perceived as a young, dynamic leader, who campaigned using modern methods and was a charismatic speaker.
- He offered attractive policies which gave simple targets for blame and tapped into popular prejudice.

Weaknesses and mistakes of others

- Splits in the Left after suppression of Spartacist revolt made joint action in the 1930s very unlikely.
- Roles of von Schleicher and von Papen. Underestimation of Hitler.
- Weakness/indecision of Hindenburg.

Any other relevant factors.

42. The Nazis used a variety of methods to stay in power. These ranged from policies that pleased the German people to the development of State terror.

Fear and terror

- Opponents liable to severe penalties, as were the families.
- The use of fear/terror through the Nazi police state; role of the Gestapo.
- Concentration camps set up; the use of the SS.

Other factors

Success of economic policies

- Nazi economic policy — attempted to deal with economic ills caused by the Great Depression affecting Germany, especially unemployment.
- Nazis began a massive programme of public works; work of Hjalmar Schacht.
- Nazi policy towards farming eg Reich Food Estate — details of various policies.
- Goring's policy of 'guns before butter'. Popular once foreign policy triumphs appeared to justify it.

Social policies

- Attempts to create the *Volksgemeinschaft* (national community).
- Nazi youth policy.
- Nazi education policy.
- Nazi policy towards the Jews-first isolate, then persecute and finally destroy.
- Nazi family policy — Kinder, Kirche, Kuche.
- Kraft durch Freude programme.
- A Concordat with the Catholic Church was reached; a Reichsbishop was appointed as head of the Protestant churches.

Success of foreign policy

- Nazi success in foreign policy attracted support among Germans; Rearmament, Rhineland, Anschluss.
- Much of Hitler's popularity after he came to power rested on his achievements in foreign policy.

Establishment of totalitarian state

- Political parties outlawed; non-Nazi members of the civil service were dismissed eg Enabling Act following the Reichstag Fire.

- Nazis never quite able to silence opposition to the regime.
- Speed of takeover of power and ruthlessness of the regime made opposition largely ineffective.
- Anti-Nazi judges were dismissed and replaced with those favourable to the Nazis.
- Acts Hostile to the National Community (1935) — all-embracing law which allowed the Nazis to persecute opponents in a 'legal' way.

Crushing/weakness of opposition

- Opponents liable to severe penalties, as were their families.
- Opponents never able to establish a single organisation to channel their resistance — role of the Gestapo, paid informers.
- Opposition lacked cohesion and a national leader; also lacked armed supporters.
- Lack of cooperation between socialists and communists.
- The Night of the Long Knives removed internal opposition, removed the unpopular SA and earned the gratitude of the Army.

Propaganda

- Use of Nuremburg Rallies.
- Use of radio.
- Cult of the Leader: the Hitler Myth.
- Use of the Cinema: Triumph of the Will, the Eternal Jew, etc.
- Role of Goebbels.

Any other relevant factors.

Part E: Italy, 1851–1939

43. By 1850 the forces of nationalism had grown in Italy. The Revolutions of 1848 showed this, but they also illustrated the tensions within the nationalist movement and the continued strength of Austria.

Supporters of nationalism

Educated middle class

- Risorgimento saw 'patriotic literature' from novelists and poets including Pellico, and Leopardi. These inspired the educated middle class.
- Gioberti, Balbo and Mazzini promoted their ideas for a national state, this inspired nationalism amongst the middle classes.

Liberals

- Some liberals and business classes were keen to develop an economic state. Napoleon Bonaparte had built roads and encouraged closer trading. One system of weights, measures and currency appealed.

Popular sentiment

- French revolutionary ideals had inspired popular sentiment for a national Italian state.
- There was a growing desire for the creation of a national state amongst students; many joined Mazzini's 'Young Italy'.
- Operas by Verdi and Rossini inspired growing feelings of patriotism.
- The use of Tuscan as a 'national' language by Alfieri and Manzoni spread ideas of nationalism.
- Membership of secret societies such as the Carbonari grew. Members were willing to revolt and die for their beliefs which included desire for a national state.

Opponents

Austria and her dependent duchies

- Resentment against Austria and its restoration of influence in the Italian peninsula and their use of spies and censorship, helped increase support for the nationalist cause. However, any progress made by nationalists was firmly crushed by the Austrian army. Strength of the Quadrilateral. Austrians never left Italian soil. Carbonari revolts in Kingdom of Naples 1820–1821, Piedmont 1821, Modena and the Papal States 1831 all crushed by Austrian army. During 1848 revolutions, Austrian army defeated Charles Albert twice — Custoza and Modena, retook Lombardy and destroyed the Republic of St Mark.

Italian princes and rulers

- Individual rulers were opposed to nationalism and used censorship, police and spies as well as the Austrian army, to crush revolts 1820–1821, 1830 and 1848.

Attitude of the peasants

- The mass of the population were illiterate and indifferent to politics and nationalist ideas. They did revolt during bad times as can be seen in 1848 — but their revolts were due to bad harvests and bad economic times and were not inspired by feelings of nationalism.

Position of the Papacy

- Pope Pius IX. Nationalist movement had high hopes of New Pope Pius IX, initially thought of as a liberal and sympathetic to nationalist cause. Hopes dashed when Pope Pius IX denounced the nationalist movement during and after 1848 revolutions.

Failures of 1848 revolutions

- These showed that nationalist leaders would not work together, nor did they seek foreign help thus hindering progress. Charles Albert's 'Italia farad a se' declared that Italy would do it alone — she did not. Lombardy and Venetia suspected Charles Albert's motives and were reluctant to work with him. Venetians put more faith in Manin.
- All progress was hampered when Pope Pius IX denounced nationalism.
- Charles Albert hated Mazzini and would not support the Roman Republic.
- Austrian military might based on the Quadrilateral defeated Charles Albert twice — at Custoza and Modena, retook Lombardy and destroyed the Republic of St Mark.
- The French crushed the Roman Republic.

Any other relevant factors.

44. By 1925, Mussolini and the Fascists had gained power in Italy. A number of factors contributed to Mussolini's rise to power, including the economic difficulties facing Italy after the First World War.

Economic difficulties

- The First World War imposed serious strain on the Italian economy. The government took huge foreign loans and the National Debt was 85 billion lira by 1918. The lira lost half of its value, devastating middle class savers. Inflation was rising; prices in 1918 were four times higher than 1914. This led to further major consequences:
  - no wage rises
  - food shortages
  - two million unemployed 1919
  - firms collapsed as military orders ceased.

Weaknesses of Italian governments

- Parliamentary government was weak — informal 'liberal' coalitions. Corruption was commonplace (trasformismo). Liberals were not a structured party. New parties formed: PSI (socialists), PPI (Catholic Popular Party) with wider support base threatening existing political system.
- WWI worsened the situation; wartime coalitions were very weak. 1918; universal male suffrage and 1919 Proportional Representation; relied on 'liberals' — unstable coalitions. Giolitti made an electoral pact with Mussolini (1921); fascists gained 35 seats then refused to support the government. Over the next 16 months, three ineffective coalition governments.
- Fascists threatened a 'March on Rome' — King refused to agree to martial law; Facta resigned; Mussolini was invited to form coalition. 1924 Acerbo Law.

Resentment against the Peace Settlement

- Large loss of life in frustrating campaigns in the Alps and the Carso led to expectation that these would be recognised in the peace settlement; Wilson's commitment to nationalist aims led to the creation of Yugoslavia and a frustration of Italian hopes of dominating the Adriatic.
- 'Mutilated victory' — Italian nationalists fuelled ideas that Italy had been betrayed by her government.

Role of the King

- The King gave in to fascist pressure during the March on Rome. He failed to call Mussolini's bluff.
- After the Aventine Secession the King was unwilling to dismiss Mussolini.

Appeal of the Fascists

- They exploited weaknesses of other groups by excellent use of Mussolini's newspaper 'Il Popolo D'Italia'.
- The Fascio Italiano di Combattimento began as a movement not a political party and thus attracted a wide variety of support giving them an advantage over narrower rivals.
- By 1921 fascism was anti-communist, anti-trade union, anti-socialist and pro-nationalism and thus became attractive to the middle and upper classes.
- Fascism became pro-conservative, appealed to family values, supported church and monarchy; promised to work within the accepted political system. This made fascism more respectable and appealing to both the monarchy and the papacy.
- Squadristi violence was directed against socialism so it gained the support of the elites and middle classes.
- Violence showed fascism was strong and ruthless. It appealed to many ex-soldiers.
- Fascists promised strong government. This was attractive after a period of extreme instability.
- Fascists promised to make Italy respected as a nation and thus appealed to nationalists.
- Fascist policies were kept deliberately vague to attract support from different groups.

Role of Mussolini

- Key role in selling the fascist message: Powerful orator-piazza politics.
- He seized his opportunities. He changed political direction and copied D'Annunzio.
- He used propaganda and his newspaper effectively and had an ear for effective slogans.
- He dominated the fascist movement, kept support of fascist extremists (Ras).
- He relied on strong nerve to seize power and to survive the Matteotti crisis.

- Mussolini manipulated his image, kept out of violence himself but exploited the violence of others.

Weaknesses and mistakes of opponents

- D'Annunzio's seizure of Fiume was not stopped by the government.
- Government failed to get martial law to stop fascist threat. Some liberals supported the Acerbo Law.
- Socialist General Strike July 1922 – failed. Socialists' split weakened them; refused to join together to oppose fascism.
- Liberals fragmented into four factions grouped around former PMs. They were too weak to effectively resist. Hoped to tame fascists.
- PPI was divided over attitude to fascism – right wing supported fascism. Aventine Secession backfired; destroyed chance to remove Mussolini.

Any other relevant factors.

45. **By 1925, Mussolini and the Fascists had achieved power in Italy. The establishment of the Fascist State had in part been achieved by economic and social policies, which were important in maintaining power up to 1939.**

Economic and social policies

- Fascists tried to develop the Italian economy in a series of propaganda-backed initiatives eg the 'Battle for Grain'. While superficially successful, they did tend to divert resources from other areas.
- Development of transport infrastructure, with building of autostrade and redevelopment of major railway terminals eg Milan.
- One major success was the crushing of organised crime. Most Mafia leaders were in prison by 1939.
- Dopolavoro had 3.8 million members by 1939. Gave education and skills training; sports provision, day-trips, holidays, financial assistance and cheap rail fares. This diverted attention from social/economic problems and was the fascist state's most popular institution.

Crushing of opposition

- Liberals had divided into four factions so were weakened.
- The Left had divided into three – original PSI, reformist PSU and Communists – they failed to work together against fascists.
- Pope forced Sturzo to resign and so PPI (Catholic Popular Party) was weakened and it split.
- Acerbo Law passed. n1924 elections – fascists won 66% of the vote.
- Opposition parties failed to take advantage of the Matteotti crisis. By walking out of the Chamber of Deputies (Aventine Secession) they gave up the chance to overthrow Mussolini; they remained divided – the Pope refused to sanction an alliance between PPI and the socialists. The King chose not to dismiss Mussolini.
- Communists and socialists did set up organisations in exile but did not work together. Communist cells in northern cities did produce some anti-fascist leaflets but they suffered frequent raids by OVRA.
- PPI opposition floundered with the closer relationship between Church and State (Lateran Pacts).

Fear and intimidation

- Mussolini favoured complete State authority with everything under his direct control. All Italians were expected to obey Mussolini and his Fascist Party.
- The squadristi were organised into the MVSN Milizia Voluntaria per la Sicurezza Nazionale the armed local Fascist militia (Blackshirts). They terrorised the cities and provinces with tactics such as force-feeding with toads and castor oil.
- After 1925–6 around 10,000 non-fascists/opposition leaders were jailed by special tribunals.
- The secret police, OVRA was established in 1927 and was led by Arturo Bocchini. Tactics included abduction and torture of opponents. 4,000 people were arrested by the OVRA and sent to prison.
- Penal colonies were established on remote Mediterranean islands such as Ponza and Lipari. Conditions for those sentenced to these prisons were primitive with little chance of escape.
- Opponents were exiled internally or driven into exile abroad.
- The death penalty was restored under Mussolini for serious offences but by 1940 only ten people had been sentenced to death.

Establishment of the Fascist state

- Nov/Dec 1922 Mussolini was given emergency powers. Nationalists merged with PNF 1923. Mussolini created MSVN (fascist militia) – gave him support if the army turned against him – and Fascist Grand Council – a rival Cabinet. These two bodies made Mussolini's position stronger and opposition within PNF weaker. The establishment of a dictatorship began:
  - 1926 – opposition parties were banned. A one party state was created.
  - 1928 – universal suffrage abolished.
  - 1929 – all Fascist Parliament elected.

Social controls

- Workers were controlled through 22 Corporations, set up in 1934; overseen by National Council of Corporations, chaired by Mussolini.
- Corporations provided accident, health and unemployment insurance for workers, but forbade strikes and lock-outs.
- There were some illegal strikes in 1930s and anti-fascist demonstrations in 1933 but these were limited.
- The majority of Italians got on with their own lives conforming as long as all was going well. Middle classes/elites supported fascism as it protected them from communism.
- Youth knew no alternative to fascism, were educated as fascists and this strengthened the regime. Youth movements provided sporting opportunities, competitions, rallies, camps, parades and propaganda lectures – 60% membership in the north.

Propaganda

- Press, radio and cinema were all controlled.
- Mussolini was highly promoted as a 'saviour' sent by God to help Italy – heir to Caesar, world statesman, supreme patriot, a great thinker who worked 20 hours a day, a man of action, incorruptible.

Foreign policy

- Mussolini was initially extremely popular, as evidenced by huge crowds who turned out to hear him speak.
- Foreign policy successes in the 1920s, such as the Corfu Incident, made him extremely popular. He was also able to mobilise public opinion very successfully for the invasion of Abyssinia.
- Mussolini's role in the Munich Conference of 1938 was his last great foreign policy triumph.

- As Mussolini got more closely involved with Hitler his popularity lessened. His intervention in Spain proved a huge drain on Italy's resources. The invasion of Albania was a fiasco.

Relations with the Papacy

- Lateran treaties/Concordat with Papacy enabled acceptance of regime by the Catholic majority.
- Many Catholics supported Mussolini's promotion of 'family values'.

Any other relevant factors.

Part F: Russia, 1881–1921

46. By 1905 Russia's problems had led to open opposition to the Tsarist state. Poor military performance in the war with Japan exposed the social, economic and political weaknesses of the state.

Military defeat

- Land battle: decisive defeat at Mukden.
- Sea battle: defeat at Tsushima Strait. They sailed 18,000 miles before being defeated in under an hour.
- The Russo-Japanese War was disastrous for Russia. Defeats by Japan were humiliating and led to discontent in Russia over the Tsar's leadership, the incompetence of the Tsar's government and the inadequate supplies and equipment of Russia's armed forces.
- Russian soldiers and sailors were unhappy with their poor pay and conditions.
- The incompetence of their leaders and their defeats led to low morale.
- Naval mutiny in the Black Sea fleet, battleship *Potemkin*, over poor conditions and incompetent leadership threatened to spread and weakened support for the Tsar.

Other factors

Economic problems

Working-class discontent

- Russia had been experiencing a number of economic problems in the period before 1905. Russia had started the process of industrialisation, however its cost meant that Russia used foreign loans and increased taxes to fund it.
- The working and living conditions in the cities were very poor and this, along with long working hours and low pay, led to discontent.

Peasantry discontent

- The vast majority of Russians were peasant farmers who lived in poverty and were desperate to own their own land. Many peasants were frustrated at paying redemption payments and at the unwillingness of the government to introduce reforms. An economic slump in Russia hurt the newly-created Russian industries and, coupled with famine in 1902/1903, led to food shortages.
- There was an outcry when Russian grain was still being exported to pay for the foreign loans.

Political problems

- Growing unhappiness with Tsarist autocratic rule. The middle class and the industrial workers were calling for a constitutionally-elected government as they were so frustrated at the incompetence of the Tsar's government, especially during the war with Japan. During 1905, workers set up groups called soviets to demand better pay and conditions. The Russian nobility feared a revolution if moderate reforms were not introduced.
- Tsar Nicholas II was seen as being too weak and unable to make good decisions for Russia in a crisis.

- National minorities hated the policy of Russification as it ignored their language, customs and religion and many felt so isolated that the desire for independence intensified.
- As the war with Japan progressed there were a growing number of protests from different parts of Russian society calling for the war to end and the Tsar to share his power.

Events

- Bloody Sunday, on Sunday 9 January 1905, led by Father Gapon. Troops fired on the unarmed crowd which led to strikes in all major towns and cities.
- Terrorist acts followed towards government officials and landowners.
- Peasant violence in the countryside when peasants took over land and burned landowners' estates started after the government threatened to repossess the land of those behind with their redemption payments.

Any other relevant factors.

47. In 1917, the Bolsheviks successfully overthrew the Provisional Government. A reason for this was the appeal of the Bolsheviks under the leadership and organisation of Lenin.

Appeal of the Bolsheviks

- Lenin returned to Russia announcing the April Theses, with slogans such as "Peace, Land and Bread" and "All Power to the Soviets" which were persuasive.
- Lenin talked of further revolution to overthrow the Provisional Government and his slogans identified the key weaknesses of the Provisional Government.
- The Bolsheviks kept attending the Petrograd Soviet when most of the others stopped doing so and this gave them control of the Soviet, which they could then use against the Provisional Government.
- The Bolsheviks did not return their weapons to the Provisional Government after they defeated Kornilov.
- Bolsheviks were able to act as protectors of Petrograd.

Other factors

Weaknesses of the Provisional Government

- The Provisional Government was an unelected government; it was a self-appointed body and had no right to exercise authority, which led it into conflict with those bodies that emerged with perceived popular legitimacy.
- The Provisional Government gave in to the pressure of the army and from the Allies to keep Russia in the War.
- Remaining in the war helped cause the October Revolution and helped destroy the Provisional Government as the misery it caused continued for people in Russia.
- General Kornilov, a right wing general, proposed to replace the Provisional Government with a military dictatorship and sent troops to Petrograd.
- Kerensky appealed to the Petrograd Soviet for help and the Bolsheviks were amongst those who responded.
- Some Bolsheviks were armed and released from prison to help put down the attempted coup.

Dual power – The role of the Petrograd Soviet

- The old Petrograd Soviet re-emerged and ran Petrograd.
- The Petrograd Soviet undermined the authority of Provisional Government especially when relations between the two worsened.
- Order No. 1 of the Petrograd Soviet weakened the authority of the Provisional Government as soldiers were not to obey orders of Provisional Government that contradicted those of the Petrograd Soviet.

Economic problems
- The workers were restless as they were starving due to food shortages caused by the war.
- The shortage of fuel caused lack of heating for the workers in their living conditions.
- The shortage of food and supplies made the workers unhappy and restless.

The Land Issue
- All over Russia peasants were seizing nobles land and wanted the Provisional Government to legitimise this.
- The failure of the Provisional Government to recognise the peasants' claims eroded the confidence in the Provisional Government.
- Food shortages caused discontent.

Any other relevant factors.

48. **In order to secure power the Bolsheviks had to fight a vicious Civil War with their opponents. That they won was due to their strengths, such as the role of Trotsky as well as disunity among their enemies.**

Role of Trotsky
- Trotsky had a completely free hand in military matters.
- HQ was heavily armed train, which he used to travel around the country.
- He supervised the formation of the Red Army, which became a formidable fighting force of three million men.
- He recruited ex Tsarist army officers and used political commissars to watch over them, thus ensuring experienced officers but no political recalcitrance.
- He used conscription to gain troops, and would shoot any deserters.
- Trotsky helped provide an army with great belief in what it was fighting for, which the whites did not have.

Other factors

Disunity among Whites
- The Whites were an uncoordinated series of groups whose morale was low.
- The Whites had a collection of different political beliefs who all wanted different things and often fought amongst themselves due to differences. All of the Whites shared a hatred of Communism but other than this they lacked a common purpose.
- No White leader of any measure emerged to unite and lead the White forces whereas the Reds had Trotsky and Lenin.

Organisation of the Red Army
- The Red Army was better organised than the White army and better equipped and therefore able to crush any opposition from the White forces.
- Use of ex-officers from old Imperial Army.
- Reintroduction of rank and discipline.
- Role of Commissars.

Superior Red resources
- Once the Reds had established defence of their lines they were able to repel and exhaust the attacks by the Whites until they scattered or surrendered.
- By having all of their land together it was easier for the Reds to defend. With the major industrial centres in their land (Moscow and Petrograd) the Reds had access to factories to supply weapons etc and swiftly due to their control of the railways.

- Control of the Railways meant they could transport troops and supplies quickly and efficiently and in large numbers to the critical areas of defence or attack.
- The decisive battles between the Reds and Whites were near railheads.
- The Reds were in control of a concentrated area of western Russia, which they could successfully defend due to the maintenance of their communication and supply lines.
- Having the two major cities of Moscow and Petrograd in their possession meant that the Reds had the hold of the industrial centres of Russia as well as the administrative centres.
- Having the two major cities gave the Reds munitions and supplies that the Whites were unable to therefore obtain.

Use of Terror (Cheka)
- The Cheka was set up to eradicate any opposition to the Reds.
- There was no need for proof of guilt for punishment to be exacted.
- There was persecution of individual people who opposed the Reds as well as whole groups of people, which helped to reduce opposition due to fear, or simply eradicate opposition.
- The Cheka group carried out severe repression.
- Some of the first victims of the Cheka were leaders of other political parties.

Foreign Intervention
- The Bolsheviks were able to claim that the foreign "invaders" were imperialists who were trying to overthrow the revolution.
- The Reds were able to stand as Champions of the Russian nation from foreign invasion.
- The help received by the Whites from foreign powers was not as great as was hoped for.
- The Foreign Powers did not provide many men due to the First World War just finishing and their help was restricted to money and arms.

Propaganda
- Whites were unable to take advantage of the brutality of the Reds to win support as they often carried out similar atrocities.
- The Whites were unable to present themselves as a better alternative to the Reds due to their brutality.
- The Reds kept pointing out that all of the land that the peasants had seized in the 1917 Revolution would be lost if the Whites won. This fear prevented the peasants from supporting the Whites.

Leadership of Lenin
- Introduction of War Communism
- By forcing the peasants to sell their grain to the Reds for a fixed price the Reds were able to ensure that their troops were well supplied with and well fed.
- The Whites' troops were not as well supplied and fed as the Reds' troops.
- Skilled delegation and ruthlessness

Any other relevant factors.

Part G: USA, 1918–1968

49. **Between 1918 and 1941 the USA was a racist society to a large extent. Black Americans faced hostility due to racist attitudes. Such racism was underpinned by a lack of political influence, legal sanction, social attitudes and organisations that persecuted black Americans.**

Lack of political influence

- 1890s: loopholes in the interpretation of the 15th Amendment were exploited so that states could impose voting qualifications.
- 1898 case of Mississippi v Williams — voters must understand the American Constitution.
- Grandfather Clause: impediment to black people voting.
- Most black people in the South were sharecroppers they did not own land and some states identified ownership of property as a voting qualification.
- Therefore black people could not vote, particularly in the South, and could not elect anyone who would oppose the Jim Crow Laws.

Activities of the Ku Klux Klan

- Racist organisation formed in 1860s to prevent former slaves achieving equal rights. Suppressed by 1872, but in the 1920s there was a resurgence.
- Methods horrific: included beatings, torture and lynching.
- Roosevelt refused to support a federal bill to outlaw lynching in his New Deal in 1930s — feared loss of Democrat support in South.
- Activities took place at night — men in white robes, guns, torches, burning crosses.
- The 'second' Klan grew most rapidly in urbanising cities which had high growth rates between 1910 and 1930, such as Detroit, Memphis, Dayton, Atlanta, Dallas, and Houston.
- Klan membership in Alabama dropped to less than 6,000 by 1930. Small independent units continued to be active in places like Birmingham, where in the late 1930s members launched a reign of terror by bombing the homes of upwardly mobile African-Americans.
- Their activities in the 1930s led to continued migration of black Americans from the South to the North.

Legal impediments

- 'Jim Crow Laws' — separate education, transport, toilets etc — passed in Southern states after the Civil War
- 'Separate but Equal' Supreme Court Decision 1896, when Homer Plessey tested their legality
- Attitudes of Presidents eg Wilson 'Segregation is not humiliating and is a benefit for you black gentlemen'.

Divisions in the black community

- Booker T. Washington, accommodationist philosophy, regarded as an 'Uncle Tom' by many.
- In contrast W. E. B De Bois founded the NAACP — a national organisation whose main aim was to oppose discrimination through legal action. 1919 he launched a campaign against lynching, but it failed to attract most black people and was dominated by white people and well off black people.
- Marcus Garvey and Black Pride — he founded the UNIA (Universal Negro Improvement Association) which aimed to get blacks to 'take Africa, organise it, develop it, arm it, and make it the defender of Negroes the world over'.

Popular prejudice

- Since the institution of slavery the status of Africans was stigmatized, and this stigma was the basis for the anti-African racism that persisted.
- The relocation of millions of African-Americans from their roots in the Southern states to the industrial centres of the North after World War I, particularly in cities such as Boston, Chicago, and New York (Harlem). In northern cities, racial tensions exploded, most violently in Chicago, and lynchings increased dramatically in the 1920s.

Any other relevant factors.

50. **After 1945, the Civil Rights Movement was active in campaigning to improve the lives of African-Americans. There are many reasons why this mass movement developed after 1945 and the role of Martin Luther King is a significant factor.**

The role of Martin Luther King

- Martin Luther King — inspirational. Linked with SCLC. Peaceful non-violence and effective use of the media. 'I have a dream' speech.
- 1957 Martin Luther King and other black clergy formed the Southern Christian Leadership Conference (SCLC) to coordinate the work of civil rights groups.
- King urged African-Americans to use peaceful methods.
- Leadership during Montgomery Bus Boycott 1955.
- Use of media to gain publicity for the cause.

The emergence of effective black leaders

- Malcolm X — inspirational, but more confrontational. Articulate voice of Nation of Islam.
- Stokely Carmichael — Black Power and rejection of much on MLK's non-violent approach. A 'direct ideas' descendant of Marcus Garvey.
- All leaders attracted media coverage, large followings and divided opinion across USA.
- Black Panthers attracted attention but lost support by their confrontational tactics.
- Other leaders and organisations eclipsed by media focus on main personalities.

The formation of effective black organisations

- 1960: groups of black and white college students organised Student Non-violent Coordinating Committee (SNCC) to help the civil rights movement.
- They joined with young people from the SCLC, CORE and NAACP in staging sit-ins, boycotts, marches and freedom rides.
- Combined efforts of the civil rights groups ended discrimination in many public places including restaurants, hotels, and theatres.

Continuation of prejudice and discrimination

- The experience of war emphasised freedom, democracy and human rights yet in USA Jim Crow laws still existed and lynching went unpunished.
- The Emmet Till murder trial and its publicity.
- Education: 1954 Brown v Board of Education of Topeka; 1957 Little Rock Central High School.
- Transport: 1955 Rosa Parks and the Montgomery Bus Boycott.

The experience of black servicemen in the Second World War

- Black soldiers talked about 'the Double-V-Campaign': Victory in the war and victory for Civil Rights at home.
- Philip Randolph is credited with highlighting the problems faced by black Americans during World War Two.
- Planned March on Washington in 1941 to protest against racial discrimination.
- Roosevelt's response — Executive order 8802.
- Roosevelt also established the Fair Employment Practices Committee to investigate incidents of discrimination.
- Creation of the Congress of Racial Equality (CORE) 1942.
- Beginning of a mass movement for Civil Rights.

Any other relevant factors.

51. After 1945, the Civil Rights Movement was active in campaigning to improve the lives of black Americans. This mass movement was successful, in part, in solving the problems facing black Americans, up to 1968.

Aims of the Civil Rights Movement

- Was mainly pacifist and intended to bring Civil Rights and equality in law to all black Americans.
- More radical segregationist aims of Black Radical Movements.

Role of NAACP

- Work of NAACP in the Brown v Topeka Board of Education, 1954.
- Work of NAACP in the Montgomery Bus Boycott, 1955.

Role of CORE

- Organised sit-ins during 1961 and freedom rides.
- Helped organise march on Washington.
- Instrumental in setting up Freedom Schools in Mississippi.

Role of SCLC and Martin Luther King

- Emergence of Martin Luther King and the SCLC.
- Little Rock, Arkansas — desegregation following national publicity.
- Non-violent protest as exemplified by Sit-ins and Freedom Rides.
- Birmingham, Alabama 1963: use of water cannon: Reaction of Kennedy.
- March on Washington, August 1963 — massive publicity.
- Martin Luther King believed that the Civil Rights Act of 1964 'gave Negroes some part of their rightful dignity, but without the vote it was dignity without strength'.
- March 1965, King led a march from Selma to Birmingham, Alabama, to publicise the way in which the authorities made it difficult for black Americans to vote easily.

Changes in Federal Policy

- Use of executive orders: Truman used them to appoint black appointments, order equality of treatment in the armed services: Kennedy signed 1962 executive order outlawing racial discrimination in public housing, etc
- Eisenhower sent in federal troops and National Guardsmen to protect nine African-American students enrolled in a Central High School: Kennedy sent troops to Oxford, Mississippi to protect black student: James Meredith
- Johnson and the 1964 Civil Rights Act banning racial discrimination in any public place, Voting Rights Act of 1965: by end of 1965 over 250,000 Blacks newly registered to vote, Affirmative Action, etc

Social, economic and political changes

- Civil Rights Acts of 1964 and 1965 irrelevant to the cities of the North.
- Economic issues more important in the North.
- Watts Riots and the split in the Civil Rights movement.
- King and the failure in Chicago.
- Urban poverty and de facto segregation still common in urban centres — failure of King's campaign to attack poverty.

Rise of black radical movements

- Stokely Carmichael and Black Power.
- Malcolm X publicised the increasing urban problems within the ghettos of America. The Black Panthers were involved in self-help schemes throughout poor cities.
- Kerner Commission 1968 recognised US society still divided.

Any other relevant factors.

Part H: Appeasement and the Road to War, to 1939

52. By its nature the fascism espoused by Hitler and Mussolini was expansionist in nature. However, the methods used to fulfil their aims varied owing to the circumstances faced by the fascist powers. There was considerable skill on display as well as the ability to use opportunity when it arose. However, the inevitable end of such actions was war.

Military agreements, pacts and alliances

- The German-Polish Non-Aggression Pact between Nazi Germany and Poland signed on January 26, 1934 — normalised relations between Poland and Germany, and promised peace for 10 years. Germany gained respectability and calmed international fears.
- Anglo German Naval Treaty 1935 — Germany allowed to expand navy. Versailles ignored in favour of bi-lateral agreements. A gain for Germany.
- Rome-Berlin axis — treaty of friendship signed between Italy and Germany on 25 October 1936.
- Pact of Steel — an agreement between Italy and Germany signed on May 22, 1939 for immediate aid and military support in the event of war.
- Anti-Comintern Pact between Nazi-Germany and Japan on November 25th, 1936. The pact directed against the Communist International (Comintern) but was specifically directed against the Soviet Union. In 1937 Italy joined the Pact Munich Agreement — negotiations led to Hitler gaining Sudetenland and weakening Czechoslovakia.
- Nazi Soviet Non-Aggression Pact August 1939 — Both Hitler and Stalin bought time for themselves. For Hitler it seemed war in Europe over Poland unlikely. Poland was doomed. Britain had lost the possibility of alliance with Russia.

Other Factors

Fascist strategies: use of Military threat and force

- Italy's naval ambitions in the Mediterranean — 'Mare Nostrum'.
- Italian invasion of Abyssinia — provocation, methods, and relatively poor performance against very poorly equipped enemy.
- German remilitarisation of Rhineland — Hitler's gamble and timing, his generals' opposition, lack of Allied resistance.
- Spanish Civil War — aid to Nationalists, testing weapons and tactics, aerial bombing of Guernica.
- Anschluss — attempted coup 1934; relations with Schuschnigg; invasion itself relatively botched militarily; popularity of Anschluss in Austria.
- Czechoslovakia — threats of 1938; invasion of March 1939.
- Italian invasion of Albania — relatively easy annexation of a client state.
- Poland — escalating demands; provocation, invasion.
- The extent to which it was the threat of military force which was used rather than military force itself — eg Czechoslovakia in 1938; and the extent to which military force itself was effective and/or relied on an element of bluff — eg Rhineland.

German Rearmament

- Open German rearmament from 1935.
- The speed and scale of rearmament, including conscription.

- The emphasis on air power and the growing threat from the air.
- By 1939, Hitler had an army of nearly 1 million men, over 8,000 aircraft and 95 warships.
- Germany's perceived military strength may have had an effect on other countries. Britain, for example feared aerial power, especially after the bombing of Guernica by the German Condor Legion.

Fascist diplomacy as a means of achieving aims:

- Aims can be generally accepted as destruction of Versailles, the weakening of democracies, the expansion of fascist powers and countering communism.
- Diplomacy and the protestation of 'peaceful' intentions and 'reasonable' demands.
- Appeals to sense of international equality and fairness and the righting of past wrongs eg Versailles.
- Withdrawal from League and Disarmament Conference.
- Prior to Remilitarisation of Rhineland Hitler made offer of 25 year peace promise. Diplomacy used to distract and delay reaction to Nazi action.

Fascist strategies: Economic

- Use of economic influence and pressure, eg on south-eastern European states.
- Aid supplied to Franco (Spain) was tactically important to Hitler. Not only for testing weapons but also access to Spanish minerals.

Any other relevant factors.

53. **Czechoslovakia was created by the break-up of Austria-Hungary, at the end of World War One, by the Treaty of St Germain. It was a successful democracy in Eastern Europe, though there was a significant minority of Sudeten Germans. This Germanic population became very restless after relentless Nazi propaganda. Hitler threatened invasion to 'protect' the 'persecuted' German minority. In September of 1938 Chamberlain flew out to meet Hitler directly at Berchtesgaden in order to avoid war. He met with Hitler again at Bad Godesberg and finally at a four-power conference in Munich, conceding the Sudetenland 'peace for our time'.**

Munich Agreement was a reasonable settlement

- Czechoslovakian defences were effectively outflanked anyway following the Anschluss.
- Britain and France were not in a position to prevent German attack on Czechoslovakia in terms of difficulties of getting assistance to Czechoslovakia.
- British public opinion was reluctant to risk war over mainly German-speaking Sudetenland.
- Military unpreparedness for wider war — especially Britain's air defences.
- Lack of alternative, unified international response to Hitler's threats:
  - Failure of League of Nations in earlier crises
  - French doubts over commitments to Czechoslovakia
  - US isolationism
  - British suspicion of Soviet Russia
  - Strong reservations of rest of British Empire and Dominions concerning support for Britain in event of war.
- Attitudes of Poland and Hungary who were willing to benefit from the dismemberment of Czechoslovakia.
- Munich bought another year for rearmament which Britain put to good use.
- Views of individuals, politicians and media at this time.

Munich Agreement was not a reasonable settlement

- A humiliating surrender to Hitler's threats.
- Another breach in the post-WW1 settlement.
- A betrayal of Czechoslovakia and democracy.
- Czechoslovakia wide open to further German aggression as happened in March 1939.
- Further augmentation of German manpower and resources.
- Furtherance of Hitler's influence and ambitions in Eastern Europe.
- Further alienation of Soviet Union.
- Poland left further exposed.
- A British, French, Soviet agreement could have been a more effective alternative.
- Views of individuals, politicians and media at this time.

Any other relevant factors.

54. **The Nazi occupation of the Sudentenland could be justified in the eyes of Appeasers as Hitler was absorbing fellow Germans into Greater Germany. However, by the time of the Nazi-Soviet Pact, any illusion of justified grievances had evaporated.**

Importance of Nazi-Soviet Pact

- Pact — diplomatic, economic, military co-operation; division of Poland.
- Unexpected — Hitler and Stalin's motives.
- Put an end to British-French talks with Russia on guarantees to Poland.
- Hitler was freed from the threat of Soviet intervention and war on two fronts.
- Hitler's belief that Britain and France would not go to war over Poland without Russian assistance.
- Hitler now felt free to attack Poland.
- But, given Hitler's consistent, long-term foreign policy aims on the destruction of the Versailles settlement and lebensraum in the east, the Nazi-Soviet Pact could be seen more as a factor influencing the timing of the outbreak of war rather than as one of its underlying causes.
- Hitler's long-term aims for destruction of the Soviet state and conquest of Russian resources — lebensraum.
- Hitler's need for new territory and resources to sustain Germany's militarised economy.
- Hitler's belief that British and French were 'worms' who would not turn from previous policy of appeasement and avoidance of war at all costs.
- Hitler's belief that the longer war was delayed the more the balance of military and economic advantage would shift against Germany.

Other factors

Changing British attitudes towards appeasement

- Czechoslovakia did not concern most people until the middle of September 1938, when they began to object to a small democratic state being bullied. However, most press and population went along with it, although level of popular opposition often underestimated.
- Events in Bohemia and Moravia consolidated growing concerns in Britain.
- The anti-appeasement movement gained more support as Hitler's intentions became clearer.
- German annexation of Memel [largely German population, but in Lithuania] further showed Hitler's bad faith
- Actions convinced British government of growing German threat in south-eastern Europe.
- Guarantees to Poland and promised action in the event of threats to Polish independence.

The occupation of Bohemia and the collapse of Czechoslovakia

- British and French realisation, after Hitler's breaking of Munich Agreement and invasion of Czechoslovakia in March 1939, that Hitler's word was worthless and that his aims went beyond the incorporation of ex-German territories and ethnic Germans within the Reich.
- Promises of support to Poland and Rumania.
- British public acceptance that all attempts to maintain peace had been exhausted.
- <u>Prime Minister Chamberlain</u> felt betrayed by the Nazi seizure of Czechoslovakia, realised his policy of appeasement towards Hitler had failed, and began to take a much harder line against the Nazis.

British diplomacy and relations with the Soviet Union

- Stalin knew that Hitler's ultimate aim was to attack Russia.
- Lord Halifax, the British Foreign Secretary was invited by Stalin to go to Russia to discuss an alliance against Germany.
- Britain refused as they feared Russian Communism, and they believed that the Russian army was too weak to be of any use against Hitler.
- In August 1939, with war in Poland looming, the British and French eventually sent a military mission to discuss an alliance with Russia. Owing to travel difficulties it took five days to reach Leningrad.
- The Russians asked if they could send troops into Poland if Hitler invaded. The British refused, knowing that the Poles would not want this. The talks broke down.
- This merely confirmed Stalin's suspicions regarding the British. He felt they could not be trusted, especially after the Munich agreement, and they would leave Russia to fight Germany alone. This led directly to opening talks with the Nazis who seemed to be taking the Russians seriously by sending Foreign Minister von Ribbentrop and offering peace and land.

The position of France

- France had signed an agreement with Czechoslovakia offering support if the country was attacked. However, Hitler could all but guarantee that in 1938, French would do nothing as their foreign policy was closely tied to the British.
- French military, and particularly their air force, allowed to decline in years after 1919.
- After Munich, French more aggressive towards dictators and in events of 1939 were keen on a military alliance with the Soviet Union, however despite different emphasis on tactics were tied to the British and their actions.

Developing crisis over Poland

- Hitler's long-term aims for the destruction of Versailles, including regaining of Danzig and Polish Corridor.
- British and French decision to stick to their guarantees to Poland

Invasion of Poland

- On 1 September 1939, Hitler and the Nazis faked a Polish attack on a minor German radio station in order to justify a German invasion of Poland. An hour later Hitler declared war on Poland stating one of his reasons for the invasion was because of "the attack by regular Polish troops on the Gleiwitz transmitter."
- France and Britain had a defensive pact with Poland. This forced France and Britain to declare war on Germany, which they did on September 3.

Any other relevant factors.

Part I: The Cold War, 1945–1989

55. Although Soviet motives in creating a buffer zone of states with sympathetic pro-Stalinist governments made sense to the Russians many of those in the satellite states did not see it that way. Resentment within the satellite states grew, especially when the standard of living did not rise. The death of Stalin seemed to offer an opportunity for greater freedom. However, Soviet tolerance of change only ran so far.

The international context

- 1955 — emergence of Nikita Khrushchev as leader on death of Stalin. He encouraged criticism of Stalin and seemed to offer hope for greater political and economic freedom across the Eastern European satellite states.
- Speech to 20th Party Congress, Feb 1956: Khrushchev attacked Stalin for promoting a cult of personality and for his use of purges and persecution to reinforce his dictatorship. Policy of de-Stalinisation.
- Development of policy of peaceful co-existence to appeal to the West.
- Development of policy of different roads to Socialism to appeal to satellite states in Eastern Europe who were becoming restless.

Demands for change and reaction: Poland (1956)

- Riots sparked off by economic grievances developed into demands for political change in Poland.
- On the death of Stalinist leader Boleslaw Bierut in 1956 he was replaced by Wladyslaw Gromulka, a former victim of Stalinism which initially worried the Soviets.
- Poles announced their own road to Socialism and introduced reforms.
- Release of political prisoners (incl. Cardinal Wyszynski, Archbishop of Warsaw); collective farms broken up into private holdings; private shops allowed to open, greater freedom given to factory managers.
- Relatively free elections held in 1957 which returned a Communist majority of 18.
- No Soviet intervention despite concerns.
- Gromulka pushed change only so far. Poland remained in the Warsaw Pact as a part of the important 'buffer zone'. Political freedoms were very limited indeed. Poland was a loyal supporter of the Soviet Union until the 1980s and the emergence of the Solidarity movement. Limited challenge to Soviet control.

Demands for change and reaction: Hungary (1956)

- Hungarians had similar complaints: lack of political freedom, economic problems and poor standard of living.
- Encouraged by Polish success, criticism of the Stalinist regime of Mátyás Rákosi grew and he was removed by Khrushchev.
- Popular upsurge of support for change in Budapest led to a new Hungarian government led by Imre Nagy, who promised genuine reform and change.
- Nagy government planned multi-party elections, political freedoms, the withdrawal of Hungary from the Warsaw Pact and demands for the withdrawal of Soviet forces.
- Nagy went too far. The Soviet Union could not see this challenge to the political supremacy of the Communist Party and the break-up of their carefully constructed buffer zone. They intervened and crushed the rising brutally.
- Successful intervention against a direct challenge to Soviet control, but lingering resentment from mass of

Hungarian people, through some economic flexibility allowed the new regime of Janos Kadar to improve economic performance and living standards.

Demands for change and reaction: Berlin (1961)

- Problem of Berlin — a divided city in a divided nation.
- Lack of formal boundaries in Berlin allowed East Berliners and East Germans to freely enter the West which they did owing to the lack of political freedom, economic development and poor living standards in the East.
- Many of those fleeing (2.8 million between 1949 and 1961) were skilled and young, just the people the communist East needed to retain. This was embarrassing for the East as it showed that Communism was not the superior system it was claimed to be.
- Concerns of Ulbricht and Khrushchev: attempts to encourage the Western forces to leave Berlin by bluster and threat from 1958 failed.
- President Kennedy spoke about not letting the Communists drive them out of Berlin. Resultant increase in tension could not be allowed to continue.
- Building of barriers: barbed wire then stone in August 1961 to stem the flood from East to West.
- Success in that it reduced the threat of war and the exodus to the West from the East to a trickle. To an extent it suited the West as well as they did not like the obvious threat of potential conflict and escalation that Berlin represented.
- Frustration of many in East Germany. Propaganda gift for the US and allies, though Soviets had controlled the direct challenge.

Military and ideological factors

- Buffer zone could not be broken up as provided military defence for Soviet Union.
- Use of force and Red Army to enforce control in late 40s and early 50s.
- Need to ensure success of Communism hence policy.

Domestic pressures

- Intention to stop any further suffering of Soviet Union in aftermath of WW2 made leadership very touchy to change.
- Some economic freedoms were allowed, but at the expense of political freedoms.
- Need to stop spread of demands for change.

Any other relevant factors.

56. Events during the Cuban Missile crisis had concentrated the minds of the superpowers leaders and led to a more conciliatory relationship between the USSR and USA. However, each side also had its own reasons for engagement. The USSR wished to restructure its economic focus from weapons production and heavy industry to more consumer goods. The USA felt that there were other ways to contain Communism and wished for more engagement in the context of their involvement in Vietnam.

Economic cost of arms race

- Developments in technology raised the costs of the arms race.
- The development of Anti-Ballistic Missile technology and costs of war led to SALT 1, and the ABM treaty
- Limiting MIRV and intermediate missile technology led to SALT 2.
- The cost of 'Star Wars' technology also encouraged the Soviet Union to seek better relations.

- Khrushchev's desire for better relations between the superpowers in the 50s and 60s was, in part, about freeing up resources for economic development in the USSR. He hoped this would show the superiority of the Soviet system.
- Gorbachev wanted to improve the lives of ordinary Russians and part of this was by reducing the huge defence budget eg Intermediate Nuclear Forces Treaty, December 1987.

Other factors

Mutually Assured Destruction

- The development of vast arsenals of nuclear weapons from 1945 by both superpowers as a deterrent to the other side; a military attack would result in horrific retaliation.
- So many nuclear weapons were built to ensure that not all were destroyed even after a first-strike, and this led to a stalemate known as MAD. Arms race built on fear.

Dangers of military conflict as seen through Cuban Missile Crisis

- In this it worked as the threat of nuclear war seemed very close on the discovery of Soviet nuclear missiles on Cuba in 1962. Before Khrushchev backed down nuclear war was threatened. It also illustrated the lack of formal contact between the superpowers to defuse potential conflicts.
- Introduction of a 'hot-line' between the Kremlin and White House in order to improve communication between the superpowers. Khrushchev and Kennedy also signed the Limited Nuclear Test Ban Treaty, the first international agreement on nuclear weapons.

Technology: The importance of verification

- American development of surveillance technology (U2 and satellites) meant that nuclear weapons could be identified and agreements verified.
- Example of U2 flight over Cuba where Anderson photographed nuclear sites.
- Also U2 and satellite verification to make sure the Soviets were doing as promised at the negotiating table.
- Some historians think Arms Control would never have taken root, but for the ability of the sides to verify what the other was doing.

Co-existence and Détente

- Policies of co-existence and détente developed to defuse tensions and even encourage trade.
- Role of others like Brandt in West Germany in defusing tension through their policies of Ostpolitik, etc.

Any other relevant factors.

57. Ronald Reagan became President of the United States in 1981. He brought an aggressive anti-Communism to Cold War relations. This showed itself through new defence initiatives as well as tough talk. By 1985 Mikhail Gorbachev had become General Secretary of the Communist Party in Soviet Russia. He was very aware of the economic problems building up for Russia and sought reform at home and engagement abroad.

Actions of President Ronald Reagan

- Unlike many in the US administration Reagan actively sought to challenge Soviet weakness and strengthen the west in order to defeat Communism. In 1983 he denounced the Soviet Union as an 'Evil Empire'.

- Programme of improving US armed forces, including nuclear weapons and he proposed a Star Wars missile shield to challenge the belief in MAD (SDI).
- He was very charming when he met Gorbachev and visited the Soviet Union.

Other factors

Failure of Communism in Eastern Europe

- Strong Polish identity and history of hostility with Russia. By 1970s, Poland in economic slump. Emergence of opposition around Gdansk in 1980: industrial workers strike led by Lech Walesa, who argued for the creation of an independent trade union. Solidarity grew to nine million members in a matter of months. Movement suppressed in 1981 by General Jaruzelski's government.
- Multiparty elections in Poland, after Soviet troops left, victory for Solidarity.
- Czechoslovakia, political prisoners released in November 1989 and by the end of the month, the communist government had gone. No Soviet intervention.
- Opening of the Berlin Wall: division of Germany finally came to an end.
- Soviet domination ended.
- Perestroika and Glasnost and end of Communist rule in USSR.

Role of President Mikhail Gorbachev

- Gorbachev saw that the USSR could not afford a new arms race. The Soviet economy was at breaking point. Commitments to the arms race and propping up allied regimes meant consumer goods and other things such as housing that mattered to Russian people were neglected.
- Gorbachev implemented policies of Perestroika and Glasnost which aimed to reform the Soviet economy and liberalise its political system.
- Gorbachev worked to improve relations with the USA. He took ideology out of his foreign policy, as exemplified by arms agreements to allow the USSR to concentrate on internal matters: Intermediate Nuclear Forces Treaty, Dec 1987, Nuclear Weapons Reduction Treaty, 1989.
- Gorbachev told leaders of the satellite East European states in March 1989 that the Soviet army would no longer help them to stay in power.

Western economic strength

- Allowed America to embark on the Star Wars weapons programme.
- Perception of the affluent West through television and consumer goods undermined Communist claims of the superiority of their economic system.

Withdrawal of the Soviet Union from Afghanistan

- Symptom of the problems of Soviet Union
- Intervention in Dec 1979: conflict with the Mujahidin. Russian army morale crumbled when over 20,000 Soviet soldiers died, as did support at home.
- The conflict showed the weaknesses of the Soviet economy. War led to a slump in living standards for ordinary Russians.
- Russians began to question the actions of their own government. Gorbachev withdrew troops in 1988.

Any other relevant factors.

2016
SECTION 1: SCOTTISH

Part A: The Wars of Independence, 1249—1328

1. Evaluate the usefulness of Source A as evidence of the succession problem.

*Candidates can be credited in a number of ways **up to a maximum of 6 marks**.*

Examples of aspects of the source and relevant comments:

Aspect of the source — Author
Scottish nobles

Possible comment
Useful as the nobles spoke on behalf of the Scottish political leaders therefore they were speaking with authority and in the absence of a king; their reply would have been considered an official statement.

Aspect of the source — Type of source
Statement by the Scottish nobles

Possible comment
Useful as the statement was a prepared and considered response by the Scottish nobles.
Less useful as it may be a biased response by the Scottish nobles during a three week adjournment after the break-up of the meeting at Norham.

Aspect of the source — Purpose
Reply to Edward's demand at Norham to be recognised as overlord of Scotland

Possible comment
Useful as the response of the Scottish nobles was to reject Edward I's demand of overlordship of Scotland showing that during the succession crisis, the Scots were concerned to safeguard the independence of the Scottish kingdom.

Aspect of the source — Timing
May 1291

Possible comment
Useful as the statement was made only seven months after news reached Scotland that the Maid of Norway had died on her way to Scotland resulting in the succession crisis, a struggle for the throne and a fear that there would be civil war between the rival claimants.

Content
In response to Edward I's demand at Norham that he is recognised as overlord of Scotland before he can judge between the claimants to the Scottish succession.

Possible comment
Useful as it provides insight of Edward's intentions towards Scotland during the succession crisis. It provides details of how Edward I claimed the overlordship of Scotland during a period of weakness in Scotland.

Content
We have no power to reply to Edward I's claim as we lack a king to whom the demand ought to be addressed and only a king has the power to answer.

Possible comment
Useful as the nobles claim that they could not respond to Edward's demand themselves as this part of the statement was a reminder to Edward that such an important demand could only be dealt with by the king of Scotland.

Less useful as their denial of competence to reply to Edward's demands could be viewed as a delaying tactic and an attempt to avoid Edward's demand.

Content
King Edward has himself guaranteed the kingdom of Scotland's independence in the Treaty of Birgham-Northampton.

Possible comment
Useful as it provides evidence of the importance attached to the Treaty of Birgham by the Scots during the succession crisis. Despite the collapse of the marriage treaty after the death of the Maid of Norway, the Scots wanted to ensure the survival of their customs and rights and to maintain the independence of the kingdom of Scotland.

Possible points of significant omission may include:
- Edward I had in fact claimed overlordship as recently as 1278 when it was rejected by Alexander III.
- The death of Alexander III in March 1286 posed a succession problem as there was no male heir.
- When Alexander died, his grand-daughter, Margaret, was aged three or four and was in Norway, where her father, Eric II was king.
- There was no precedent in Scotland for a queen ruling in her own right. The succession of a female, even as an adult, posed potential difficulties.
- Bishop Fraser of St Andrews was afraid of civil war when Robert Bruce the elder arrived in Perth with an army. Bishop Fraser asked Edward to come to the Scottish border in order to maintain peace.
- The seriousness of the situation after the death of Alexander III required the Scottish nobles to carry on the government of the country. Six Guardians were elected (two bishops, two earls, two barons) in a parliament in Scone.
- The Guardians compromised the independence of Scotland by asking Edward I for advice and protection.
- There were concerns to maintain the independence of Scotland. The Treaty of Birgham, the marriage of Margaret, Maid of Norway and King Edward's son, Edward, Prince of Wales, appeared to solve the potential threat of civil war and to establish a secure relationship with England through marriage. The Guardians however, were concerned to keep Scotland's separate customs and laws.
- A problem arose over the succession after Margaret's death on her way to Scotland in 1290. Her death left no obvious heir to the kingdom of Scotland.
- Following the invitation to be arbiter in the issue of Scottish succession, Edward showed his authority by inviting the Scottish leaders to meet him at his parliament at Norham rather than Edward travelling over the border into Scotland.
- Edward also showed his strength by ordering his northern armies to assemble at Norham. In addition, Edward organised his navy for a blockade of Scotland and raised taxes to prepare for a possible war.
- Edward put further pressure on the Scots representatives by asking them to prove that he, Edward, was not their overlord. The Scottish leaders replied they could not be asked to "prove a negative".
- The Scottish representatives were granted three weeks to reply to Edward's demands.
- Edward responded to the refusal of the Scots representatives to acknowledge his overlordship by asking the claimants to the throne to accept it instead.
- In the Award of Norham, nine claimants, fearing they would be left out of the judgement, accepted Edward's overlordship, and in so doing, compromised the independence of the kingdom.

- The Guardians and other leading Scots eventually took an oath of fealty to Edward. An English baron, Brian fitzAllan was appointed by Edward to the Guardians.
- The task of choosing a new king, known as the Great Cause was a long drawn out process, lasting over 15 months from August 1291 until November 1292. Thirteen claimants, not including Edward himself, presented themselves although only three, John Balliol, Robert Bruce and John Hastings, had a strong legal claim.
- Edward continued to exercise his overlordship over Scotland even after deciding in favour of John Balliol in November 1292. Balliol had the strongest legal claim, based on primogeniture, being a descendent of the eldest daughter of Earl David.
- Balliol had to swear fealty to Edward. Balliol also did homage to Edward in December 1292 at Newcastle. Edward exercised such authority which created problems for King John's reign.

Any other valid point that meets the criteria described in the general marking instructions for this kind of question.

2. Compare the views of Sources B and C about the role of William Wallace and Scottish resistance.

Candidates can be credited in a number of ways up to a maximum of 5 marks.

Possible points of comparison may include:

Source B	Source C
Overall: The sources agree that Wallace's military leadership at the Battle of Stirling Bridge and his political leadership as Guardian made a positive contribution to Scottish resistance to Edward I.	
Source B suggests there were divisions among the nobility and some reluctance to accept Wallace's Guardianship. However **Source C** suggests that, on the whole, Wallace had the support of the traditional nobility.	

Source B	Source C
In the weeks which followed Wallace and Murray's victory at Stirling Bridge, English garrisons across central and southern Scotland surrendered.	Wallace and Murray's startling defeat of the largely cavalry force brought against them by Surrey and Cressingham at Stirling on the 11 September 1297 led to the near collapse of the English military control in Scotland.
Wallace was knighted and named guardian of the realm, thus reviving the office used between 1286 and 1292.	Wallace ... was knighted and afterwards elected as guardian, still in the name of King John but also of the Community of the Realm.
Wallace appointed William Lamberton, a supporter of Scottish independence, as the new bishop of St Andrews.	Wallace ... appointed new bishops — most importantly his friend William Lamberton to succeed William Fraser as bishop of St Andrews.
Many of the nobles, clergy and others who opposed Edward's rule accepted Wallace as the best hope for the defence of the kingdom.	Scotland's traditional leaders fought under Wallace's command.

3. How fully does Source D explain the reasons for the rise and triumph of Robert Bruce?

Candidates can be credited in a number of ways up to a maximum of 9 marks.

A maximum of 2 marks may be given for answers which refer only to the source.

Possible points which may be identified in the source include:

- The Comyns never displayed any outstanding talent in military matters.
- Bruce himself had quickly matures into a cunning and effective guerrilla leader.
- The new king was also blessed with an ability to attract and sustain a close-knit team of military commanders who were as effective in military terms as Bruce.
- Bruce could maintain a war on more than one front, sending his only surviving brother, Edward and the enthusiastic James Douglas, down into Galloway to deal with Balliol supporters there, while he himself tackled the Comyn heartland.

Possible points of significant omission may include:

- Bruce's decisive victory over the Earl of Buchan in the battle of Inverurie and the destruction of Comyn lands in the "Herschip of Buchan" removed the threat from the powerful Comyn family.
- Bruce was increasingly able to leave much of the conduct of the war to such men as Edward Bruce, James Douglas and Thomas Randolph. Bruce's lieutenants were especially important in capturing castles such as Linlithgow, Edinburgh and Roxburgh from English garrisons.
- Edward Bruce, along with James Douglas, led the attack on Galloway and by 1309 was being styled lord of Galloway, a title formerly held by John Balliol.
- The death of King Edward I in 1307 while leading an army against Bruce removed Bruce's main military adversary. Edward's death also weakened English resolve to prosecute the war in Scotland.
- Edward II did not share his father's obsession with Scotland, and he lacked his father's drive and ability. King Edward II did not lead a major campaign into Scotland for several years which allowed Bruce to concentrate on fighting his Scottish enemies.
- Bruce reconquered Scotland from 1310—14 by conducting a successful campaign against English held castles in Scotland, e.g. Dundee, Perth, Dumfries, Linlithgow, Roxburgh and Edinburgh.
- Raids were made on the north of England after 1311 and Bruce and his lieutenants led regular raids into England after 1314 to force Edward II to the negotiating table. Bruce attacked England in 1315, 1316, 1318, 1322, 1323 and 1328.
- The raids on England did not succeed in bringing Edward II to the negotiating table but did result in war weariness which contributed to a series of truces in the 1320s.
- Berwick, England's last major outpost in Scotland was captured by the Scots in 1318.
- Bruce inflicted a major defeat on the English at Old Byland in 1322 which almost resulted in the capture of Edward II.
- The support of the Scottish Church was also significant in Bruce's triumph. Most bishops supported Bruce as they saw him as the best hope of securing the independence of the kingdom which would ensure the independence of the Scottish Church. Churchmen preached Bruce propaganda thus promoting Bruce's struggle against his Scottish enemies in the Civil War.

- In the Declaration of the Clergy in 1310 Scotland's bishops declared their support for Bruce as the legitimate king of Scotland.
- Bruce's triumph over a huge English army at the Battle of Bannockburn (23—24 June 1314) completes Bruce's military control of Scotland and gains him increased support thereby securing his position as king of Scots.

Bruce also weakened English power by sending Scottish armies under his brother Edward to campaign in Ireland. Despite the failure of the Scots to conquer Ireland and the defeat and death of Edward Bruce in 1318, the possibility of a Celtic fringe alliance diverted English attention and forces from Scotland.

- Diplomacy also contributed to Bruce's triumph. Bruce's position was strengthened by king Philip of France's recognition of Bruce in 1310 which helped to raise Scottish morale.
- A powerful case for Scottish Independence was presented to the pope, in the letter known as the Declaration of Arbroath in 1320 and in the Treaty of Edinburgh Bruce made major concessions to gain recognition of his kingship and of Scotland's independence.
- At a parliament held at Cambuskenneth Abbey in 1314, Bruce gave the nobles the opportunity to pledge their allegiance and keep their Scottish lands whilst disinheriting those who chose to side with England.
- Bruce's position was also strengthened by his brutal crushing of the 1320 "Soulis Conspiracy". However Bruce also showed leniency towards former enemies. Bruce gathered support and ensured loyalty by rewarding his followers.
- Bruce triumphed when he finally secured peace between Scotland and England. Bruce exploited the weakness of the English government after the deposition of Edward II by once more launching attacks into northern England and into Ireland which succeeded in forcing the insecure government of Isabella and Mortimer to negotiate. The Treaty of Edinburgh (1328) formally recognised Bruce as king of an independent Scotland.

Any other valid point of explanation that meets the criteria described in the general marking instructions for this kind of question.

Part B: The Age of the Reformation, 1542—1603

4. Evaluate the usefulness of Source A as evidence of the reasons for the Reformation of 1560.

Candidates can be credited in a number of ways up to a maximum of 6 marks.

Examples of aspects of the source and relevant comments:

Aspect of the source	Possible comment
Author: 'Beggars' Summons'	Useful as it claims to be from the poor in Scotland. However, it was in fact written anonymously and is thought to be the work of Protestants who were leading the Reformation in Scotland. It is biased against the Friars as they are one part of the Catholic Church which the Protestants see as corrupt and open to bribery so may be less useful.

Type of source: A summons — A written notice which was pinned to the door of friaries across the country.	This is useful because it shows the discontent of the poor towards the Catholic Church in Scotland, in particular their resentment towards the friars.
Purpose: The Summons was written to act as a threat to the friars. It was to demand that the friars leave their friaries by next Whitsunday (12 May 1559).	The source shows that they were prepared to take action against the friaries which makes it useful as it shows the anger and resentment that had built up in Scotland amongst Protestants prior to the Reformation.
Timing: 1st January 1559	Useful as it is a contemporary document written the year before the Reformation of 1560 as discontent was growing against the Catholic Church.
Content	**Possible comment**
We the blind, crooked, bedridden widows, orphans and all other poor have grievances with all friars within the realm.	Useful as it shows how the most vulnerable in society appear to have grievances against the friars.
Steal from us our lodgings, and then leave us to perish and die from the effects of poverty.	Useful as it shows how the friars appear to have taken advantage of the poor.
We have thought it wise to warn you by this public writing fixed to your gates, that between now and the Feast of Whitsunday next, you must remove yourselves from the friaries.	Useful as it shows the strength of feeling and threats made by Protestants towards the Catholic Church.

Possible points of significant omission may include:
- Increase in popular support of Protestant sentiment between 1547 and 1559 despite the absence of the figurehead Knox. This support can be seen in the Perth riot 11th May 1559 and stealing of the image of St Giles on the day of the saints celebration (1st September) 1558 in Edinburgh.
- Return of Knox as a figurehead. Hugely influential in gathering support for the movement through his preaching.
- Unhappiness under Mary of Guise due to heavy taxation and her pro-French policies.
- English military intervention crucial in early 1560.
- Increase of Protestant literature.
- Protestant martyrs such as George Wishart (1546) and Walter Myln (1558) helped garner popular support for the Protestant cause.
- Wish for Scots to create their own national cultural identity. Wish for no interference from England or France.

- Lack of strong leadership from the Catholic Church in Scotland. Particularly following the murder of Cardinal Beaton.
- Scotland disliked being ruled by a woman Mary of Guise.
- Protestant religious commitment. Hard-line and unwavering commitment to the cause.
- The Lords of the Congregation were encouraged by the prospect of support from the English after Elizabeth became Queen in 1558.
- Protestant ideas had been coming into Scotland for some time.
- English Bibles and books critical of the Catholic Church were distributed in Scotland following the Reformation in England.
- The Catholic Church failed to make sufficient reform to satisfy its critics.
- Increased numbers of the nobility opted for the new faith.
- The Lords of the Congregation had increasing support and took up arms against Mary of Guise.
- The weaknesses of the Catholic Church — decline and corruption; pluralism had not been addressed.
- Minors being given top positions in the church.
- Crown and nobility taking much of churches' revenues.

Any other relevant points.

5. Compare the views of Sources B and C about the relationship between monarch and Kirk in the reign of James VI.

Candidates can be credited in a number of ways up to a maximum of 5 marks.

Possible points of comparison may include:

Source B	Source C
Overall: Sources B and **C** agree about the fact that the Kirk viewed James with distrust. The sources also agree about James's attempts to exert control over the Kirk over his attendance at General Assemblies.	
Source B	**Source C**
James had inherited a poor country divided by religious factions which viewed the monarch with mistrust.	James VI was viewed with a degree of distrust by his Kirk.
James's main claim was that the Sovereign's right came straight from God.	This was in part due to his relentless view that Kings were in charge of the church by divine rule.
While James's views were questioned by extremist Presbyterians, his resolve to exercise authority over the Kirk strengthened and in 1597, Andrew Melville was deposed as rector of St Andrews.	The initiative passed to the king, and with the dismissal of Melville many ministers who had previously been happy to criticise him were more willing to accept.
Thereafter, the King attended all General Assemblies between 1597 and 1603, cementing his influence.	By 1603, James had exerted his influence with attendance at every General Assembly since 1597.

6. How fully does Source D explain the impact of the Reformation on Scotland, to 1603?

Candidates can be credited in a number of ways up to a maximum of 9 marks.

A maximum of 2 marks may be given for answers which refer only to the source.

Possible points which may be identified in the source include:

- However, by 1573 there were over 500 such men preaching to the people showing the growing influence of the Kirk, in many parishes the people were being served by ministers who were well informed on religious matters.
- The Kirk also remained committed to improving education throughout the land.
- Above all, the people now heard the Word of God in their own language, a matter of indescribable worth.
- Kirk services became more serious as the sound of music, and the playing of the organ in particular, were associated with the Catholic faith and became a thing of the past.

Possible points of significant omission may include:

- The *Second Book of Discipline* led indirectly to a regular meeting of ministers from 10 to 20 parishes for discussion of doctrine, which became the presbytery.
- It proved impractical to dispossess the Catholic clergy of their benefices so they were allowed to retain two-thirds of their revenues for life.
- Concessions made to Catholic clergy, on the grounds of old age or ill-health.
- At the beginning of 1560, Scotland was a Catholic country with a Protestant minority. By 1603, it was a Protestant country with a small Catholic minority.
- The Reformation did not lead to a significant transfer of wealth from the Church and much of the lands of the Catholic Church remained in the hands of the nobility.
- The new church still had the problem of not having enough revenue for the parishes.
- James VI was reluctant to enforce anti-Catholic laws.
- Kirk sessions were instruments of moral and religious control.
- The elaborate interiors of Catholic churches were replaced with plain, whitewashed parish kirks.
- Observance of Catholic festivals and saints' days and festivals were discouraged.
- Literary works and Kirk sermons were conducted in English rather than Latin. The only Protestant bibles available to lowland Scots were in English. However, through time the English language became more familiar as English bibles were used in church.
- Assistance given to the poor from the friaries ended. New plans to help the poor by the Presbyterian Church faced difficulty.
- The aim of a school in every parish not achieved but some advances were made in central Scotland.
- Literacy rates improved during this period.
- Many of the issues prevalent within the Catholic Church prior to the Reformation remained, such as: attendance; poverty of some parishes; and poor quality of preaching.
- Scots merchants continued to trade with England and trading ports across the North Sea.
- Scots focused on trade with the Protestant Dutch.
- Trade with France continued despite the change in religion.
- Former Catholics were required to dispose of all religious objects which in the past might have provided a sense of comfort.

- Abolition of Christmas and Easter reflected fear of Catholic custom.
- Respect for the Sabbath.
- The observance of Catholic festivals and the performance of plays were actively discouraged.
- Kirk Sessions were preoccupied with keeping wedding and other celebrations under control. Even though the Kirk decided to remove all organs from places of worship, there is evidence that in some areas music during services survived.
- Great emphasis was laid upon attendance at both daily and Sunday services.
- Prose writers tended to write in English rather than Latin or Scots — this also applied to sermons.
- The catechism was used by ministers, school masters and elders to teach the principles of Protestantism to young Scots. Young people would be examined on their knowledge during the Sunday afternoon service.

Any other relevant points.

Part C: The Treaty of Union, 1689–1740

7. Evaluate the usefulness of Source A as evidence of worsening relations between Scotland and England.

Candidates can be credited in a number of ways up to a maximum of 6 marks.

Examples of aspects of the source and relevant comments:

Aspect of the source	Possible comment
Author: John Dalrymple — Earl of Stair	Useful as Stair was a prominent figure who was known to support future Union, but opposed any deal that would be bad for Scotland. Could argue less useful as author will be biased.
Type of source: Speech	Useful as it reveals strength of feeling amongst some MPs about Scotland's relations with England.
Purpose: To remind Scots of treatment by England during Darien Scheme.	Useful as treatment of Scots by English created further resentment of King William and the English government.
Timing: 1706	Useful as contemporary to the period when the merits of Union were being debated.

Content	Possible comment
Scotland suffered from a lack of co-operation from England.	Useful as it informs MPs of cause for resenting English government.
England treated Scots as pirates and enemy aliens, not fellow British subjects.	Useful as it reveals how Scots were directly affected by English actions in Darien.
No security from union of crowns — Spain attacked Scots.	Useful as it suggests English influence had impact upon safety of Scots in Darien.

Possible points of significant omission may include:

- King William, under influence of English MPs, objected to Darien as it threatened English trade in the Caribbean.
- William persuaded many English investors to withdraw from the Company.
- William used his connections in Holland and persuaded the Dutch to refuse to manufacture or sell ships to the Scots.
- East India Company stopped foreign investment in Company of Scotland as it perceived it as a threat.
- William instructed English colonists in Jamaica not to offer any help to the Scots at Darien.
- William was influenced by English foreign policy towards Spain and France which governed his policy towards Darien.
- King William firmly controlled Scotland to reduce threat of Jacobite rebellion in support of James VII and II.
- Glencoe Massacre (in which Stair himself had been complicit) was announced as murder by the Scottish parliament.
- England's war with France affected English dealings with Scotland.
- Jacobite plot to assassinate William further strained relations between the two countries.
- Continued effects on trade of English Navigation Acts of the 1660's preventing Scots trade with English colonies.
- Issues concerning the succession – Act of Settlement (England).
- Act of Security (Scotland) – threat to restore the Stuarts.
- Wool Act and Wine Act in Scotland were declarations of Scottish independence in matters of trade.
- Alien Act in England threatening Scottish trade with England created hostility in the Scottish parliament.
- Consequence of 1688–89 Revolution: Scottish Parliament – no longer willing to "rubber stamp" decisions taken in England.
- Scotland's economic problems – seven ill years, no help from England or William during this time.
- England's fear that France may use Scotland as "back door" – threat of invasion from France made English wary of Scots who may choose to aid France.
- Influence of the English Court on Scottish government – Queen Anne would employ only those who would support the Hanoverian Succession.
- Queen Anne's determination to settle the Scottish succession on Sophia of Hanover and her heirs – would upset Jacobites and Episcopalians.
- Distrust existing between Episcopalian Anglican Church and Presbyterian Church of Scotland.
- Execution of Captain Green by mob in Leith highlighted anti-English feeling in Edinburgh as Union became more likely.
- Covenanters still agitating for Covenant of 1638 to be observed.

Any other valid point that meets the criteria described in the general marking instructions for this kind of question.

8. Compare the views of Sources B and C about the reasons for the passing of the Union by the Scottish Parliament.

Candidates can be credited in a number of ways up to a maximum of 5 marks.

Possible points of comparison may include:

Source B	Source C
Overall: Sources **B** and **C** agree that rather than a persuasive argument, bribery in the form of cash payments, land and the Equivalent was more important in the passing of the Treaty of Union.	
Source B emphasises the role of Defoe in attempting to persuade MPs of the arguments in favour of union. **Source C** gives additional details about the Earl of Glasgow's role in the cash payments to MPs.	

Source B	Source C
Any Court party arguments in favour of union, however well meaning, persuaded only a few despite winning their votes.	The Court party won all the votes, without making much effort or troubling themselves with reasoning.
Sums of money were certainly distributed to various MPs in order to secure the necessary votes for the passage of the Act of Union through the Scottish parliament.	A sum of £20,000 advanced from the Queen to ease the passage of the Treaty was distributed to various members of the Scottish Parliament by the Earl of Glasgow.
Promises of English landed estates were dangled before members of the Scottish nobility who supported the Treaty.	The English government was determined to secure the Treaty by offering Scottish nobles large and prosperous estates as means of making money after union.
The biggest sweetener was £398,085.10s – the precise "Equivalent" of all the losses of the Darien expedition.	The Equivalent seemed to offer repayment to the many Scots, including members of the Scottish parliament, who had lost their savings through the collapse of Darien.

9. How fully does Source D explain the effects of the Union to 1740?

Candidates can be credited in a number of ways up to a maximum of 9 marks.

A maximum of 2 marks may be given for answers which refer only to the source.

Possible points which may be identified in the source include:

- One irony of the Union is that it did not in the end extinguish Scotland as a nation; it retained its own distinctive identity, attitudes and ideas, and its traditions were so strong that they were not easily removed.
- The Treaty in this respect were not as harmful as they might have been, although it did exert a strong Anglicising influence.
- Guarantees to the Scottish legal system in the Treaty and to the Church in the Act of Security for the Kirk had more influence on Scotland.
- The continuation of the Scottish systems of education and local government were a significant achievement of Union.

Possible points of significant omission may include:

- Scottish tradition still evident in other areas – culture, music, art, literature, Scottish Enlightenment, Scott, Smith, Hume, Burns.

- Influence of English agricultural techniques and innovations after Scottish landowners travelled south to parliament in London.
- Political effects: 1711 – parliament banned Scottish peers with English titles.
- Highland clans divided between Hanoverian and Jacobite loyalties.
- 1713 – Motion to repeal Act of Union defeated by 4 votes.
- Whig election victory in 1715 led to government delaying Malt Tax.
- 1725 – Secretary of State for Scotland replaced by Home Secretary.
- Economic effects: Scottish industry could not compete with English competition; only small number of Scots engaged successfully with colonies.
- New taxes particularly on imports led to increases in smuggling in Scotland and loss of revenue for government.
- Paper industry failed.
- Scottish linen industry suffered.
- Merchant shipping benefited, particularly trade with Baltic and Caribbean.
- Tobacco industry developed in Glasgow although not until around 1740 and only benefited a small amount of merchants.
- Agriculture improved; increased investment; 1727 – Royal Bank of Scotland.
- 1730s – Favourable economic climate; industries such as linen recovered.
- Jacobite reaction: Jacobites led national sentiment in literature and songs.
- 1708 – Abortive French-sponsored invasion by the Old Pretender.
- Jacobite rising of 1715; Earl of Mar played leading role; Battle of Sheriffmuir in November 1715 claimed as victory by both government and Jacobites.
- 1716 Disarming Act banned holding of weapons by Highlanders.
- 1719 – failed attempt at rising in north-west Scotland by earl Marischal.
- Other effects: claims of the unpopularity of union made vocally by opponents.
- 1712 – House of Lords became court of appeal for Scottish cases.
- 1724 – Outbreak of fence-smashing by levellers; 1725 – Shawfield riots in Glasgow in response to Malt Tax; 1736 – Porteous riots in Edinburgh.
- Military road-building; establishment of forts in Highlands.
- 1710 – Tories in parliament failed to remove Church of Scotland's privileges; 1711 – Greenshields case; 1712 – Toleration Act and Patronage Act.
- 1722 Marrow affair in Church of Scotland; 1733 secession from state church after some ministers objected to their support of certain religious writings.

Any other valid point of explanation that meets the criteria described in the general marking instructions for this kind of question.

Part D: Migration and Empire, 1830–1939

10. Evaluate the usefulness of Source A as evidence of the reasons for the migration of Scots.

Candidates can be credited in a number of ways up to a maximum of 6 marks.

Examples of aspects of the source and relevant comments:

Aspect of the source	Possible comment
Author: Editor of Chambers' Journal, a weekly Scottish magazine.	Useful as the editor provides a well-informed description of the attractions of emigration.
Type of source: Article from a popular weekly magazine.	Useful as it was a popular publication which attracted a wide range of readers.
Purpose: To encourage emigration to Canada.	Useful as an example of how publications were used to inform, promote and recruit emigrants.
	Less useful as it is a biased/ one sided view focusing only on the benefits of Canadian farming and attractions of emigration to Canada and omitting the hard work and difficult experiences which was often the reality encountered by many emigrants in clearing the land and building homes.
Timing: 1872	Useful as the article was written at a time when it was easier and cheaper for ordinary Scots to emigrate due to transport innovations.

Content	Possible comment
Experienced farmers and skilled agricultural workers can earn far more overseas than they can here at home.	Useful as it explains that material gain was an important reason why Scots chose to emigrate. Useful as many Scots who emigrated earned higher wages.
The familiarity and neighbourliness of living among fellow Scots who had already emigrated in the past.	Useful as it explains that for many, a powerful attraction was the familiarity and security of community support offered by joining an established Scottish settlement. The thought of joining a community already created by families and friends reduced concerns about emigration.
The confident prospect that the poorest may become landowners thereby earning sufficient to make a living and to comfortably settle one's children.	Useful as it explains that a key factor in emigration was the prospect of owning land which for many Scots of modest means, only emigration could make real.
	Useful as the possibility of taking the future into their own hands was a big attraction for Scottish farmers and is corroborated by many eye-witness accounts.

Possible points of significant omission may include:

- Newspapers in Scotland also published articles in support of emigration to the United States of America, Australia

and New Zealand. Guidebooks to help emigrants, such as "Hints on Emigration to Upper Canada" were also produced along with posters with information and encouragement for potential Scottish emigrants.
- In the nineteenth century a network of emigration agencies developed across Scotland which advertised for passengers and organised their travel arrangements. The Canadian Government appointed agents in Scotland who toured markets, hiring fairs and agricultural shows in an effort to encourage able Scots to emigrate.
- Scots were encouraged to emigrate due to the help offered by charities and societies. The Highland and Islands Emigration Society raised money and helped poor crofters to leave Scotland for Australia and Canada.
- Emigration was also encouraged by the Government through the Colonial Land and Emigration Commissioners. Support offered included land grants and help with the costs of passage. Direct funding of emigration was provided by the Empire Settlement Act of 1922.
- Canada and New Zealand were attractive to Scottish farmers as they offered cheaper, fertile land.
- Letters home from relatives and friends who had already emigrated describing the attractions of colonial life and recounting the successes of Scots emigrants was important in encouraging Scots to move overseas.
- Scots emigrated due to the financial support of relatives. Relatives often paid for fares and provided help on arrival.
- Skilled workers from the towns, for example, textile workers, were attracted to emigrate by higher wages and better careers prospects.
- Some Scots were attracted to emigrate by the investment opportunities abroad in farming, mining and in the railways.
- Scots were encouraged to emigrate in search of gaining quick wealth as a result of the discovery of gold.
- Scots were encouraged to emigrate due to cheaper and more efficient transport.
- Although the Clearances were at their height earlier in the 1840s and early 1850s, some Highlanders emigrated due to the fear of forced evictions happening again.
- Many Highlanders were forced to consider emigration as a result of poverty and near starvation, for instance, during the potato blight. Rising rents, the poor quality of housing and the lack of good farming land as a result of the population increase pushed many to emigrate.
- Countries overseas offered a pleasant climate which contrasted with the wet weather, hardships and poor living of the Highlands.
- Highlanders emigrated due to the encouragement of landowners paying the fares of local people to emigrate.
- Scots from farming areas in the Lowlands of Scotland in particular were forced out of farming and encouraged to emigrate due to the lack of opportunities due to the effects of the agricultural revolution (mechanisation, specialisation, selective breeding) which led to a decrease in the number of workers required on the land.
- Scottish farmers and agricultural workers were forced to emigrate during the agricultural depression between 1880 and 1914.
- Scots from coastal towns were forced to emigrate as a result of the decline of the kelp and herring industries and later as a result of a depression in the fishing industry between 1884 and 1894.
- Scots were forced to emigrate due to unemployment and a lack of opportunities. Many Scottish workers emigrated due to the effects of the economic depression of the 1920s and 1930.

- Scots migrated from the countryside to the towns due to increased opportunities for work. Employment in the towns was seen as being more attractive due to shorter hours and more leisure time in contrast to the drudgery, isolation and long hours of farm work.
- Highlanders migrated to the towns to escape their difficult and poverty stricken lives farming poor soil in harsh weather.
- Scots migrated to the towns to gain access to the increased social and leisure opportunities such as shops, the pub, cinema, dance hall and football. Railways made moving to enjoy the "bright lights" of the town much easier.
- Scots migrated due to the effects of increased mechanisation. Labour saving machinery reduced opportunities particularly in areas of the Lowlands of Scotland. Industrialisation also affected rural craftspeople. Such workers could not compete with factory produced goods and were forced to migrate in search of work in the towns and cities.
- Scots migrated to England which offered better opportunities in trades and profession such as medicine. Scots also took up farming opportunities in England, in Essex, in the south of England.

Any other valid point that meets the criteria described in the general marking instructions for this kind of question.

11. Compare the views of Sources B and C about the impact of Scots emigrants on the Empire.

Candidates can be credited in a number of ways up to a maximum of 5 marks.

Possible points of comparison may include:

Source B	Source C
Overall: Sources B and **C** agree that Scots played an important role in the development of Australian industries such as sheep farming and coal mining.	
Both sources also agree that the arrival of Scots emigrants in Australia was accompanied by the setting up of Presbyterian churches and that the Scots were involved in the development of education.	
While both sources highlight the importance of the Scots exporting agricultural skills, **Source B** suggests that some Scots became innovative by their experimentation with farming techniques such as irrigation.	

Source B	Source C
There was a strong Scottish presence in the pastoral (sheep and cattle) industry, especially in eastern Australia.	All over eastern Australia Scots played a large part in covering the land with homesteads and sheep stations.
Miners were also among the Scottish emigrants to Australia and were mainly to be found in coal mining.	In the coal mining industry, particularly influential were James and Alexander Brown, originally from Lanarkshire whose mining business employed many fellow Scots and produced most of the coal in New South Wales by 1868.

The Presbyterian Church was by far the most important Scottish institution brought to Australia which was to influence many areas of Australian life.	An indication of the distribution of the Scots in Australia is given by the establishment of Presbyterian churches.
Scots and Presbyterians were prominent in the teaching profession with Presbyterian secondary schools established in great numbers in Victoria.	In areas where the Scots were strong, they were usually also associated with educational effort; for example, the support of the Church of Scotland for Melbourne Academy was so significant that it became known as "the Scotch College".

12. How fully does Source D explain the effects of migration and empire on Scotland, to 1939?

Candidates can be credited in a number of ways up to a maximum of 9 marks.

A maximum of 2 marks may be given for answers which refer only to the source.

Possible points which may be identified in the source include:

- The shipbuilding industry still possessed a world reach and remained pre-eminent as in 1914 the Clyde yards built almost a fifth of the world's total output.
- the interlinked coal, steel, iron and engineering industries, employing over a quarter of the Scottish labour force all dependent upon access to overseas markets in the Empire.
- Other manufacturing sectors — carpets, thread and woollens — covering the country from the Borders to the north-east Lowlands — were also dependant on overseas trade.
- The role of the Scots as key junior partners in Empire was maintained after 1918 with the careers of numerous professional and middle class Scots continuing to be pursued within the Empire.

Possible points of significant omission may include:

- Empire contributed to the Clyde becoming the centre of the shipbuilding industry. Shipyards such as Fairfield's, Beardmore's and Denny's were world leaders in the production of shipping in the years up to 1914.
- Empire created a market for Scottish goods. Heavy industries of Scotland exported a high proportion of their products. American grain might well be taken in sacks made in Dundee, by locomotives manufactured in Springfield near Glasgow (which produced one quarter of the world's locomotives in 1914), to be loaded onto ships built on the Clyde.
- Empire provided raw materials for Scottish factories such as jute. The jute trade was closely associated with the Empire: the raw material came from the Indian province of Bengal. The textile manufactured from the raw material from the Indian province of Bengal was subsequently exported all over the world. Dundee textile firms became internationally known.
- Empire enabled some firms and individuals to make great commercial fortunes. Examples include Scottish businessmen such as Sir Charles Tenant (chemicals), Sir James and Peter Coats (cotton) and William Weir (coal and iron).

- Many wealthy Scots invested their profits at home by building mansions in the suburbs. Broughty Ferry near Dundee is an example of the display of wealth created by the jute industry.
- Empire provided many middle-class Scots with successful careers, especially in India, as civil servants, doctors and as soldiers.
- Empire encouraged Scottish martial tradition. Scottish soldiers often from the Highlands were used to protect the Empire and helped create the identity and reputation of the Scots as brave soldiers.
- Empire provided a destination for large numbers of Scottish emigrants.
- Empire also had negative effects on Scotland. The low-wage economy encouraged in Scotland by the export market led to considerable poverty for many.
- Empire left Scotland vulnerable to international trade slumps due to the importance of commerce with the Empire. Due to an over dependence on exports Scotland was adversely affected after the First World War due to the world economic downturn.
- Empire created competition for Scottish goods. Other countries in the Empire came to produce goods more cheaply. Examples of industries where this happened were sheep farming in Australia and New Zealand and the linen and jute industry in India.
- Empire created investment opportunities. By the 1880s 40 per cent of all Australian borrowing was from Scotland. The Scots also invested in India.
- Investment a double-edged sword as Scottish industrial magnates sometimes used their profits to finance projects abroad which meant capital left Scotland.
- Italian immigration had an impact on Scottish society. Italian families contributed to the growing leisure industry. In 1903 there were 89 cafés in Glasgow, growing to 336 by 1905.
- Italian families settled in many towns on the coast and in the main towns. The Nardini family developed what was to become the largest café in Britain. Small sea side towns also had their own Italian cafés.
- In the late 1920s the College of Italian Hairdressers was set up in Glasgow.
- Jewish immigrants helped to develop the commercial life of Scotland. Jews settled in central Glasgow, typically setting up small businesses.
- Jewish immigrants were also important in the tobacco industry. Cigarette making was a common job for the Jewish immigrants to Scotland as there was no local workforce that could produce cigarettes.
- Jewish immigrants made an important contribution to the tailoring trade and helped produce affordable, quality clothing, especially men's suits.
- Lithuanian immigration contributed to the economic development of Scotland mainly through employment in the coal industry.
- Lithuanians joined the Scottish miners in bringing about improved working conditions through trade union activity.
- Lithuanian immigrants also contributed a distinctive culture to Scotland through their language and community activities. However the Lithuanian community integrated effectively into Scottish society therefore left less of a lasting impact. Lithuanians were also fewer in numbers than Irish immigrants and were not perceived as a threat to the Scottish way of life by native Scots. In addition many Lithuanians returned to Eastern Europe during First World War.

- Migration had a positive economic effect on Scotland. The immigrant Irish provided a workforce prepared to tackle the hardest of jobs. The Irish contributed to industrial developments in Scotland through the building of roads, canals and railways across Scotland.
- Irish immigration had a lasting cultural impact on Scottish society reflected in the creation of separate Catholic schools across most major urban centres in Scotland.
- Migration had an impact on Scottish sporting life — Edinburgh Hibernian was founded in 1875 by Irishmen living in the Cowgate area of Edinburgh. Glasgow Celtic was founded in 1887 by Brother Walfrid, a Catholic priest. A Catholic team in Dundee called Dundee Harp also existed for a short time. Dundee United was founded in 1909 and was originally called Dundee Hibernian.
- Irish immigrants also contributed to the culture of Scotland through the Protestant Orange Lodge Order.
- Irish immigrants and their descendants had an impact on Scottish politics. The Irish were important in the Scottish Trade Union movement and the development of the Labour Party in Scotland. The Irish community produced important political leaders like John Wheatley and James Connolly.
- A negative effect of Irish immigration was the presence of sectarian rivalries.

Any other valid point of explanation that meets the criteria described in the general marking instructions for this kind of question.

Part E: The Impact of The Great War, 1914—1928

13. Evaluate the usefulness of Source A as evidence of the experience of Scots on the Western Front.

Candidates can be credited in a number of ways **up to a maximum of 6 marks.**

Examples of aspects of the source and relevant comments:

Aspect of the source	Possible comment
Author: Scottish soldier on the Western Front.	It is useful as it is from the diary of a private from the Royal Scots. It is the view of someone who experienced the war first-hand and who will be well informed about the Scots military involvement on the Western Front.
	Less useful as this diary extract only reflects the experience of one soldier.
Type of source: A diary.	It is useful as it is a personal account of his experience which reflects the broader experience of Scots on the Western Front. It is an eyewitness account to some of the events at High Wood. May be less guarded, so source may be more useful.
Purpose: To record personal experiences during the war.	It is useful as it is a record of a Scottish soldier's experience of particular aspects of life on the Western Front.

Timing: 21st July 1916.	The source is useful as it dates from a time when Scottish soldiers were heavily involved in the war. It is useful as a contemporary account written at the time of the events at High Wood during the Battle of the Somme.
Content	**Possible comment**
We got a whiff of tear gas still lingering after German bombardment, which made our eyes sore and watery.	Useful as it tell us that tear gas was used (against the Scots) by the Germans and what the effects were.
We plunged into a hail of shells. The air was full of the roar of their approach and the drawn out shattering detonations of their explosions.	Useful as it provides an insight of what an enemy bombardment of shells was like for Scottish soldiers who had to experience these.
We were then sent to relieve the survivors of the Division which had suffered terrible losses in the unsuccessful attempt to occupy High Wood.	Useful as it provides insight into a failed attempt at High Wood in July 1916 during which there had been high levels of loss. A common experience for Scottish units during the war.

Possible points of significant omission may include:

- Experience of trench warfare eg rats, lice, trench foot, snipers, boredom, fear of death, lack of sanitation, food rations, shell shock.
- By December 1914, 25% of the male labour force of western Scotland had already signed up.
- 13% of those who volunteered in 1914–15 were Scots.
- Young Scots urged to join the army through a mixture of peer pressure, feelings of guilt, appeals to patriotism, hopes for escapism and adventure, heroism, self-sacrifice and honour. For the unemployed, the army offered a steady wage.
- Kitchener's campaign was a huge success: examples such as by the end of August 20,000 men from the Glasgow area had joined up.
- In Scotland there were no official "Pals Battalions" but in reality — the Highland Light Infantry/Tramway battalion; the 16th battalion/the Boys Brigade.
- In Edinburgh, Cranston's battalion and McCrae's battalions became part of the Royal Scots. McCrae's battalion was the most famous because of its connection with Hearts football club.
- Gas first used by the British at Loos 1915.
- Gas cylinders were replaced by gas-filled shells. Different types of gas, chlorine, phosgene, mustard and their effects.
- More soldiers killed on the Western Front by artillery fire than by any other weapon.
- Partly due to the static nature of trench warfare, the wounded suffered horribly.
- Bloody minded attitude of the survivors who used it to stimulate them for future battles.
- Losses were replaced and the Scottish units carried on though grousing and criticisms became more common.

- A British first field dressing was issued to all servicemen during the First World War. They were intended for use as soon after injury as possible, often applied by the wounded soldier himself.
- Medical support improved as the war went on.
- Loos: for many of Scotland's soldiers in Kitchener's New Army the initial taste of action for the volunteers came at Loos in September 1915.
- The 9th and 15th Scottish Divisions were involved in the attack; 9th lost almost 3,000 men killed and missing from 25 to 28 September; 15th lost over 3,000 in a single day.
- Loos was part of a series of British battles of Neuve Chapelle, Aubers Ridge, Festubert and Loos. Scottish losses were huge and all parts of Scotland were affected; of the 20,598 names of the missing at Loos a third of them are Scottish.
- Bravery and fighting spirit of Scottish units: 5 Victoria Crosses given to Scots after the battle in recognition of their extraordinary bravery; The Somme: Three Scottish divisions 9th, 15th (Scottish) and 51st (Highland) took part in the battle of the Somme, as well as numerous Scottish battalions in other units, ie the Scots Guards in the Household Division. 51 Scottish infantry battalions took part in the Somme offensive at some time.
- Piper Daniel Laidlaw of the KOSB played the pipes during an attack at Loos to encourage Scottish troops to charge. Laidlaw was awarded the Victoria Cross for his bravery.
- Huge Scottish sacrifice: 15th (Cranston's) Royal Scots lost 18 officers and 610 soldiers wounded, killed or missing. 16th (McCrae's) Royal Scots lost 12 officers and 573 soldiers; 16th HLI lost 20 officers and 534 men – examples of Scottish losses on the first day. The 9th (Scottish) Division performed well during the five months of fighting. Casualties were high: 314 officers and 7,203 other ranks, yet morale remained high.
- Battle of Arras in 1917 saw concentration of 44 Scottish battalions and seven Scottish named Canadian battalions, attacking on the first day, making it the largest concentration of Scots to have fought together. One third of the 159,000 British casualties were Scottish.
- High numbers of Scottish deaths at Loos, Somme Arras.
- The official figure given at the end of the war calculated that Scotland had suffered 74,000 dead.
- Huge sacrifice of Scots during the war: of 557,000 Scots who enlisted in the services, 26.4% lost their lives. One in five British casualties was Scottish.
- Experience of Scottish women on Western Front.
- Scottish leadership: role of Douglas Haig; strong Presbyterian background; believed in his mission to win; stubborn and stoical; famous for order in 1918 not to give ground and to fight to the end.
- Debate over Haig's role: considered to be one of the soldiers of his generation, he had a reputation as an innovative commander. In a balanced judgment the historian John Terrain calls him "The Educated Soldier". He had to deal with a military situation which was unique and no other general had had to deal with.
- That he did so with a vision of what was needed – he embraced the use of tanks for example – is to his great credit. He could be distant and was touchy, but he did visit the front and was aware of the sacrifices made; he was the architect of eventual victory.

Any other valid point of explanation that meets the criteria described in the general marking principles for this kind of question.

14. **Compare the views of Sources B and C about the domestic impact of war on the land issues in the Highlands and Islands.**

Candidates can be credited in a number of ways up to a maximum of 5 marks.

Possible points of comparison may include:

Source B	Source C
Overall: Sources **B** and **C** broadly agree about the land issue in Scotland. They agree about promises of land, raiding, imprisonment and the failure of the Land Settlement (Scotland) Act. **Source B** highlights the specific role of propaganda. However, **Source C** highlights the wider effects of the war.	

Source B	Source C
The reaction from ex-servicemen might not have been so violent had the propaganda during and after the war not been so effective **OR** "During the war agents appointed by the government flooded Sutherland with literature containing guarantees to all of land."	The promise of land for men who served in the war was a central part of government policy.
Only weapon that had proved successful since the late nineteenth century was land seizure.	The frustration generated land seizures on a scale not seen in the Highlands for forty years.
The landlord could have them arrested for breaking the law.	The illegal occupation of land in the Highlands led to the arrest and imprisonment of many.
In 1919 the Land Settlement (Scotland) Act came into operation, the stage now seemed to be set for rapid settlement, but it did not work out that way.	The Land Settlement (Scotland) Act was unable to redistribute land according to the precise nature of the demand put by crofters.

15. **How fully does Source D explain the impact of the war on politics in Scotland?**

Candidates can be credited in a number of ways up to a maximum of 9 marks.

A maximum of 2 marks may be given for answers which refer only to the source.

Possible points which may be identified in the source include:

- After the war more people were listening to the Labour Party.
- The Conservatives in the aftermath of the Great War emerged as a major force.
- (In Scotland) voices were raised in calls for a separation of powers and the Scottish Home Rule Association re-established itself in 1918.
- From the time of the "Red Clydeside" rising of 1919 Scots had found much in common with firebrands such as John MacLean.

Possible points of significant omission may include:

- The ILP MPs from Clydeside elected November 1922 were committed to home rule.
- It was difficult for Home Rule to make progress in Westminster parliament.

- Private members' Home Rule bills failed.
- Glasgow University Scottish National Association formed 1926.
- Support for Home Rule waned within the Labour Party.
- 1927 John MacCormick and Roland Muirhead, formed the National Party of Scotland. It distanced itself from the Labour Party. Drew support from intellectuals like Hugh McDiarmid.
- Some Liberals and Conservatives formed the Scottish Party at the end of the 1920s and proposed some form of devolution in an effort to attract Liberal and Unionist supporters.
- The latter formed the National Party of Scotland but it had little electoral impact. (MacCormick and Muirhead each got less than 3,000 votes in the 1929 election.)
- 'Scottish Renaissance' of the 1920s had strong leanings towards Home Rule and Independence — they challenged both the cultural and political relationship between Scotland and England.
- Beginnings of change in Scottish attitudes to the Empire — linked with the "profound crisis which overwhelmed the nation between the wars" (Devine).
- Scots' faith in their role as the economic power-house of the Empire had been shattered.
- Extension of the franchise to women. Many working class women had become politicised by their war work and the rent strikes. Women, such as Mary Barbour, Agnes Dollan and Helen Crawfurd became role models for women keen to make their voice heard politically for the first time.
- Initial instances of radicalism after war: 1919 — George Square.
- The Clyde Workers Committee (CWC) was formed to control and organise action for an extension of workers' control over industry.
- Forty Hours Strike and demonstration at George Square, waving of red flag, riot, troops and tanks appeared on streets of Glasgow. Riot Act was read. The Cabinet agreed with the Scottish Secretary Robert Munro, that the confrontation was not strike action but a "Bolshevist rising".
- Class conflict — breaking of shop stewards, engineers and miners by 1926.
- Splits and decline of the Liberal Party: Coalition Liberals supported Lloyd George and the coalition with the Conservatives at the end of the war. The supporters of Herbert Asquith, the old party leader, stood as Liberals.
- Old Liberal causes died in the aftermath of the war.
- The Liberal Party, which had claimed guardianship of workers' interests on the pre-war era, was increasingly perceived as defending the well-being of employers and capital.
- In the second 1924 election the Liberals won only 9 seats in Scotland.
- Protestant/Orange vote foundered on the Conservatives' support for the 1918 Act giving state support to Catholic secondary schools; separate Orange and Protestant party established in 1922, splitting 'Moderate' (Conservative) vote.

Any other valid point of explanation that meets the criteria described in the general marking principles for this kind of question.

2016
SECTION 2: BRITISH

Part A: Church, State and Feudal Society, 1066–1406

16. To what extent were the peasant classes the most important part of feudal society?

Context

Feudalism is a term that is used to describe a society that is organised around relationships that emerge from the holding of land in exchange for service or labour.

There is debate about what this means in detail, but the relationship between king, nobility, knights and the peasantry is generally agreed to form the basis of feudalism.

Peasants
- Feudal lords depended on the peasant classes; without their work in the fields the feudal system would not have worked.
- The peasants were used to form the bulk of the armies.
- Their importance was highlighted after the Black Death when they were able to demand a lot of money for their labour.
- The Peasants' Revolt (1381) demonstrates that when required the peasants could work together and make demands.

Other factors

The King
- Kings exercised control over their kingdoms, through patronage and gifts of land.
- The Barons were indebted to the king for the lands given to them.
- The king could therefore demand military service in return for a charter that granted the land to the baron and his descendants.

Justice
- The king granted judicial rights to the barons.
- He retained the right to hear any case in his own court.

Revenue
- The king received revenue, from not only his own lands, but from feudal dues from all of his barons.
- The king received money in the form of scutage (shield tax), from those followers who refused to fight.
- The king could apply taxes (feudal aids and reliefs etc.) across the kingdom.

Knights and chivalry
- Royalty understood the importance of the idea of chivalry if properly harnessed ie in favour of the monarchy. Kings hoped to encourage knights and keep their loyalty; romantic stories of the Arthurian Legends were a way of keeping knights loyal.
- The English crown attempted to recreate Camelot and the spirit of the round table. In a way, this way Edward I and Edward III kept the importance of chivalry alive in their realm.

The great Magnates
- Barons accounted for ownership of almost half the arable land in England; they could have lands from several lords or kings.
- Like the king, barons had control over the people under them; they could demand military service and raise an army of knights.
- Like kings they could raise revenue from their lands.

Any other relevant factors.

17. *David I was successful in increasing royal power in Scotland*. How valid is this view?

Context

David I was the youngest son of King Malcolm III and St Margaret. By the time he succeeded to the throne in 1124, he was well connected with a good marriage, a rich inheritance and estates in Normandy, north England and southern Scotland. He sought to impose his authority on the kingdom of Scotland on his succession to the throne.

Introduction of feudal landholding

- During his time in England, David became an admirer of the feudal landholding system. He introduced a form of military feudalism into areas of Scotland, notably the southwest, Lothian and the northeast.
- Noble families were imported from his lands in England and France and given grants of land. In return they offered David their support, both politically and militarily. Examples include Robert de Brus in Annandale and Walter fitz Allan in Renfrewshire and East Lothian.
- There was penetration in to Fife and beyond. Even land given in feudal due to Flemish knights in Moray.
- However, the Mormaers in Scotland were semi-independent and held autonomous power over large parts of Scotland. The Earls of Moray had a long tradition of independence, even going so far as to claim the crown during the reign of Macbeth. However, when its earl rebelled in 1130 and was killed near Brechin, David annexed the province for the crown and set up feudatories there.
- Leaders in the far west and north of Scotland also had a history of independence. In the south the lordship of Galloway, was under the leadership of Fergus, who from 1124 styled himself as King of the Gallowegians.
- There was no whole scale replacement of the native aristocracy. By the 1160s there were still 10 native earls and David was close to those in Fife and Dunbar.

The need to develop the economy

- Before David I, revenue in Scotland was mostly limited to the incomes from royal demesnes.
- The lack of royal burghs limited international trade and early medieval Scottish kings lacked the financial resources to tackle the Mormaers directly without the Community of the Realm backing them.
- As a result David sought to develop more burghs, for example Perth, in order to generate revenue. Burghs allowed for privileged merchant communities. The rents, tolls and fines that the burghs provided were David's earliest and most important sources of money. By the end of his reign there were even burghs in Forres and Elgin in Moray.
- Moneyers were appointed by David and silver pennies were introduced.

Law and order

- Royal justice was usually reserved for more serious crimes. Issues of land, an important aspect of justice, were often poorly judged or unfairly settled.
- Expansion of Royal Castles: Motte and Bailey.

Development of royal government

- Development of offices during David I's reign such as Constable, Butler, Chamberlain and Chancellor. Supporters like Hugh de Moreville and Raulph de Souces became David's constable and butler.
- However, his household kept the Gaelic speaking "Rannaire" (Divider of Food) and the royal body guard; the "Durward".

- Sheriffdoms were introduced along the style of Norman Kings of England. Larger than the traditional thanages.
- Sheriffs sought to replace thanes in the remote areas of the kingdom. They offered direct royal contact for those away from the traditional seat of power.
- However the continued use of officials with Gaelic names shows how he used the structures that already existed.

Development of the royal military forces

- The new feudal forces brought to David by his introduction of feudalism offered a significant advantage when dealing with the Celtic Mormaers.
- Traditionally it was the Mormaers who controlled the summoning of the Common army of Scotland. Now David had an independent force loyal to him.
- Did not always work well together, as seen at the disastrous Battle of the Standard.
- The peace settlement established during the disputed reign of Stephen-Matilda in England, extended Scotland's border further south than ever before.

Development of the justice system

- New Scottish barons were given the rights to hold their own courts within their fiefs. This was an extension of the king's law, rather than reliance on the traditional Celtic courts led by Brechons, experts in the law. Eventually these Celtic courts died out and were replaced with sheriff courts. The gradual acceptance of the king's law led the way to the decrease of importance of the Mormaers and the acceptance of central control.
- Justiciar appointed to complement the sheriffs: highest administrative and judicial officer.

Development of the Church

- Started by David's mother Margaret, the introduction of the Roman Church at the expense of the Celtic one offered a significant support to the development of royal authority. David gave significant grants of land to Religious orders. The greatest being the Cistertian house at Melrose in 1136. Benedictine at Dunfermline and the Augustinians at St Andrews and Holyrood.
- Important in the monastic economic development of land, but also important as the Church preached the divine grace of the king, it was hard to justify any rebellions against him.
- Loyalty was given from new religious orders free from corruption; in return David constructed magnificent Abbeys at Jedburgh and Holyrood. Established Diocese at Moray and Ross and down the east coast from St Andrews to Edinburgh (East Lothian).
- However, David was also sensitive to local needs and displayed reverence to the native saints eg St Mungo of Glasgow and Columba of Iona.

Succession

- David sought a smooth succession to his son. He did however use Celtic procedures, such as taking Malcolm round the country to secure acceptance and the use of Gaelic in the inauguration.

Any other relevant factors.

18. To what extent was King John successful in increasing royal authority in England?

Context

King John was the youngest, and favourite, son of Henry II and Eleanor of Aquitaine. On the death of his elder brother Richard, he became King of England despite the claims of his nephew Arthur. He struggled to hold the widespread Angevin Empire together in the face of the challenges of the Capetian monarch of France and his own barons.

Impact of the loss of Normandy

- Had an impact on the Royal finances as it reduced John's income.
- The recovery of the Royal lands north of the Loire became the focus of John's foreign policy and led to policies which eventually led to challenges to his authority.
- The need to fund warfare to recover Normandy led to the frequent use of Scutage to raise cash. It was used much more frequently than under Henry II and Richard, levied 11 times in 17 years.

Taxation

- John was more efficient in collecting taxes.
- Used wardships to raise cash.
- Introduced new taxes: eg 1207 tax on income and moveable goods.
- Improved quality of silver coinage.

Administration of government

- John filled many of the roles in the Royal Household with new men; especially from Poitou. This was not popular with the English barons.

Military power

- Established the Royal Navy.
- Extensive use of mercenaries rather than feudal service.
- Able to exert his military strength against the nobility and the French.
- John an able military commander; ie when conflict started with France and his nephew Arthur, he defeated them and captured Arthur.
- His forces and his allies were decisively beaten at the Battle of Bouvines in 1214.

Law and justice

- Increasingly partial judgements were resented.
- John increased professionalism of local sergeants and bailiffs.
- Extended the system of coroners.

Relations with the Church

- John fell out with Pope Innocent III over the appointment of the Archbishop of Canterbury. Innocent insisted on the appointment of Langton which John opposed.
- Papal interdict laid on England and Wales for 6 years.
- In 1213 John made England a fief of the papacy.
- Noble uprising led by Archbishop of Canterbury.

Relations with the nobility

- Nobles refused to fight in France. This was especially true of the northern Barons who had little stake in France.
- Nobles felt their status was reduced by use of mercenaries.
- John became increasingly suspicious of the nobles.
- High cost of titles led to nobles becoming overly indebted.
- John took hostages to ensure nobles behaved. He showed he was prepared to execute children if the father opposed him.

Magna Carta

- Relations worsened over the course of the reign, ending with Magna Carta and rebellion of many Barons.

John's personality

- He could be generous, had a coarse sense of humour and was intelligent.
- However, could also be suspicious and cruel: vicious in his treatment of prisoners and nobles.
- Arthur, his nephew, died in mysterious circumstances.

- Powerful lords like William de Braose fell from favour and were persecuted. William's wife and son were imprisoned and died. He died in exile in France.

Any other relevant factors.

Part B: The Century of Revolutions, 1603–1702

19. *Political issues were the main cause of the problems faced by King James after the Union of the Crowns in 1603*. **How valid is this view?**

Context

During the reign of James I in England 1603–25, the House of Commons had challenged the Divine Right of Kings, and relations between crown and Parliament deteriorated over a number of issues. When James I had ascended the throne, Parliament had become used to wielding some power due to developments during the reigns of Henry VIII and Elizabeth I, but James wanted to exercise the same authority in England as he had been accustomed to in Scotland. Factors contributing towards James I's problems were economic, religious (in relation to both Presbyterianism and Roman Catholicism), political, legal and Scotland related.

Politics

- Parliament had been encouraged since the days of Henry VIII to make policy, and therefore its members felt they could criticise the Crown freely; however, James I asserted the divine right of kings as he claimed he had been accustomed to this in Scotland, which made his status as a foreigner more unattractive to the English Parliament.
- The House of Commons opposed James I to such an extent that the stability of the nation was affected.
- The King conceded defeat in the Goodwin Case which gave Parliament fresh impetus to challenge him further.
- James I attempted to curtail Parliamentary freedom of speech by imprisoning outspoken MPs in the Tower of London when Parliament was dissolved.

Economic issues

- James I wanted to exist financially independent of Parliament and manipulated the statute books to re-impose anachronistic laws which were designed merely to raise revenue.
- Fiscal devices such as monopolies and wardships were unpopular.
- The King alienated his natural allies in the House of Lords by selling honours and titles and appearing to devalue the status of the aristocracy.
- Increases in customs duties led to the Bates Case in 1606 which James I won, although Parliament declared the duties illegal in 1610.

Religious issues – Presbyterianism

- James I had a lifelong hatred of Puritanism; Puritans existed in large numbers in the House of Commons and were demanding church reform.
- The King feared moves towards Presbyterianism and rejected the Millenary Petition at the Hampton Court Conference of 1604, saying "no bishops, no king", and vowing to maintain an Episcopalian Church of England.
- Puritans existed in large numbers in House of Commons and were demanding church reform early in James I's reign.
- In 1607 the House of Commons presented a Petition for the Restoration of Silenced Ministers, requesting the reinstatement of preachers who had been previously dismissed for their Puritan views. This set MPs in direct opposition in policy terms to the sitting monarch.

Religious issues — Roman Catholicism

- James I relaxed the Recusancy Laws against Roman Catholics, which revealed that there were more Roman Catholics than many in the House of Commons had feared.
- The Gunpowder Plot of 1605 increased tension and turned many against Roman Catholics.
- Parliament was horrified that the King allowed his son to marry a Roman Catholic French princess and allow her to celebrate mass privately at court.
- Furthermore, James I admired the religious power of the monarchies in France and Spain, both Roman Catholic countries and England's traditional enemies.
- James conducted many negotiations with the Spanish Ambassador, Count Gondomar, whose influence at court many Puritans resented. In 1604 they concluded a peace, bringing their nineteen-year war to an end with the Treaty of London.
- Eventually the King issued the House of Commons with the Rebuke of 1621, a ban on discussing foreign policy so that he could forge stronger links with Spain. This generated much anti-Catholic feeling amongst James I's political opponents who disapproved of this developing relationship.

Legal issues

- James I attempted to control the court system by appointing judges who would favour the Crown; Parliament saw this as unfair and objected to the abuse of power.
- The King also made sure that only he could sack Justices of the Peace, and not Parliament. This "immovability of judges" was deeply resented by the House of Commons.
- The King used his position to influence proceedings in the prerogative law courts such as the Court of Star Chamber and protect the landed classes who were exempt from flogging. Savage punishments were imposed on poorer people who could not pay fines, with Justices of the Peace frequently pronouncing "No goods: to be whipped".
- The King imposed martial law in towns where troops were preparing to embark on foreign campaigns; Parliament opposed this.
- The King billeted troops in the homes of civilians in order to enforce the law.

The difficulties James had ruling both England and Scotland

- Parliament in London rejected the King's proposed union between Scotland and England as they felt he was making no attempt to understand the English constitution, which accorded greater powers to Parliament in London than were accorded in Edinburgh.
- James I sought to obtain greater taxation in Scotland, and employed members of loyal clans as government agents, at considerable expense, to extract payment of overdue taxes or fines.
- James I exerted his influence in the Highlands with force, giving permission for certain clans to attack clans who had not professed loyalty to him.
- As legitimate king of Scotland, James I (and VI) was carrying out a role into which he had been born; however, his position in trying to maintain rule over two kingdoms, and the dominance of England, meant Scotland proved to be more than a minor irritation in his attempts to achieve stability.

Any other relevant factors.

20. To what extent were economic issues the most important reason for the outbreak of civil war in England?

Context

The English Civil War lasted from 1642 to 1649. It was fought between the Royalist forces, who supported Charles I, and Parliamentarians, who opposed the king's authority. During the reign of James I, 1603–25, the House of Commons had challenged the Divine Right of Kings. When Charles I ascended the throne in 1625, relations between crown and Parliament deteriorated over a number of issues. Factors contributing towards the war were economic, religious, political, and legal; the legacy of James I was also a factor, as were Scottish matters and the events of 1640–2.

Economic issues

- Charles I wanted to be financially independent, but resorted to anachronistic methods of raising revenue, such as a Declaration of Forced Loans in 1625 to fund wars with France and Spain, and a continuation of the enforcement of the Forest Laws re-discovered by James I.
- The punishing of Distraint of Knighthood raised £150,000 between 1633 and 1635 by fining those with incomes of over £40, a practice unheard of since medieval times.
- The raising of Ship Money in 1635 was highly controversial, as the king demanded money to the value of a ship from towns throughout the country, extending the medieval practice of requesting this only from ports to aid the defence of the realm. The Ship Money Case of 1637 involved an MP, John Hampden, who refused to pay but was defeated in court.
- The Tunnage and Poundage allowance, which gave the king a share in profits from farm-produce in order to help fund English naval supremacy, was awarded by Parliament in 1625 for one year only as the Charles I allowed the navy to decay. However, the King continued to raise this without MPs' consent up until 1628. Opposition to this in the House of Commons would eventually be a factor in the King's dissolving parliament in 1629.
- The King encouraged trade and empire as means of raising revenue. Parts of Canada were sold to France in 1629, and a Commission for Plantations established merchants in the West Indies between 1634 and 1637. Parliament objected not so much to the notion of trade but to the King's favouritism in awarding contracts and membership of trading companies.

Religious issues

- In 1628 Charles I made William Laud Archbishop of Canterbury. Laud wanted to stamp out Puritanism and believed in the authority and discipline of the Anglican Church and sacred status of the clergy, ordering priests to wear elaborate vestments and conduct services from Communion tables railed off from the congregation.
- Laud favoured the High Church, which was the grouping of those whose ideas about liturgy and prayer were not dissimilar to Roman Catholic practice. He oversaw the Court of High Commission, in front of which those who offended the Church were brought to trial and fined heavily.
- Charles I authorised Laud's punishment of Puritan preachers and his clamp-down on conventicles, private meetings for worship. There was tight censorship of printed word to prevent criticism of the High Church. This led to 20,000 Puritans fleeing England to America in 10 years.
- Charles I allowed his queen, Henrietta Maria to celebrate Mass publicly at court. He also permitted this to take

place with a representative of the Pope in attendance. This development infuriated Puritans in Parliament.

- The King used the church for political purposes, with clergymen often holding public office in the civil service. Charles I appointed clerics to ministerial positions, including the Bishop of London who became Lord High Treasurer in 1636.

Political issues

- Charles I's employed the Duke of Buckingham as his Chief Minister and together the two men excluded Parliament from their negotiations with France and Spain.
- Parliament passed the Petition of Right in 1628 condemning Buckingham's work raising taxes and imprisoning opponents, both carried out with the King's approval and without parliamentary consent.
- Charles I believed in Divine Right, treated his promises to Parliament lightly, was a poor judge of character and surrounded himself with advisors unsuited to their positions.
- After Buckingham died, the King was increasingly influenced by three people: his wife, Henrietta Maria, who encouraged him to relax laws against Roman Catholics; Archbishop Laud, who encouraged him to promote High Church policies; and Thomas Wentworth, the Earl of Stafford, whose work as Chief Minister from 1628 to 1633 and then as Lord Deputy of Ireland made Charles I more absolute.
- Parliament tried to introduce bills and antagonised the King by impeaching serving government ministers to show that members of the His Majesty's government were responsible to Parliament as well as the crown. Charles I disapproved of this, and imprisoned critics in the Tower of London.
- When Parliament was asked to support Charles I's foreign policy it drew up the Petition of Right in 1628 and forced him to sign it in exchange for funds. This stated that taxes should not be levied without Parliament's consent, no-one could be imprisoned by the King without trial, soldiers and sailors could not be billeted in civilians' houses, and martial law should not be imposed on civilians.
- In 1629, however, Charles I dissolved Parliament because it criticised his levying of tunnage and poundage. He ruled on his own until 1640 — the "Eleven Year Tyranny".

Legal issues

- Charles I's used the prerogative law courts such as the Star Chamber to enforce royal policy. One example is the 1637 case in which 3 men were sentenced to be pilloried, have their ears cropped, and be imprisoned for life, merely for writing Puritanical pamphlets. MPs objected fiercely, believing that the Star Chamber was an instrument of the crown.
- The King also allowed the Archbishop of Canterbury to use the Court of High Commission to put on trial anyone who opposed his religious policy and to persecute Puritans. Laud even used his power in the High Commission to reverse some decisions made in common law courts.
- Thomas Wentworth, the Earl of Stafford, was the King's chief minister from 1628 to 1633, and was authorised by Charles I to use the Council of the North to enforce his ruthless "Thorough" policies in the north of England to put down rebellions and influence the justice system. After 1633, Wentworth was made Lord Deputy of Ireland, and although he revived Ireland's fishing, farming and linen industries this was merely to generate more money for the crown and make the Irish subservient to the King.

Legacy of James I

- James I, who reigned between 1603 and 1625, continually opposed the Puritan movement and resisted calls for Presbyterianism in the Anglican Church. He rejected the Millenary Petition in 1604 and persecuted Puritan leaders. This caused resentment amongst Puritan MPs.
- In addition, his adopted tolerant policy towards Roman Catholicism. He relaxed the Recusancy Laws in 1603 and approved of his son's marriage to a Roman Catholic princess from France.
- James I used anachronistic laws to increase his personal wealth, raising taxes himself and selling honours and titles to those who could afford to buy them.
- James I's imprisonment of MPs in the Tower of London showed absolutist tendencies. In addition, his assertion of Divine Right was a notion less accepted in England than in Scotland.
- James I intervened continually the English judicial system, as he had done in Scotland. He allowed martial law in coastal towns.
- James I attempted and failed to bring about a political union between the England and Scotland. This meant that the issue of ruling both countries was significant in making it almost impossible to achieve the stable rule of either.

Scottish issues

- Laud's imposition of the Prayer Book in Scotland in 1637 was fiercely opposed by members of Scottish Kirk. His policies towards Scotland provoked hostility in Scottish Parliament.
- Thousands of Scots signed the National Covenant in 1638, pledging to defend Presbyterianism. The Covenanting movement was a political challenge to Laud, and was also therefore a challenge to royal power in Scotland. This led to a weakening of Charles I's position in England as the military threat from the Covenanters forced the King to attempt to reconcile his differences with Parliament.
- Charles I's defeat in the First and Second Bishops' Wars in 1639 and 1640 further weakened his authority over Parliament in England. Threats of Scottish invasion in 1640–2 led to drastic action by Parliament in forming its own army.

Events of 1640–2

- By 1640–41, Puritans and the High Church were in bitter dispute over proposed reforms of Church of England. Parliament had imposed anti-Episcopalian conditions on its co-operation with the King in his request for funds to fight Scotland.
- Charles I had asked for Parliamentary funding for the Bishops' Wars in 1639 and 1640. MPs took advantage of the situation, demanding the abolition of ship money which would be seen as a victory in the face of years of perceived financial tyranny.
- Parliament insisted on the introduction of the Triennial Act in 1641, legislating for Parliament to be called at least every three years. In response to rumours of plots against him, in January 1642, Charles I entered the House of Commons to try and arrest 5 Puritan MPs, including John Hampden, but they escaped.
- Parliament made increasing demands on the King, such as the abolition of the prerogative law courts including the Star Chamber, High Commission and Council of the North. The House of Commons impeached Wentworth who was then arrested in March 1641 and condemned to death after Charles I signed an Attainder Act agreeing to this.
- There were minor rebellions in Ireland, as hostilities broke out after people rose up against the ruthless policies

imposed by Wentworth during 1630s. In addition, threats were faced from Scotland, as with England in crisis, invasion by the Covenanters seemed likely.

- Charles I left London for the north, joined by two-thirds of the House of Lords and one-third of the House of Commons. By the end of March 1642, Parliament had completed forming its own army and the King responded by raising standard at Nottingham. The English Civil War had begun.

Any other relevant factors.

21. To what extent were religious issues the main reason for the Revolution Settlement of 1688–89?

Context
After the Interregnum, the monarchy was restored in 1660. Charles II reigned until 1685, although he used loopholes in the Restoration Settlement to rule without Parliament from 1681 onwards. His brother James II ruled from 1685, but his attempts at absolutism led to the Revolution of 1688–9, when his daughter Mary and her husband William of Orange were asked by Parliament to become joint monarchs, under terms known as the Revolution Settlement. Factors contributing towards the Revolution were religious and political; the roles of both Charles II and James II were important; the role of parliament and the absence of a Bill of Rights were also factors.

Religious issues
- James II issued the First Declaration of Indulgence in April 1687 which suspended the Test Act, which stated that all holders of civil office, both military and political, should be Anglican and should swear an oath against Roman Catholic doctrine.
- The King also issued the Second Declaration of Indulgence in May 1688, which stated that toleration towards Roman Catholics should be preached in every church in England on two successive Sundays.
- Charles II had been an Anglican, but had secretly signed the Treaty of Dover in 1670, a deal agreeing with Louis XIV that he would declare himself Roman Catholic when his relations with Parliament improved. He entered the Third Dutch War in alliance with France in 1673, and eventually declared himself a Roman Catholic on his death bed.
- James II promoted Roman Catholics to key posts in government and the army. The new heir to the throne, born in 1685, was to be raised as a Roman Catholic. This religious crisis this created in the minds of MPs drove the momentum for Parliamentarians to send for William and Mary.
- The Restoration Settlement in 1660 had stated that the Church of England would carry on using the Prayer Book approved by the Stuarts. There were hostile divisions between Episcopalians and Presbyterians.

James II
- The King, a Roman Catholic, ruled absolutely by dismissing Parliament in November 1685 before it could condemn Louis XIV's persecution of Huguenots, French Protestants. He then stationed a 16,000-strong army, including Roman Catholic officers, outside London.
- James II imposed his will on the judicial system, re-establishing Prerogative Courts in 1686. In 1687, used the monarch's Suspending Powers to suspend laws against Roman Catholics, and used the Dispensing Powers later that year to dismiss these laws from the statute books.
- James II replaced Anglican advisors and office-holders with Roman Catholic ones, including making the Earl of Tyrconnel the Lord Lieutenant of Ireland and Sir Roger Strickland the Admiral of the Royal Navy. He appointed Roman Catholics to important posts at Oxford and Cambridge Universities.
- In late 1688 as MPs made clear their determination to invite the King's Protestant daughter Mary to become queen, he tried to use the Stuarts' links with Louis XIV to appeal for military and financial assistance. However, the French King offered little more than vocal support.

Charles II
- The King, exiled in France for the Interregnum, had accepted limitations on his power when the monarchy was restored in 1660. However, loopholes in the Restoration Settlement allowed him to make policy without Parliament. This caused indignation among MPs.
- The legal terms of the 1660 Restoration had upheld the Triennial Act and the abolition of prerogative law courts, and prohibited non-Parliamentary taxation. It also stated that Charles II should live off his own finances and not receive money from Parliament, although in return, Parliament granted the King taxation on alcohol.
- In 1677 the King's Lord Treasurer, the Earl of Danby, who was anti-French, was persuaded by some MPs to arrange the marriage of the King's niece, Mary, to William of Orange, a Dutch prince. This was a response to Charles II's foreign policy which broke the 1668 Triple Alliance with Holland and Sweden against France, by allying himself with Louis XIV. This did not reduce Parliament's alarm at the King's pro-French and Roman Catholic leanings.
- Nevertheless, towards end of reign Charles II ruled alone for 4 years after dissolving Parliament in March 1681 and ignoring the Triennial Act in 1684. In 1683 he imposed a new Charter for the City of London which said that all appointments to civil office, including Lord Mayor, should be subject to royal approval.

Political issues
- James II's use of the Suspending and Dispensing Powers in 1687, although not illegal, was seen by Parliament as a misuse of royal privilege. Questions had also been raised by MPs over monarchical control of the army after the King called troops to London in 1685, which was perceived as another abuse of power.
- As in the pre-Civil War era, both post-Restoration Stuart monarchs advocated Divine Right and practised absolutism. Charles II's dismissal of Parliament in 1681 and James II's dissolution in 1685 resembled Charles I's conduct at the start of his "Eleven Year Tyranny" in 1629.
- Charles II's Lord Chancellor, the Earl of Clarendon, had been unpopular due to his mishandling of the Second Dutch War between 1665 and 1667, and was even blamed for the Great Plague of 1665 and the Fire of London in 1666. MPs opposed his influence at court and impeached him in 1667, forcing him into exile.
- So, in June 1688 as crisis approached, James II hastily promised to recall Parliament by November and announced that Roman Catholics would be ineligible to sit in it. He also replaced Roman Catholic advisors, as well as those in the high ranks of the army and navy, with Protestant ones.

The role of Parliament
- Parliament resented James II's abuses of power but took comfort from thought that he would be succeeded by his Protestant daughter Mary. However, the King's wife had a son, James Edward, in June 1688, to be raised as Roman Catholic. This led to Parliament writing to Mary, by now married to the Dutch Prince William of Orange, offering her the Crown.

- William and Mary arrived at Torbay in November with an army of 15,000, and after many in the House of Lords declared their support for William, on Christmas Day James II fled to France. Parliament had also persuaded the King's younger daughter Anne, as well as leading generals, to declare their support for Mary. Subsequent to these events, William and Mary became joint sovereigns on February 13th 1689.

Absence of a Bill of Rights between crown and Parliament

- With no document resembling a Bill of Rights that would formalise the powers held by monarch and Parliament, some MPs felt that a settlement involving William and Mary would have to include one. Without one, future monarchs, including William and Mary, could preach notions of Divine Right, absolutism and passive obedience. This meant that Parliament wanted limitations on the power of the monarchy to be written into law.
- In March 1689, therefore, Parliament drew up a Declaration of Right, which legalised a new relationship between crown and Parliament in matters such as finance, law, the succession and religion. This became the Bill of Rights in December that year, and had to be signed by William and Mary as a condition of their remaining on the throne. The importance of the Bill of Rights confirms the view that the blurred lines between monarchs and Parliament had been a problem in the past.

Any other relevant factors.

Part C: The Atlantic Slave Trade

22. To what extent was the failure of alternative sources of labour the main reason for the development of the slave trade?

Context
During the eighteenth and early nineteenth centuries a large productive work force was required as the sugar plantation system spread throughout the West Indies. As the number of indentured servants declined plantation owners increasingly turned to enslaved Africans as a source of labour.

Failure of alternative sources of labour

- The slave trade developed due to the rapid decline in the number of native Indians who were first used as a source of labour in the West Indies. Poor diet and European diseases were largely responsible for this. Although compared to the later enslavement of Africans, the use of the native populations was on a small scale. Few colonists were also willing to work voluntarily on the plantations as manual labour.
- There was a limit to the number of British criminals who could be sent as forced labour. Britain had very harsh laws in the 18th century with 300 capital crimes, examples would be pick pocketing more than 1 shilling, shop lifting 5 shillings or more, stealing a sheep or a horse, poaching rabbits. Transportation to the West Indies was seen as an alternative to hanging. Some of those transported were for political or religious reasons. For example, many Jacobite's were treated in this way. As political upheavals subsided, the number of political prisoners declined.
- There was also a lack of indentured servants. These poor Europeans would sign a contract binding them to work for a fixed period, usually 3—7 years, in return for their passage abroad although it was not unknown for poor people in cities such as London and Bristol to find themselves on ships to Jamaica after being kidnapped or plied with drink. Some Europeans were classed as

Redemptioners: They arranged with the ship's captain, to pay for their passage within a specified time after arrival or be sold to the highest bidder.
- Historian Eric Williams has argued that there were not enough indentured servants to replace those who had served their time and that escape was much easier for Europeans. As a result, for economic reasons plantation owners started to turn to African slaves for labour. Williams argues that the decisive factor was the fact that enslaved Africans were cheap and that while an indentured servant would be working for a limited number of years, the enslaved African would work for life. For a while European indentured labour existed alongside enslaved Africans but as African slavery increased, European indentured labour gradually came to an end.

Other factors

Shortage of labour

- Huge profits made from the trade in tropical crops created a demand for labour to work on plantations in the colonies. Crops such as sugar cane required a large labour force to plant; look after, harvest and process crop in harsh conditions. There was a high death rate among native populations due to lack of resistance to diseases brought by Europeans and ill-treatment at the hands of colonists created labour shortage in the West Indies.

Religious factors

- The Church of England had links to slavery through the United Society for the Propagation of the Gospel missionary organisations which had plantations and owned slaves. The Church of England supported the laws not to educate enslaved Africans. Some bible passages such as the Curse of Ham from Genesis were used to justify slavery. Other bible passages such as Exodus were banned in British colonies because they could be interpreted as being anti-slavery.
- Many believed that Africans benefited from slavery as they became "Christian". This would result in the spread of "civilisation". This however did not necessarily mean that they would be treated as equals.
- Some clergy tried to push the idea that it was possible to be a "good slave and a Christian" and pointed to St Paul's epistles, which called for slaves to "obey their masters".
- However very little missionary work actually took place during the early years. Religion got in the way of a moneymaking venture by taking Africans away from their work. It also taught them potentially subversive ideas and made it hard to justify the cruel mistreatment of fellow Christians.

Racist attitudes

- The unequal relationship that was created as a consequence of the enslavement of Africans was justified by the ideology of racism — the mistaken belief that Africans were inferior to Europeans.
- Entrenched racism among members of the merchant and landowning classes meant that enslaving African captives was accepted by colonists.
- Many Europeans claimed that African captives would suffer if slave trade was abolished eg criminals and prisoners of war would be butchered and executed at home.
- Many colonists believed that slaves were fortunate to be provided with homes, protection and employment, in the care of enlightened Europeans rather than African despots.

Legal position

- The legal status of slaves as property was long established. It took a series of court cases from the 1770s that dealt with the rights of former slaves within the British Isles to challenge the legality of slavery and the slave trade eg Granville Sharp's resolute campaign to prove the illegality of slavery in England that culminated in Lord Mansfield's decision in the Somerset case.

Military factors

- The Seven Years War was chiefly an imperial war fought between Britain, France and Spain and many of the most important battles of the Seven Years War were fought at sea to win control of valuable overseas colonies. Britain emerged from the war as the leading European imperial power, having made large territorial gains in North America and the Caribbean, as well as India. Slave labour was necessary to exploit these gains.

Importance of West Indian colonies

- The slave trade generated finance — It was an important source of tax revenue and West Indian colonies were an important source of valuable exports to European neighbours.
- Financial, commercial, legal and insurance institutions emerged to support the activities of the slave traders. Slave traders became bankers and many new businesses were financed by profits made from slave trading.

Any other relevant factors.

23. ***The fear of revolt was the most important factor governing relations between slaves and their owners. How valid is this view?***

Context

As the number of enslaved Africans increased with the growth of the slave trade, a climate of fear was created as slave owners became increasingly outnumbered. The fear of revolt was reflected in the conditions on board the slave ships on the middle passage and in the harsh discipline on the plantations.

Fear of revolt

- Both on slave ships and plantations there was a constant fear of a slave revolt. On ships, security was paramount, as crews were heavily outnumbered by their cargoes. This meant that slaves were kept under decks for long periods. It also meant that they were usually shackled for the whole passage.
- As the number of revolts on slave ships grew so did the cost as larger crews were required.
- On plantations, there was fear of slave resistance, both overt and otherwise. Draconian legal codes were enacted by island assemblies (dominated by planters) covering the treatment/punishment of runaways as well as those who resisted openly.
- Escaped ex-slaves called Maroons raided plantations, killed militia and freed slaves. Due to the inability of the planters to crush them they entered into a treaty with them which gave them some toleration in return for leaving the slave system alone.

Other factors

Financial considerations

- In essence, the slave trade and the institution of slavery were commercially based. Most participants entered the trade or owned or worked the plantations as a means of income. Financial considerations were usually paramount.

- Slave ships carried as many slaves as possible in order to make as much profit as possible. The debate over "loose" or "tight" pack on board slave ships had little to do with humanitarianism. In loose pack, slaves were treated better and had better conditions, but the prime motivation was the transport of as many slaves as possible to the auctions in the West Indies, alive.
- At auctions at the end of the Middle Passage, slaves were chosen for their ability to work. Little thought was given to family bonds.
- To extract as much work from slaves as possible on the plantations, slaves were often beaten or worse.
- As slaves were property, bought and paid for, they were valuable. On the other hand, they were cheap enough to work, or beat, to death. This was known as "wastage".
- The British Caribbean islands were particularly cursed by a culture of absentee owners; estates were managed by overseers whose main interest was to amass profits in order to gain a foothold in the plantation economy.
- Owners and overseers were aware of the risks to their own health from a lengthy stay in the West Indies and often were concerned to make as much money as quickly as possible in order to return to Britain and enjoy their wealth.

Racism and prejudice

- The harsh treatment of enslaved Africans was often justified by racism, the mistaken belief that Africans were inferior to Europeans.
- Slave traders who bought slaves at trading posts on the African coast often believed that African captives would otherwise be executed as prisoners of war or for crimes.
- There was ignorance of African culture and achievements. Africans were regarded by some Europeans as almost another species. This was used as an excuse for extreme brutality.
- Slaves were treated not as fellow human beings but as moveable property. This was illustrated by the case of the Liverpool slave ship, the Zong. The killing of slaves was not considered to be murder in the eyes of the law.

Religious concerns

- Slave traders/owners were able to point to the existence of slavery in the bible, and use this as a justification for the institution.
- Traders/owners claimed that slaves were being exposed to Christianity. Enslavement was therefore good for them, as it gave them the chance of eternal salvation.
- Some participants were religious and moderated their treatment of slaves accordingly.

Humanitarian concerns

- Humanitarian concerns had little impact on the treatment of slaves in Africa or on the Middle Passage. Participants were not in daily close contact with slaves and did not get to know them personally.
- The West Indian plantations, on the other hand, were often small communities. Where members of the owner's family were present, bonds of affection grew between slaves and free. Where such personal ties did not exist, there was less moderation of the brutalities of slavery.
- Some slave ship captains were more humane and lessened the harsh conditions of the Middle Passage.

Any other relevant factors.

24. How important were the effects of the French Revolution as an obstacle to abolition?

Context
The early progress of the abolitionist campaign was temporarily stalled by events outside Britain. One such event was the French Revolution, the effects of which led to a fear of change among Britain's politicians.

Effects of the French Revolution
- The French Revolution had a detrimental effect on the progress of the abolitionist campaign as there was the belief among many British MPs that the abolitionist cause was associated with French revolutionary ideas. For example, the abolitionist campaigner, Thomas Clarkson openly supported the French Revolution.
- Although, initially, the French Revolution was generally welcomed in Britain, the execution of Louis XVI and soon after, Britain being at war with France changed the views of both the public and Britain's politicians. Wealthy and powerful people in Britain were shocked by the events which were viewed as being far too radical. Britain's politicians became worried about the activities of British radicals and feared they had links with their French counterparts. In Britain political societies which had supported the French revolution were now forced to shut down. Basic civil freedoms began to be withdrawn, anti-republican associations were formed, and government informers became more common due to a fear that events in France may be repeated in Britain.
- A number of Acts were passed which limited civil rights. Approval for any political meeting was required if more than 50 people were in attendance. People could be arrested if they spoke or wrote in any way which could stir up hatred or criticism of the Government. Interestingly, Wilberforce although consistently for abolition gave his support to these Acts. The result was however a halt to the popular grass roots support for the Abolition Societies, which had made such an impact in the 1780s.
- Due to the similarity in tactics — associations, petitions, cheap publications, public lectures, public meetings, pressure on Parliament, some abolitionists were linked to radicals. The Anti-Republican associations produced petitions which people became frightened not to sign. In this climate it became difficult for the abolitionists as the anti-abolitionists soon linked them to French radical politics and made them appear unpatriotic. By the 1790s very few apart from hardened radicals still supported abolition.
- Britain's involvement in in the French Revolutionary Wars also delayed the abolitionist campaign. To oppose the slave trade during a major war seemed unpatriotic to many people, leading to a loss of support for the abolitionists' cause.
- It was argued that the slave trade was vital in Britain being able to sustain an expensive war effort against France. Not only did Britain need ships and sailors to protect itself and the Empire but a lot of money was required to pay for the war with France. Britain could therefore not risk ending the slave trade which might have resulted in a loss of much needed finance.

Other factors

Slave rebellion in St. Domingue
- An obstacle to abolition was the fear of the impact of ending the slave trade. Fears over the consequences of abolition were increased when slaves on the French colony of Saint-Domingue rose up against their rulers and ended slavery. There was a high loss of life, perhaps as high as 200,000. Under the leadership of Toussaint L'Ouverture, the escaped slaves set up an independent country called Haiti. Abolition was associated with this symbol of violence and exaggerated the general fear of slave revolts. Such slave violence played into the hands of the slave lobby, confirming their warnings of anarchy.
- The defeat of the colonial French by rebellious slaves on St Domingue sent shock waves throughout the Atlantic world and unsettled slave owners everywhere. British leaders were worried that similar slave rebellions might break out on neighbouring British islands such as Jamaica. They banned any moves towards abolishing the slave trade claiming it would encourage slaves in the West Indies to revolt.
- Britain suffered humiliation when it attempted to take the rebel French Colony, beaten by disease and the ex-slave army.
- When the Revolutionary government of France attempted to regain control, however, support for abolition grew as a means of striking at the French once war was declared.

The power of vested interests
- Successive British Governments were influenced by powerful vested interests in Parliament and industry that had the wealth and power to buy votes and exert pressure on others in support of the slave trade.
- Many absentee plantation owners and merchants involved in the slave trade rose to high office as mayors or served in Parliament. William Beckford, the owner of a 22,000 acre estate in Jamaica, was twice Lord Mayor of London. In the mid to late 1700s over 50 MPs in Parliament represented the slave plantations.
- Many MPs themselves had become wealthy as a result of the slave trade which made it difficult to get a law abolishing the slave trade through Parliament. These MPs were wealthy and powerful enough to bribe other MPs to oppose abolition. Liverpool MPs Banastre Tarleton and Richard Pennant used the House of Commons to protect their families' business interests.
- Members of Parliament who supported the slave trade made speeches in Parliament opposing abolition. They argued that millions of pounds worth of property would be threatened by the abolition of the slave trade. They also argued that the slave trade was necessary to provide essential labour on the plantations and that abolition of the slave trade would ruin the colonies.
- MPs with business interests which made money from the slave trade used delaying tactics to slow down any moves towards abolition or supported compromise solutions. In 1792, in a response to Wilberforce's Bill to end the slave trade, Henry Dundas proposed a compromise of gradual abolition over a number of years. Henry Dundas, termed the 'uncrowned king of Scotland' was Secretary of State for War and First Lord of the Admiralty and as such, protected the interests of Scottish and British merchants in the Caribbean.
- Wealthy merchants from London, Liverpool and Bristol also exerted pressure on governments to oppose the abolition of the slave trade. In 1775 a petition was sent to Parliament by the mayor, merchants and people of Bristol in support of maintaining the slave trade.
- The House of Commons was dominated by various interest groups, of which the West India Lobby was for long the most powerful. Tactics included producing pro slave trade witnesses to testify in Parliamentary inquiries into the slave trade. The West India Lobby included the Duke of Clarence, one of the sons of George III, and proved tough opposition to the abolitionists. Governments

were often coalitions of interests, and often relied on patronage, either through the distribution of posts or the appeasement of such interests.

Anti-abolition propaganda
- Vested interests conducted a powerful propaganda campaign to counter that of the abolitionists, though some of the arguments and evidence were specious.
- Slave owners and their supporters argued that millions of pounds worth of property would be threatened by the abolition of the slave trade. The slave trade was necessary to provide essential labour on the plantations. Abolition of the slave trade would ruin the colonies.

Importance of the trade to the British economy
- The slave trade generated finance — It was an important source of tax revenue and West Indian colonies were an important source of valuable exports to European neighbours. Taxes would have to be raised to compensate for the loss of trade and revenue. Abolition would help foreign rivals such as France as other nations would fill the gap left by Britain.
- British cotton mills depended on cheap slave produced cotton.
- Africa provided an additional market for British manufactured goods.
- Individuals, businesses and ports in Britain prospered on the back of the slave trade.
- Shipbuilding benefited as did maritime employment.

Attitudes of British governments
- Initially British governments were anxious to protect the rights of property, which attacks on slavery seemed to threaten. The tactical decision to concentrate on the abolition of the slave trade circumvented this to an extent.

Fears over national security
- Abolition could destroy an important source of experienced seamen; there was a possibility that Britain would lose its advantage over its maritime rivals. On the other hand, the Triangular Trade was as much a graveyard as a nursery of seamen. The slave trade was seen as the "nursery of seamen" — it provided training for sailors joining the Royal Navy.

Any other relevant factors.

Part D: Britain 1851–1951

25. To what extent were changing political attitudes the most important reason why Britain became more democratic, 1851–1928?

Context
By the mid-19th century changes to Britain's economy (industrialisation) were resulting in social change, such as the demand for literacy. Such changes brought about increasing demands for political change.

Changing political attitudes
- Political reform was no longer seen as a threat. In the USA and in Europe, struggles were taking place for liberty and a greater political say for the people. Britain tended to support these moves abroad, making it logical for this to happen in Britain too.
- The growing influence of the Liberal Party in challenging older vested interests — the Liberal Party opposed the power of the old land-owning aristocracy, eg the secret ballot to assist the working-class electorate to use their political voice to promote social reforms.

- Politicians combined acceptance of changes which they suspected were unavoidable while ensuring that their own party political interests would be protected.
- The death of former PM Palmerston represented the changing tone of politics as the reactionary ideas of the early 19th century gave way to new ideologies.
- The veto of the unelected chamber was removed partly as result of the 1910 elections fought on the issue of 'peers vs people' and the financing of social reform to help the poor, especially in urban areas.

Other factors

The effects of industrialisation and urbanisation
- Urbanisation and growing class identity within an industrial workforce and the spread of socialist ideas led to demands for a greater voice for the working classes. Also, the growth of the Labour party offered a greater choice.
- Demographic change, including rapid urbanisation, sparked demands for redistribution of seats.
- The growing economic power of middle-class wealth-creators led to pressure for a greater political voice.
- Basic education, the development of new, cheap, popular newspapers and the spread of railways helped to create an awareness of national issues.
- After 1860 the fear of the "revolutionary mob" had declined. Skilled working men in cities were more educated and respectable. That was an argument for extending the vote in 1867.

Role of pressure groups
- The 1867 Reform Act was passed amongst considerable popular agitations; before them the Reform League and Reform Union had been active.
- The suffragists and suffragettes were influential in gaining the franchise for women.
- Role of trade unions may also be considered.
- There was debate about the methods which should be adopted, whether direct action or peaceful protest would be more effective.
- Large-scale meetings, eg Hyde Park.

Party advantage
- In 1867 the Conservative Party became the government after 20 years out of power. To an extent the Reform Act could be seen as "stealing the Liberal's clothes" to gain support.
- The Corrupt and Illegal Practices Act of 1883 limited the amount of spending on elections; the Liberals believed the advantage held by wealthier Conservative opponents would be reduced.
- By placing the reforms of 1883 and 1884 close to the next election, the Liberals hoped to gain advantage from grateful new voters in towns more fairly represented after the redistribution of seats.

The effects of the First World War
- The war necessitated more political change. Many men still had no vote but were conscripted to fight from 1916. As further reform for males was being considered, fears of a revival of the militant women's campaign, combined with a realisation of the importance of women's war work led to the Representation of the People Act of 1918 which gave votes to more men and some women.
- The role of women can be overstated as the eventual franchise was for women aged over 30. Many munitions workers were younger than this.

- It could also be argued that the war provided an opportunity for the coalition government to give women the vote. No one political party was able to claim it was behind the idea.

The effects of examples of developments abroad

- In a number of foreign countries there was a wider franchise than in Britain; in others women could also vote. Neither development had threatened the established social order.

Any other relevant factors.

26. *The part played by women in the war effort was the main reason why some women received the vote in 1918.* How valid is this view?

Context

The campaigns for women's suffrage must be seen within the wider context of a changing society and the massive social and political changes happening in the late 19th and early 20th centuries. The campaign for women's suffrage was a clear attempt to influence the development of democracy in Britain at a time of changing attitudes about the sexes between 1851 and 1928 when women gained the right to vote on the same terms as men.

The part played by women in the war effort, 1914–18

- Britain declared war on Germany on 4 August 1914 and two days later the NUWSS suspended its political campaigning for the vote. Undoubtedly the sight of women "doing their bit" for the war effort gained respect and balanced the negative publicity of the earlier Suffragette campaign. A WSPU pro-war propaganda campaign encouraged men to join the armed forces and women to demand "the right to serve".
- Women's war work was important to Britain's eventual victory. Over 700,000 women were employed making munitions.
- The creation of a wartime coalition also opened the door to change.
- The traditional explanation for the granting of the vote to some women in 1918 has been that women's valuable work for the war effort radically changed male ideas about their role in society and that the vote in 1918 was almost a "thank you" for their efforts. But the women who were given the vote were "respectable" ladies, 30 or over, not the younger women who worked long hours and risked their lives in munitions factories.
- Another argument about the 1918 act is that it only happened because politicians grew anxious to enfranchise more men who had fought in the war but lost their residency qualification to vote and women could be "added on" to legislation that was happening anyway.
- The war acted more as a catalyst but the tide was flowing towards female franchise before it started.

The women's suffrage campaigns

- The NUWSS believed in moderate, "peaceful" tactics to win the vote such as meetings, pamphlets, petitions and parliamentary bills. Membership remained relatively low at about 6,000 until around 1909 but grew to 53,000 by 1914 as women angered by the Suffragettes' campaign found a new home.

The militant Suffragette campaign up to 1914

- Emmeline Pankhurst formed the Women's Social and Political Union (WSPU) in 1903. WSPU adopted the motto "Deeds Not Words". The new strategy gained publicity with noisy heckling of politicians. Newspapers immediately took notice. The Suffragettes had achieved their first objective – publicity. Violent protest followed eg window smashing campaign and arson attacks aimed to provoke insurance company pressure on the Government. The prisons filled with Suffragettes.
- Women used hunger strikes as a political weapon to embarrass the government. In response the government introduced the Prisoner's Temporary Discharge for Ill Health Act – the Cat and Mouse Act.
- The actions of the Suffragettes mobilised opinion for and against. It can be argued that were it not for the Suffragette campaign, the Liberal Government would not even have discussed women's suffrage before World War One. But for opponents the militant campaign provided an excellent example of why women could not be trusted with the vote.

Changing attitudes to women in society

- The campaigns for women's suffrage could also be seen within the context of societies' changing attitudes towards women in the late 19th and early 20th centuries. For example, in the words of Martin Pugh, "their participation in local government made women's exclusion from national elections increasingly untenable." Millicent Fawcett, a leader of the NUWSS, had argued that wider social changes were vital factors in the winning of the right to vote.

The example of other countries

- Women were able to vote in other countries such as New Zealand, and in some American states.

Any other relevant factors.

27. To what extent did the social reforms of the Liberal government, 1906–1914, meet the needs of the British people?

Context

Attitudes towards poverty in the 19th century were laissez-faire. Although the Liberals had not been elected on a social reform ticket in 1906, the overwhelming evidence regarding the scale of poverty, as well as developing concerns about the health of the nation (as an Empire Britain could ill afford to let her economic lead slip), led to a series of limited social reforms that were introduced by the Liberal Party.

The young

- Children were thought to be the victims of poverty and unable to escape through their own efforts. In this way they were seen as "the deserving poor". Child neglect and abuse were seen as problems associated with poverty.
- The Provision of School Meals Act allowed local authorities to raise money to pay for school meals but the law did not force local authorities to provide school meals.
- Medical inspections after 1907 for children were made compulsory but no treatment of illnesses or infections found was provided until 1911.
- The Children's Charter of 1908 banned children under 16 from smoking, drinking alcohol, or begging. New juvenile courts were set up for children accused of committing crimes, as were borstals for children convicted of breaking the law. Probation officers were employed to help former offenders in an attempt to avoid re-offending.
- The time taken to enforce all the legislation meant the Children's Charter only helped improve conditions for some children during the period.

The old

- Rowntree had identified old age as the time when most people dropped below his poverty line. Old age was inescapable and so was clearly associated with the problem of poverty.

- Old Age Pensions Act (1908) gave people over 70 up to 5 shillings a week. Once a person over 70 had income above 12 shillings a week, their entitlement to a pension stopped. Married couples were given 7 shillings and 6 pence.
- The level of benefit was low. Few of the elderly poor would live till their 70th birthday. Many of the old were excluded from claiming pensions because they failed to meet the qualification rules.

The sick

- Illness can be seen as both a cause and consequence of poverty.
- The National Insurance scheme of 1911 applied to workers earning less than £160 a year. Each insured worker got 9 pence in contributions from an outlay of 4 pence — 'ninepence for fourpence'. As a result workers would be paid 10s a week for the first thirteen weeks.
- Only the insured worker got free medical treatment from a doctor. Other family members did not benefit from the scheme. The weekly contribution was in effect a wage cut which might simply have made poverty worse in many families.

The unemployed

- Unemployment was certainly a cause of poverty.
- The National Insurance Act (Part 2) only covered unemployment for some workers in some industries and like Part 1 of the Act, required contributions from workers, employers and the government. For most workers, no unemployment insurance scheme existed.

Other reforms which could be argued helped address problems associated with poverty

- In 1906 a Workman's Compensation Act covered a further six million workers who could now claim compensation for injuries and diseases which were the result of working conditions.
- In 1909, the Trade Boards Act tried to protect workers in the sweated trades like tailoring and lace making by setting up trade boards to fix minimum wages.
- The Mines Act and the Shop Act improved conditions.

Any other relevant factors.

Part E: Britain and Ireland, 1900–1985

28. To what extent was the Nationalist response to the Home Rule Bill responsible for the growth of tension in Ireland to 1914?

Context

Local self-government for Ireland in the late nineteenth century had created a number of politically experienced leaders. This, coupled with land reform, gave political nationalism an economic base from which to demand self-government. There was also an increasingly radical edge to this, albeit at the margins, through James Connolly and the Irish Socialist Republican Party. Tension was exacerbated by the reaction from the Protestant dominated north of Ireland.

Nationalist response to the Home Rule Bill

- The Irish Volunteer Force (IVF) was set up as a reaction. Members from the Gaelic League, the Gaelic Athletic Association, Sinn Fein and the IRB all joined hoping to use the IVF for their own purposes. By May 1914 it had 80,000 members.
- In 1913, a third private army was set up, the Irish Citizen Army, under the leadership of James Connolly, a socialist. It had two clear aims — to gain independence for Ireland

and set up a socialist republic, for working class of all religions to join up with to improve their lives.

Other factors

Unionist response to the Home Rule Bill

- The roles of Carson and Craig: Sir Edward Carson's theatrical political performances caught the public imagination and brought the case of the Unionists to the nation. At the signing of the Solemn League and Covenant in Belfast at Town Hall, to the world's press, 250,000 Ulstermen pledged themselves to use "all means necessary" to defeat Home Rule.
- Setting up of the UVF.
- Curragh Mutiny: British officers stationed in Ireland declared they would not use force against the Unionists.

The Irish Cultural Revival and Re-emergence of Irish Republicanism

- In 1884 the Gaelic Athletic Association was set up "for the preservation and cultivation of our national pastimes." Games like Gaelic football and hurling became very popular. In 1883 the Gaelic League was also set up whose aim it was to revive, and preserve the Irish language and Gaelic literature.
- Sinn Fein (Ourselves Alone) was founded by Arthur Griffith in 1904 to boycott all things British and to press for the Irish to set up their own parliament in Ireland, which Griffith thought would cause the British Government to collapse. The IRB was revived with Thomas Clarke recruiting young men in Dublin for the movement. Both these groups wanted an Ireland separate from Britain and both willing to use force.

The British Position over Ireland — the effects of the 1910 elections

- After 1910 the Liberals needed the help of the Irish Nationalists to run the country as they would not have a majority otherwise; they passed the third reform bill. In 1908 Campbell-Bannerman had been replaced as Prime Minister by Asquith, who in 1909 had declared that he was a supporter of Home Rule.
- With the support of John Redmond, leader of the Nationalists, a Bill was passed to reduce the power of the House of Lords, which was dominated by Conservatives, from being able to block a Bill to only being able to hold up the passing of a Bill for two years. As a result the Home Rule Bill for Ireland, which was previously blocked by the House of Lords, could now be passed.

Redmond and Home Rule

- Redmond claimed that the Home Rule Bill would lead to greater unity and strength in the Union, ending suspicion and disaffection in Ireland, and between Britain and Ireland. It would show Britain was willing to treat Ireland equally, as part of the empire. Redmond's Party was consistently strong throughout southern Ireland, where there was strong support for Home Rule.

Distinctive economic and religious features of the Northern Counties

- Ulster was mainly Protestant and feared that a government led by Dublin would see the imposition of laws on Northern Ireland based on Catholic faith; this they were opposed to.
- Ulster people were worried they would lose the economic benefits they enjoyed from being part of the British Empire, such as the linen industry and the shipbuilding industry.

Any other relevant points.

29. *The policies and actions of the British government were the main obstacle to peace in Ireland, 1918–1921*. How valid is this view?

Context

The radicalisation of Irish politics engendered during the First World War, led to conflict between the British State and Irish nationalists. Attempts to solve the problem of who was to govern in Ireland led to the 1920 Government of Ireland Act, which effectively created two governments, one in Belfast and one in Dublin. However, this gave only very limited devolved power which was unacceptable to the Irish nationalists.

The policies and actions of the British government

- The British aim between 1918 and 1921 was to reduce Ireland to obedience within the United Kingdom and in doing this relied increasingly on military force. The best houses in local areas were taken and used, with the occupants evicted, if the local police station had been burned or destroyed.
- RIC members were instructed to challenge civilians from ambush and shoot them if they did not obey the RIC officers. RIC officers were encouraged to shoot suspicious looking people, sometimes innocent people were killed. RIC officers were protected by their superiors.
- The Black and Tans were responsible for violence, theft, drunken rampages, attacks on villages such as the burning of Balbriggan, village creameries being burnt down and houses destroyed. In March 1919 the Lord Mayor of Cork was shot dead by RIC men. At Croke Park, where there was a Gaelic football match taking place, the Black and Tans fired in to the crowd, killing 12 people and injuring 60.
- The violence led to a drift to extremism, culminating in the sacking of Cork City by the Black and Tans.

Other factors

The legacy of the First World War — 1918 election, and the growth of Sinn Fein

- The aftermath of the Easter Rising, and the anti-conscription campaign, led to a decline in support for the Nationalist Party and a huge growth in support for Sinn Fein (Sinn Fein membership reached 112,000). In the 1918 General Election Sinn Fein won 73 seats, compared to winning none in 1910, 34 representatives were in prison, one had been deported, two were ill and seven were absent on Sinn Fein business, so there was only 25 present when they held their first public meeting in January 1919. This meant control of the nationalist movement largely moved to the IRB and the IVF. With the support of the majority of the population, the IRA was prepared to wage an armed struggle against the British.

The Declaration of Independence and the establishment of the Dail

- Republicans led by Sinn Fein, who did not attend Westminster, met at the Mansion House in Dublin and declared themselves "Dail Eireann". De Valera was made the President of Ireland, Arthur Griffith Vice President and Michael Collins Minister of Finance. Most local councils in Ireland, except in Ulster, recognised the rule of this new assembly. By 1921 1,000 Sinn Fein law courts had been set up and Collins raised £350,000 as many people paid their taxes to the Minister of Finance, Collins, rather than the British Government.

- The Dail failed to meet very regularly but worked using couriers carrying communications between those in hiding. Law and order was maintained though, as the Dail relied on "alternative" courts, presided over by a priest or lawyer and backed up by the IRA. This system won the support of the Irish communities as well as the established Irish legal system.
- The Dail had won the support of masses, the Catholic Church and professional classes in Ireland. The Dail wrested power away from Britain to a considerable extent due to military wing of the Dail.

The position of the Unionists in the North

- Ulster Unionists won an extra 10 seats and now had 26 seats in Westminster, making partition increasingly likely. Additionally, Unionists had made a huge blood sacrifice in the First World War (eg on the Somme) and naturally expected this to be reflected in any post-war settlement in Ireland.

IRA tactics and policies

- The IRA campaign used guerrilla tactics against a militarily stronger foe eg attacks on agencies of law and order, RIC, magistrates and police barracks, ambush, assassination, the disappearance of opponents, the sabotage of enemy communications and the intimidation of local communities into not supporting the British forces, attacks on British troops and G-men (detectives concentrating on IRA atrocities), the attempted assassination of Lord French (Viceroy). British forces found these increasingly frustrating to contend with, and this ramped up the violence and bitterness on both sides.

Any other relevant factors.

30. **To what extent was the Unionist ascendancy the main reason for the developing crisis in Northern Ireland by 1968?**

Context

By the early 1960s Northern Ireland was relatively stable. However, the Northern Ireland Nationalists were discriminated against in terms of housing, employment and electorally. In 1964 a peaceful civil rights campaign started to end the discrimination against Catholics in Northern Ireland.

The Unionist ascendancy in Northern Ireland and challenges to it

- Population of Northern Ireland divided: two-thirds Protestant and one-third Catholic: it was the minority who were discriminated against in employment and housing.
- In 1963, the Prime Minister of Northern Ireland, Viscount Brookeborough, stepped down after 20 years in office. His long tenure was a product of the Ulster Unionist domination of politics in Northern Ireland since partition in 1921.
- Unionist ascendancy: Before 1969 elections not held on a "one person, one vote" basis: gerrymandering used to secure unionist majorities on local councils. Local government electoral boundaries favoured unionist candidates, even in mainly Catholic areas like Derry/Londonderry. Also, right to vote in local elections restricted to ratepayers, favouring Protestants, with those holding or renting properties in more than one ward receiving more than one vote, up to a maximum of six. This bias preserved by unequal allocation of council houses to Protestant families.
- Challenges as Prime Minister O'Neill expressed desire to improve community relations in Northern Ireland and create a better relationship with the government

in Dublin, hoping that this would address the sense of alienation felt by Catholics towards the political system in Northern Ireland.
- Post-war Britain's Labour government introduced the welfare state to Northern Ireland, and it was implemented with few concessions to traditional sectarian divisions. Catholic children in the 1950s and 1960s shared in the benefits of further and higher education for the first time. This exposed them to a world of new ideas and created a generation unwilling to tolerate the status quo.
- Many Catholics impatient with pace of reform and remained unconvinced of Prime Minister O'Neill's sincerity. Founding of the Northern Ireland Civil Rights Association (NICRA) in 1967. NICRA did not challenge partition, though membership mainly Catholic. Instead, it called for the end to seven "injustices", ranging from council house allocations to the "weighted" voting system.

Economic issues
- Northern Ireland was left relatively prosperous by World War Two, with the boom continuing into the 1950s. But by the 1960s, as elsewhere in Britain, these industries were in decline eg Harland and Wolff profitable 'til early '60s, but government help in 1966. Largely Protestant workforce protected as a result.
- Catholic areas received less government investment than their Protestant neighbours. Catholics were more likely to be unemployed or in low-paid jobs than Protestants in N. Ireland. Catholic applicants also routinely excluded from public service appointments.
- The incomes of mainly Protestant landowners were supported by the British system of "deficiency payments" which gave Northern Ireland farmers an advantage over farmers from the Irish Republic.
- Brookeborough's failure to address the worsening economic situation saw him forced to resign as Prime Minister. His successor, Terence O'Neill set out to reform the economy. His social and economic policies saw growing discontent and divisions within his unionist party.

Role of the IRA
- Rioting and disorder in 1966 was followed by the murders of two Catholics and a Protestant by a "loyalist" terror group called the Ulster Volunteer Force, who were immediately banned by O'Neill.
- Peaceful civil rights marches descended into violence in October 1968 when marchers in Derry defied the Royal Ulster Constabulary and were dispersed with heavy-handed tactics. The RUC response only served to inflame further the Catholic community and foster the establishment of the Provisional IRA by 1970 as the IRA split into Official and Provisional factions.
- The Provisional IRA's strategy was to use force to cause the collapse of the Northern Ireland administration and to inflict casualties on the British forces such that the British government be forced by public opinion to withdraw from Ireland.
- PIRA were seen to defend Catholic areas from Loyalist attacks in the summer of 1970.

Cultural and political differences
- The Catholic minority politically marginalised since the 1920s, but retained its distinct identity through its own institutions such as the Catholic Church, separate Catholic schools, and various cultural associations, as well as the hostility of the Protestant majority.
- Catholic political representatives in parliament refused to recognise partition and this only increased the community's sense of alienation and difference from the Unionist majority in Northern Ireland.
- Nationalists on average 10–12 in NI Parliament compared to average 40 Unionists. In Westminster 10–12 Unionists to 2 Nationalists.
- As the Republic's constitution laid claim to the whole island of Ireland, O'Neill's meeting with his Dublin counterpart, Seán Lemass, in 1965, provoked attacks from within unionism, eg the Rev. Ian Paisley.
- Violence erupted between the two communities, in 1966 following the twin 50th anniversaries of the Battle of the Somme and the Easter Rising. Both events were key cultural touchstones for the Protestant and Catholic communities.

The issue of Civil Rights
- From the autumn of 1968 onwards, a wide range of activists marched behind the civil rights banner, adopting civil disobedience in an attempt to secure their goals. Housing activists, socialists, nationalists, unionists, republicans, students, trade unionists and political representatives came together across Northern Ireland to demand civil rights for Catholics in Northern Ireland.
- The demand for basic civil rights from the Northern Ireland government was an effort to move the traditional fault-lines away from the familiar Catholic-Protestant, nationalist-unionist divides by demanding basic rights for all citizens of Britain.
- Civil rights encouraged by television coverage of civil rights protest in USA and student protests in Europe. Also by widening TV ownership: 1954, 10,000 licences, by 1962 there were 200,000 leading to increased Catholic awareness of the issues that affected them.
- As the civil rights campaign gained momentum, so too did unionist opposition. Sectarian tension rose: was difficult to control, and civil disobedience descended into occasions of civil disorder.

Any other relevant factors.

2016
SECTION 3: EUROPEAN AND WORLD

Part A: The Crusades, 1071–1204

31. To what extent were attempts to assert Papal authority the main reason for the calling of the First Crusade?

Context
In 1095 Pope Urban II urged Christians from all over Europe to fight a holy war to drive out the Muslims from the Holy Land. Among Urban II's reasons for launching a crusade was a desire to increase the power of the papacy. Pope Urban II saw the appeal from Byzantium as an opportunity to assert papal power and authority not only over western European leaders and people, but to assert the influence of Rome onto the Byzantine and Muslim East.

Attempts to assert Papal authority
- The new style of pope, influenced and trained at the monastery of Cluny, heralded a shift in the emphasis of Christianity. The papal reforms influenced by the Cluniac establishment demanded actual, as well as spiritual, power. No longer were popes to be subservient to the monarchs or warlords of Europe. A Cluniac reformer himself, Pope Urban II was keen to build on the reforms of previous popes.
- The papacy was anxious to re-join the two halves of the Christian church. Since the Great Schism of 1054, where the Pope of Rome and Patriarch of Constantinople excommunicated each other, it had been the goal of every pope to become head of the Greek Orthodox Church and to extend Roman influence into the eastern Mediterranean. Now the Crusade seemed to offer Pope Urban the opportunity to achieve this.

Other factors

The ongoing struggle between church and state — the Investiture Contest
- Popes now actually challenged kings and demanded the right to appoint priests, bishops and cardinals as they saw fit. This led to the development of the Investiture Contest, a prolonged war between Pope Gregory VII and the German Emperor, Henry IV. A low point was reached in 1080 when Henry appointed a separate Pope and attacked Rome with his armies. This power struggle had damaged the reputation of the papacy and directly affected Urban, possibly influencing his decision.
- A crusade would increase the papacy's political status in Europe. The Pope would be seen as a great leader, above princes and emperors.
- It is believed the Investiture Contest may have delayed the calling of a crusade. There may have been a crusade to drive back the Seljuk as early as the mid-1070s but Gregory's struggle against the German Emperor meant he was too weak to see it through.

Fear of Islamic expansion
- Founded by the Prophet Muhammad, the Islamic religion had exploded onto the world in the late seventh century, advancing across the Christian principalities of North Africa, through Spain and into southern France, where it had been halted in the eighth century and pushed back into Spain.
- Pope Urban used the fear of Islamic expansion in his famous speech at Clermont in 1095. He pointed to the successful Reconquista in Spain. El Cid had only captured Valencia from the Moors in 1094.
- He pointed to the threat of the Turks to Byzantium, a topic that was already talked about across Europe. He claimed that the loss of Anatolia had "devastated the Kingdom of God".
- He detailed claims of Turkish activities such as torture, human sacrifice and desecration.

The threat to Byzantium
- The Seljuk Turks had been threatening the Empire for decades. The Byzantines had been defeated in 1071 at the Battle of Manzikert in eastern Anatolia. Between 1077 and 1092 the Byzantines had been driven out of the eastern regions of Anatolia, and the Turks were now encroaching further west towards the Byzantine capital of Constantinople. There was fear in Europe that if Byzantium was allowed to fall then the expansion of this new aggressive Islamic group into central Europe would be inevitable.
- The Byzantine Emperor, Alexius was seen as a bulwark against this eventuality and his letter asking for help was taken very seriously.
- The threat to Byzantium was perhaps exaggerated by the Emperor Alexius who had negotiated a treaty with Kilij Arslan in 1092 and was hiring more and more mercenaries from Europe to protect the Empire.

The threat to Mediterranean trade
- The development of trade within the Mediterranean Sea had been in the hands of ambitious cities in Italy, notably Venice, but also Pisa and Genoa. By 1095 Venice had bound its future to Byzantium.
- Their preferential trade agreements with Constantinople for silk, spices and other luxury goods meant that they were keen to see Byzantium saved from the expansion of the Turks.

The emergence of a knightly class
- The introduction of Norman feudalism across Western Europe had created a knightly class. Their dedication to learning the arts of war had created a culture based around the skills of fighting. Even the tournaments had come to be seen as an integral part of the culture and as entertainment.

Papal desire to channel the aggressive nature of feudal society
- Urban's appeal specifically targeted the nobility of France and northern Europe in the hope of diverting the violence of the warring European kingdoms in order to create peace within Europe. For knights to use their skills in anger was a sin. Pope Urban had long considered how he could turn the nature of the Western knights to a less aggressive, less damaging activity.
- The Church was determined to reverse what it perceived as the breakdown of society in many parts of Western Europe. As a man of God, Urban II saw a crusade as an opportunity to avoid the evils of civil war in Europe.
- The Church had already successfully introduced the Peace of God, an agreement that non-combatants would be spared in any conflict. Urban saw the Crusade as a way to channel this aggression out of Europe and into the Middle East which would be of benefit to Christianity.

Any other relevant factors.

32. To what extent were divisions among the Islamic states the main reason for the success of the First Crusade?

Context

Despite many hardships, the First Crusade was a unique and overwhelming success. Muslim disunity and the lack of a single Muslim leader were very much to the crusaders' advantage and assisted the crusaders in their victories.

Divisions among the Islamic states

- The division in the Islamic faith was between the Sunni and the Shia, a split dating back to the death of the prophet Muhammad (AD 632).
- By the 1070s, the Sunni controlled Asia Minor and Syria, under the leadership of the caliph of Baghdad while the Shia ruled Egypt under a caliph based in Cairo. The two groups hated each other more than they hated the crusaders and were known to form alliances with the crusaders in order to make gains on their fellow Muslim enemy.
- At the time of the First Crusade, there was a lack of stable leadership in Anatolia due to the death of several leaders from both the Sunni and the Shia branches of Islam. A series of petty rulers fought for leadership.
- As a result, the Islamic response to the First Crusade was slow in getting under way. Not only were the Islamic leaders more willing to fight among themselves than join forces against the common enemy, many did not even realise that the crusaders were a common enemy. Kilij Arslan, for example, expected the "Princes Crusade" to be no more of a concern than Peter the Hermit's followers. Thus he was off raiding his Muslim neighbours when Nicaea came under attack.
- Further evidence of division amongst the Islamic states was when Kerbogha's army abandoned him at the battle of Antioch in 1098. Many had feared that his victory would allow him to gain a semblance of authority over the other Seljuk Turkish leaders. There was tension in his army as the Turks mistrusted the Arab speaking Muslims and the different tribes of nomads. The lack of unity was clear among the divisions of Ridwan of Aleppo and Duquaq of Damascus. Infighting among the Turkish leaders led to Kerbogha being abandoned at the battle's critical moment.
- The fundamental division of Muslim between the Fatimids and the Seljuk is illustrated in the Egyptian's seizure of Jerusalem. The Egyptian army used siege engines to reduce the walls of Jerusalem in a siege that lasted 6 weeks. This not only damaged the defences of the city but reduced the number of defenders available. The Fatimids even sent embassies to the crusaders offering them Jerusalem in exchange for an alliance against the Seljuk.
- For the Muslims the First Crusade was not seen as a holy war, at least not at the outset. To the Muslims, unifying to face the Christians was a more dangerous idea than the crusaders themselves.

Other factors

The religious zeal of the Crusaders

- Without their belief in what they accepted as God's Will, the First Crusade would have disintegrated long before it reached Jerusalem. The sheer determination of the Crusaders helped them through incredible hardships during their passage through the Taurus Mountains and at the sieges of Antioch and Jerusalem.

- Because they believed God would help them, the Crusaders attempted the impossible, where most armies would have surrendered. Visions during the siege of Antioch and the discovery of the Holy Lance were much needed boosts to morale. The Lance had become a mystical weapon to be wielded on Christ's behalf. The fact that the crusading army was now in possession of such a relic caused the majority of the crusaders to believe in their own invincibility. The miracle perceived by the crusaders lifted their spirits and brought them victory over Kerbogha's army at Antioch and gave them the energy and confidence for the next stage of their crusade — Jerusalem.
- Another vision came to the rescue of the Crusaders at Jerusalem. Peter Desiderous announced he had received a vision from Bishop Adhemar saying the city would fall to them if they would fast and walk on barefoot in procession around the city. God's Hand was even clearer when the crusaders fought their way across the city wall on 15 July 1099, the date that Adhemar, in vision, had foretold as the day by which the Christian army would capture Jerusalem.
- Despite Nicaea falling to the Byzantine emperor through negotiation and the skill of Bohemond of Taranto who saved the crusaders at their first real battle at Dorylaeum, many crusaders considered their success as part of God's plan.

The military power of the Crusader knights

- The First Crusade had been unexpected by local Muslim leaders. Those that had witnessed the ineptitude of the People's Crusade expected Christian knights to be as inept in combat. However Christian knights were often ferocious fighters, used to long campaigns in Europe, whereas the knights of the East were seen as gentlemen of culture and education.
- The mounted tactics of the knights were relatively unknown in the east and the sight of the largest concentration of knights in history assembled on the field was a truly awesome sight. This full frontal charge of the knights was in contrast to the tactics deployed by the Islamic forces. Their hit and run horse archers were not prepared for this aggressive style.
- It was the strategic skill of Bohemond of Taranto and the discipline that he had instilled in his men which saved the crusaders from a ferocious Turkish attack near Dorylaeum.
- Crusading knights used aggressive combat tactics, and utilised heavier armour and barding for their horses. The constant fighting of the 12th century had well prepared the organised and disciplined knightly classes for warfare. Many, such as Raymond of Toulouse, had combat experience against the Moors in Spain.

Misunderstanding of the Crusaders' intent

- Muslims misunderstood the threat of the Western knights. Many saw this as another expedition from Byzantium and thought them soldiers of Alexius. Such raids had occurred before; however this was different. Here the Christians had an ideological motivation not yet encountered by the Islamic leaders.

Aid from Byzantium

- The First Crusade was the only Crusade to have significant support from Constantinople. Even though Alexius's army did not participate in the Crusade itself, they did cause problems, diverting a lot of Muslim resources.
- Alexius also provided much needed supplies at the sieges of Antioch and Jerusalem.

Any other relevant factors.

33. *During the Third Crusade Richard was more successful than Saladin both as a military leader and as a diplomat.* **How valid is this view?**

Context

The Third Crusade is viewed as the greatest-ever crusade in Europe to be launched against the Muslim East. Both heroic military leadership and diplomatic negotiations were features of the Third Crusade. Despite defeating Saladin in battle and forcing Saladin to a peace treaty, Richard ultimately failed to recapture Jerusalem.

Richard's military strengths

- Despite Muslims and Christians having fought a on and off battle over Acre over two years, Richard's leadership and expertise broke the deadlock and forced the surrender of Acre after 5 weeks of bombardment, mining and repeated assaults.
- Richard's arrival in June 1191 with money and with the cutting edge of western military technology in the form of enormous siege engines which struck the fear of God into opponents. This enabled Richard to seize control of the battle and to intensify the bombardment.
- Richard switched tactics at Acre after the destruction of his great war machines. He offered his soldiers four gold coins for every stone they could remove from the base of one of the towers, putting so much effort on the one point that a breach in the wall was created.
- Further evidence of Richard's leadership skills at Acre, were shown when, despite falling ill with "arnaldia" he ordered himself to be carried to the walls in a silken quilt and there, protected by a screen, fired his crossbow at the city which further inspired his troops.
- The capture of Acre was a major boost for the crusaders and brought the unimpeded rise of Saladin to a halt.
- Richard demonstrated firm, if brutal, leadership in August 1191 when he took the drastic decision to massacre the 2700 Muslim prisoners taken at Acre when Saladin failed to meet the ransom payment. Richard knew feeding and guarding the prisoners would be a considerable burden and suspecting that Saladin was deliberately using delaying tactics to pin Richard down, Richard resolved the situation quickly and effectively in order to carry on his momentum and capitalise on his victory at Acre.
- Richard demonstrated that he was a great military strategist on the march from Acre down the coast to Jaffa. Under Richard's leadership, the Crusader army of 12 000 men set out along the coast in immaculate formation. Inland were the foot soldiers with their vital role of protecting the heavy cavalry, the cavalry themselves were lined up with the Templars at the front and the Hospitallers at the back, the strongest men to protect the most vulnerable parts of the march. Between the cavalry and the sea was the baggage train, the weakest, slowest and most difficult part to defend. Finally out to sea was the crusader fleet to provide the well-defended columns with essential supplies.
- Richard's military leadership was crucial to the survival of the crusaders on the march to Jaffa. Forced to face terrible conditions, Richard allowed the soldiers rest days and prevented fights over the meat of dead horses. Despite the constant attacks, Richard showed enormous discipline as he kept his troops marching even as they were being peppered by arrows. Richard was insistent that no crusader should respond and break formation denying Saladin an opportunity to inflict a crushing defeat on the crusader forces. Richard wanted to charge on his own terms. Such discipline showed Richard to be a true military genius.
- At the battle of Arsuf, Richard reacted immediately to the breaking of the Crusader ranks and personally led the attack which eventually swept the Muslims from the battlefield. Richard turned his whole army on the Muslims and fought off two fierce Muslim counter attacks. Led by Richard, the Crusader charge smashed into Saladin's army forcing them to retreat. Richard's planning and meticulous attention to detail created the circumstances in which his personal bravery could shine through. The victory of Richard's army over Saladin's forces at the Battle of Arsuf and the success of the Crusaders in reaching Jaffa was an important turning point in the Third Crusade. Saladin's aura of success had been breached.
- Richard displayed inspired military leadership and immense personal bravery at Jaffa. When Richard heard that Saladin had stormed the port of Jaffa in July 1192, Richard responded with characteristic brilliance. Richard rushed south from Acre with a tiny force of only 55 knights and crossbowmen at the head of a sea borne counter attack. Despite being heavily outnumbered Richard ordered his men to attack and was one of the first to wade ashore at the head of his small army. The surprise of his attack turned the battle around and gave the crusaders an improbable and dramatic victory. The Muslim troops themselves were overawed by Richard's courage and nerve. Richard's highly disciplined and organised army had again proved too much for Saladin's men and they retreated.
- Richard's ability as a military tactician was shown by his caution on the march to Jerusalem. To ensure his advance on Jerusalem could be properly sustained, Richard carefully rebuilt several fortresses along the route.
- Richard also demonstrated his strategic competence when he withdrew twice from Jerusalem, realising that once recaptured, Jerusalem would be impossible to defend due to insufficient manpower and the possibility that their supply lines to the coast could be cut off by the Muslims. Despite his personal desire to march on Jerusalem, Richard was a general and knew that military sense told him that his depleted force of 12 000 men and lack of resources couldn't hold Jerusalem against Saladin's vast army drawn from across the Muslim world.
- That Richard was a military strategist of the highest order was also demonstrated on his journey to the Holy Land when he captured Cyprus and sold part of it to the Templars. Richard recognised the long term importance of Cyprus as a base for crusading armies to use when supplying and reinforcing expeditions to the Holy Land.
- Richard also realised that Egypt was the key to Saladin's wealth and resources. Ever the military strategist Richard wanted to take the mighty fortress of Ascalon which would threaten Saladin's communications with Egypt. Richard was aware that in order to keep Jerusalem after it was captured; Egypt would need to be conquered first. Richard wrote to the Genoese asking for a fleet to support a campaign in the summer of 1192 but the crusader army was not interested in Jerusalem and wanted to proceed to Jerusalem. Richard reluctantly agreed to march on Jerusalem before campaigning in Egypt.
- Although the Third Crusade failed in its ultimate aim of the recovery of Jerusalem, Richard's leadership played a crucial role in providing the Crusaders with a firm hold on the coastline which would provide a series of bridgeheads for future crusades. Compared to the situation in 1187, the position of the Crusaders had been transformed.

Richard's military weaknesses

- Richard was ultimately unable to recapture Jerusalem, the main objective of the Third Crusade.
- Richard also failed to draw Saladin into battle and inflict a decisive defeat. He failed to comprehensively defeat Saladin.

Saladin's military strengths

- Saladin counter attacked at Acre. Saladin's troops launched fierce attacks on the Crusaders at given signals from the Muslim defenders and launched volley after volley of Greek fire putting Richard on the defensive as all three of his giant siege towers went up in flames. Saladin also sent a huge supply ship with 650 fighting men in an attempt to break into Acre's harbour. After destroying a number of English vessels, it scuttled itself rather than have its cargo fall into Christian hands. On the march south to Jaffa, Saladin's army unleashed a relentless series of forays and inflicted constant bombardment, tempting the Christians to break ranks. Saladin's skilled horsemen made lightning strikes on the Crusaders showering the men and their horses with arrows and crossbow bolts. The crusaders lost a large number of horses and the crusaders themselves resembled pincushions with as many as ten arrows or crossbow bolts protruding from their chain mail.
- Saladin massed his forces from Egypt and all across Syria and launched an intense bombardment on the Crusaders which tested the Crusader knights' discipline and patience, not to react, to the absolute limits.
- At the Battle of Arsuf, despite the devastating impact of the Crusader charge, Saladin's own elite Mamluk units rallied and offered fierce resistance.
- To prevent the crusaders taking Ascalon, Saladin made the decision to pull down Ascalon's walls and sacrifice the city.
- While the crusaders remained in Jaffa and strengthened its fortifications Saladin took the opportunity to destroy the networks of crusader castles and fortifications between Jaffa and Jerusalem.
- In October 1191 as the crusaders set out from Jaffa and began the work of rebuilding the crusader forts along the route to Jerusalem, they were repeatedly attacked by Saladin's troops.
- At the end of July Saladin decided to take advantage of the crusader's retreat from Jerusalem by launching a lightening attack on Jaffa in an attempt to break the Christian stranglehold on the coast. In just four days the Muslim sappers and stone throwers destroyed sections of Jaffa's walls which left only a small Christian garrison trapped in the citadel. Saladin's forces blocked help coming from overland which meant that relief could only arrive by sea.
- Arguably Saladin's greatest military achievement was to gather and hold together (despite divisions) a broad coalition of Muslims in the face of setbacks at Acre, Arsuf and Jaffa. Although the consensus is that Saladin was not a great battlefield general (It could be argued that his triumph at Hattin was down more to the mistakes of the crusaders than his own skill), Saladin was still able to inspire his troops and fight back. Saladin's continued resistance had ensured that Jerusalem remained in Muslim hands.

Saladin's military weaknesses

- Saladin found it increasingly difficult to keep his large army in the field for the whole year round. In contrast to the Crusading army, many of his men were needed back on their farms or were only expected to provide a certain number of days' service.

- Saladin's authority was ignored when the garrison at Acre struck a deal with Conrad of Montferrat to surrender. Saladin lost control of his men at Jaffa.
- The stalemate at Jaffa showed that Saladin was incapable of driving the Crusaders out of southern Palestine.

Richard's diplomatic strengths

- During the siege of Acre and despite his illness Richard opened negotiations with Saladin showed his willingness to use diplomacy.
- That Richard was skilled in the art of diplomacy was shown in his negotiations with Saladin's brother, Al-Adil. A bond was forged between them and Richard even offered his sister Joan to be one of al-Adil's wives as part of a deal to divide Palestine between the crusaders and the Muslims. Richard's connection with Al-Adill was enough of an incentive for Saladin to agree to a truce with Richard.
- Richard negotiated a five year truce over Jerusalem.

Richard's diplomatic weaknesses

- Richard showed poor diplomacy towards his allies. After the victory at Acre, Richard's men pulled down the banner of Count Leopold of Austria, claiming his status did not entitle him to fly his colours alongside the king of England, even though Leopold had been fighting at Acre for almost two years. This resulted in Leopold leaving Outremer in a rage, taking his German knights with him (Eighteen months later he imprisoned Richard after the king was captured returning through Austria).
- Richard also failed to show subtlety in his dealings with King Philip. Richard's inability to share the spoils taken during this attack on Cyprus with Philip helped persuade the ill King of France that he was needed at home. The one thing Richard had wished to do was keep Philip with him on the Crusade; now he had to worry about French incursions into his Angevin Empire.
- Against advice Richard backed Guy de Lusignan to become King of Jerusalem, against the popular Conrad of Montferrat, perhaps because he was the favorite of Philip. This continued support of Guy resulted in a compromise that no one liked. The assassination of Conrad was even whispered by some to be Richard's fault. The end result was the withdrawal of the support of Conrad's forces and those of the Duke of Burgundy's remaining French knights.

Saladin's diplomatic strengths

- During the siege of Acre and alongside the military skirmishes as the crusaders set out on their march to Jerusalem, Saladin and Richard were engaged in diplomacy. Both sides were willing to find areas of agreement at the same time as engaging in brutal combat.
- Following Richard's victory at Jaffa, Saladin knew he could not maintain such a level of military struggle indefinitely. He recognised the need to make a truce with Richard. On 2 September 1192, the Treaty of Jaffa was agreed which partitioned Palestine in return for a three year truce. While Saladin was to retain control of Jerusalem, the Crusaders were allowed to keep the conquests of Acre and Jaffa and the coastal strip between the two towns. Christian pilgrims were also allowed access to the Church of the Holy Sepulchre in Jerusalem.

Saladin's diplomatic weaknesses

- Saladin faced increasing discontent from his Muslim allies.
- Saladin negotiated a five year truce over Jerusalem despite his strong position.

Any other relevant factors.

Part B: The American Revolution, 1763—1787

34. To what extent was George III the main reason for colonial resentment towards Britain by 1763?

Context

By 1763, Britain had ruled the thirteen American colonies for over a century. The harmony with Britain which colonists had once held had become indifference during Whig Ascendancy of the mid-1700s. The ascendancy of George III in 1760 was to bring about further change in the relationship between Britain and America. When the Seven Years War ended in 1763, the King strengthened Britain's control over the colonies. Factors contributing towards colonial resentment included George III, the Navigation Acts, the old colonial system, political differences between the colonists and the British, and British neglect of the colonies.

George III

- George III increased the number of British soldiers posted to the colonies after the Seven Year War ended in 1763.
- One function of the King's Proclamation of 1763 was to protect the colonies from future threats posed by foreign powers. However, all colonies and even some larger towns and cities within the colonies had their own militia already, and felt that the British Army in fact posed a threat to the colonists' freedom to defend themselves.
- In addition, George III ensured there was a highly visible Royal Navy attendance on the Atlantic coast, whose job it was to patrol for smugglers importing from Holland, France or Spain and ensure compliance with the Navigation Acts.
- This measure, to support the Revenue Bill proposed in Parliament 1763 was seen as equivalent to foreign invasion by many colonists who had acted in an independent spirit during Whig Ascendancy.
- On the other hand, it can be debated that George III was aiming to guarantee the protection of the colonies by maintaining British military presence and that together with Parliament he was planning a sensible economic strategy to raise money from the colonists to pay for their own security.
- However, cynics in America argued that the King was merely working to ensure continued revenue for Britain, whose national debt had grown from £75 million to £145 million between 1756 and 1763.

Other factors

Navigation Acts

- The Navigation Acts stated that colonists in any parts of the British Empire could only sell their goods to British merchants, they could only import goods from British traders, and they could only use British shipping in the transportation of goods in and out of the colonies.
- This meant that colonist merchants were being denied access to European markets for their produce such as tobacco or whale products, reducing their potential income and creating opposition to this aspect of British rule.
- Moreover, although colonists had ignored the acts during the Whig Ascendancy, the laws were re-enforced by Prime Minister Grenville after the Seven Years War ended in 1763.
- This caused deep resentment, since the presence of the Royal Navy, patrolling the Eastern Seaboard for rogue Dutch, French or Spanish ships, restricted the trading ability of the colonists who felt their enterprising spirit was being penalised.
- It could, however, be argued that the Navigation Acts gave the colonists a guaranteed market for their goods. Generally though, the Navigation Acts were disliked by those wishing to trade freely with European merchants.

The old colonial system

- The thirteen colonies in North America had been used by Britain for almost two centuries as a source of revenue and convenient market.
- Valuable raw materials such as timber or cotton or fur were plundered from the continent and then used to manufacture goods which were then sold in Europe and around the world. This meant that the profits from North American goods were being made by British trading companies, which was resented by those colonists whose labour produced the raw materials to make goods such as fur-trimmed hats or rifles.
- In addition, colonists in the more populated New England and Middle Colonies objected to being used as a dumping ground for British goods.
- Poverty led to minor rebellions by tenant farmers against their landlords throughout the 1740s, including the Land Riots in New Jersey and the Hudson River Valley Revolt in New York.
- Elsewhere, wealthy Southern plantation owners, who considered themselves the aristocracy of the continent, objected to members of British government attempting to control them through trading restrictions on sugar, cotton and molasses.
- Some historians would point out that being part of the British Empire meant British Army protection for the colonists against the threat of the French and Indians; the British had fought the Seven Years War which prevented the colonies being ruled by France. Despite this advantage, colonists greatly resented the efforts of Britain to restrict their movements and economic development.

The Proclamation of 1763

- The Proclamation Line drawn up by Parliament in 1763 led to Frontiersmen feeling frustrated at British attempts to prevent them from settling beyond the Appalachian Mountains.

Political differences

- The colonies were more enlightened politically than Britain, as each had its own elected Assembly which had passed local laws and raised local taxes since the 1630s.
- Britain appointed a Governor for each colony, but the Governor was paid by the colony, which ensured a slight element of control for colonists over whoever was in the post.
- Lack of representation for the colonists in the British Parliament which sought to control their lives, however, frustrated many.
- In addition, radical proposals in the colonies were rejected by the British authorities, such as the abolition of slavery, favoured by the Massachusetts Assembly led by lawyer James Otis and brewer Samuel Adams but continually vetoed in the early 1760s by the British Governor Hutchinson.
- Nevertheless, some understood that the British Empire provided an order to the existence of the colonies, and Britain acted out the role of Mother Country in a protective manner. This did not stop many colonists from wishing to have a greater say in their own daily lives.

British neglect

- During the Whig Ascendancy from 1727 to 1760, colonist Assemblies had assumed the powers which should have been exercised by Governors, such as the settlement in new territories acquired during that time including the Ohio Valley and Louisiana. Although they objected Parliament's attempt to reverse this after the Royal Proclamation of 1763, they were politically impotent and could not prevent it.
- In addition, individual colonists and land companies expanding west into the Michigan area unwittingly violated agreements between Britain and Native American Indians such as the 1761 Treaty of Detroit.
- Therefore, quarrels arose as it appeared that the British government, and in particular Secretary of State William Pitt, was ignoring colonist aspirations to explore new regions in the continent.
- One school of thought suggests that Britain's policies highlighted the status of the colonies as lands to be fought over with imperial powers like France and Spain who viewed America as potential possessions, and that British legislation maintained colonist security under the Union Jack.
- However, colonists such as planter and lawyer Patrick Henry of Virginia believed by 1763 that, whilst the right of the King to the colonies was indisputable, the right of the British Parliament to make laws for them was highly contentious.

Any other relevant points.

35. To what extent did the views of Thomas Paine represent British opinion towards the conflict in the colonies?

Context

In the 1760s and 1770s, the thirteen colonies in America witnessed resentment from colonists towards Britain. Several crises including the Stamp Act in 1765, the Boston Massacre in 1770 and the Tea Act in 1773 created a momentum of hostility. The colonists' last hope of compromise, the Olive Branch Petition, was rejected by Britain in 1775 and the Continental Congress declared independence in 1776, leading to a five year war which the colonists won. Factors to be considered amongst British opinion are the views of Thomas Paine, Edmund Burke, George III, parliament, the Earl of Chatham and other British people such as politicians, industrialists and the working classes including those living in England, Scotland and Ireland.

Thomas Paine

- Paine had attacked the notion of hierarchical monarchy in debating clubs in London and in revolutionary pamphlets in the 1770s. His views were radical for his time, and people in Britain read his work out of fascination rather than because they agreed with him. This suggests Paine's opinions on the monarchy were out of step with his contemporaries.
- Paine had met Benjamin Franklin in London and he assisted Paine to settle in Philadelphia in October 1774.
- Paine believed he could further the cause of American independence, and made republican speeches and met with notable colonists, although his revolutionary ideas were regarded as too radical for many, including Franklin, who favoured compromise with Britain. Paine, therefore, was very much against the stem of British opinion on the situation.
- On 10 January 1776 Paine published "Common Sense", a propagandist pamphlet in favour of American independence which sold 100,000 copies in the colonies, and more than that in Britain and France.

- During the war, his writings continued to encourage colonists to keep fighting as Britain would one day recognise America's independence. The popularity of his work demonstrates the willingness of colonists to expose themselves to his radical views.

Other factors

Edmund Burke

- As a new MP in 1765, Burke spoke against the Stamp Act in the House of Commons, having studied the American situation and taken the colonists' demands seriously.
- He made speeches citing the common bond of "Englishness" which existed between Britain and America, and urging Parliament to "loosen the reins" on colonists or lose America for good. This shows Burke's insight into colonist feeling about rule by Parliament.
- He opposed the Quebec Act 1774 as both impractical and ill-timed, stating that it appeared to be punitive because it was being passed simultaneously with the Coercive Acts.
- He proposed a Motion of Conciliation from Britain to the 1st Continental Congress in November 1774, but was heavily defeated in the House of Commons. Burke's actions demonstrate an awareness of the need to maintain good relations with America.
- Burke believed George III's actions to have accelerated colonists' moves towards independence, but his views were dismissed as alarmist by many Parliamentarians in the pre-war years.
- During the war, in 1777 in Parliament, Burke predicted a colonist victory based on his knowledge of their rebellious spirit and Britain's impotence to crush their determination.
- One school of thought is that Burke was an imperialist who merely sought to maintain the colonies within the British Empire by compromising with their political demands. However it is certain that Burke was viewed as a sympathetic figure by many colonists who applauded his common sense and humanist approach to their plight.

George III

- The King re-imposed British authority on America soon after ascending the throne in 1760.
- When the Seven Years War ended in 1763 he ordered the strict application of the Navigation Acts. This led to colonists immediately resenting Parliament, who enforced the king's will by sending the army and navy to America.
- Popular in Britain, he brought about the dismissal or resignations of successive Prime Ministers in the 1760s, in part due to his desire to see firmer policies enforced on the colonies.
- He supported Parliament's right to tax America, which created more radical opinions in the colonies against British policy.

Parliament

- The Proclamation Act in 1763, Stamp Act in 1765, Declaratory Act in 1766, Tea Act in 1773 and Coercive Acts in 1774 enforced British authority over the colonies.
- Repeated speeches by significant figures such as Lord Sandwich displayed a disregarded for warnings of the impending crisis, and seriously underestimated colonists' forces. This showed that the majority of Lords and MPs endorsed the views of the King.
- Several ministries between 1763 and 1776 sought to control America through the military enforcement of policy.

- Prime Ministers were supported in the House of Lords in their assertions of Parliament's absolute sovereignty over the American colonies as in all parts of the British Empire. This led them to view taxation as fair and lenient.
- In House of Commons, country gentlemen MPs favoured taxation in the colonies, as it allowed cuts in taxation in Britain. Many viewed the developing American situation as one to be resolved purely in terms of what was best for Britain, which demonstrates Parliamentary opinion against the colonists' interests.

Earl of Chatham

- As William Pitt, he had been Secretary of State during the Seven Years War, and became regarded as architect of the Empire in America, favouring trade restrictions and British military presence.
- Nevertheless, he condemned the Stamp Act as an unfair. This suggests Pitt support Parliamentary legislation for the colonies but disagreed with taxation.
- He was ennobled as the Earl of Chatham when he became Prime Minister in 1766, and proclaimed himself a friend of America.
- However, he seemed to object only to taxation, and pushed through the Quartering Act of 1765, which forced the colonies to pay for supplies and billets for British troops. This was opposed, particularly by the New York Assembly.
- After he resigned amidst domestic political manoeuvrings in 1768, Chatham became increasingly aware of the colonists' plight in his final years, speaking against harsh measures towards America in the 1770s, and repeatedly cautioning the government about the impending crisis as war approached.
- However, his warnings fell on deaf ears, as Parliament ignored his pleas for conciliation and his assertion that America could not be beaten if war broke out.

Differing British views of the situation in the colonies

- Lord Grenville was Prime Minister 1763–5, and favoured British merchants in the colonies. His Currency Act of 1764 protected debts owed to British traders. He imposed the Stamp Act, though privately feared it could not be enforced.
- Lord Rockingham was Prime Minister 1765–6, and was inclined to be lenient towards America. However, after he repealed the Stamp Act he passed the Declaratory Act, proclaiming British Parliamentary supremacy over America.
- The Duke of Grafton was Prime Minister 1768–70, and believed in the removal of duties in America but stood firm on the notion of British supreme authority. Despite his opposition to taxation, he insisted that duties on tea remain.
- Lord North was Prime Minster from 1770 until 1782. He believed Parliament should enforce British interests and supremacy in the colonies. He was supported by the British landed classes as long as he did not attack their interests and had the confidence of George III. North oversaw the Coercive Acts and Quebec Act. He led Britain through the war and spent a fortune on military supplies in America and the West Indies, believing the war could be won.
- John Wilkes was elected as an MP in 1768, although Parliament refused to allow him to take his seat as he was so radical. He was recognised by American radicals as honest and freedom-loving, fighting against the tyranny of Crown and Parliament. He favoured "rights and privileges of freeborn subjects in a land of liberty", and spoke out against British policy in the House of Commons.

- British cotton industrialists and mill owners, including some MPs, favoured the Navigation Acts as they guaranteed a supply of raw materials from the colonies. However, as the crisis approached war, they merely wanted a speedy resolution in order to allow trade to continue. Cotton mill workers — workers wanted trade to be maintained in order to preserve jobs, and so favoured any moves by the British government which would resolve the crisis.
- In Scotland and Ireland, some people sympathised with the colonists' resentment of "English" rule and understood their calls for greater autonomy.
- In America, British settlers and other Empire Loyalists in the colonies favoured the status quo, and after the Revolution 70,000 left the new states to settle in Canada.

Any other relevant factors.

36. How important was British military inefficiency in the colonists' victory in the War of Independence?

Context

The American War of Independence took place between 1776 and 1781, between Britain and its thirteen colonies of North America. For many colonists, this was a revolutionary conflict fought by people fighting for freedom against tyranny, monarchy and the threat of enslavement. The war was fought not only on American soil, but on the high seas and across the world once other European Powers became involved. Factors which contributed to the colonists' victory were British military inefficiency, George Washington's military capability and leadership, France's entry to the war and its contribution worldwide, local knowledge held by the Continental Army and other worldwide factors.

British military inefficiency

- On several occasions British generals did not act appropriately to instructions, such as when Lord George Germain, the British Secretary of State for America, hatched a plan to separate the New England colonies from the others in mid-1777. This involved General Howe moving his forces north from New York, but Howe misinterpreted his orders and moved south during August, rendering the plan futile.
- Meanwhile, General Burgoyne, commander of British forces in Canada, had received orders to march south into the Hudson valley towards Ticonderoga in early 1777. Burgoyne, however, was left isolated in the Hudson valley after capturing Ticonderoga because Howe had gone south and General Clinton was too slow to move north in place of Howe, and so, confronted by large American forces, Burgoyne was forced to surrender his 3,500 men and equipment at Saratoga in October 1777.
- Furthermore, changes in personnel hindered operations, as politicians such as Lord North and Lord Germain promoted or appointed officers frequently, causing inconsistency and lack of stability at command level.
- Petty jealousies amongst military leaders also obstructed progress, so that even after military campaigns had been waged successfully or battles had been won, there was no co-operation, leading to the British losing land gained, particularly after French entry in 1778.

Other factors

Washington's military capability

- Washington was aware that the British forces would hold the advantage in open battle, so he fought using guerrilla warfare effectively, for example at the significant crossing of the Delaware River in December 1776.

- This was part of a surprise raid on British posts which resulted in Washington's small bands of men crossing the river back to their positions in Pennsylvania with captured supplies and arms. Guerrilla warfare, therefore, was an effective weapon in Washington's armoury.
- In addition, Washington taught his troops to fire accurately from distance on those occasions when they were engaged in open battle, particularly in the fight to control the New Jersey area in the first half of the war.
- During the attack on Princeton in January 1777 and the Battle of Monmouth in June 1778, Washington's forces successfully drove the British from the battlefield.
- Washington's "scorched earth" campaign during the summer of 1779 was aimed at Iroquois settlements in New York in revenge for their co-operation with the British early in the war.
- This policy deterred further collaboration between Native Americans and the British Army. Although brutal, this strategy increased colonists' chances of winning the war on land.
- Moreover, Washington had experience of serving with British Army during Seven Years War, and had been a leading figure in the British capture of Pittsburgh in 1758. He was aware of British military practice and the weaknesses in the chains of communication between London and North America.

Washington's leadership

- He was a self-made Virginian who had become a successful tobacco planter in the 1760s and involved himself in local politics as a member of the Virginia legislature.
- As a military hero from the Seven Years War, his choice as Commander of the Continental Army in 1775 gave heart to many. So Washington's business and political reputation were key features of his authority during the war.
- His personal qualities included the ability to give speeches to his troops, emphasising the incentive of independence if they won the war. Washington was aware of the political aspect of the conflict, and turned military defeats, of which he suffered many, into opportunities to inspire his forces to fight on.
- Washington's leadership at Valley Forge during the winter of 1777–8 saw him preserve the morale of his 10,000-strong army in terrible conditions, particularly by his allowing soldiers' families, known as Camp Followers, to remain with the troops.
- His appointment of celebrated Prussian drill sergeant Baron Friedrich von Steuben to maintain discipline meant firearms skills stayed at a high quality.
- His promotion of Nathaniel Greene through the ranks from Private to Quartermaster-General meant regular food for the soldiers as well as adequate supplies of ammunition and uniforms, including boots.
- The trust he showed in the French General Lafayette led to Congress commissioning Lafayette into the Continental Army before the French entered the war, allowing him an important role in strategic planning.

French entry into the war

- The Franco-American Treaty of Alliance was signed Franklin and Louis XVI at Versailles in February 1778. This formalised French recognition of the United States, the first international acknowledgement of American independence.
- From this period onward, the French guaranteed the colonists abundant military support in the form of troops sent to fight on land and a naval contribution on the Eastern seaboard, around Britain and across the world.

- In addition, France provided the Continental Army with ammunition, uniforms, expertise, training and supplies.
- Importantly, the forces under the command of Count Rochambeau who landed at Rhode Island in 1780 hampered the British army's attempts to dislodge colonist strongholds in Virginia throughout 1780 and 1781.
- Rochambeau's co-operation with the colonist General Lafayette and the clear lines of communication he established between himself and de Grasse led to the trapping of Cornwallis at Yorktown and the French navy's arrival in Chesapeake Bay.

French contribution worldwide

- The strength of French navy meant Britain had to spread its forces worldwide, particularly as France attacked British colonies in the Caribbean Sea and Indian Ocean. In addition, there were attempts to raid Portsmouth and Plymouth in order to land soldiers on the British mainland.
- Admiral d'Orvilliers defeated the Royal Navy in the Battle of Ushant in the English Channel in July 1778, weakening British defences in preparation for further attacks on the south-coast of England.
- Admiral de Grasse successfully deceived British fleets in the Atlantic to arrive at Chesapeake Bay in September 1781 prior to the Yorktown surrender.
- The entry of France into the conflict encouraged Spain and Holland to follow suit within next two years, declaring war against Britain in June 1779 and December 1780 respectively.
- French action against the Royal Navy gave these European Powers confidence to attack British interests in India and the southern colonies.

Local knowledge

- The main theatre of the land war was on American soil, with the main battles being fought out in Massachusetts, the Middle Colonies and Virginia. Even if the British gained ground, the revolutionary forces knew the terrain well enough to find ways of re-occupying lost territory.
- Key colonist victories such as the Battle of Princeton on 3 January 1777, the Battle of King Mountain on 7 October 1780, and the Battle of Yorktown between September and October 1781 were in no small part due to colonist forces' ability to utilise local geography to advantage.
- British forces constantly found themselves having to react to the movement of the Continental Army.
- Furthermore, as witnessed in British victories such as the Battle of New York City between August and October 1776, the Battle of Fort Ticonderoga on 6 July 1777, and the Battle of Brandywine on 25 August 1777, colonist troops had intimate knowledge of the surrounding areas and were able to avoid capture, and so withdrew to safety in order to fight another day.
- On occasions, such as during the Saratoga campaign, local people burned their crops rather than let them fall into British hands. The distance between Britain and the colonies already meant that supplies were slow in arriving at the front.

Other worldwide factors

- Spain entered into the war in June 1779, intent on mounting an attack on the British mainland.
- Dutch entry into war came in December 1780, providing another threat of invasion.
- These European Powers stretched British resources even further and made British less effective in its overall military effort.
- The Armed League of Neutrality was formed in December 1780. The involvement of Russia, Denmark and Sweden

in an agreement to fire on the Royal Navy, if provoked, placed extra pressure on Britain.

- The war at sea was a vital feature of Britain's weaknesses. British concentration was diverted from maintaining control of the colonies on land towards keeping control of maritime access to its wider Empire. Ultimately, with the surrender at Yorktown, it was loss of control of the sea which led to the eventual British defeat.

Any other relevant factors.

Part C: The French Revolution, to 1799

37. *Taxation was the main cause of the threats to the security of the Ancien Régime before 1789*. How valid is this view?

Context
In France, the Ancien Régime was the old order, which came to an end with the French Revolution of 1789. The king was at the centre of the Ancien Régime, governing through Councils and Ministries. Taxes and laws were set by royal edict. The absolute monarchy ruled in provinces through Intendants, and in towns through Parlements. The Ancien Régime consisted of Three Estates. Factors contributing to the threat to security included taxation, corruption, the royal family, financial issues, the position of the clergy, the role of the nobility, and grievances held by the peasantry and bourgeoisie.

Taxation
- Unfair nature of the system.
- Privileged orders of the First and Second Estates were exempt from many taxes.
- The Church received the tithe from peasants who lived on its lands — one tenth of their produce.
- The nobility could tax the peasantry for hunting, shooting and fishing on their land.
- Cumbersome administration — tax collected by the Farmers General, who had a vested interest in collecting as much as they could.
- The Third Estate (peasantry, urban workers and bourgeoisie) had to pay indirect taxes such as the gabelle (on salt), aides (on luxury goods) and the douanes (on imported goods).
- The Third Estate paid direct taxes such as the capitation (to local government) and the vingtieme (to central government).

Other factors

Corruption
- Absolutist nature of the monarchy meant that many resented the lack of political representation.
- Much of the functioning of central and local government was carried out with favour shown to individuals.
- Court advisors were concerned with protecting their position rather than contradicting the king or warning him against bad decisions.

Royal family
- Louis XVI was viewed as a wasteful monarch, creating an excess of court expenditure.
- The King was seen as weak and indecisive, surrounded by incompetent sycophants.
- The King never called the Estates General (before 1789).
- Marie-Antoinette was despised by many in the population for her Austrian nationality.
- The Queen was unwilling to improve her political knowledge.

- Monarchy perceived as being ignorant of the lifestyles of the peasantry.
- Decadence of the court.

Financial issues
- Financial problems were arguably the biggest threat to the Ancien Régime.
- Created in part by France's involvement in wars — most recently the American War of Independence — brought France to bankruptcy.
- By the 1780s, the Treasury deficit was estimated at 112,000,000 livres.
- Failure to reform — several finance ministers suggested changes to the taxation system but were thwarted by the privileged classes.
- Turgot, Controller-General 1774–76 was dismissed after suggesting physiocratic reform and the abolition of town guilds.
- Necker, 1776–81, reduced court expenses, cut the number of tax-farmers, but had to borrow heavily to finance the war in America. Disclosure of court expenditure brought about his dismissal.
- Calonne, 1783–87, floated loans and spent freely, and attempted to persuade nobles to accept a land tax but resigned when they refused this.
- Brienne, 1787–88, tried to impose taxes on the privileged classes but the Parlements refused to confirm this and he was dismissed.

The position of the clergy
- The clergy was split into the upper and lower clergy, the latter identifying more closely with the Third Estate. The church hierarchy was resented by the lower clergy.
- Parish priests often sided with the peasants in their locality but the upper clergy viewed peasants with contempt and merely as a source of taxation.
- The Church owned a large amount of land and paid relatively little taxation. The upper clergy were concerned to protect their privileges.

The role of the nobility
- Like the clergy, the upper nobility were concerned to protect their privileged status, particularly access to posts at court and in the army, and their exemptions from taxation.
- Natural supporters of the monarchy, they saw some threat from the rise of the bourgeoisie.
- There were also tensions between the traditional nobility (of the sword) and the newly ennobled nobility (of the robe).
- The "old" sought to hold onto their control of key positions of the State, the Army and the Church, much to the annoyance of the "new".

Grievances held by the peasantry
- The 3rd Estate was liable for compulsory military service.
- The peasantry were liable for forced labour on public roads and buildings — this service was called the corvée.
- The peasantry had to pay to use their landlords' ovens to bake bread.
- The peasantry would be likely willing to support change when it came.
- Poor pay and high food prices.
- During times of poor harvests and bad winters, resented the lack of help from the 1st and 2nd Estates.

Grievances held by the bourgeoisie

- The bourgeoisie had to pay the taille if they did not want to do military service.
- The bourgeoisie desired political power but the Estates General, the collective group of representatives from each of the Three Estates, had not been called since 1614.
- Resented the extravagant lifestyle of the 2nd Estate.
- The bourgeoisie were educated and were aware of the criticisms made of the Ancient Regime by the French philosophical movement of the 18th century.

Any other relevant factors.

38. To what extent was the character of Louis XVI the main reason for the failure of constitutional monarchy, 1789–92?

Context

The French Revolution of 1789 brought about the downfall of the Ancien Regime, the collapse of absolutism and ultimately in 1792 the end of the French monarchy. The constitution was established in 1789 and was an attempt to retain the French monarchy with limited powers and according representation to royalists, Jacobins and Girondists. Factors contributing to the failure of the constitution included the character and actions of Louis XVI, weaknesses in the constitution and government, financial problems and the effects of the outbreak of war in Europe in 1792.

Character of Louis XVI

- Even before the outbreak of revolution in July 1789, Louis had shown himself incapable of making the strong decisions necessary to save the monarchy.
- The King was seen as weak and indecisive, surrounded by incompetent sycophants.
- The King was viewed as a wasteful monarch, creating an excess of court expenditure.
- The King placed no trust in the Estates General.
- Monarchy perceived as being ignorant of the lifestyles of the peasantry.
- Decadence of the court.
- Marie-Antoinette was despised by many in the population for her Austrian nationality.
- The Queen was unwilling to improve her political knowledge.

Other factors

The King's attitudes and actions

- The King never called the Estates General (before 1789).
- Flight to Varennes had already stirred anti-royalist feelings.
- Louis was from the start unsupportive of the principle of constitutional monarchy.
- He dismissed Controller-General (Finance Minister) Calonne in the face of opposition from the nobility to the major tax reforms needed to save France from bankruptcy.
- Even in the weeks before the Declaration of the Rights of Man, the king seemed to be preparing for a counter-revolution through the build-up of troops at Versailles.
- After the Declaration of the Rights of Man in August 1789, Louis failed to openly endorse its principles.
- There was considerable suspicion about the King, which made the achievement of a constitutional monarchy unlikely.
- Even before his veto on decrees against "refractory" clergy and émigrés in December Louis' actions during 1791 had done the monarchy immeasurable harm.

- His lukewarm support for the reforms of the Constituent Assembly had generated popular hostility in Paris from the spring of 1791 onwards.
- The King was likely to seek support from European allies to increase his powers.

Weaknesses in the constitution and the government

- The constitution still accorded the king a power-sharing arrangement with the Legislative Assembly.
- Limitations on the power of the monarch would never be accepted by Louis.
- Within 6 months of the first meeting of the Assembly in October 1791 the King had been exercising his veto in a manner unacceptable to the Girondists and Jacobins.
- The government's actions against the Church were unpopular with the peasantry.
- The Civil Constitution of the Clergy made clergymen state employees which Roman Catholic priests objected to.

Financial problems

- The economy had been damaged by events of the Revolution (and was already in crisis before 1789).
- Inflation was spiralling, making the constitutional monarchy unpopular in the provinces.
- In towns and cities increased bread prices were unpopular amongst industrial workers in urban areas.
- Continued heavy taxation of the poorest sections of society.
- The financial benefits of the Revolution were perceived as being enjoyed by the wealthy and bourgeoisie.

The outbreak of war

- The Revolution was radicalised to the point where the position of the monarchy became impossible because of the king's identification with the enemy.
- Partly, as was said above, this was Louis' own fault but it should be remembered that France declared war on Austria in April 1792.
- However, radical anti-monarchists believed that a successful war against Austria would bring them increased support at home and prove a decisive blow to the monarchy.
- The final overthrow of the monarchy in August 1792 had become inevitable under the pressures exerted by the war.

Any other relevant factors.

39. To what extent was political instability the most important reason for the establishment of the Consulate?

Context

The French Revolution of 1789 brought the end of the Ancient Regime. After a failure to establish a constitutional monarchy between 1789 and 1792, the monarchy was abolished, and the King and Queen were later executed. The period of Terror then took place until 1795, at the end of which the new Directory was created, but this was brought to an end with the creation of the Consulate by Napoleon Bonaparte in 1799. Amongst the factors which led to this were political instability, the increasing intervention of the army in politics, the role of Sieyes, the constitution of 1795, and the role of Bonaparte himself.

Political instability

- In the late summer of 1794 France was emerging from two years of increasing radicalisation.
- Growing bitterness between opposing factions within the country.

- The Jacobins, under Robespierre, had been overthrown and a "White Terror" was soon to sweep the country in revenge for the excesses of the radical left during the Terror.
- France had been torn apart by civil war, with suspicions existing within communities in both urban and rural areas.
- The country was threatened by foreign armies egged on by émigré nobles seeking to overthrow the Revolution.
- France was riven by religious conflict occasioned by the State's opposition to the primacy of the Catholic Church.

Other factors

Increasing intervention of the army in politics

- Even before the 1795 constitution was ratified the army had been used to quell sans-culottes insurgents who sought to invade the Convention and to repel an émigré invasion at Quiberon.
- Napoleon's use of a "whiff of grapeshot" to put down the disturbances in October merely underlined the parlous nature of politics at the time.
- The army was deployed in May 1796 to put down the left-wing Babeuf Conspiracy.
- The Directory reacted with the Coup of Fructidor in September 1797 when the first "free" Convention elections returned a royalist majority.

Role of Abbe Sieyes

- Sieyes was afraid that France would descend into anarchy as a result of the on-going political conflict, and deemed the 1795 constitution unworkable.
- Sieyes enlisted the aid of Bonaparte in mounting a coup against the constitution.
- The Convention, the Directory and the legislative councils had run their course and few, if any, mourned their passing.

The Constitution of 1795

- Policy-makers framed a new constitution which sought to reconcile the bitterness of the preceding years by imposing checks and balances against the emergence of one dominant individual, group or faction. In so doing, many historians argue that the new constitution was a recipe for instability in the years which followed.
- A bi-cameral legislature was established wherein each chamber counter-balanced the power of the other. By so doing it inhibited strong and decisive government.
- To ensure continuity, the new Convention was to include two-thirds of the outgoing deputies from the old. This enraged sections of the right who felt that the forces of left-wing radicalism still prevailed in government.
- The resulting mass protests in October 1795 were put down by the army under Bonaparte. The principle of using extra-parliamentary forces to control the State had been established with Bonaparte right at the heart of it. It was to prove a dangerous precedent.
- Annual elections worked against consistent and continuous policy-making.
- So did the appointment of an Executive — the Directory — one of whose members rotated on an annual basis.
- Again, the counter-balance between the legislature and the executive may have been commendable but it was to prove inherently unstable in practice.

Role of Bonaparte

- Following participation in warfare in Europe and the Middle East, Bonaparte returned in October.
- Public perception was of Bonaparte as a hero, someone who could restore France to its former glory after years of revolutionary chaos and confusion.

- Bonaparte himself had political ambitions and planned to support Sieyes in the dissolution of the Directory and then seize power himself.
- Bonaparte cited the Coup of Fructidor to the Council of Five Hundred as evidence of their own culpability in the imminent downfall of the Directory.
- Bonaparte led the army in deposing the Directory in November 1799.
- Bonaparte's use of the military gave him greater authority in later dealings with Sieyes.

Any other relevant factors.

Part D: Germany, 1815–1939

40. How important were cultural factors as a reason for the growth of nationalism in Germany, 1815–50?

Context

In 1815 "Germany" was not a unified state but a loose confederation made up of 39 separate states with their own rulers and systems of government. However, the development of a German sense of culture after 1815 created a greater feeling of unity and led to a growth of nationalism.

Cultural factors

- Main unifying force was language — 25 million Germans spoke the same language and shared the same culture and literature.
- Writers and thinkers (eg Heine, Fichte, Goethe, Brothers Grimm, Schiller and Hegel) encouraged the growth of a German consciousness.
- Post-1815 nationalist feelings first expressed in universities.
- Growth of Burschenschaften pre-1815 dedicated to driving French from German soil — zealous but lacking a clear idea of how best to accomplish the task.
- The Hambacherfest and student demonstrations — little was accomplished by the students.
- Early 19th century was a time of great change in all European states and it has been suggested that the political changes of the time can be partly explained by an understanding of the cultural developments of the time.

Other factors

Economic factors

- Urbanisation and industrialisation of the German states — political fragmentation — can be argued to be the most important obstacle to German economic development.
- Middle-class businessmen called for a more united market to enable them to compete with foreign countries. They complained that tax burdens were holding back economic development.
- Prussian economic expansion — drift in power away from Austria and towards Prussia as the latter began to build on rich resources such as coal and iron deposits.
- Prussia's gain of territory on the River Rhine after 1815 meant it had good reason to reach an agreement with neighbours to ensure relatively free travel of goods and people between its lands in the East and the West.
- Prussia created a large free-trade area within Prussia itself.
- Railway/road development — post-1830s the development of railways/roads ended the isolation of German states from each other. This enabled the transport and exploitation of German natural resources. Economic cooperation between German states encouraged those seeking a political solution to the issue of German unity.

The Zollverein

- Zollverein — the "mighty lever" of German unification. By 1836, 25 of the 39 German states had joined this economic free-trade area (Austria excluded).
- Members of the Union voluntarily restricted their sovereignty (even if only for selfish interests) to allow for economic gain through joining the Prussian-led Customs Union.
- German nationalists in the late 1830's saw it as a step towards a wider political union.

French Revolution and the Napoleonic Wars

- Ideas of the French Revolution appealed to the middle classes in the German states.
- Impact of Napoleonic wars — many Germans argued that Napoleon/France had been able to conquer German states pre-1815 due to their division as separate, autonomous territories. German princes had stirred national feeling to help raise armies to drive out the French, aiding the sense of a common German identity with common goals.

Political factors

- 1848 revolutions in Germany raised consciousness greatly even though they failed.
- Many Liberals were middle-class and were also receptive to nationalist ideas.

Military weakness

- The French Revolution led to a realisation that, individually, the German states were weak.
- French troops had marched across Germany for over 20 years, and had humiliated Prussia, the strongest "German" state at Jena and Auerstadt. Germany had been carved up by Napoleon, the North Sea coast being incorporated into France itself, and the Confederation of the Rhine set up as a puppet state. Divided, the German states could not defend their territorial integrity.
- Germany had been used as a recruiting ground by Napoleon: Germans had died to protect France. Even the enlarged post-Vienna states would be powerless, with the exception of Prussia, to prevent this happening again.

Any other relevant factors.

41. To what extent was Austrian strength the main obstacle to German unification, 1815—50?

Context

Between 1815 and 1850 there was a growth in German nationalism across the German confederation made up of 39 separate states with their own rulers and systems of government. Due to a variety of divisions ranging from religious to political, there were many who did not support German unification.

Austrian strength

- The states within "Germany" had been part of the moribund Holy Roman Empire, traditionally ruled by the Emperor of Austria.
- Post — 1815 the chairmanship of the *Bund* was given to Austria on a permanent basis, partly as she was considered to be the major German power.
- Metternich's work — to oppose liberalism and nationalism. His use of the weapons of diplomacy and threats of force eg Karlsbad Decrees and the Six Articles. Use of the police state, repression and press censorship.
- Austrian control over the administration and management of the empire, stamping authority on the *Bund*.

- Treaty of Olmutz, 1850 — signalled the triumph of Austria and humiliation of Prussia which showed that Austrian military strength was an important obstacle. Although Austrian military strength was in decline, this was not apparent until the 1860s.

Other factors

German Princes

- The leaders of the German states obstructed unification — protective of their individual power and position. They wanted to maintain the status quo which would safeguard this for them.
- Particularism of the various German states — autonomous and parochial in many ways.
- Self-interest among German rulers led to opposition to the actions at Frankfurt.

Resentment towards Prussia

- Smaller states, particularly in the south, resented the economic and political predominance of Prussia.
- There was a reluctance to accept unification within the Prussian state, which had a significant non-German population and which contained a large conservative/reactionary landed class.

Divisions among the nationalists

- Nationalists were divided over which territory should be included in any united Germany; *grossdeutsch* and *kleindeutsch* arguments.
- Failure of the Frankfurt Parliament — lack of clear aims and without an armed force to enforce its decisions. Lack of decisive leadership. Divisions among the "revolutionaries" regarding aims and objectives.

Religious differences

- Religion — northern German states were mostly Protestant and southern states mainly Catholic; thus the north looked to Prussia for help and protection while the south looked to Austria.

Economic differences

- The smaller states of the West had more advanced economies than the Prussian heartlands.
- Even within Prussia there were significant social differences between the industrially advanced territories on the Rhine and the largely agricultural areas in the East, which were dominated by the Junkers (although less so than in the 18th century), who were adversely affected by the agricultural depression of the 1820s.
- Austria's failure to join the Zollverein led her to create her own customs union.

Indifference of the masses

- Popular apathy — most Germans had little desire to see a united Germany; nationalism affected mainly the educated/business classes.
- Lack of coincidence between political boundaries and ethnic/linguistic ones.
- However, politically based literature and propaganda also reached the masses, helping to bond their ideals and strengthen their resolve for both reform and unification.

Attitudes of foreign states

- France had been able to dominate central Europe for centuries due to its lack of unity. Although most of Germany had been united by Napoleon into the Confederation of the Rhine, it was not in French interests for Germany to be united, particularly as that would present a barrier to France achieving a frontier on the Rhine.

Any other relevant factors.

42. To what extent were weaknesses of the Weimar Republic the main reason why the Nazis achieved power in 1933?

Context
In 1933, Hitler had become chancellor of Germany. A number of factors contributed to Hitler and the Nazis' rise to power, including economic difficulties caused by the hyperinflation crisis of 1923, the Wall Street Crash of 1929 and the Great Depression which followed.

Weaknesses of the Weimar Republic
- "A Republic without Republicans"/"a Republic nobody wanted" — lack of popular support for the new form of government after 1918.
- "Peasants in a palace" — commentary on Weimar politicians.
- Divisions among those groups/individuals who purported to be supporters of the new form of government eg the socialists.
- Alliance of the new government and the old imperial army against the Spartacists — lack of cooperation between socialist groups — petty squabbling rife.
- The Constitution/Article 48 ("suicide clause") — arguably Germany too was democratic. "The world's most perfect democracy — on paper."
- Lack of real, outstanding Weimar politicians who could strengthen the Republic, with the exception of Stresemann.
- Inability (or unwillingness) of the Republic to deal effectively with problems in German society.
- Lukewarm support from the German Army and the Civil Service.

Other factors

Resentment towards the Treaty of Versailles
- The Treaty of Versailles: acceptance by Republic of hated terms.
- Land loss and accepting blame for the War especially hated.
- Led to growth of criticism; "November Criminals", "Stab in the back" myth.

Appeal of the Nazis after 1928
- Nazi Party had attractive qualities for the increasingly disillusioned voting population: they were anti-Versailles, anti-Communist (the SA took on the Red Front in the streets), promised to restore German pride, give the people jobs.
- The Nazis put their message across well with the skillful use of propaganda under the leadership of Josef Goebbels.
- Propaganda posters with legends such as "Hitler — our only hope…" struck a chord with many.
- The SA were used to break up opponents meetings and give the appearance of discipline and order.
- Gave scapegoats for the population to blame from the Jews to the Communists.

The role of Hitler
- Hitler was perceived as a young, dynamic leader, who campaigned using modern methods and was a charismatic speaker.
- He offered attractive policies which gave simple targets for blame and tapped into popular prejudice.

Social and Economic divisions
- Over-reliance on foreign loans left the Weimar economy subject to the fluctuations of the international economy.

- 1923 (hyperinflation) — severe effects on the middle classes, the natural supporters of the Republic; outrage and despair at their ruination.
- The Great Depression — arguably without this the Republic might have survived. Germany's dependence on American loans showed how fragile the recovery of the late 1920s was. The pauperisation of millions again reduced Germans to despair.
- The Depression also polarised politics in Germany — the drift to extremes led to a fear of Communism, which grew apace with the growth of support for the Nazis.

Weaknesses and mistakes of opponents
- Splits in the left after suppression of Spartacist Revolt made joint action in the 1930s very unlikely.
- Roles of von Schleicher and von Papen. Underestimation of Hitler.
- Weakness/indecision of Hindenburg.

Any other relevant factors.

Part E: Italy, 1815—1939

43. To what extent were cultural factors the main reason for the growth of nationalism in Italy, 1815—50?

Context
The origins of Italian nationalism can be traced back to the Renaissance and the writings of Machiavelli who urged Italians to seize Italy from the "barbarians". However, the ideas of Mazzini and his anti-Austrian views led to the development of more political nationalism in the 19th century.

Cultural factors
- The Risorgimento was inspired by Italy's past. Poets such as Leopardi glorified and exaggerated past achievements, kindling nationalist desires. Poets and novelists like Pellico inspired anti-Austrian feelings amongst intellectuals, as did operas such as Verdi's "Nabucco" and Rossini's "William Tell".
- There was no national Italian language — regional dialects were like separate languages. Alfieri inspired Italian language based on Tuscan. The poet and novelist Manzoni wrote in Italian. Philosophers spread ideas of nationalism in their books and periodicals.
- Moderate nationalists such as Gioberti and Balbo advocated the creation of a federal state with the individual rulers remaining, but joining together under a president for foreign affairs and trade. Gioberti's "On the moral and civil primacy of the Italians" advocated the Pope as president whilst Balbo, in his book "On the hopes of Italy", saw the King of Piedmont/Sardinia in the role.

Other factors

Economic factors
- Economic factors were not important directly. Wealth lay in land (landowners were often reactionary) and trade (where the educated bourgeoisie were more receptive to ideas of liberalism and nationalism).
- The election of a new, seemingly reformist Pope, Pius IX, in 1846 inspired feelings of nationalism particularly amongst businessmen and traders as he wished to form a customs union.
- Tariff walls between the Italian states and the disorganised railway system prevented economic development of Italy, which did lead businessmen to be interested in unification.

Military weakness

- The French Revolution led to a realisation that, individually, the Italian states were weak. The fragmentation of Italy in the Vienna Settlement restored Italy's vulnerability to foreign invasion.

Effects of the French Revolution and Napoleonic wars

- Italian intellectuals had initially been inspired by the French Revolution with its national flag, national song, national language, national holiday and emphasis on citizenship.
- Napoleon Bonaparte's conquest inspired feelings of nationalism — he reduced the number of states to three; revived the name "Italy"; brought in a single system of weights and measures; improved communications; helped trade, inspiring desire for at least a customs union. Napoleon's occupation was hated — conscription, taxes, looting of art.

Resentment of Austria

- After the Vienna settlement in 1815, hatred of foreign control centred on Austria. The Hapsburg Emperor directly controlled Lombardy and Venetia; his relatives controlled Parma, Modena, Tuscany. Austria had strong ties to the Papacy and had alliances with other rulers. Conscription, censorship, the use of spies and the policy of promotion in the police, civil service and army only for German speakers was resented.
- Austrian army presence within towns like Milan and the heavily garrisoned Quadrilateral fortresses ensured that Italians could never forget that they were under foreign control and this inspired growing desire for the creation of a national state.

Role of Mazzini

- Radical nationalist Mazzini not only inspired dreams of a united, democratic Italian republic through his written works, but also formed an activist movement — "Young Italy" — whose aim was to make these dreams a reality.

Secret societies

- The growth of secret societies, particularly the Carbonari, led to revolts in 1820, 1821, 1831. Also Young Italy and their revolts in the 1830s.

Any other relevant factors.

44. How important was the dominant position of Austria and her dependent duchies as an obstacle to Italian unification, 1815–50?

Context

By 1850 the forces of nationalism had grown in Italy. The revolutions of 1848 showed this. However, there were many obstacles which prevented unification from happening before 1850 such as the dominant position of Austria and her dependent duchies.

Dominant position of Austria and her dependent duchies

- Following Vienna Settlement Austria Emperor Francis I had direct control of Lombardy and Venetia. Relatives of the Austrian Hapsburg Emperor controlled Parma, Modena and Tuscany (Central Duchies). Austria had agreements with the other states.
- Lombardy and Venetia were strictly controlled — censorship, spies, conscription (8 years), policy to employ German speakers (Austrian) in law, police, army civil service so controlled others (non Austrian).
- Austrian army was a common sight in major cities and in the Quadrilateral fortress towns on Lombard/Venetian border (Verona, Peschiera, Legnano, and Mantua). The Austrian army was sent in by Metternich to restore order following the Carbonari-inspired revolts in 1820, 1821 and 1831.

- Austria had first class commander, Radetsky. In 1848 Charles Albert's army won two skirmishes but Radetsky awaited reinforcements then defeated Albert at Custozza forcing an armistice. Radetsky re-took Milan in August.
- After Albert's renewal of war Radetsky took just three days to defeat him again (Novara). He then besieged Venetia until the Republic of St Mark surrendered on 22 August 1849. Austrians re-established control across north and central Italy.

Other factors

Divisions among the nationalists

- Secret societies lacked clear aims, organisation, leadership, resources and operated in regional cells.
- Moderate nationalists feared extremists like Mazzini.
- The 1848/49 revolutions showed that nationalist leaders did not trust one another (Manin and Charles Albert) or would not work together (C. Albert and Mazzini).
- Failure to capitalise on Austrian weakness in 1848.

Social, economic and cultural differences

- Geographical difficulties hindered the spread of nationalist ideas.

Political differences

- There was division between those desiring liberal changes within existing states and those desiring the creation of a national state.

Attitude of the Papacy

- Pope Pius IX denounced nationalism in 1848.

Italian princes

- Individual rulers were opposed to nationalism. They feared for their position within a united Italy.

Indifference of the masses

- Patriotic literature inspired intellectuals and students but did not reach the vast majority of the population who were illiterate (90% in some areas). The mass of the population were indifferent to nationalist ideas.

Any other relevant factors.

45. To what extent was the role of Mussolini the main reason why the Fascists achieved power in Italy, 1919–1925?

Context

By 1925, Mussolini and the Fascists had gained power in Italy. A number of factors contributed to the Fascist rise to power in Italy, such as Mussolini's personality and oratory skills.

Role of Mussolini

- Powerful orator — piazza politics.
- He seized his opportunities. He changed political direction and copied D'Annunzio.
- He used propaganda and his newspaper effectively and had an ear for effective slogans.
- He dominated the fascist movement kept support of fascist extremists (Ras).
- He relied on strong nerve to seize power and to survive the Matteotti crisis.

Other factors

Economic difficulties

- WWI imposed serious strain on the Italian economy. The government took huge foreign loans and the National Debt was 85 billion lira by 1918. The Lira lost half of its value, devastating middle class savers. Inflation was rising;

prices in 1918 were four times higher than 1914. This led to further major consequences:
- no wage rises
- food shortages
- two million unemployed 1919
- firms collapsed as military orders ceased.

Weaknesses of Italian governments
- Parliamentary government was weak — informal "liberal" coalitions. Corruption was commonplace (trasformismo). Liberals were not a structured party. New parties formed: PSI (socialists), PPI (Catholic Popular Party) with wider support base threatening existing political system.
- WWI worsened the situation; wartime coalitions were very weak. 1918; universal male suffrage and 1919 Proportional Representation; relied on "liberals" — unstable coalitions. Giolitti made an electoral pact with Mussolini (1921); fascists gained 35 seats then refused to support the government. Over the next 16 months, three ineffective coalition governments.
- Fascists threatened a "March on Rome" — King refused to agree to martial law; Facta resigned; Mussolini was invited to form coalition. 1924 Acerbo Law.

Resentment against the Peace Settlement
- Large loss of life in frustrating campaigns in the Alps and the Carso led to expectation that these would be recognised in the peace settlement; Wilson's commitment to nationalist aims led to the creation of Yugoslavia and a frustration of Italian hopes of dominating the Adriatic.
- "Mutilated victory" — Italian nationalists fuelled ideas that Italy had been betrayed by her government.

Appeal of the Fascists
- They promised strong government. This was attractive after a period of extreme instability.
- Violence showed fascism was strong and ruthless. It appealed to many ex-soldiers.
- Squadristi violence directed against socialism so it gained the support of elites and middle classes.

Role of the King
- The King gave into fascist pressure during the March on Rome. He failed to call Mussolini's bluff.
- After the Aventine Secession the King was unwilling to dismiss Mussolini.

Social and economic divisions
- Membership of Trade unions and PSI rose — strikes, demonstrations, violence. 1919/20 "Biennio Rosso" in towns — general strike 1920; army mutiny; occupation of factories.
- Industrialists/middle classes were fearful of revolution. Governments failed to back the police so law and order broke down.
- In the countryside, there was seizure of common land — peasant ownership increased.

Weaknesses and mistakes of opponents
- D'Annunzio's seizure of Fiume was not stopped by the government.
- Government failed to get martial law to stop fascist threat. Some liberals supported the Acerbo Law.
- Socialist General Strike July 1922 — failed. Socialists' split weakened them; refused to join together to oppose fascism.
- Liberals fragmented into four factions grouped around former PMs. They were too weak to effectively resist. Hoped to tame fascists.

- PPI were divided over attitude to fascism — right wing supported fascism. Aventine Secession backfired; destroyed chance to remove Mussolini.

Any other relevant factors.

Part F: Russia, 1881–1921

46. *Opposition groups were unable to effectively challenge the security of the Tsarist state before 1905*. How valid is this view?

Context
Opposition groups were weak in the Tsarist state before 1905. The main reasons for making this possible were the "Pillars of Autocracy". Each of these "Pillars" strengthened the Tsar's position, and made it almost impossible for opposition groups to challenge the state.

Opposition groups
- Opposition groups, eg Social Democrats (supported by industrial workers) and Liberals (who wanted a British-style parliament), were fairly weak. However, these groups were not powerful or popular enough to effect change.
- There were various revolutionary groups like the Social Revolutionaries (supported by peasants seeking land reform). Moreover these groups were further weakened by the fact they were divided and disorganised.
- The leaders were often in prison or in exile.

"Pillars of Autocracy"
- **The Fundamental Law** stated "To the emperor of all Russia belongs the supreme and unlimited power. God himself commands that his supreme power be obeyed out of conscience as well as out of fear". This was the basis of the Tsarist state.
- **The army** was controlled by the officers who were mainly upper-class, conservative and loyal to the Tsar. They ensured that the population and the peasantry in particular, was loyal to the Tsar. They crushed any insurgence and were used to enforce order in the country and loyalty to the Tsar.
- **The secret police (Okhrana)** was set up to ensure loyalty to the Tsar and weed out opposition to the Tsar. They did this by spying on all people of society irrespective of class. Those showing any sign of opposition to the Tsar were imprisoned or sent into exile. Large numbers were exiled.
- **The civil service** mainly employed middle-class people, therefore ensuring the loyalty of that class. The civil service was responsible for enforcing laws on censorship and corruption and controlling meetings which made it very difficult for the revolutionaries to communicate.
- **The Church** helped to ensure that the people, particularly the peasants, remained loyal to the Tsar. They preached to the peasants that the Tsar had been appointed by God and that they should therefore obey the Tsar. Ensured the peasants were aware of the Fundamental Law.

Censorship
- This controlled what people could read, what university lecturers could say, access to schools, and limited the number and type of books available in libraries.

Russification
- This was the policy of restricting the rights of the national minorities in the Russian Empire by insisting that Russian was the first language. As a result, law and government were conducted throughout the Russian Empire in the Russian language. This maintained the dominance of

the Russian culture over that of the minorities. State intervention in religion and education. Treated subjects as potential enemies and inferior to Russians.

Zubatov unions

- Organised by the police, these were used to divert the attention of the workers away from political change by concentrating on wages and conditions in the factories, thus reducing the chances of the workers being influenced by the revolutionary groups. Unions in 1903 became involved in strikes and so were disbanded due to pressure from employers.

Any other relevant factors.

47. *The Tsar was successful in strengthening his authority between 1905 and 1914.* **How valid is this view?**

Context

After the 1905 Revolution the Tsar had to strengthen his authority and weaken the threat of any opposition. He attempted to restore authority between 1905 and 1914 by introducing a variety of political and economic reforms led by Stolypin.

Role of the Tsar

- Tsar Nicholas II appointed Stolypin to restore order. He used a "divide and conquer" policy to deal with each of the threats individually. He secured the loyalty and control of the armed forces by promising overdue pay, improved conditions and training.
- The Tsar issued the October Manifesto and the Fundamental Laws which were crucial in strengthening the Tsarist state. He ruled by divine decree which along with the support of the Russian Orthodox Church, helped the Tsar use religion to secure his power.

Restoring order

- Stolypin was given the job of restoring order after the rural violence, industrial strikes and terrorism during and after the 1905 Revolution. He used measures such as military courts which issued death penalties — "Stolypin's necktie" — as well as sentences of hard labour in Siberia. He used the Okhrana and censorship to silence the Tsar's opponents.
- Stolypin also enforced Russification and disenfranchisement to suppress the national minorities. Public order was restored as ringleaders were dealt with severely and this acted as a deterrent, thereby strengthening the Tsarist state. However, there was still discontent in some areas.

Political Reforms — Dumas

- Stolypin believed that the Tsarist system would only survive if there were some political and social reforms which would reduce social bitterness and therefore reduce opposition. Stolypin wanted middle class support so he showed respect for the Duma and tried to work with it rather than against it. He changed the franchise in 1907 which prevented many national minorities, peasants and workers from voting although they did still have a say in the Zemstvos. This allowed him to obtain a more co-operative Third Duma which passed his land reforms.
- Stolypin's work with the Dumas helped to strengthen the Tsarist state as he helped secure the support of the middle class and Liberals for the Tsarist state.

Economic Reforms

- Stolypin's main plan was preventing another revolution through economic reform, particularly land reforms. He tried to address some of the economic problems facing Russia like food shortages and rural over-population. Stolypin felt that if the peasants and industrial workers were happy then they would be loyal to the Tsar and therefore any revolutions would fail. Stolypin's land reform details such as cancelling redemption payments, Kulaks, freedom from commune, Peasant Loan Bank and more land available. Peasants were encouraged to leave their overcrowded communes and relocate to Siberia or Central Asia.
- Stolypin also introduced reforms in education which became compulsory and Stolypin hoped this would allow them to get more highly skilled jobs. He introduced improvements in industrial working conditions and pay and as more factories came under the control of inspectors, there were signs of improving working conditions. As industrial profits increased, the first signs of a more prosperous workforce could be detected.
- In 1912 a workers' sickness and accident insurance scheme was introduced. Stolypin's economic reforms tried to strengthen the Tsarist state by improving life and work for the vast majority of the population.
- However, the land reforms did not modernise as much as had been hoped. Despite the record harvest of 1913, there was an economic slump which made life difficult for people and affected their loyalty to the Tsarist state.

Any other relevant factors.

48. **To what extent were the weaknesses of the Provisional Government the main reason for the success of the October Revolution, 1917?**

Context

After the abdication of the Tsar in March 1917 the Provisional Government took control of Russia. However, they were not an elected body but a provisional government put in place to keep Russia stable and to continue her war effort. Yet, by October 1917 the Provisional Government had been swept from power by Lenin and the Bolshevik's who carried out a successful revolution.

Weaknesses of the Provisional Government

- The Provisional Government was an unelected government; it was a self-appointed body and had no right to exercise authority, which led it into conflict with those bodies that emerged with perceived popular legitimacy.
- The Provisional Government gave in to the pressure of the army and from the Allies to keep Russia in the War.
- Remaining in the war helped cause the October Revolution and helped destroy the Provisional Government as the misery it caused continued for people in Russia.
- Failure to deal with the main issues of the Russian people.

Other factors

Political discontent

- The July Days was an attempt by the Bolsheviks to seize power. Rising in support of the Kronstadt sailors who were in revolt.
- The revolt was easily crushed by the Provisional Government but showed increasing opposition to the Provisional Government, especially from the forces.
- The impact of the Kornilov Revolt.
- Kerensky appealed to the Petrograd Soviet for help and the Bolsheviks were amongst those who were helped.
- Some Bolsheviks were armed and released from prison to help put down the attempted coup.

Appeal of the Bolsheviks

- Lenin returned to Russia announcing the April Theses, with slogans such as "Peace, Land and Bread" and "All Power to the Soviets".
- Lenin talked of further revolution to overthrow the Provisional Government and his slogans identified the key weaknesses of the Provisional Government.
- The Bolsheviks kept attending the Petrograd Soviet when most of the others stopped doing so and this gave them control of the Soviet, which they could then use against the Provisional Government.
- The Bolsheviks did not return their weapons to the Provisional Government after they defeated Kornilov.
- Bolsheviks were able to act as protectors of Petrograd.

Dual power — the role of the Petrograd Soviet

- The old Petrograd Soviet re-emerged and ran Petrograd.
- The Petrograd Soviet undermined the authority of Provisional Government especially when relations between the two worsened.
- Order No. 1 of the Petrograd Soviet weakened the authority of the Provisional Government as soldiers were not to obey orders of Provisional Government that contradicted those of the Petrograd Soviet.

Economic problems

- The workers were restless as they were facing starvation due to food shortages caused by the war.
- The shortage of fuel caused problems for the workers.
- The shortage of food and supplies made the workers unhappy and restless.
- The Bolsheviks' slogans appealed too many such as the workers control of industry.

The land issue

- All over Russia peasants were seizing nobles' land and wanted the Provisional Government to legitimise this.
- The failure of the Provisional Government to recognise the peasants' claims eroded their confidence in the Provisional Government.
- Food shortages caused discontent, and they were caught up by revolutionary slogans such as "Peace, Land and Bread".

Any other relevant factors.

Part G: USA, 1918–1968

49. To what extent were the effects of the First World War the main reason for changing attitudes towards immigration in the 1920s?

Context

By the 1920s the USA's open door policy on immigration had closed. New laws were introduced to further restrict immigration. The traumas of the First World War changed many Americans' attitudes towards immigrants.

The effects of the First World War

- Many immigrants during the First World War had sympathies for their mother country which led to resentment within the USA.
- A large part of the US immigrant population was of German or Austrian origin. Many of these immigrants had supported the German side in the war and society was split when the USA joined the war against Germany. Anti-German propaganda containing stories of German atrocities increased dislike and suspicion of immigrants from Germany and the old Austrian Empire.
- Irish Americans were suspected of being anti-British.
- Many citizens felt hostile to anything foreign. During the war, many Americans resented having to become involved in Europe's problems. After the First World War the USA was even more in favour of an isolationist policy. By 1918 the USA wanted to leave Europe behind especially after the November armistice, when ships began to bring the wounded back to the United States from the European Western Front. Many Americans therefore did not want new waves of immigrants bringing "European" problems to the USA.

Other factors

Isolationism

- Attitudes towards immigration in the 1920s were in some respects a development of existing attitudes towards immigration apparent in the 19th century. Before the 1920s, the USA's "open door" policy did not apply to everyone. Before 1900 the USA had reduced Asian immigration. The first significant law to restrict immigration into the USA was the Chinese Exclusion Act of 1882 which banned Chinese immigration.
- The first general Federal Immigration Law in 1882 imposed a head tax of 50 cents on each immigrant admitted and denied entrance into the USA of "any convict, lunatic, idiot, or any person unable to take care of himself or herself without becoming a public charge".
- The Immigration Restriction League was founded in 1894 to oppose "undesirable immigrants" from southern and eastern Europe who, it was believed, threatened the American way of life.
- The 1913 Alien Land Law prohibited "aliens ineligible for citizenship" from owning agricultural land or possessing long term leases. This particularly affected Chinese, Indian, Japanese and Korean immigrant farmers.
- At the beginning of the First World War, American public opinion was firmly on the side of neutrality and wanted to keep out of foreign problems and concentrate solely on America. When the war ended, most Americans were even more in favour of a return to the USA's traditional policy of isolationism.
- Despite Woodrow Wilson's support of a League of Nations to sort out future disputes between countries, in November 1919 and March 1920 the US Senate voted against US membership of the League of Nations, and refused to accept the terms of the League of Nations covenant. The USA was determined not to be involved in Europe's problems or become dragged into another European war. The USA was now firmly committed to a policy of isolationism.

Fear of revolution

- Attitudes towards immigration changed due to the "red scare" which increased suspicion of immigrants. The Russian Revolution in 1917 had established the first Communist state in Russia which was committed to spreading revolution and destroying capitalism. As many immigrants to the USA came from Russia and Eastern Europe, it was feared that these immigrants would bring communist ideas into the USA.
- In 1919 there was a wave of strikes in the USA. Many of the strikers were unskilled and semi-skilled workers and recent immigrants from southern and eastern Europe. People opposed to the strikes linked the strikes with communism as it was believed that revolution was imminent.

- The American public's fear of red revolution appeared to be confirmed when the US Attorney General Mitchell Palmer's house in Washington, DC, was blown up and letter bombs were sent to government officials. The red scare reached a peak of hysteria in January 1920 when, one night, Palmer ordered the arrest of 4000 alleged communists in 33 cities in what became known as the Palmer Raids.

Prejudice and racism

- Attitudes towards immigration changed due to fears concerning the changing nature of immigration. Up until the 1880s most immigrants to the USA came from northern and western Europe from, for example, Britain, Germany and Scandinavia. After 1880 the majority of immigrants came from southern and eastern Europe, from countries such as Russia, Poland and Italy. Descendants of the more established immigrants, known as WASPs (White, Anglo-Saxon Protestants) were concerned there would be a flood of new immigrants from southern and Eastern Europe which they believed would threaten their way of life. Some new immigrants continued to wear traditional dress which was not viewed as being "American".
- Many new immigrants were Catholic or Jewish which led to the belief that the arrival of new immigrants would threaten the Protestant religion.
- Many new immigrants were unfamiliar with democracy. This was viewed as a threat to the American constitution.

Social fears

- Attitudes towards immigration changed due to fears that immigration would lead to competition for housing and jobs. White working class Americans experienced rising rents due to the high demand for housing.
- The majority of new immigrants settled in cities in the north – east of the USA and often congregated with people from their own culture in ghettos. Some Americans felt this was a threat to their way of life.
- There were also fears that immigrants would increase the already high crime rates in cities. Such fears were heightened by the existence of organised crime gangs such as the Mafia with its Italian roots. Nicola Sacco and Bartolomeo Vanzetti were two Italian immigrant anarchists who were convicted of robbery and murder. Their trial linked crime, immigration and "un-American" political revolutionary ideas in the minds of many Americans.
- The activities of Al Capone, the son of Italian immigrants, also reinforced the stereotype that all Italian immigrants were in some way linked to crime.

Economic fears

- Attitudes towards immigration changed due to increased fears that the jobs of "Americans" would be threatened. Due to new production methods employers realised they could make huge profits by employing immigrants and paying them low wages. Trade unions believed that anything they did to improve conditions or wages was wrecked by Italian or Polish workers who were prepared to work longer hours for lower wages.
- New immigrants were also used as "strike breakers" as long hours and low wages in the USA were often better than what they were used to. There was huge resentment towards immigrant strike breakers which led to an increase in the desire to stop immigrants coming into the country.

Any other relevant factors.

50. *The weaknesses of the US banking system was the main reason for the economic crisis of 1929—33.* **How valid is this view?**

Context

Although the collapse of the New York Stock Exchange in October 1929 symbolises the start of the US economic crisis which in turn led to a worldwide Depression, problems in the American economy went beyond the stock market, and began before 1929. The weakness of the American banking system, for example, was highlighted in the autumn of 1929 when many banks failed to cope with the sudden rush to withdraw savings.

Weaknesses of the US banking system

- A major problem was the lack of regulation of banks.
- The US banking system was made up of hundreds of small, state-based banks. In hundreds of small communities local people put their money into the banks for safe keeping and a small amount of interest. Banks then used that money to make investments that made some money for the banks. As the economic boom grew, banks invested savers' money in stocks and shares in the hope of making a large profit.
- When people began to withdraw their savings, the banks could not cope with the demand as funds had been invested elsewhere. The collapse of one bank often led to a "run" on other banks, resulting in a banking collapse. By the end of 1932, twenty per cent of the banks that had been operating in 1929 had closed down. The normal banking system almost ceased to exist and without an efficient banking system, the economy could not function.

Other factors

Overproduction of goods

- New mass-production methods and mechanisation meant that the production of consumer goods had expanded enormously creating a consumer boom in the 1920s. Items such as irons, ovens, washing machines, vacuum cleaners, refrigerators, radios and telephones became very popular. The production of automobiles rose from 1.9 million in 1920 to 4.5 million in 1929.
- By 1929 those people who had the money to buy consumer goods – even on credit, had already bought them. Cars, radios and other electrical goods had flooded the market and more was being made than people could buy. The USA was experiencing the serious problem of over production. Radios, telephones, washing machines, refrigerators and other goods were piling up in warehouses across the country.

Under consumption — the saturation of the US market

- The enormous output of goods required a corresponding increase of consumer buying power, ie higher wages. However, workers' income in the 1920s did not rise with the increased productivity. The purchasing power of farmers had also declined. Between 1920 and 1932 the total income of farmers dropped by approximately 70%. Many small farmers lived in appalling conditions and many lost their farms due to outstanding debts.
- Throughout the 1920's business had benefited from low tax policies. The result of this was that the bottom 40% of the population received only 12.5% of the nation's wealth. The economic boom of the 1920s was not a good time for everyone. In 1928 it was estimated that 42% of Americans did not earn enough to buy adequate food, clothing or shelter. Many American people were too poor to afford the new consumer goods.

- In contrast, the top 5% of the population owned 33% of the nation's wealth. Only a wealthy minority of the US population could afford the new consumer goods that rolled off factory production lines.
- Therefore, domestic demand never kept up with production. By the end of the 1920s the market for the new consumer goods was saturated. By 1929 automobile factories had to lay off thousands of workers because of reduced demand.

Republican government policies in the 1920s

- The Republican administrations followed a policy of laissez-faire. Under Harding and Coolidge, the USA enjoyed a period of great prosperity. Most Republicans believed that governments should be involved as little as possible in the day to day running of the economy. If business people were left alone to make their own decisions, it was thought that high profits, more jobs and good wages would be the result. The only role for the government was to help business when requested.
- There was a failure to help farmers who also did not benefit from the 1920's boom.
- Low capital gains tax encouraged share speculation which resulted in the Wall Street Crash.
- The depression was also due to the actions — or inactions — of President Hoover. Few politicians realised the seriousness of the economic crisis and believed the economy would eventually recover by itself without the need for federal intervention. It is believed that the Hoover administration took the narrow interests of business groups to be the national interest which turned out to be catastrophic. Republican attempts to bring America out of the Depression were described as "too little too late".

International economic problems

- Results of the First World War on European economies.
- All European states, except Britain, placed tariffs on imported goods which meant American companies were failing to sell the extra goods they were producing to foreign countries.
- US economy could not expand its foreign markets.
- US tariff barriers meant that other countries found it difficult to pay back loans, which they had to refinance, becoming increasingly indebted.

The Wall Street Crash

- During the 1920s many people were encouraged to buy shares in American companies. As the share prices went up, the demand for shares increased further as people saw the chance to make easy money. The boom of the 1920s however was very fragile and the rise in share prices was based on the confidence that prosperity would continue.
- By the late 1920s ordinary people, banks and big businesses were buying shares "on the margin", paying only a fraction of the full price at the time of purchase, intending to sell on the shares at a profit before the rest of the payment became due. This meant that share buyers were forcing up share prices with money they did not really have.
- During the late 1920s, the economic boom started to slow down. There was an atmosphere of uncertainty in October 1929 and some shareholders began to sell their shares, believing that prices were at their peak.
- On 21 October prices began to fall. On 24 October 1929 Black Thursday, the Wall Street Crash began. On 29 October 1929 Black Tuesday, the US Stock market collapsed completely. As hardly anyone wanted to buy

shares, the shares were sold for very low prices. The share collapse caused panic. Many firms went out of business and thousands of Americans were financially ruined.

- The stock market crash did play a role in the depression but its significance was more as a trigger. The Wall Street Crash led to a collapse of credit, and of confidence. The Wall Street Crash revealed how fragile and unstable the economic boom of the 1920s really was.

Any other relevant factors.

51. How important was the continuation of prejudice and discrimination in the development of the Civil Rights campaign, after 1945?

Context

Despite modest progress in black Americans' civil rights, a number of events highlighted the continuing problem of prejudice and discrimination in post war America. While these events publicised the full horrors of segregation, they also demonstrated that segregation could be challenged and changed which was a significant factor in the development of a more organised mass movement for civil rights in the 1950s and 1960s.

The continuation of prejudice and discrimination

- Continuing racial discrimination pushed many black Americans to demand civil rights. The experience of war emphasised freedom, democracy and human rights yet in the USA Jim Crow laws still existed and lynching went unpunished.
- The continuing problem of prejudice and discrimination was highlighted when Emmett Till, a 14-year-old black boy from Chicago was murdered in Mississippi. The Emmett Till case had a big effect on the development of the civil rights movement due to the publicity of the trial. Despite being virtually unrecognisable due to being beaten up so badly, Emmett's mother insisted on showing her son's corpse in an open coffin which shocked both local people and the nation.
- The US Supreme Court's 1954 decision to end segregation in schools (Brown v the Topeka Board of Education) followed by the protest at Little Rock High School, Arkansas, in 1957, encouraged civil rights campaigners. The sight of Elizabeth Eckford being bullied and threatened for attending a white school made national and world news headlines.
- The bus boycott in Montgomery, Alabama (over the arrest of Rosa Parks, who refused to give up her seat on a segregated bus) was one of the first successful protests and showed the effectiveness of united peaceful, non-violent protest.

Other factors

The experience of black servicemen in the Second World War

- Despite the US army being segregated, black servicemen in Europe had freedoms they had never experienced in America. Even in prisoner of war camps, black airmen were treated as officers regardless of their colour.
- As a result, black soldiers, sailors and airmen supported the "Double-V" campaign: victory against the enemy abroad in the war and victory for Civil Rights at home in America.
- A. Philip Randolph is credited with highlighting the problems faced by black Americans during World War Two which planted the seeds that grew into the civil rights movement of the 1950s and 1960s. A. Philip Randolph was the president of the Brotherhood of Sleeping Car Porters,

a mainly black union. The porters, who travelled on long-distance overnight trains, could carry news between black communities in the rural South and those in northern cities.

- During the Second World War, A. Philip Randolph threatened a mass protest march in Washington unless discrimination in defence industry jobs and in the armed forces was ended. In 1941 Randolph and other black leaders met President Roosevelt with three demands: an end to segregation and discrimination in federal government jobs, an end to segregation of the armed forces and government support for an end to discrimination and segregation in all jobs in the USA.

- As the USA was fighting against Hitler's racist policies in Europe and unwilling to highlight the US's own racism, Roosevelt gave in to some of Randolph's demands and issued Executive Order 8802 which stated that there would be no discrimination in the employment of workers in defence industries and in government on the basis of race, colour or religious beliefs.

- Roosevelt also established the Fair Employment Practices Committee to investigate incidents of discrimination.

- Not all Randolph's demands were met. Segregation in the armed forces and in jobs in the USA continued.

- A positive outcome of the Double-V campaign was the creation of the Congress of Racial Equality (CORE) in 1942 which was the beginning of a mass movement for civil rights. CORE was to play a large part in the civil rights protests of the 1950s and 1960s.

The role of Martin Luther King

- Martin Luther King was an inspirational speaker and leader who was prepared to be arrested, criticised and even put his own life at risk for the cause of civil rights.

- Martin Luther King believed that non-violent, peaceful civil disobedience was the best weapon in the fight for civil rights. King felt that if a law was wrong then the citizens of a country had both the right and responsibility to protest about it. He believed in endless protests to wear down the resistance of white racists.

- Martin Luther King presented a non-threatening image of black protest to the US television audience.

- In 1960 King became president of the Southern Christian Leadership Conference (SCLC) formed in 1957 to coordinate the work of the Civil Rights groups. King became more involved and well known for his use of non-violent civil disobedience in the campaign for civil rights.

- King led many demonstrations in the South which encouraged the development of the civil rights movement. During the Montgomery Bus Boycott 1955, King's leadership inspired the black population of Montgomery to keep up the pressure for Civil Rights.

- Through the effective use of the media, King became famous and publicised the civil rights movement throughout the world in 1964 with the hugely influential "I Have a Dream" speech.

- King urged African Americans to use peaceful methods in the campaign for civil rights. King won international recognition for the Civil Rights campaign when he won the Nobel Peace Prize, also in 1964.

The emergence of effective black leaders

- The Civil Rights campaign was also inspired by the ideas of the black activist, Malcolm X. Malcolm X was an articulate although confrontational speaker who became a preacher for the Nation of Islam and spoke against King's belief in non-violence. Malcolm X believed non-violence meant being defenceless and stated that black people had to

work out their own futures without relying on white help. Malcolm X was one of the first black Civil Rights activists to draw attention to the problems of crime, and unemployment in the ghettos of American cities.

- Many young black Americans living in the ghettos were attracted to the more extreme ideas of Stokely Carmichael and "Black Power". A direct ideas descendant of Marcus Garvey and his "Back to Africa" movement. Many black Americans no longer believed that non-violence was the way forward.

- The Black Panthers attracted attention and headline news contributing to the Civil Rights campaign. The Black Panther Party for Self-Defence was founded in 1966 by Huey P. Newton and Bobby Seale. The Black Panthers represented the opposite of Martin Luther King's ideas and supported the anti-white, black separatist ideas of Stokely Carmichael and Malcolm X. The Black Panthers became very popular among young black Americans in the big cities and gained a lot of publicity. On the other hand, even at the height of their popularity, membership was relatively low and they lost support due to their confrontational tactics.

- The Civil Rights leaders were all effective in attracting media coverage and large followings although other leaders and organisations were eclipsed by media focus on the main personalities.

- The black radicals attracted support for the Civil Rights campaign but also divided opinion across the USA.

The formation of effective black organisations

- In 1960 a group of black and white college students created the Student Non-violent Coordinating Committee (SNCC) to help coordinate, support and publicise the sit-in campaign. Their first target was segregated lunch counters and their use of non-violent protest in the face of provocation gained the Civil Rights movement support across the country.

- The SNCC joined with young people from the SCLC, CORE and NAACP in boycotts, marches and freedom rides. TV news coverage of attacks on the Freedom Riders, for example, shocked the American public.

- The combined actions of these organisations breathed new life into the Civil Rights movement and ended discrimination in many public places including restaurants, hotels, and theatres. These successes furthered encouraged the development of the Civil Rights campaign to demand more.

Any other relevant factors.

Part H: Appeasement and the Road to War, to 1939

52. How important was Fascist ideology as a reason for the aggressive nature of the foreign policies of Germany and Italy in the 1930s?

Context

Fascist belief was founded on the idea of national unity. It totally opposed the idea of internal class division. In the cases of Italy and Germany it was also expansionist in outlook. Mussolini looked to create a new Roman Empire while Hitler sought living space for the "excess" German population. A number of factors led to this.

Fascist ideology

- Fascism was nationalistic in nature; emphasising the importance of loyalty to country (and superiority over others).

- Fascism is often defined by what it dislikes. One fundamental belief was a pathological hatred of communism which led to an anti-Soviet crusade as well as contempt for the "weak" democracies.
- Fascism as seen through Nazism was racist. This belief in the superiority of the "German/Aryan" people [through a crude Social Darwisim] allowed Nazis to perpetuate the idea of a racial mission to conquer the world and cleanse it of "weaker" races.
- Fascism was Militaristic in nature — fascist glorification of war; Prussian/German military traditions/harking back to the glories of the Roman Empire in Italy.
- Fascist foreign policies were driven by Hitler's and Mussolini's own belief, but also their personalities and charismatic leadership.
- Irredentism or the intention to reclaim and reoccupy lost territory, eg Hitler's commitment to incorporation of all Germans within Reich.
- Fascism between the wars was expansionist. Mussolini's "Roman" ambitions in the Mediterranean and Africa; Hitler's ambitions for lebensraum or living space in Eastern Europe and Russia.

Other factors

Economic difficulties after 1929
- In 1929 the US economy crashed leading the world into economic recession. This had a particularly dramatic effect on Germany as unemployment soared to 6 million.
- By 1929 Italy's fascist economic policy was failing; an aggressive foreign policy was useful in distracting the people at home.
- An aggressive foreign policy was also useful in gaining resources for the fascist powers eg Italian invasion of Abyssinia and Hitler's obsession with lebensraum.
- Germany also developed policies to use their economic and political power to make the countries of Southern Europe and the Balkans dependent on Germany. Germany would exploit their raw materials and export manufactured goods to them. It was not a big step to invasion.

The Peace Settlement of 1919
- Determination to revise/overturn Paris Peace Settlement — German resentment of Article 48 which made Germany accept guilt for starting the war, hatred of the reparations bill of £6,600,000,000, disarmament clauses were also a cause of resentment as the German army was reduced to 100,000 men and was not allowed heavy weaponry, lost territory, in particular in the east to Poland was bitterly resented.
- German desire to get revenge for defeat in WW1. Hitler called the treat a Diktat; a dictated treaty forced on a helpless Germany.
- Italy came into the war on the side of the Allies in 1915. She suffered during the war, but hoped to gain land at the expense of Austria-Hungary, in particular the Dalmatian coast. In fact Italian territorial gains were small scale. It was felt that the Italians had suffered and gained little.
- Mussolini in Italy promised to make Italy great again and wipe out the embarrassment of the peace treaties when he gained power in 1922.

Weakness of the League of Nations
- Purpose of the league was to ensure world peace through collective security and disarmament. This the league conspicuously failed to do allowing Fascism to grow unchecked.

- The League was divided politically. Its main supporters had their own domestic audiences which dictated their policies, which led to confusion and inconsistency in the international response to aggression.
- British policy of appeasement and concerns over their Empire.
- French political divisions between the left and right.
- The USA retreated into isolationism.
- There was suspicion of Communist Soviet Russia from the democracies.
- The Peace treaties created many small states in Eastern Europe which were difficult to defend.
- Determined aggression worked as the League failed to stop the Italian invasion of Abyssinia. Even when the League did act, by putting mild sanctions on Italy they were too little, too late.

The British policy of appeasement
- Appeasement was intended to solve genuine foreign policy grievances that had arisen from the 1919 peace treaties, through negotiation.
- British public opinion broadly supported the policy of Appeasement, though there were voices raised in dissent. Many felt that Germany had genuine grievances which deserved to be settled.
- British appeasement to an extent encouraged both Germany and Italy to increase their demands and do so increasingly forcefully. They certainly reinforced fascist belief in the weakness of democracies.
- British attempts to keep Mussolini away from Hitler's influence during the Abyssinian crisis resulted in the Hoare-Laval Pact, which produced a popular outcry when the terms were leaked. Mussolini saw that Britain and France were not opposed in principle to gains for Italy in East Africa and he was able to defy sanctions and keep Abyssinia.
- Hitler knew of British reservations about some terms of the Versailles Treaty and was able to play on these, increasingly realising that he would not be stopped eg rearmament, the reoccupation of the Rhineland and then the Anschluss.

Any other relevant factors.

53. *Military weakness was the most important reason for the British policy of appeasement, 1936—38. How valid is this view?*

Context
Appeasement is the policy of making concessions to another power in order to avoid conflict. Historically, the term is frequently associated with the Prime Minister Neville Chamberlain. The context to the policy is more long term, but the failure of the League of Nations and collective security in the aftermath of the First World War, known at the time as the war to end all wars, forms the backdrop to the policy.

Military weakness
- Run-down state of armed forces following WW1 as Britain disarmed.
- Army: conscription ended post-WW1, scaled right down in size. This plus the demands of Empire meant that the British army was stretched. There was also a lack of investment in developing military technology.
- Navy: not so run-down as other military arms due to the Empire, but not fully maintained. There were many obsolete ships, plus a disturbing lack of awareness of the power of aerial attack.

- Air Force: lack of adequate air defences and fear of aerial bombing. However, there were technological innovations that would save Britain in 1940 such as the development of Radar and effective fighter aircraft, but time was needed to develop military strength. Some believe that Appeasement gave Britain that time.
- Exaggerated assessments of German military strength.

Other factors

Economic difficulties

- In common with other world economies Britain was affected by the 1929–32 economic crisis. Unemployment rose as businesses struggled. This led to the belief that Britain could not sustain a war against the European dictators and maybe Japan in the Far East.
- There was an understandable reluctance to further damage international trade and commerce by threatening war. Commerce thrived on stability and peace.
- Difficulty of financing any large scale rearmament in the face of other economic commitments. At a time when many people were anti-war it was difficult to justify increased military spending.

Attitudes to the Paris Peace Settlement

- Even though Britain was a signatory to the 1919 Peace Settlement, it was seen as too harsh on Germany by many and there was sympathy for what were seen by many as genuine grievances. Reasonable discussion and careful concession would ensure that such grievances would be addressed.
- This led to beliefs such as, "they are only going into their own backgarden" (Lord Lothian) when remilitarising the Rhineland and even sympathy for the Anschluss between Austria and Germany from people like John Buchan who was Governor-General of Canada who states that, "I do not quite see what the fuss is about".

Public opinion

- The fear of another World War had an impact on public opinion. Even though the war had been fought on mainland Europe casualties meant that everyone knew someone who had died and there were visible reminders of the effects of war with injured veterans.
- The memories of losses/horrors of WW1 were vivid and had a real impact on many politicians, especially Neville Chamberlain, the Prime Minister from 1937.
- Isolationist feelings, summed up in Chamberlain's pre-Munich speech where he made the famous statement about, "how horrible, fantastic, incredible it is that we should be digging trenches and trying on gas masks here because of a quarrel in a faraway country between people of whom we know nothing."

Pacifism

- Public anti-war feeling — Peace Ballot, Oxford "King and Country" debate where the students carried the motion that, "This House would not fight for King and Country" by 275 votes to 153. There was a huge reaction to this in Britain and beyond. Fascists saw it as evidence of Britain's weakness.
- East Fulham by-election in 1933 showed strength of anti-war feeling. A Conservative candidate who supported military rearmament saw a majority of 3,000 overturned into a majority of 7,000 for his pacifist Labour opponent. In a democracy such things mattered and the government saw this as evidence of pacifist attitudes.

Concern over the Empire

- The British Empire was huge and its defence was a concern for the government.
- The Empire was thought to be crucial to British economic well-being and to her status as a Great Power.
- Fears that Britain could not defend the Empire against simultaneous threats in Northern Europe, the Mediterranean and the Far East. In 1934 the Committee for Imperial Defence warned that Britain was not strong enough to fight Japan, Germany and Italy together.
- Some accommodation with at least one of the unsated powers was thought essential.
- There was also concern about whether the Empire would answer the call to help Britain in the event of war. At the 1937 Imperial Prime Ministers' Conference, the leaders of the Empire Dominions were unwilling to give a firm commitment to resist Hitler. All had their own memories of sacrifice during World War One.

Lack of reliable allies

- Failure of the League of Nations to police world conflict through Disarmament and Collective Security as well their lack of action in Abyssina.
- France was considered to be unreliable. She had severe political divisions between the political left and right.
- US isolationism after World War One meant a previous powerful ally could not be relied upon to help in the event of war.
- Suspicion of Soviet Russia and their reliability due to the fact it was Communist.
- The relative weakness of successor states in Eastern Europe. Many were small, militarily weak and susceptible to German economic influence.
- Italy was also appeased in vain attempt to prevent alliance with Germany, but after Abyssinia closely allied itself with the Nazi regime.

Fear of the spread of Communism

- Too many in Britain, Communism was the greater political threat to Britain: there was suspicion of Soviet Russia as a result.
- Nazi Germany was also seen as a buffer against Communism by some and destabilising the Nazi regime might lead to questions over communist revolution in Germany.
- Fear of spreading Communism into Western Europe; distrust of French popular Front government; alarm at actions of the Left (more than of the Right) in Spain.

Beliefs of Chamberlain

- Chamberlain's personal control of foreign policy after 1937.
- Chamberlain believed that problems could be solved rationally, by negotiation.

Any other relevant factors.

54. To what extent was the Munich agreement a success?

Context

Czechoslovakia was created after World War One. It contained 3 million German speakers in the Sudetenland. It had a good army and native arms industry. The Czechs had created strong defences along their border with Germany. These Sudeten Germans had not fitted into the successful Czech democracy and were fired up the Sudeten German Party which was financed and controlled by the German Nazi Party. The ensuing crisis was managed by the British Prime Minister through a series of meetings with Hitler.

This culminated in the Munich Agreement which gave the Sudetenland to Germany. The Czechs were not consulted on this agreement.

Munich reasonable under circumstances

- Czechoslovakian defences were effectively outflanked anyway following the Anschluss.
- Britain and France were not in a position to prevent German attack on Czechoslovakia in terms of difficulties of getting assistance to Czechoslovakia.
- British public opinion was reluctant to risk war over mainly German-speaking Sudetenland. This seemed to be true from public reaction to the agreement. Chamberlain was mobbed on his return and spoke to cheering crowds outside 10 Downing Street. He received gifts and thousands of letters of support.
- Britain was military unprepared for a wider war. Her Navy was large and airforce growing, but her army was small and poorly equipped. Britain could not practically intervene on mainland Europe even if she wanted to.
- Lack of alternative, unified international response to Hitler's threats, Britain could not go it alone in the circumstances.
- Failure of League of Nations In earlier crises so there was no alternative to discussion.
- French doubts over commitments to Czechoslovakia. To his surprise, the French Premier was mobbed by enthusiastic supporters of the Agreement on his return.
- US isolationism meant that no help could be expected from the Americans if conflict broke out.
- British suspicion of Soviet Russia in terms of Communism and possible actions in the event of conflict.
- Strong reservations of rest of British Empire and Dominions concerning support for Britain in event of war.
- Attitudes of Poland and Hungary who were willing to benefit from the dismemberment of Czechoslovakia.
- Munich bought another year for rearmament which Britain put to good use.
- Much of the British media was supportive of Chamberlain's actions. There was support from abroad as well with some foreign commentators saying Chamberlain should receive the Nobel Prize for Peace.

Munich not reasonable

- Munich was a humiliating surrender to Hitler's threats.
- Another breach in the post-WW1 settlement. Duff Cooper was the only Government minister to resign over Munich and he commented on the way Hitler had continually broken the Treaty of Versailles over the years.
- A betrayal of Czechoslovakia and democracy. The Czechs had not been consulted and were forced to give up significant resources and their border defences.
- Czechoslovakia wide open to further German aggression as happened in March 1939.
- Further augmentation of German manpower and resources. Germany now controlled the important Skoda works as well as significant coal deposits and other industries.
- Furtherance of Hitler's influence and ambitions in Eastern Europe.
- Further alienation of Soviet Union from the Allies. The Soviets were very suspicious of British and French motives and saw Appeasement as giving into Germany. They could not be trusted. This would have repercussions in 1939.
- A British, French, Soviet agreement could have been a more effective alternative.

- Public opposition was greater than was reported at the time. For example; 15,000 demonstrated in Trafalgar Square against the Agreement.
- Significant political opposition to the Agreement from Labour leader Attlee, Liberal leader Archibald Sinclair and Conservatives like Winston Churchill.
- Cartoonists such as David Low made pointed comments about Chamberlain and the Munich Agreement.

Any other relevant factors.

Part I: The Cold War, 1945–1989

55. To what extent were tensions within the wartime alliance the most important reason for the emergence of the Cold War, up to 1955?

Context
The wartime alliance had always been one of convenience owing to the common enemy of Nazism. America had not recognised the Soviet Communist government's legitimacy until 1933. As the Second World War came to an end the inherent tensions between a Capitalist America and her allies and Communist Russia became all too clear.

Tensions within the wartime alliance

- WW2: suspicion of USSR by allies because of Nazi-Soviet Pact of 1939. Tensions within the wartime alliance as the defeat of Nazism became clear. Soviet Union felt they had done the bulk of the land fighting and wanted security for the USSR.
- USSR suspicions of the USA and Britain over failure to open a second front before 1944.
- Yalta Conference: Stalin determined to hang on to land gained and create a series of sympathetic regimes in Eastern Europe. The USA wanted to create a free trade area composed of democratic states. Soviet actions in Poland, Romania, Bulgaria, etc. in creating pro-Communist regimes and Allied actions in Western Europe, Greece further increased tensions.

Other factors

The US decision to use the atom bomb

- One aim of the use of atom bombs on Hiroshima and Nagasaki was to impress the USSR and make them ready to make concessions in Eastern Europe.
- Stalin knew about the Manhattan Project and refused to be intimidated and in fact it made him even more suspicious of the USA.

The arms race

- Stalin was determined to make the Soviet Union a nuclear power as soon as possible; the development of the arms race.
- British and French were also developing their independent nuclear deterrents — which, realistically, were only aimed at the USSR.
- Development of technologies to deliver nuclear weapons.

Ideological differences

- Impact of 1917 Bolshevik revolution in Russia on relations with the western powers: Soviet withdrawal from WW1, involvement of West with anti-Bolshevik Whites: ideological differences between Communist and Capitalism.
- Fears in the West that Communism was on the march led President Truman to the policy of containment: British power was in retreat: WW2 had been expensive so the British aimed to reduce their world commitments,

specifically in Greece where civil war raged between Communists and Royalists. Fear of similar problems in Italy when allied troops left; activities of Mao in China.

- Truman acknowledged world dividing into two hostile blocs in his speech to support free peoples and proposals to oppose totalitarian regimes — exemplified by the Marshall Plan. Fulton speech by Churchill. Creation of competing military alliances: NATO and Warsaw Pact further polarised the world. The Soviet Union rejected the Western economic model and set up its own economic bloc: Comecon.

Disagreements over the future of Germany

- The Potsdam Conference and policy over Germany whereby the allied sectors remained free as compared to Soviet sector which was stripped of assets as reparations. The economic status of Germany: creation of Bizonia in West. Contrast between the developing capitalist west and centrally controlled east: introduction of Deutsche mark in West led to the Berlin Blockade in 1949.

The crisis over Korea

- Stalin encouraged Communist North Korea to invade Capitalist South. This led to American-led UN intervention on behalf of the South, and resultant Chinese intervention. Soviet and American pilots fought each other across Korea. Stalemate along 38th parallel. The Cold War had been sealed with a Hot War.

Any other relevant factors.

56. To what extent was US foreign policy the main reason for the Cuban Crisis of 1962?

Context

In the years before 1959, Cuba was ruled by a military dictatorship led by General Batista. Batista's government was corrupt and inefficient. A revolution led by Fidel Castro successfully overthrew Batista. Castro eventually moved into the Communist sphere of influence.

US foreign policy

- The presence of a Communist country so close the US mainland was objectionable to the US governments who feared the spread of Communism.
- The United States had placed their Jupiter missiles in Turkey and now the USSR felt very threatened. Kennedy had originally placed the Jupiter missiles in Turkey in 1961 because the United States had feared the possible nuclear capabilities of the Soviet Union. These missiles became a major threat to the Soviets because they were capable of striking anywhere in the USSR.
- In order to defend themselves, and let the United States know what it was like to be surrounded by a deadly threat, the Soviets placed missiles in Cuba. Counter view that the missiles were obsolete.

Other factors

Kennedy's domestic context

- US interests and investments in Cuba had been lost in the revolution.
- Cuban exiles in Florida were vocal in their demands for US action against Castro.
- Background of attempts by the CIA to destabilise Cuba. Kennedy inherited a plan to invade Cuba by exiles in order to overthrow Castro's regime. Bay of Pigs incident, 1961, where 1400 exiles landed and were crushed by Castro's army.
- American aggression seemed to be confirmed by the United States practising the invasion of a Caribbean island with a dictator named Ortsac: Operation Mongoose overseen by Robert Kennedy.

Castro's victory in Cuba

- Castro had come to power in 1959–60 after overthrowing the corrupt, American-backed Batista regime in a Communist revolution.
- Castro was not liked by the US who objected to his policies which redistributed wealth and took over large sugar plantations controlled by US business interests. Castro increasingly pushed towards the USSR, who, for example, bought Cuba's sugar crop when the USA did not.
- Khrushchev was sympathetic to Castro. Some historians argue that he wanted to use Cuba as a launch pad for revolution in Central America. Missile deployment would provide protection for the revolution.
- Argument that Bay of Pigs incident forced Castro to start preparing to defend himself against another attack and drew him closer to Khrushchev and the Soviet Union. Castro asked for significant conventional military aid.

Khrushchev's domestic position

- Criticism of Khrushchev at home over cuts in the armed forces, economic failures and the issues surrounding de-Stalinisation. He believed a foreign policy coup would help improve matters for him at home.
- Foreign policy criticisms: ongoing deadlock over Berlin; shadow of events in Hungary 1956, etc.
- Rise of China as a rival for leadership of the Communist world; pressure on Khrushchev from influential circles within USSR to assert Soviet leadership.

Disagreements over the future of Germany

- The Potsdam Conference and policy over Germany whereby the allied sectors remained free as compared to Soviet sector which was stripped of assets as reparations. The economic status of Germany: creation of Bizonia in West. Contrast between the developing capitalist west and centrally controlled east: introduction of Deutsche mark in West led to the Berlin Blockade in 1949.

The crisis over Korea

- Stalin encouraged Communist North Korea to invade Capitalist South. This led to American-led UN intervention on behalf of the South, and resultant Chinese intervention. Soviet and American pilots fought each other across Korea. Stalemate along 38th parallel. The Cold War had been sealed with a Hot War.

Any other relevant factors.

57. *The danger of Mutually Assured Destruction was the main reason why the superpowers attempted to manage the Cold War, 1962–1985.* How valid is this view?

Context

Events during the Cuban Missile crisis had concentrated the minds of the superpowers leaders and led to a more conciliatory relationship between the USSR and USA. However, each side also had its own reasons for engagement.

Mutually Assured Destruction

- The development of vast arsenals of nuclear weapons from 1945 by both superpowers as a deterrent to the other side; a military attack would result in horrific retaliation.
- So many nuclear weapons were built to ensure that not all were destroyed even after a first-strike, and this led to a stalemate known as MAD. Arms race built on fear.

Other factors

Economic cost of arms race

- Developments in technology raised the costs of the Arms Race.

- The development of Anti-Ballistic Missile technology and costs of war led to SALT 1, and the ABM treaty.
- Limiting MIRV and intermediate missile technology led to SALT 2.
- The cost of "Star Wars" technology also encouraged the Soviet Union to seek better relations.
- Khrushchev's desire for better relations between the superpowers in the 50s and 60s was, in part, about freeing up resources for economic development in the USSR. He hoped this would show the superiority of the Soviet system.
- Gorbachev wanted to improve the lives of ordinary Russians and part of this was by reducing the huge defence budget eg Intermediate Nuclear Forces Treaty, December 1987.

Dangers of military conflict as seen through the Cuban Missile crisis

- In this it worked as the threat of nuclear war seemed very close on the discovery of Soviet nuclear missiles on Cuba in 1962. Before Khrushchev backed down nuclear war was threatened. It also illustrated the lack of formal contact between the superpowers to defuse potential conflicts.
- Introduction of a "hot-line" between the Kremlin and White House in order to improve communication between the superpowers. Khrushchev and Kennedy also signed the Limited Nuclear Test Ban Treaty, the first international agreement on nuclear weapons.

The development of surveillance technology

- American development of surveillance technology (U2 and satellites) meant that nuclear weapons could be identified and agreements verified.
- Example of U2 flight over Cuba where Anderson photographed nuclear sites.
- Also U2 and satellite verification to make sure the Soviets were doing as promised at the negotiating table.
- Some historians think Arms Control would never have taken root, but for the ability of the sides to verify what the other was doing.

Softening of the ideological conflict through policies of co-existence and détente

- Policies of co-existence and détente developed to defuse tensions and even encourage trade.
- Role of others like Brandt in West Germany in defusing tension through their policies of Ostpolitik, etc.

Any other relevant factors.

Part A: The Wars of Independence, 1249–1328

1. *Candidates can be credited in a number of ways **up to a maximum of 5 marks**.*

Possible points of comparison may include:

Source A	Source B
Overall: Both sources agree that events in late 1290 led to a contest for the throne revolving around two candidates Robert Bruce, Lord of Annandale and John Balliol, Lord of Galloway. Both sources also agree that the prospect of civil war led Bishop Fraser, one of the Guardians to ask Edward for help. Both sources also highlight that in writing to Edward, Bishop Fraser took the opportunity to make known his preference for John Balliol as Scotland's future king.	
Source B places slightly greater emphasis on the threat to peace posed by Robert Bruce.	

Source A	Source B
Tragic events in late September 1290 set in motion a struggle for the throne between a number of claimants of whom two were of outstanding importance: Robert Bruce and John Balliol.	It was a second royal death, which heralded the eruption of the rival campaigns of the Bruce and Balliol families to secure the Scottish throne.
While the nobles were gathering at Perth, Robert Bruce, in his seventieth year or thereabouts, had arrived unexpectedly with a strong body of armed men.	At a meeting between the Scots and English ambassadors at Perth Robert Bruce of Annandale arrived with a great following.
It looked as though the question of the succession would be settled by open war between the two claimants and their supporters.	He was also concerned at the terrible prospect of "the shedding of blood" between the rival candidates and their allies.
Bishop Fraser went so far as to write to the English king in October 1290 suggesting that if John Balliol was to come to Edward, the king would be well advised to reach an understanding with him, as the likely king of Scots.	At the same time, one of the Guardians, William Fraser, the bishop of St Andrews wrote to Edward recommending Edward "deal" with John Balliol, whom he believed to be the best claimant to the throne.

2. *Candidates can be credited in a number of ways **up to a maximum of 9 marks**.*

Possible points which may be identified in the source include:

- John Balliol travelled south to Newcastle where on 26 December 1292 he paid homage to Edward I for his kingdom.
- Even as he began to assert his authority it was undermined by Edward's intention to accept appeals from King John's Court.
- When the case of Macduff of Fife came before the Court of King Edward at the November parliament, John was subjected to the most public humiliation.
- King John was made to promise Scottish participation in Edward's proposed expedition against Philip IV of France.

Possible points of significant omission may include:

- King Edward's determination to exercise his authority as overlord undermined and weakened John's authority as King of Scotland throughout his three and a half year reign.
- John swore fealty (loyalty) to Edward at Norham shortly after being awarded the kingship.
- John's inauguration as King of Scots on 30 November 1292 at Scone was attended by English officials.
- Balliol was summoned by Edward to pay homage in December 1292 at Edward's court in NE England. John was summoned, more than once, to Northern England by Edward and crumbled in face of demand he renew his homage.
- Edward's influence was shown when John had to agree to some English members of his government. The new chancellor, Master Thomas of Hunsingore came from Yorkshire and John's chief financial officer was described as a treasurer rather than chamberlain.
- Edward insisted he hear appeals as supreme judge from Scottish courts at Westminster, despite the promises made in the Treaty of Birgham-Northampton that Scottish legal cases would not be heard outside Scotland.
- It was only a week into John's reign when a Burgess of Berwick appealed to Edward, as his Superior Lord, over a court decision made by the Guardians that John had upheld. Edward undermined John's legal authority by overturning one of the verdicts given in the Scottish courts.
- On 30 December Edward declared that any promises made between 1286 and John's enthronement was no longer applicable. On 2 January 1293, under pressure John released Edward from the terms of the Treaty of Birgham, with its guarantees of Scottish independence.
- Edward appeared to use the legal appeals, concerning judgements given in the Scottish courts, as one way of reminding John that he, Edward had ultimate authority over the king of Scots.
- In June 1294 Edward I demanded military service from John, 10 Scottish barons and 16 Scottish barons for his war with King Philip IV of France.
- In 1295, twelve new Guardians were elected by the Community of the Realm to help John stand up to Edward I.
- In October 1295 an alliance was made with France, Edward I's enemy.
- In rebellion against Edward's treatment of John and the Scottish kingdom, the Scottish host assembled in the Borders in March 1296 and attacked villages around Carlisle before retreating back to Scotland.
- Edward laid siege to Berwick, Scotland's largest and most wealthy port, in revenge.
- After a Scottish army was defeated at Dunbar, Edward and his army advanced north, marching as far as Elgin.
- John entered into negotiations with Anthony Bek but was ultimately made to endure a number of humiliations. At Kincardine Castle he was forced to confess his rebellion; on 7th July at Stracathro he was made to formally renounce the treaty with France; finally, on 8 July at Montrose John was made to resign his kingdom to Edward.
- John was brought before Edward and ceremoniously stripped of his royal regalia. The royal coat-of-arms embroidered on his tabard was torn off (Toom Tabard) and his crown, sceptre, sword and ring removed.
- John and his son were taken to England by ship where they spent three years under house arrest, being moved from castle to castle until they were handed over to the Pope. John retired to his estates in France.

Any other valid point of explanation that meets the criteria described in the general marking instructions for this kind of question.

3. *Candidates can be credited in a number of ways up to a maximum of 6 marks.*

Examples of aspects of the source and relevant comments:

Aspect of the source	Possible comment
Author: Monks of Westminster Abbey An English source.	The source is useful as it was written by medieval chroniclers/historians who would have been educated and well informed of important events such as the resistance of William Wallace. The source is less useful as it was written from an English point of view and is likely to be biased against William Wallace.
Type of source: A chronicle.	The source is useful as the chronicle records key local, national and international events and therefore would include details of Wallace's resistance.
Purpose: To record a narrative of contemporary events such as the execution of William Wallace.	The source is useful as this account and commentary on Wallace's execution provides an insight into how the English viewed Wallace's resistance and shows there was still strong feeling against Wallace in England as late as 1305.
Timing: 1305 A contemporary source.	The source is useful as it dates from the time when the Scottish resistance to Edward I had collapsed and Scotland was once more under Edward's rule. Wallace's execution in 1305 finally marked the English defeat of the Scottish resistance.

Content	Possible comment
• A certain Scot, by the name of William Wallace, collected an army of Scots in 1289 at the battle of Falkirk against the King of England.	Useful as it tells us details of how Wallace raised and strengthened a Scottish army and engaged in battle with an English army at Falkirk.
• For acts of treason against the English king, Wallace was dragged to a gallows where he was hanged.	Useful as this accusation of resistance is an insight into the English definition of resistance and treason. Edward's view was that Balliol's surrender of the kingdom of Scotland in 1296 made all the inhabitants of Scotland, and therefore Wallace, his subjects.
• For his sacrilege, the burning of churches in England, his heart, liver, and entrails were cast upon a fire.	Useful as it provides details of how Wallace led resistance against Edward's attempts to control Scotland by leading devastating and destructive raids into England.

Possible points of significant omission may include:

- Wallace killed William Heselrig, the English Sheriff of Lanark.
- Wallace led a resistance movement amongst commoners in the south-west of Scotland, possibly backed by Scottish nobles.
- Wallace, accompanied by Sir William Douglas, led an attack on Scone and attempted to kill the English Sheriff William Ormesby.
- Wallace led attacks on castles and an assault on Dundee.
- There was localised resistance to the English administration in Scotland, especially Cressingham's attempts to raise taxes.
- Robert Wishart, Robert Bruce and James Stewart led a revolt in the south-west of Scotland before surrendering at Irvine.
- Andrew Murray led resistance against Edward's rule in the North. Murray raised his standard at Avoch, in the Black Isle and led a guerrilla campaign, capturing Urquhart, Inverness, Elgin, Duffus, Banff and Aberdeen castles. By August 1297 Murray had succeeded in driving out the English garrison's north of Dundee.
- Wallace along with Andrew Murray led the Scottish army to victory at the Battle of Stirling Bridge, 11th September 1297.
- Wallace and Moray resisted by proclaiming Scotland's freedom from English rule in the Lubeck Letter of 11 October 1297.
- Wallace continued to play a part in the Scottish resistance after the defeat at Falkirk, 1298 and the end of his period as Guardian. It is believed Wallace travelled to the court of Philip IV and later to Rome on diplomatic missions to petition the release of King John.
- Wallace rejoined the resistance in 1303 and was involved in further guerrilla activity in Annandale, Liddesdale and Cumberland.
- There was a rebellion of the McDougal family against the MacDonalds in the Western Isles.
- John Comyn and Robert Bruce were named joint Guardians and carried on the resistance to Edward I. Bruce continued to play a part in the Scottish resistance until 1302. Comyn continued to resist until his surrender in 1304.

Any other valid point that meets the criteria described in the general marking instructions for this kind of question.

Part B: The Age of the Reformation, 1542—1603

4. *Candidates can be credited in a number of ways up to a maximum of 5 marks.*

Possible points of comparison may include:

Source A	Source B
Overall: Both sources agree about the breakdown of the relationship between the Protestant Lords and Mary of Guise. Both sources also agree that Scotland welcomed English intervention. While **Source A** speaks in a negative tone about hopes of reinforcement fading away **Source B** focuses on Scottish resistance.	

Source A	Source B
(In 1559) the Protestant Lords now styling themselves 'the Congregation' mobilised to defend themselves against her forces.	Military operations by the Lords of the Congregation against Mary of Guise began in the summer of 1559.
In January 1560, Queen Elizabeth granted the Lords help: a naval blockade of Leith, followed by an army.	While the arrival of an English fleet and army to assist the Lords between January and March 1560 was helpful, the fortress of Leith still held out.
Guise's forces were besieged in Leith from April till July 1560 and while they were able to repel assaults, their hopes of reinforcement were melting away.	Mary of Guise's French troops were based on a strongly fortified position at Leith, well placed to maintain communications with France and they fiercely resisted the Lords.
Worse, Guise herself was gravely ill with dropsy, and died on 11 June by which time France sent not an army but ambassadors to negotiate peace with the English.	It was Mary of Guise's death, on the night of 10—11 June which opened the way for peace arranged between the English and French commissioners.

5. *Candidates can be credited in a number of ways up to a maximum of 9 marks.*

Possible points which may be identified in the source include:

- As consort to the King of France, Mary's refusal to recognise the Reformation Parliament in Scotland made her position difficult.
- The Catholics of Europe, the Pope, the Kings of France and Spain, and the Earl of Huntly saw her return as the beginning of a Scottish Counter-Reformation.
- Mary made a deal with her half-brother Lord James Stewart, raising concerns when she became the only Catholic in Scotland entitled to hear Mass.
- Mary was driven by her ambition to sit on the English throne and England fearing a revival of French influence in Scotland remained cautious of her.

Possible points of significant omission may include:

- In 1560 Scotland was declared Protestant by Parliament. Mary remained in France. As a Catholic she did not accept the decision of Parliament.
- Mary had the difficult situation of being a Catholic monarch in a land which had become Protestant.
- Mary faced pressures regarding her position towards religion within Scotland. Many Protestants suspected that she would restore Catholicism to Scotland.
- On her return Mary did nothing to reverse the Reformation. Indeed, she gave no encouragement to Catholics and enforced the law against the celebration of Mass.
- Mary was slow to return to Scotland — she did not come back until August 1561 — Francis' death was December 1560.
- She often preferred to hide away with servants and favourites. Having been brought up in France she remained open to French influences.
- As a young woman, working with dominant and ambitious nobles Mary was at an immediate disadvantage.

- Mary became known for her lack of attention to matters of State. By 1564 her attendance at Privy Council meetings had dropped to only five out of fifty meetings.
- When Mary accepted support from half-brother Lord James Stewart and other moderate reformers (she granted James the Earldom of Moray), she faced a revolt from her cousin, the Earl of Huntly. While the reformers guaranteed her personal religion, Mary demonstrated her strength by putting Huntly's corpse on trial and finding him guilty as a result of which his family lost their property. His son was executed. It was clear that being a Catholic did not excuse disobedience. This ambiguity was problematic for Mary.
- On arrival to Scotland Mary showed tolerance to the Protestant church.
- Nobles were to feel neglected by Mary which was one of the reasons for the Riccio murder.
- Mary's marriages created difficulties for her and increased opposition amongst her nobles. Her marriage to Darnley was unpopular amongst nobles.
- The Chaseabout Raid occurred as a result of Mary's marriage to Darnley. After the marriage in July, nobles complained that Mary was wrong to make Darnley 'King' because only a Parliament could do so. England gave refuge to a number of earls including the Earl of Moray after the raid. Mary lost good and trusted servants through this.
- Once Mary had given birth to her son and heir, her opponents believed it easier to replace her.
- Shortly after Darnley's death in 1567, she married Bothwell according to Protestant rites — an unpopular decision which led to the Confederate Lords taking up arms against her.
- Mary believed herself to be the rightful heir to Queen Elizabeth of England. Elizabeth saw her as a threat and was suspicious of her.

Any other valid point of explanation that meets the criteria described in the general marking instructions for this kind of question.

6. *Candidates can be credited in a number of ways **up to a maximum of 6 marks**.*

Examples of aspects of the source and relevant comments:

Aspect of the source	Possible comment
Author: Black Acts were written by advisers to King James VI.	The source is useful as it was written by those in government (Earl of Arran) in consultation with King James. As such, it reflects the views of those influential in ruling Scotland at the time.
Type of Source: Act of Parliament.	The source is useful as it gives an outline of the views of the King as regards the role of bishops in the Kirk as well as asserting the authority of the sovereign over the Kirk.
Purpose: This Act asserts the authority of James VI over the Kirk. In particular, it demonstrates that James favoured a Kirk governed by bishops (and not presbyteries).	The source is useful as it is an assertion of the authority of the King over the Kirk.

Timing: 1584	The source is useful as it was produced during the period when the role of the monarch in the Kirk was subject to debate.
Content	**Possible comment**
Patrick, Archbishop of St Andrews, and the bishops, shall direct and put order to all matters ecclesiastical by visiting the kirks and the ministers.	Useful as it displays James VI's view that bishops should have a prominent role in the Kirk. As a result, the role of Presbyteries was undermined.
Where they shall find persons worthy and qualified they should appoint them to parishes and where those appointed fail in their duties they will be tried by their bishops and lose their livings.	Useful as it recognised that the power of bishops should be extended to both appointing and deposing ministers.
None of his highness's subjects should gather together for holding of councils, conventions or assemblies, where any matter civil or religious is to be discussed, without his majesty's special commandment, and licence obtained to that effect.	Useful as it demonstrates further royal control of religious assemblies. All ministers were required to accept the 'Black Acts' abolishing Presbyteries and asserting royal authority over the Kirk.

Possible points of significant omission may include:
- James's belief that kings should have control over the church led to a powerful struggle which was present throughout his reign.
- Although James had a Protestant education, the Kirk remained suspicious of the King. As the son of Mary, Queen of Scots, James was viewed with suspicion.
- James favouring of Catholic nobility further increased the suspicion of the Kirk.
- The Second Book of Discipline (1578) had proposed a Presbyterian Kirk which could make the church independent of the King and his nobility.
- By 1581 plans to establish 13 Presbyteries appeared to challenge royal authority.
- In 1582, a group of Presbyterians sought to take control of the government by kidnapping the King. The 'Ruthven Raid', as it is known, was designed to increase their hold on power by controlling the King.
- In 1589 the King took action against the Catholic nobles who rebelled in March of that year, gaining support from the Kirk.
- James marriage to a Protestant princess, Anna, daughter of the Danish king in the same year also gained greater approval.
- From 1588–1590 harmony between the Kirk and the King increased.
- In 1592 the 'Golden Act' accepted the recovery of Presbyterian influence within the Kirk, but did not reduce the power of the King.
- Relations with the Kirk deteriorated after 1592, leading to conflict in 1596.
- Extreme Presbyterians like Andrew Melville were marginalised on account of James' views.

- James' belief in the divine right of monarchs clashed with Melvillians' view that the monarch should be accountable to the authority of the Kirk.
- James sought to extend the power of the monarch and bishops over the Kirk by having bishops recognised as moderators of Presbyteries.
- Elders were excluded from Presbyteries and the monarch had the power to determine the time and place of the General Assembly.
- James would ensure that the General Assembly would meet in Perth or Aberdeen where he could expect more ministers to support him.
- 1597 riot in Edinburgh after a sermon preached against the King. James VI had the ministers of Edinburgh briefly imprisoned. The King ordered that no minister was to be appointed without his consent.
- In 1597, Andrew Melville was deposed as rector of St Andrews.
- James attended every General Assembly from 1597 to 1603, by which time assemblies were becoming more agreeable to the King's aims.
- In his writings, James asserted that no human institution could limit the powers of a monarch.
- James' preferred form of Church government was by bishops and in 1600 he appointed three bishops to Parliament.
- Further detail of Trew Law and Basilikon Doron asserting James' views about royal authority.

Any other valid point that meets the criteria described in the general marking instructions for this kind of question.

Part C — The Treaty of Union, 1689–1740

7. *Candidates can be credited in a number of ways up to a maximum of 5 marks.*

Possible points of comparison may include:

Source A	Source B
Overall: Sources A and **B** agree that England and King William were at fault for the failure of the Darien scheme.	
Both sources suggest England was attempting to protect its own interests in its negative approach towards the Scots in Panama. Also, **Source A** emphasises that this led to anti-English riots in Edinburgh. **Source B** suggests that the scheme had a pitiful outcome.	

Source A	Source B
There was significant English political opposition to the scheme.	We lacked the political co-operation of England.
Because of the perceived threat to the English-owned East India Company.	Because the English wanted to protect their East India Company.
King William who viewed the Scots settlers as aliens.	The British king treated us as pirates and enemies, as if we were aliens.
Spanish military opposition to the Scots settlers in Central America.	English did not prevent us being exposed to the hostile rivalry of Spain.

8. *Candidates can be credited in a number of ways up to a maximum of 9 marks.*

Possible points which may be identified in the source include:

- Many MPs knew that the standing of Scotland in the British Parliament would not be that of a kingdom, but of a province of England.
- Cornwall would send almost as many members to Parliament as the whole of Scotland.
- The people cried out that they were Scotsmen and they would remain Scotsmen.
- Scotland had always had a famous name in foreign courts, and had enjoyed privileges and honours there for many years, bought with the blood of their ancestors.

Possible points of significant omission may include:

Arguments against union:

- British Parliament would favour English trade over Scottish.
- Fear of loss of European trade.
- Royal Burghs would be deprived of rights.
- Manufactures may be ruined.
- English currency, weights and measures to be introduced.
- Public opinion against union.
- Protestants feared a British Parliament dominated by Anglican Episcopalian church with bishops' seats in the House of Lords.
- Reduction in status of Scottish nobility in British parliament.
- Scots Episcopalians opposed union and Hanoverian Succession — only Stuart dynasty might restore Episcopacy to Scottish church.
- The creation of 'Scotlandshire' was a genuine fear for opponents of union.
- 45 Scots MPs in the House of Commons was felt to be under-representation.
- Many cherished what Lord Belhaven called 'Mother Caledonia'.
- Opponents of union wanted Scotland to remain an independent nation.

Arguments for union:

- Advantages in commerce and trade.
- Economy would improve — national product would increase.
- Scotland's trade would catch up with other European nations'.
- Free trade with English colonies.
- Protection of being in Great Britain.
- Common interests already with England eg both Protestant countries, geographical proximity.
- Advantages of Scottish politicians being part of the court of the king in London.
- Hanoverian Succession offered security to Protestantism.
- Threat from "Popery" reduced.
- Property rights in England preserved for Scottish people who owned land in England.
- Reduction in civil discord, poverty, oppression from bad ministries.

Any other valid point of explanation that meets the criteria described in the general marking instructions for this kind of question.

9. *Candidates can be credited in a number of ways up to a maximum of 6 marks.*

Examples of aspects of the source and relevant comments:

Aspect of the source	Possible comment
Author: Scottish Parliament	The source is useful as Scottish MPs debated the treaty in parliament for several months.
Type: Act of Parliament	The source is useful as it is official and accurate.
Purpose: To lay out the terms of union with England	The source is useful as the terms contained incentives for MPs to vote for the treaty.
Timing: 1707	The source is useful as this is exactly when union was passed.

Content	Possible comment
There shall be full freedom of trade from the United Kingdom to the Colonies.	The source is useful as it shows one of the economic incentives for voting for union.
Scotland shall be free from paying the Salt Tax for 7 years after the union.	The source is useful as it shows one of several last minute concessions made by the English parliament.
Three hundred and ninety eight thousand and eighty-five pounds and ten shillings shall be granted by the English parliament to Scotland before union, the Equivalent of debts owed to Scotland by England.	The source is useful as it shows the promise of payment to be made to Darien investors, including some Scottish MPs.

Possible points of significant omission may include:
- Votes of presbyterians will secure Union vote in way that it can never be undone.
- Some will vote for Union because it ensures Hanoverian Succession and future security for Scotland.
- Political management of Court Party.
- Squadrone Volante's hold on the balance of power.
- Role of Hamilton as weak leader of Country Party.
- Hamilton's failure to lead planned walkout of parliament.
- Divisions amongst opponents eg Jacobites, Cavalier party, Covenanters.
- Economic assurances about tax rises made to MPs.
- Trade incentives given to parliament.
- Last minute concessions on wool and liquor.
- Financial payments to individual Scots through Lord Godolphin.
- £20,000 paid to Scottish MPs through the Earl of Glasgow.
- Incentives for Scottish nobles such as legal protection to remain.
- Act of Security for the Kirk guaranteeing Presbyterianism in Church of Scotland.
- English spies; Daniel Defoe's role in informing English government about Scottish MPs' views.
- Future stability and security.
- Military argument regarding Scottish protection.
- Scots feared English invasion as English forces were moving north towards end of 1706.

- Scots law to remain.
- Historical argument, all factors for Union in place at same time for the first time.
- Royal Burgh rights to remain.

Any other valid point that meets the criteria described in the general marking instructions for this kind of question.

Part D — Migration and Empire, 1830–1939

10. *Candidates can be credited in a number of ways up to a maximum of 5 marks.*

Possible points of comparison may include:

Source A	Source B
Overall: Both sources agree that Scots migrated due to the Empire Settlement Act of 1922. The sources also both mention that subsidies encouraged people to emigrate. Both sources also agree that emigration allowed Scots to escape from depression and unemployment and finally, to become independent land owners.	
Both sources agree that Canada was perceived as a land of opportunity.	

Source A	Source B
In 1923, 600 Hebrideans took advantage of the year-old Empire Settlement Act to secure passage to Canada.	Rural populations of Canada and other parts of the British Empire were increased by the Empire Settlement Act of 1922.
The unprecedented subsidised state funding also encouraged lowland workers to emigrate.	Travel was possible as subsidies were paid to the emigrants who agreed to work the land for a certain amount of time.
This provided opportunity to escape from the depression and unemployment that blighted the heavy industries of the Central Belt after the First World War.	Both town and country workers also seized this opportunity to escape from the grip of depression and the lack of employment opportunities that existed in Scotland.
Rural lowlanders had been attracted to Canada precisely because it offered the prospect of changing from tenancy to independent ownership.	Many went to Canada where they were offered the chance to become independent landowners, something that there was little opportunity to achieve in Scotland.

11. *Candidates can be credited in a number of ways up to a maximum of 9 marks.*

Possible points which may be identified in the source include:
- Immigration from Lithuania was met with hostility as it was believed that foreigners had been brought into the Ayrshire coalfields to break strikes and dilute the power of the Unions.
- Friction further intensified after 1900 as depression in the coal trade caused successive reductions in miners' wages while Lithuanian immigration into the labour market continued.
- To enhance their economic advantage Lithuanians gave a convincing display of loyalty to the Trade Union which improved relations with Scots.
- Due to their smaller numbers the Lithuanians were not viewed as a threat to the Scottish way of life.

Possible points of significant omission may include:

- Lithuanian immigrants were largely employed in the coal industry.
- Many Lithuanians changed their names to integrate more easily into Scottish society.
- Members of Catholic Irish communities were involved in strikes, trades unions and trades union campaigns which was both welcomed and sought by Scottish workers.
- In the 1830s and 1840s many Scots were repelled by the poverty and disease of Irish immigrants, Catholic and Protestant alike.
- Mixed marriages between Catholics and Protestants became more common as the century progressed, particularly in smaller communities where the choice of marriage partners was less.
- The Catholic Church took steps to develop Catholic organisations and institutions (eg Celtic FC) to develop a distinct Catholic community.
- Pius X's "Ne Temere" decree of 1908 on invalid marriages applied to every marriage of a Catholic, even when marrying someone who was not of his or her faith; this caused much heartache amongst non-Catholics who felt they were continually losing out.
- The 1918 Education Act led to the establishment of Catholic schools.
- In the 1920s the Church of Scotland became overtly hostile to Roman Catholicism.
- As the Scottish economy collapsed in the 1920s and 1930s, workplace discrimination against Catholics grew.
- In the 1920s and 1930s, a few anti-Catholic councillors were successful in local elections in Glasgow and Edinburgh (though many lost their seats at the first defence).
- Anti-Catholic (rather than anti-Irish) disturbances in Edinburgh in 1935 were condemned by the press and punished by the courts.
- The Protestant Irish assimilated more easily into Scottish society.
- Italians were accepted into Scottish society fairly readily, providing a service through cafes etc.
- Italians suffered hostility in the years before World War II as concerns grew about Mussolini's actions.
- Jews settled in central Glasgow, typically setting up small businesses. As they prospered they moved to more affluent suburbs.
- Most immigrant groups suffered minor harassment at various times, both from native Scots and from other immigrant groups.
- Immigrants often settled initially in the poorest areas of towns and cities; in the nineteenth century this meant they suffered from deprivation in overcrowded slums.
- Immigrants in Glasgow particularly suffered alongside the poorer sections of native society from the epidemics of mid-century.
- By the 1890s, both Catholic and Protestant Irish were gaining apprenticeships and beginning to move up the social ladder.
- The First World War and the ensuing slumps led to the collapse of the Scottish economy; this prevented further upward social mobility to a large extent. It also meant there was little further immigration, so that those near the foot of the social structure tended to stay there.

Any other valid point of explanation that meets the criteria described in the general marking instructions for this kind of question.

12. *Candidates can be credited in a number of ways up to a maximum of 6 marks.*

Examples of aspects of the source and relevant comments:

Aspect of the source	Possible comment
Author: Sir Charles Dilke	Useful as Dilke had travelled to India and experienced first-hand the significant impact of Scots on India.
Type of source: Diary	Useful as a personal account of his experience which reflects the broader impact of Scots on India. May be less guarded so source may be more useful.
Purpose: To recount the impact of Scots on India.	Useful as it is a record of the positive impact of Scots in India.
Timing: 1868	Useful as a contemporary account at a time when many Scots had an impact on India eg serving as soldiers and as civil servants.
Content	**Possible comment**
• The stories of the tea and jute industries begin with the Scots and their impact on these industries.	Useful as shows Scots were prominent in the development of tea plantations and the jute industry.
• I was struck by the importance of Scots within the business classes of one of India's largest cities, as Bombay merchants were all Scotch.	Useful as it illustrates the dominance of Scots in the business class of India.
• It is strange indeed that Scotland has not become the popular name for the United Kingdom, particularly with their impact on education, not only in India but across the Empire.	Useful as it illustrates many Indian educational institutions, such as elite schools, owed much to Scottish emigrants.

Possible points of significant omission may include:

Examples of Scots contributing to India:

- Scottish missionaries played an important role in the development of education in India. For example, Reverend Alexander Duff from Perthshire was linked to the founding of the University of Calcutta in 1857 as well as the establishment of the first medical school in the country.
- James Dalhousie used his time as Governor General of India (1848–56) to ban practices of suttee (human sacrifice) and thugee (ritual murder). He also pushed for changes in Indian attitudes to female education.
- In 1857, Scottish soldiers played an important role in crushing the Indian Mutiny. Sir Colin Campbell played a key role.

Examples of Scots who contributed to the development of Canada:

- Some had an impact on politics in Canada, eg John A. MacDonald became first Prime Minister of Canada.

- Scots had a major impact on the development of transport systems in Canada, eg in the Canadian Pacific Railway, George Stephen at the Bank of Montreal helped finance it and Sanford Fleming was the main engineer.
- Scots contributed to the religious development of Canada through the Church of Scotland.
- Scots also influenced educational development in Canada, eg the world-famous McGill University was established with money from the estate of James McGill, a Glasgow emigrant.

Examples of Scots contributing to New Zealand:

- Scots had a major impact on banks and financial institutions. Scots merchants in Dunedin did much for the commerce and prosperity of the Otago region.
- Scots influenced education in New Zealand, eg the 1872 Education Act formed the basis of the education system in New Zealand. Learmouth Dalrymple was behind New Zealand's first school for girls, opened in 1871.
- Scots contributed to political development, eg Sir Robert Stout and Peter Fraser played significant roles.
- Presbyterian settlers created the town of Dunedin, which became an important settlement in New Zealand.
- Scottish settlers established a very strong Scottish community in the Otago region.
- Some Scots had a positive impact on native Maori people, eg Donald Maclean from Tiree learned native language and became the first Native Minister from 1877–80.
- Some Scots had a negative impact as they were involved in taking land from the Maoris.

Examples of Scots contributing to Australia:

- Scots made a major impact in farming in Australia. John MacArthur introduced the first merino sheep.
- A considerable number of Scots came to Australia to invest in mining. Many Scots came for the Gold Rush and some gold camps had a distinctive Scottish character.
- Scots excelled in shipping and trade. McIllwrath, McEacharn and Burns Phillips established a very successful shipping business.
- Many of the pioneers of the sugar industry were Scots and they contributed to the sugar boom of the 1880s in Queensland.
- The Church of Scotland played an important role in developing education in Australia. In Victoria there were a large number of Presbyterian secondary schools and Melbourne Academy was known as the 'Scotch College'.
- Negative impact on native Aboriginal populations, eg Warrigal Massacre.

Any other valid point that meets the criteria described in the general marking instructions for this kind of question.

Part E — The Impact of The Great War, 1914–1928

13. *Candidates can be credited in a number of ways up to a maximum of 5 marks.*

Possible points of comparison may include:

Source A	Source B
Overall: Both sources agree that soldiers of the 16th Battalion, Highland Light Infantry were surrounded after an attack on Frankfurt Trench in what was the last phase of the Battle of the Somme. The sources also agree that the Scots held out with limited resources, despite German attacks, for eight days.	
Both sources highlight the action taken by the Scots showing a determined attitude and fighting spirit.	

Source A	Source B
The Glasgow Boys Brigade Battalion — officially the 16th Highland Light Infantry, who fought their way into the Frankfurt Trench where they were stranded.	The 16th Highland Light Infantry had been trapped by the German counter-attack and were lying low in Frankfurt Trench some distance behind the recaptured German line.
They set about barricading a section of the trench to repel the expected German counter attack.	The Scots who had blocked a stretch of the Frankfurt Trench.
It soon became painfully clear that the men of the 16th Highland Light Infantry were in no position to offer prolonged resistance — of their number only half were uninjured and they only had four Lewis guns with limited ammunition.	Far from being armed to the teeth however, all the Scots had, were four Lewis-guns and a small amount of ammunition.
Against the odds they managed to hold out until 25 November, over a week after the original attack.	It was now Tuesday 21 November and three days had passed but still the Scots soldiers had the fixed intention of defending their position: they held out until Sunday.

14. *Candidates can be credited in a number of ways up to a maximum of 9 marks.*

Possible points which may be identified in the source include:

- Scottish society had to reacquaint itself with mass mortality with the census of 1921 suggesting a figure of 74,000 for war related mortality, nearly 11 per cent of the Scots who enlisted.
- Prior to 1914 the loss of a relative in battle was not a common experience for most Scottish families, but mounting losses now brought this to the forefront of Scottish life.
- The dead of the Great War however were glorified and idealised by the culture of remembrance.
- The Scottish landscape is littered with war memorials, in towns and villages and in places where the number of names on the memorial outnumbers the current population.

Possible points of significant omission may include:

- The Scots responded in great numbers to the call to arms in 1914. The Daily Record reported that within two days of war being declared, six thousand men 'from all classes' enlisted in Glasgow alone.
- By December 1914, 25% of the male labour force of western Scotland had signed up.
- Recruitment levels in Scotland began to fall by the beginning of 1916.
- The Military Service Act of January 1916 imposed conscription on single men in Scotland aged eighteen to forty-one, with exemption clauses covering those in ill-health, engaged in work of national importance, or acting as sole breadwinner with dependents. It also recognised the right of individuals to refuse military service on conscientious grounds. Such cases were to be heard by a local tribunal. In May 1916 the Military Service Act was extended to include married men.

- The ILP, whose main aim was opposition to the war, gradually gained increased strength in Scotland. Branches of the ILP had also taken root in rural locations such as Inverurie, Buckie, Keith and Craigellachie during the war years.
- The No-Conscription Fellowship (NCF) had branches in various locations around Scotland by 1915.
- The Union of Democratic Control (UDC) also opposed conscription and included influential Scottish anti-war protesters.
- Thousands of Scots opposed the war on religious, ethical or political grounds, although only a very small percentage of the Scottish population were pacifists.
- By the end of 1915, the ILP had begun its own register of conscientious objectors and claimed to represent 10,000 men in Scotland.
- Scottish tribunals were not always consistent in their decisions. Glasgow tribunals, for example, were seen to be harsher than others due perhaps to the high number of cases they heard or as claimed by Forward, due to the fact that most COs in Glasgow were members of the ILP.
- By 1917 many cases in Scotland on conscientious grounds were being rejected. Not all COs were treated harshly but those who chose prison rather than non-combat duties, accepted that their sentence would entail hard labour.
- At first the Scottish public accepted increased government control and increased security under the terms of the Defence of the Realm Act, (DORA) as necessary to win the war.
- Scots became increasingly tired of restrictions which were not seen as being directly linked to the war effort such as reduced opening times of pubs.
- Many felt DORA was being used by the government to restrict individual freedoms such as speaking out against the war. DORA allowed the government to censor the press and imprison war protestors.
- Many Scots resented how the government used DORA to make legitimate protest appear unpatriotic. In the reporting of strikes on Clydeside in 1915, the strikers were shown as undermining the war effort.
- During the war years there was an increase in the number of Scottish women employed in the military and manufacturing industries and a temporary decline in employment in some service industries.
- Before the war less than 4,000 women worked in heavy industry in Scotland. By 1917 over 30,000 women in Scotland were employed making munitions. The figure had risen to 31,000 by October 1918, with the vast majority employed in the industrial west.
- A munitions factory at Gretna employed 9000 women workers and a women's police force to keep order.
- Scottish women also worked as conductors on trams and buses, as typists and secretaries and nearly 200,000 women found work in government departments.
- Many Scottish women were involved in the process of dilution, especially in munitions manufacture, strongly represented in the west of Scotland.
- Many Scottish women did not keep their wartime jobs after 1918.
- Some Scottish women were granted the vote in national elections in 1918.
- Rent Strikes saw a prominent role played by women like Mary Barbour, Helen Crawfurd, Agnes Dollan and Jessie Stephens who helped form the Glasgow Women's Housing Association to resist rent rises and threatened evictions.
- These women would even physically oppose sheriff officers ordered to carry out evictions of those who could not pay the increased rents. Their direct action helped win the passing of the Rent Restriction Act freezing rent levels and introducing state intervention in the private housing rental market for the first time. Scottish women became more politicised during the war.
- Unofficial estimates of the Scottish war dead are much higher — at 110 000 deaths.
- The Scottish people wanted their own memorial in tribute to their special sacrifice: Sir Robert Lorimer's Scottish National War Memorial at Edinburgh Castle was opened in 1927 as a national symbol of Scotland's sacrifice and as an attempt to express a sense of indebtedness. Over 148,000 Scottish names are carved on the national war memorial.
- In 1921 the British Legion and British Legion Scotland under Douglas Haig were created to help care for veterans. The Poppy Appeal started at the same time.
- The act of remembrance with a silence at 11am on 11 November started in 1919.

Any other valid point of explanation that meets the criteria described in the general marking instructions for this kind of question.

15. *Candidates can be credited in a number of ways **up to a maximum of 6 marks**.*

Examples of aspects of the source and relevant comments:

Aspect of the source	Possible comment
Author: The Ministry of Munitions.	The source is useful as it has been produced by the Ministry of Munitions who will have expert and detailed knowledge of the impact of the war on Scotland's industries.
Type of source: A report.	Useful because it is an official Government document which will be a factual and accurate account of the impact of war on Scotland's heavy industries. Less useful as it only focuses on the impact of war on Clydeside's heavy industries.
Purpose: To inform the Government of the amount of shells and ammunition being produced in Scotland.	Useful as it highlights the role of Scotland's industries during the war which provides an insight into how the war impacted Scottish industry and the economy.
Timing: 1916	Useful because it is a contemporary account from the time when there was a fear that there would be a serious shortage of shells on the Western Front.

Content	Possible comment
• The increase in the number of workers employed by these great establishments is suggestive of a substantial expansion in business with practically the whole of the output being for the purposes of the war.	Useful as it accurately states that the war gave a big temporary boost to Scotland's engineering industries and to Scotland's old traditional industries which had been facing problems in the years before the war.

• Mr Beardmore and Company, in addition, undertook the management of various National Projectile (shell) factories for the government.	Useful as it accurately illustrates how, during the war, Scottish industries, for example, engineering works were organised to supply the country's need for weapons. Useful as it explains how existing industries were given financial support by the government to manufacture shells.
• Existing works have been supplemented by entirely new factories established for the express purpose of supplying munitions.	Useful as it accurately shows that new factories had to be introduced in Scotland in order to meet the needs of war.

Possible points of significant omission may include:

Wartime effects of war on industry, agriculture and fishing

- Scottish shipbuilding benefited from an increased demand for warships and replacement orders for lost shipping.
- Wartime was good for the steel industry due to the increased demand to build weapons. Ninety per cent of plate armour was produced in the west of Scotland.
- Coal benefited during the war years due to increased demand to power the machinery and fuel the ships built on the Clyde.
- The Jute industry in Dundee benefited during the war due to the increased demand for sandbags and feedbags for horses.
- Scottish agriculture benefited through the government purchase of wool for uniforms and oats for horse feed.
- There was a shortage of farmworkers on many Scottish farms due to so many young men joining up. Women, boys, older men, prisoners and conscientious objectors were all used as farm workers during the war.
- The war resulted in increased mechanisation in Scottish farming as thousands of farm horses were taken for the war effort.
- The fishing industry suffered during the war due to Scotland's east coast ports being taken over by the Admiralty. Ports were at first almost totally closed to fishing although restrictions on fishing were lifted when food supplies became scarce.
- Many boats and crews were used as support to the navy as coastal patrols or for searching for mines.
- In 1918 the Scottish fishing industry faced rising fuel costs and the need to repair and equip boats after war service.
- Revolution in Russia and post war changes in Eastern Europe resulted in traditional export markets for herring in Germany, Eastern Europe and Russia being lost.

Price rises and rationing

- In March 1917, the Board of Trade Labour Gazette published an article on the steady rise of the price of food across Britain. In comparing the price of food from March 1916 to March 1917, the journal reported that there was an average increase of 32%. Potatoes had more than doubled in price; cheese and eggs were 45% more expensive; meat, bacon and butter rose by 30%–35%, flour, milk and sugar by 20%–25%; bread, margarine and fish by 13%–18% and tea by 7%. Those with money could afford the higher prices but ordinary working people suffered the most.
- By the end of the war almost all foods were subject to price control by the government.

- As the war continued, trade and the transport of goods with overseas countries were affected. Certain foodstuffs were in short supply, made worse by panic buying. In February 1918, the Ministry of Food approved a scheme for rationing butter, margarine and tea to maintain levels of distribution throughout the country.
- Full scale rationing was in force in Scotland by April 1918.

Post-war economic change and difficulties

- The Scottish economy suffered as a result of the war due to the disruption of overseas trade. This trade was slow to recover.
- Shipbuilding went into decline when the war ended due to a number of factors including a return to competitive tendering, a decline in the demand for steel and for ships, foreign competition, labour disputes and a shortage of manpower. Between 1921 and 1923 the tonnage built on the Clyde declined from 510,000 to 170,000.
- Heavy industries like iron and steel also faced problems post war. The demand for iron decreased during the war years and although the demand for steel increased during the war other countries increased their steel making during the war years and Scots manufacturers could not compete. As a result, the iron and steel industries were severely affected by the downturn in demand from 1921 onwards.
- The fishing industry faced difficulties due to the loss of markets in Russia and Germany. European countries started to compete strongly with Scottish fleets and in 1920 the government removed the guaranteed price for the herring. The price of herring dropped dramatically; it was no longer profitable; and for twenty years the industry went into a steep decline.
- After the war the jute industry went into decline due to falling orders, worn-out machinery and direct competition from Calcutta in world markets. The price of goods collapsed resulting in mass unemployment, deep social misery and discontent especially in Dundee and several firms went into liquidation.
- Problems in agriculture continued as competition came after the war from cheap foreign imports of food like refrigerated meat from Argentina, frozen lamb and tinned fruit from Australia and New Zealand.
- Post-war Scotland suffered badly from the slump in the world economy.
- Industries like shipbuilding, mining and engineering were badly hit and because these were the main industries in Scotland, the economy suffered more than in the rest of Britain.
- Those returning from war faced poor prospects of getting jobs in agriculture, fishing and heavy industries and unemployment grew in the 1920s.
- Diversification of firms like Beardmores from shipbuilding to tanks to airships.

Post-war emigration

- The 1920s also saw significant emigration from Scotland by people seeking a better life elsewhere. In the inter-war period Scotland had the highest rate of emigration of any European country.
- Many Scots saw emigration as an escape from unemployment, overcrowding and poor housing, at home. In the 1920s three out of ten migrants to New Zealand came from Scotland, many from the depressed industrial areas of central Scotland.
- Many of the people who emigrated came from rural Scotland, where the on-going land issue and land raids continued to be problems.

- Thousands of Scots decided to emigrate helped by the Empire Settlement Act of 1922, a government assisted migration programme.
- Many Scots were also persuaded due to the actions of Canadian government agents travelling around Scotland advertising the attractions of emigrating to Canada such as the availability of land and better employment opportunities.

The land issue in the Highlands and Islands

- Propaganda, recruitment statements and speeches had made a firm link between the Highland men and their land. Some landowners made promises of gifts of land from their own estates to men who had joined up to fight.
- Poverty, overcrowding and hunger in the Highlands, mainly due to the shortage of available land, were exacerbated by the post war decline in fishing especially the collapse of the herring trade which deprived many of seasonal work which had helped sustain many in the past.
- The Land Settlement Act in December 1919 stated that land would be made available for men who had served in the war. It soon became clear however that due to adverse post war economic conditions, the government could not afford to purchase land from the previous owners.

Any other valid point that meets the criteria described in the general marking instructions for this kind of question.

2017
SECTION 2: BRITISH

Part A: Church, State and Feudal Society, 1066–1406

16. *The landed classes played the most important role in feudal society.* How valid is this view?

Context

Feudalism is a term that is used to describe a society that is organised around relationships that emerge from the holding of land in exchange for service or labour. There is debate about what this means in detail, but the relationship between king, nobility, knights and the peasantry is generally agreed to form the basis of feudalism.

The role of the landed classes

- Barons and other powerful magnates received land from the feudal overlords. These lands offered rights and privileges that in turn led to wealth and a comfortable lifestyle.
- These privileges usually gave the barons judicial control and the right to bear arms, build castles and hold tournaments. This often supplemented their income.
- Barons enjoyed a relatively leisured life, with pastimes such as hunting and hawking.
- The main drawback for the landed classes was the requirement to provide military service. This was occasionally dangerous, even fatal. Many circumvented this by providing substitutes or making excuses for non-appearance.

Other factors

The role of the peasant classes

- Peasants played an important part of feudal society, beyond the need for a productive class working in agriculture. It was expected that peasants would run their own day-to-day lives without the need for the feudal lord's presence. Local reeves and bailiffs, appointed by the peasants or the lord himself, would act in his stead.
- Villeins had to organise themselves through the local manor court. The court dealt with sharing the land, fined those that broke the rules, and even brought murderers to trial.
- The feudal term of villein or serf indicated a peasant who was not free to leave his home farm or village. They were bought and sold along with the land and were expected to work at least 3 days a week in the lord's lands without recompense and hand over the best of their produce in exchange for the rent of their farmland.
- Peasants, or villeins, tended to work hard, mostly in the agricultural sector. All the work had to be done by hand and this resulted in long hours of backbreaking work.
- Improvements in agricultural equipment and the use of ploughs drawn by horses instead of oxen speeded up the work and reduced the hours required in the field.
- While work was hard the manor court ensured that everyone had a fair share of the good land to grow their crops. During bad times there were systems in place to share out food so that no one in the village went hungry.
- Not all peasants received the same amount of good farming land, and often it was the case that land was rotated amongst the peasants. This dissuaded them from attempts to improve the land; many did not put in the extra effort when next year their neighbour would reap the benefit.

- Accommodation was often very poor, especially for the lower strata of peasant society. Many peasants lived in poorly constructed one-bedroom dwellings, which they shared with their animals. A single hearth provided all the heat, lighting and cooking facilities.
- Firewood was at a premium; peasants were forced to pay a penny to their lord for the right to pick up fallen wood for the fires.
- Food was basic and, in times of famine, starvation was a real threat. As the 12th century progressed famine became rare in England, since the manor system pulled in isolated communities and helped create new more viable villages throughout the kingdom.
- Archaeological evidence points to homes occupied by small nuclear families, some with upper rooms that indicate a level of privacy previously thought impossible. Evidence of leisure activities included cards, chess pieces, musical instruments and even a football.

Social divisions

- Social stratification was relatively rigid, though it was possible for landowners to rise through the ranks of the nobility, through ability or exceptional service.
- Some peasants famously left behind their humble beginnings, proving that social mobility was possible in the 13th and 14th centuries. William of Wykeham became bishop of Winchester but such rises outside the church were rare.

The changing role of knights — the development of chivalry

- The medieval knightly class was adept at the art of war, trained in fighting in armour, with horses, lances, swords and shields. Knights were taught to excel in the arms, to show courage, to be gallant and loyal. As time went by, the idea developed that they had a duty to protect the weaker members of society and women in particular. This ideal did not always extend beyond their own class.
- Christianity had a modifying influence on the classical concept of heroism and virtue. The Truce of God in the 10th century was one such example, with limits placed on knights to protect and honour the weaker members of society and also help the church maintain peace. At the same time the church became more tolerant of war in the defence of faith, espousing theories of the Just War.

Any other relevant factors.

17. To what extent was the increase of central royal power in the reign of Henry II in England due to the need to develop the economy?

Context

Henry was the son of Geoffrey of Anjou and Matilda, daughter of Henry I of England. Matilda was involved in a dispute with Stephen of Blois, over who should rule, resulting in civil war. Stephen was appointed King of England by the Church and reigned, 1135–1154. However, on Stephen's death, Matilda's son, Henry became King of England. Henry's aims were to preserve the Angevin dominions, strengthen royal authority and increase royal revenues.

Need to develop the economy

- Henry II established the exchequer under Nigel of Ely to rein in sheriffs who failed to pay taxes and ensure scutage and other forms of aid and direct taxes were paid on time. Constant warfare during the Civil War between Stephen and Matilda meant barons and sheriffs had become increasingly lax in paying their taxes.
- Nigel of Ely, a cleric, was installed by Henry to administer revenue eg feudal dues, scutage, justice, towns and land.

- In general Henry oversaw a more settled age in England, which encouraged trade as did Henry's acquisitions abroad. This in turn helped Henry with revenue, but also stimulated Henry's positon in the international world eg his acquisition of Guienne stimulated the west-country ports.
- The industrial centres of Flanders depended on English wool and welcomed grain from fertile East Anglian and Kentish fields.
- There was a European demand for English metals.
- Henry's England was at the centre of the Angevin Empire and the French speaking world.
- The period saw an increase in literacy eg all of his sons (Richard, Geoffrey & John) had some education.

Other factors:

Impact of the Civil War

- Civil War had developed during the disputed reign between Stephen and Matilda, after the death of Henry I.
- Bulk of the fighting was in Wiltshire, Gloucestershire and nearby private wars developed.
- There was some devastation of land due to the Civil War eg 1143–4 Geoffrey de Mandeville laid waste to the Fens and in 1147 Coventry and surroundings was laid to waste by the king.
- In financing the Civil War Stephen began with a full treasury, however, the Exchequer was disorganised and yields from land were low. During the Civil War barons and sheriffs had become increasingly lax in paying their taxes. So the development of the royal administration during Henry II's reign is due, in part to the need to increase the Royal finances eg this led to changes to the Exchequer, which improved the methods for receiving his revenues, as well as development of the Chamber and the use of sheriffs.

Growth of the nobility

- During the time of the Civil War in England the barons had increased in stature and political importance due to both sides vying for their support. As a result, barons built castles without royal permission, increased the numbers of knights beyond limits agreed by their charters, acquired land illegally and many hired large armies of Flemish mercenaries. Henry, as King of England exiled those barons who did not support him. He successfully restored order in England by dismantling illegally built castles.
- Changes in taxes were also needed to firm up revenue, but also to formalise Henry's relationship with his main tenants-in-chief.
- Many of his actions were to re-establish the authority of the king after the chaos of the Civil War and that meant action against those who had used the Civil War as an opportunity to extend their own power.
- Henry vigorously pursued the destruction of illegally built castles and the recovery of former royal strongholds that were now in baronial hands. For example, he took action against resistance from William of Amuale who refused to surrender Scarborough castle.
- Henry's introduction of scutage allowed him to get around the problem of 40 days' knight service.
- Many lesser nobles were employed as his royal administration expanded.

Cost of warfare

- In part royal government developed in order to fund warfare, which had become increasingly expensive in the 12th century.

- Henry recovered land lost during the Civil War between Stephen and Matilda eg Northumbria from the Scots, he forced Owen Gwynedd of Wales to do homage.
- Scutage was levied on the knight's service owed to the baron, rather than owed to the king. In the process it also enabled Henry II to ensure they had sworn allegiance to their king as well as their lord.
- Henry had various military needs, to defend his lands across the Angevin Empire, to recover lost territories, to keep vassals abroad in check and to crush uprisings across the extensive Angevin Empire. The Great Baronial Rebellion of 1173—4 also shook him, although they were won in Henry's favour. In short he needed an army at times and that had to be paid for.
- Previously direct taxation had been on landed property, but to get money for crusades Henry ordered a tax on moveably property and in 1188 a Saladin tithe [one tenth of the value of rents].
- By the end of the period there was a soundly organised field army with the administration to produce the money for this.
- Fortifications were also repaired and by the end of the period all Norman castles were part of a general defence plan.
- This increased organisation can be seen in the Assize of Arms of 1181 — a survey of resources.

Law and order

- Key appointments to the office of Justiciar, such as Richard de Lucy and Robert de Beaumont, helped run a more effective the legal system for Henry, dealing with land matters, criminal matters and overseeing the sheriffs of England.
- Henry favoured the extension of royal jurisdiction, partly for its contribution to the domestic peace and partly for its financial rewards to the crown, but also to extend control over his tenants-in-chief.
- Henry II is remembered as the creator of Common Law. He inherited the 'Good Laws' from his grandfather Henry I. He had first used feudalism to enhance the power of the Crown. Henry II developed a central administration beyond previous lines.
- There was a general need to rationalise law and marry the Anglo Saxon with the Norman practices in order to simplify the system and stop people playing the system. Change was gradual throughout Henry's reign and did not conform to some grand plan, but royal power did increase as a result of them.
- Henry believed that too few offenders were put on trial or caught. He reasserted royal jurisdiction over major crimes and sought to improve the efficiency of the legal process.
- Henry II extended the power of the Curia Regis, the royal court. Writs were issued. Royal officials gave judgements in local courts. In some areas Henry appointed local magnates to act as permanent royal justice. This gave Henry a notable increase in royal authority and the power of the crown. Restoring the law and order established by his grandfather, Henry I.
- The Assizes of Clarendon (1166), modified by the Assize of Northampton (1176) for example, widened the scope of royal justice, now including indictment and prosecution of local criminals.
- Regional inquest juries should meet periodically under the royal eye to identify and denounce neighbourhood criminals.
- Extension of the king's justice into land disputes, which had once been dominated by the baronial courts, through the Assize of Novel Disseisin and Grand Assize. These rationalised a mass of local laws and customs into a uniform royal law — a 'common law' by which all subjects were ruled. They speeded up the judicial process, but also placed decisions in the hands of the king's own justices-in-eyre, going over the heads of the powerful local tenants-in-chief.
- Henry II recognised the need to assert Royal Authority over Church Authority in matters of criminal law. Thomas Becket, Henry's loyal Chancellor, was appointed Archbishop of Canterbury in 1162. The Constitution of Clarendon listed the state-church relations. Henry's failure, and the death of Becket 1170, did little to harm his royal authority.

Effects of foreign influence

- Henry reigned for almost 35 years, but he spent 21 years away from England, in France. Henry II inherited Normandy from his mother and his father, Anjou, Maine and Touraine. In 1152 his marriage to Eleanor, saw Henry become Duke of Aquitaine. However, revolt from his sons and wife in 1173—4. Crushed, but further rebellion from young Henry over fears of Henry II favouring John. Ended when young Henry died of a fever. Succession passed to Richard. Henry II lost his authority before his death as Richard and King Philip II of France combined their forces against the dying English king.
- The Angevin Empire ranged from the border with Scotland, to the border with Spain, and was united on only one sense, loyalty to Henry II.
- Arguably, the demands of holding this disparate group of lands together led to the need for taxation and a capable army.
- Foreign influence in England, especially from the Norman Lords who had extensive landholdings in both Normandy and England.
- Some unity of government was necessary, however, and can be seen with the use of the Exchequer system throughout the Empire.
- Use of the Seneschal's court — use of same legal procedure and interpretation of laws.

Any other relevant factors.

18. How important was the Black Death as a reason for the decline of feudal society?

Context
The decline of feudalism happened as the previous order of society where land was exchanged for economic or military service was challenged. Economic developments, which changed the relationship between peasants and lord as well as the development of new ways to trade and pay for labour/service led to its decline.

The Black Death
- The population decreased between 33% and 50% during the Black Death.
- The decline in the population meant that the survivors, particularly of the lower classes, could demand and often received better wages for their labour. Wage levels in England roughly doubled. Indeed, the shortage of labourers is often seen as causing the decline of serfdom in Western Europe.
- Landowners for the first time needed to negotiate for their serfs' services, leading to higher wages and better living conditions for those that survived.

Other factors

The Peasants' Revolt

- In England, the attempts of the Statute of Labourers in 1351 to force peasants back into serfdom were widely and strongly resisted. The extent of the revolt and the impressive way in which it was organised shows that the old feudal consensus had broken down.
- There is an argument that the Peasants' Revolt was a reaction to the attempts to force peasants to return to the old ideas of labour services.
- The use of the Poll Tax was a trigger to the revolt by secular leaders, John Ball and Wat Tyler.

The growth of towns

- Many found the freedom of burgh life allowed them to develop trade without the burden of labour services or restrictions in movement.
- There was a movement from the countryside to the towns which saw a growth.
- Economy in towns did not depend on the ownership of land, rather on the production and selling of goods.

The growth of trade/mercantilism

- With markets for their goods fluctuating considerably, many nobles came to understand their weak economic position. For some it was better to let their peasants become tenants who rented their land than to continue as their feudal protector.
- Others discovered that sheep were a far more profitable resource than peasants could ever be. The monasteries in particular turned over large areas to sheep pasture to capitalize on the strong demand for wool.
- Peasants who could afford to purchase or rent extra land could propel themselves upwards on the social ladder.

Changing social attitudes

- Social mobility was increasing for a number of reasons, including the move to an economy based more on cash than service. In England the wars against France had brought riches to some, and enabled them to climb the social ladder.

Any other relevant factors.

Part B: The Century of Revolutions, 1603–1702

19. *Religious issues were the main reason for the problems faced by King James after the Union of the Crowns in 1603.* **How valid is this view?**

Context
James VI of Scotland became James I of England in 1603. He had been used to absolute rule in Scotland and expected the same in England. However, the English parliament would not accept the Divine Right of Kings, and expected to wield some power itself.

Religious issues – Presbyterianism

- James I had a lifelong hatred of Puritanism; Puritans existed in large numbers in the House of Commons and were demanding church reform.
- The king feared moves towards Presbyterianism and rejected the Millenary Petition at the Hampton Court Conference of 1604, saying 'no bishops, no king', and vowing to maintain an Episcopalian Church of England.
- Puritans existed in large numbers in the House of Commons and were demanding church reform early in James I's reign.

- In 1607 the House of Commons presented a Petition for the Restoration of Silenced Ministers, requesting the reinstatement of preachers who had been previously dismissed for their Puritan views. This set MPs in direct opposition in policy terms to the sitting monarch.

Religious issues – Roman Catholicism

- James I relaxed the Recusancy Laws against Roman Catholics, which revealed that there were more Roman Catholics than many in the House of Commons had feared.
- The Gunpowder Plot of 1605 increased tension and turned many against Roman Catholics.
- Parliament was horrified that the king allowed his son to marry a Roman Catholic French princess and allow her to celebrate mass privately at court.
- Furthermore, James I admired the religious power of the monarchies in France and Spain, both Roman Catholic countries and England's traditional enemies.
- James conducted many negotiations with the Spanish Ambassador, Count Gondomar, whose influence at court many Puritans resented. In 1604 they concluded a peace, bringing their nineteen-year war to an end with the Treaty of London.
- Eventually the king issued the House of Commons with the Rebuke of 1621, a ban on discussing foreign policy so that he could forge stronger links with Spain. This generated much anti-Catholic feeling amongst James I's political opponents who disapproved of this developing relationship.

Other factors

Economic issues

- James I wanted to exist financially independent of Parliament and manipulated the statute books to re-impose anachronistic laws which were designed merely to raise revenue.
- Fiscal devices such as monopolies and wardships were unpopular.
- The king alienated his natural allies in the House of Lords by selling honours and titles and appearing to devalue the status of the aristocracy.
- Increases in customs duties led to the Bates Case in 1606 which James I won, although Parliament declared the duties illegal in 1610.

Divine Right of Kings

Political issues

- Parliament had been encouraged since the days of Henry VIII to make policy, and therefore its members felt they could criticise the Crown freely; however, James I asserted the Divine Right of Kings as he claimed he had been accustomed to this in Scotland, which made his status as a foreigner more unattractive to the English Parliament.
- The House of Commons opposed James I to such an extent that the stability of the nation was affected.
- The king conceded defeat in the Goodwin Case which gave Parliament fresh impetus to challenge him further.
- James I attempted to curtail Parliamentary freedom of speech by imprisoning outspoken MPs in the Tower of London when Parliament was dissolved.

Law

- James I attempted to control the court system by appointing judges who would favour the Crown; Parliament saw this as unfair and objected to the abuse of power.

- The king imposed martial law in towns where troops were preparing to embark on foreign campaigns; Parliament opposed this.
- The king billeted troops in the homes of civilians in order to enforce the law.

The difficulties of ruling both countries — England and Scotland

- Parliament in London rejected the king's proposed union between Scotland and England as they felt he was making no attempt to understand the English constitution, which accorded greater powers to Parliament in London than were accorded in Edinburgh.
- James I sought to obtain greater taxation in Scotland, and employed members of loyal clans as government agents, at considerable expense, to extract payment of overdue taxes or fines.
- James I exerted his influence in the Highlands with force, giving permission for certain clans to attack clans who had not professed loyalty to him.
- As legitimate king of Scotland, James I (and VI) was carrying out a role into which he had been born; however, his position in trying to maintain rule over two kingdoms, and the dominance of England, meant Scotland proved to be more than a minor irritation in his attempts to achieve stability.

Any other relevant factors.

20. How important were foreign matters as a reason for the failure to find an alternative form of government, 1649—1658?

Context

The English Civil War formally ended in January 1649, with the execution of Charles I. Oliver Cromwell ruled during the Interregnum. He abolished the monarchy and attempted at constitutional rule through including the Council of State, the Barebones Parliament, and the First and Second Protectorate Parliaments.

Foreign matters

- Faced with possible invasion, Cromwell was forced to fight several battles to control Scotland.
- He had to put down rebellions in Ireland by Royalists and Catholics brutally, which caused further resentment and hostility.
- War was waged on Holland to enforce the Navigation Acts.
- In the mid-1650s war with Spain caused increased taxes.
- Foreign affairs led to social issues such as coal shortages in winter 1652—3 not being addressed appropriately, and increasing instability in England.

Other factors

Dependence on the army

- Army officers formed the Council of State with the Rump Parliament. Extremists in the army opposed Parliament's role in governing the country.
- The creation of a military dictatorship from 1653 drew comparisons with the Stuarts' martial law, as did the formation of the first Protectorate in September 1654 and the drawing up of military districts under major-generals during the second Protectorate from October 1656.
- Parliamentarians resented the influence of the army on constitutional affairs throughout the Interregnum.

Cromwell's dominance

- Cromwell dominated politics and was in a unique position to influence the direction of the country; however, he was a contrary character.

- Cromwell espoused democratic principles but acted in a dictatorial manner, as he knew an elected government would contain his enemies.
- Cromwell's roots were in Parliament but his rise to the rank of general during the Civil War meant he favoured the military during the Interregnum.
- Cromwell was conservative but many policies were ahead of his time, such as relief for the poor and insane during the Barebones Parliament.
- Cromwell was a Puritan but passed progressive reforms, such as civil marriages, which horrified many Puritans.

Parliament

- The Rump Parliament consisted of MPs who had failed to avert Civil War in 1642 and who now had to address the same problems in 1649.
- Puritans amongst MPs viewed church reform as their priority.
- Parliament was opposed to the role of the army, and wanted to have a greater say in drawing up the constitution.
- Quarrels between MPs and army officers were a feature of the Interregnum.
- Parliament opposed toleration, thus preventing religious wounds healing.

Absence of monarchy

- After Charles I's execution in 1649, the Council of State abolished the monarchy and declared a Republic, or Commonwealth; now there was no monarchical check on Parliamentary power.
- In Scotland, Charles II was crowned king and some of his supporters wanted him to ascend the throne in England also.
- Without a king in England, Cromwell ruled on his own during the Interregnum, drawing comparisons with Charles I's 11-year tyranny.

Unpopular legislation

- The Treason Law and Censorship Law were introduced in 1649; in 1650 the Oath of Allegiance was imposed for all men over 18.
- The High Court was abolished in 1654, causing a backlog of 23,000 cases.
- The Barebones Parliament was accused of introducing too many reforms in too short a space of time.
- The constitution was drawn up solely by army officers.
- Roman Catholics and Anglicans were excluded from voting by the First Protectorate, which also introduced strict moral codes that curtailed popular forms of entertainment and enforced the Sabbath.
- The Commission of Triers and Committee of Ejectors, who appointed clergymen and schoolmasters, were unpopular with the church.
- A 10% land tax was resented by the aristocracy; taxation in general was increased in order to fund wars with Spain.
- Cromwell's approval of his son Richard as his successor led many to feel that Cromwell viewed himself as a monarchical figure.
- Royalists accused Cromwell of regicide.
- Army extremists pushed for greater martial authority.
- Presbyterians impatiently demanded church reforms.

Inexperience

- The Barebones Parliament consisted of many well-intentioned but inexperienced figures who proved incapable of using power effectively.

Doomed from the start

- All the pre-Civil War problems — such as religious, political, legal and economic issues — plus additional foreign policy issues, meant that Cromwell was always going to encounter difficulties.

Any other relevant factors.

21. To what extent did the Revolution Settlement significantly alter the authority of the monarch, 1688–1702?

Context

After the reign of Charles II, James II ruled between 1685 and 1688. His attempts at absolutism led to the Revolution of 1688–9. Parliament invited the king's daughter Mary and her husband William to become joint monarchs. A series of agreements made between 1689 and 1701, legalising the division of power between Parliament and the crown, became known as the Revolution Settlement. This included the Bill of Rights, limiting the power of the monarch.

Finance

- Parliament granted William III and Mary III £1,200,000 for court expenses in 1689, including £700,000 to pay civilians working for the state; these became fixed annual amount in the Civil List Act of 1697.
- A Procedure of Audit was established for MPs to check royal expenditure; crown financial independence was no longer possible.
- The 1689 Bill of Rights stated the monarch could no longer levy taxes without Parliamentary consent; House of Commons now agreed an annual Budget proposed by the Chancellor of the Exchequer, who between 1690 and 1695 was Richard Hampden; fiscal power now lay in the hands of Parliament rather than the crown.
- However, the monarch benefited from no longer having to resort to unpopular methods of raising revenue; from now on it would be Parliament that incurred the wrath of citizens for increasing taxation.

Religion

- Parliament passed the Toleration Act of 1689: toleration of all Protestants except Unitarians, those who did not acknowledge the Holy Trinity, and Roman Catholics. Parliament ensured Roman Catholicism could no longer be accepted.
- Although Non-Conformist Protestants could now worship freely, the new law maintained an Exclusion from Public Office clause, so they could not obtain teaching positions at universities or elected posts in towns or the House of Commons.
- The Toleration Act insisted that Non-Conformists take the Oath of Allegiance and Supremacy as a condition of their religious freedom.
- Toleration Act stated the king was supreme Head of the Church of England. 400 Non-Jurors — priests and bishops refusing to acknowledge William III — were expelled from their posts by Parliament.
- However, the king, as head of the church, now had the power to appoint bishops and archbishops.

Legislation

- 1689 Bill of Rights stated monarchs could no longer require excessive bail to be demanded from defendants nor ask judges to impose cruel punishments.
- Ministers impeached by the House of Commons could not be pardoned by the crown.
- In 1695 the Treason Act was altered to give defendants' rights to be told the indictment against them, to be defended by Counsel, to call witnesses in their defence, and to demand that there be two witnesses against them to prove a case instead of the previous one.
- Act of Settlement 1701 stated judges could only be removed from their positions if Parliament demanded this.
- However, monarchs could still appoint judges.

Parliament

- William and Mary agreed to the Bill of Rights in December 1689, legalising new relationship between Crown and Parliament.
- Bill of Rights made it clear monarchs could no longer use royal prerogative to suspend or dispense with laws passed by Parliament, and could not interfere in Parliamentary elections.
- Bill of Rights also stated from now on MPs and peers could not be punished for exercising Parliamentary freedom of speech.
- Licensing Act was repealed in 1695, removing restrictions on freedom of the press to report Parliamentary criticism of Crown.
- Revolution Settlement provided for a Triennial Act passed in 1694. This was intended to keep MPs more closely in touch with public opinion. Parliament was now more relevant to voters than ever before, although voters were still the landed classes.
- However, the Revolution Settlement still allowed monarchs executive power, so they could dismiss Parliament at will and also rule alone for up to three years, and could still appoint peers.

The succession

- Bill of Rights of December 1689 declared no Roman Catholic could become king or queen in the future, and all future monarchs should be members of Church of England.
- Act of Settlement 1701 stated if William and Mary had no heirs the throne would pass to Sophia of Hanover, Protestant daughter of Elizabeth of Bohemia, sister of Charles I. However, the Hanoverian Succession was desired by William anyway, and so the crown was getting its own way.

Scotland

- In April 1689, the Scottish Parliament passed the Claim of Right removing James VII (James II of England) from the throne and approving William II (William III of England) and Mary II as his successors. The new monarchs' acceptance of this suggests that in Scotland there was a contract between crown and the people.
- Scotland was to be allowed to have its own Presbyterian Kirk.
- Scottish Parliament would have a greater share in the government of Scotland and more say in the passing and enforcement of Scots law.
- However, the crown influenced Scotland by appointing ministers who would not challenge English policy.

Ireland

- Treaty of Limerick 1691 brought an uprising led by James II's French and Irish volunteers to an end and stated Irish Roman Catholics would enjoy same freedoms as under Charles II, and land confiscated from Roman Catholics by Oliver Cromwell was given back.
- The Treaty also stated Jacobite soldiers captured at the Battle of the Boyne in July 1690 were allowed to flee to France. 14,000 soldiers and their families left. However, promises to treat Roman Catholics better were broken by the Penal Laws of 1693–94, excluding Roman Catholics from the learned professions and elected public office.

The status of the army
- Bill of Rights stated the monarch could not maintain a standing army during peacetime. The Mutiny Act of 1689 legalised the army, and had to be passed annually by Parliament, forcing the king to summon Parliament.
- However, the king controlled foreign policy, had the final say on the decision to send the army to war or to sign peace treaties, and used his patronage to appoint officers in both the army and navy.

Any other relevant factors.

Part C: The Atlantic Slave Trade

22. How important were racist attitudes as a reason for the development of the slave trade?

Context
The Atlantic Slave Trade developed as West Indian plantation owners increasingly looked to the continent of Africa for a new supply of labour. The enslavement of millions of Africans was justified by racist beliefs that Africans were inferior to Europeans.

Racist attitudes
- The unequal relationship that was created as a consequence of the enslavement of Africans was justified by the ideology of racism — the belief that Africans were inferior to Europeans.
- Entrenched racism among members of the merchant and landowning classes meant that enslaving African captives was accepted by colonists.
- Many Europeans claimed that African captives would suffer if the slave trade was abolished eg criminals and prisoners of war would be butchered and executed at home.
- Many colonists believed that slaves were suited to work on the plantations and were fortunate to be provided with homes, protection and employment, in the care of enlightened Europeans rather than African despots.

Other factors:

Military factors
- The European wars of the 17th and 18th centuries impacted on the development of the Atlantic Slave Trade. As result of these battles Britain came to play a dominant part in the Atlantic Slave Trade.
- The Seven Years War was chiefly an imperial war fought between Britain, France and Spain and many of the most important battles of the Seven Years War were fought at sea to win control of valuable overseas colonies. Britain emerged from the war as the leading European imperial power, having made large territorial gains in North America and the Caribbean, as well as India. Slave labour was necessary to exploit these gains. As the number and size of Britain's colonies grew, so did the number of British plantation owners and slave traders.

Importance of West Indian colonies
- Crops such as sugar cane became highly profitable which led to planters buying enslaved Africans in growing numbers. Islands such as Jamaica which specialised in sugar production became one of the largest disembarkation points for slaves in the West Indies.
- The slave trade generated finance — it was an important source of tax revenue and West Indian colonies were an important source of valuable exports to European neighbours.

- Financial, commercial, legal and insurance institutions emerged to support the activities of the slave traders. Slave traders became bankers and many new businesses were financed by profits made from slave trading.

Shortage of labour
- Large scale plantations became big businesses and required larger labour forces to sustain production.
- Huge profits made from the trade in tropical crops created a demand for labour to work on plantations in the colonies. Crops such as sugar cane required a large labour force to plant, look after, harvest and process crop in harsh conditions.
- There was a labour shortage in the West Indies due to the high death rate among native populations due to the lack of resistance to diseases brought by Europeans and the harsh conditions and ill-treatment at the hands of colonists.

Failure of alternative sources of labour
- The slave trade developed due to the rapid decline in the number of indigenous peoples who were first used as a source of labour in the West Indies. Poor diet and European diseases were largely responsible for this. Although compared to the later enslavement of Africans, the use of the native populations was on a small scale. The number of indigenous peoples on the islands was not large enough to meet the planters' demands. Few colonists were also willing to work voluntarily on the plantations as manual labour.
- There was a limit to the number of British criminals who could be sent as forced labour. Britain had very harsh laws in the 18th century with 300 capital crimes, examples would be pick pocketing more than 1 shilling, shop lifting 5 shillings or more, stealing a sheep or a horse, poaching rabbits. Transportation to the West Indies was seen as an alternative to hanging. Some of those transported were for political or religious reasons. For example, many Jacobites were treated in this way. As political upheavals subsided, the number of political prisoners declined.
- There was also a lack of indentured servants. These poor Europeans would sign a contract binding them to work for a fixed period, usually 3—7 years, in return for their passage abroad and food, clothes and shelter although it was not unknown for poor people in cities such as London and Bristol to find themselves on ships to Jamaica after being kidnapped or plied with drink. Some Europeans were classed as Redemptioners: they arranged with the ship's captain, to pay for their passage within a specified time after arrival or be sold to the highest bidder.
- Historian Eric Williams has argued that there were not enough indentured servants to replace those who had served their time and that escape was much easier for Europeans. As a result, for economic reasons plantation owners started to turn to African slaves for labour. Williams argues that the decisive factor was the fact that enslaved Africans were cheap and that while an indentured servant would be working for a limited number of years, the enslaved African would work for life. For a while European indentured labour existed alongside enslaved Africans but as African slavery increased, European indentured labour gradually came to an end.

Legal position
- The legal status of slaves as property, which meant they were considered commodities rather than humans, was long established.

- It took a series of court cases from the 1770s that dealt with the rights of former slaves within the British Isles to challenge the legality of slavery and the slave trade eg Granville Sharp's resolute campaign to prove the illegality of slavery in England that culminated in Lord Mansfield's decision in the Somerset ruling. However the legal position of African slaves remained unclear until the early 19th century.

Religious factors

- The Church of England had links to slavery through the United Society for the Propagation of the Gospel missionary organisations which had plantations and owned slaves. The Church of England supported the laws not to educate enslaved Africans.
- Some Bible passages such as the Curse of Ham from Genesis were used to justify slavery. Other Bible passages such as Exodus were banned in British colonies because they could be interpreted as being anti-slavery.
- Many believed that Africans benefited from slavery as they became 'Christian'. This would result in the spread of 'civilization'. This however did not necessarily mean that they would be treated as equals.
- Some clergy tried to push the idea that it was possible to be a 'good slave and a Christian' and pointed to St Paul's epistles, which called for slaves to 'obey their masters'.
- However very little missionary work actually took place during the early years. Religion got in the way of a moneymaking venture by taking Africans away from their work. It also taught them potentially subversive ideas and made it hard to justify the cruel mistreatment of fellow Christians.

Any other relevant factors.

23. To what extent did the slave trade have negative implications for African societies?

Context
It has been estimated that at least 12 million enslaved Africans were forcibly transported to the West Indies as a result of the Atlantic Slave Trade. In addition, the long term implications of the slave trade for African societies affected many millions more.

The slave-sellers and European 'factories' on the West African coast

- Europeans seldom ventured inland to capture the millions of people who were transported from Africa as captives. African middlemen usually sold slaves to European factors who collected the slaves on the coast. In the areas where slavery was not practised, such as among the Xhosa people of southern Africa, European slave ship captains were unable to buy African captives.
- European 'factories' were developed on the coast to control the slave trade. These 'factories' or forts held slaves until the arrival of the slave ships.

The development of slave-based states and economies

- Africans could become slaves as punishment for a crime, as payment for a family debt, or — most commonly of all — by being captured as prisoners of war. With the arrival of European ships offering trading goods in exchange for captives, Africans had an added incentive to enslave each other, often by abducting unfortunate victims.
- Some societies preyed on others to obtain captives in exchange for European firearms, in the belief that if they did not acquire firearms in this way to protect themselves, they would be attacked and captured by their rivals and enemies who did possess such weapons.

At the height of the Atlantic Slave Trade only states equipped with guns were able to resist attacks from their neighbours. The acquisition of guns by rulers also provided an edge over rivals and increased their drive to capture and sell slaves. This led to the growth of states such as Dahomey whose raison d'être was the slave trade. The mass importation of guns for slaves altered the conduct of warfare in Africa and changed the balance of power between kingdoms.

- As the Atlantic Slave Trade developed, more African societies accommodated themselves to the trade in slaves.

The destruction of societies

- Rich and powerful Africans were able to demand a variety of consumer goods, including textiles, glassware, pottery, ironmongery and — in some places — even gold for captives, who may have been acquired through warfare or by other means, initially without massive disruption to African societies.
- By the end of the 17th century, European demand for African captives — particularly for the sugar plantations in the Americas — became so great that they could only be acquired through initiating raiding and warfare; large areas of Africa were devastated and societies disintegrated. As the temptation to go to war increased, existing systems of rule based on kinship and consent were destroyed.
- It is estimated that around 12 million people were transported from Africa over the 18th century. In addition, many captured Africans died during the journey from the interior to the coast which could take weeks and sometimes months. This was a huge drain on the most productive and economically active sections of the population and this led to economic dislocation and falls in production of food and other goods.
- Europeans also brought diseases which contributed to the decline in population of African societies.

The development of foreign colonies

- West Africa was impoverished by its relationship with Europe while the human and other resources that were taken from Africa contributed to the economic development and wealth of Europe and the European colonies in the New World.
- The transatlantic trade also created the conditions for the subsequent colonial conquest of Africa by the European powers.

The roles played by leaders of African societies in continuing the trade

- African slave-sellers grew wealthy by selling African captives to European traders on the coast. They were able to deal on equal terms with European traders who built "factories" on the West African coast to house captives before selling them onto the slave-ship captains, who in turn transported the captives to the colonies of the New World.
- On the African side, the slave trade was generally the business of rulers or wealthy and powerful merchants, concerned with their own selfish or narrow interests, rather than those of the continent. At that time, there was no concept of being African — identity and loyalty were based on kinship or membership of a specific kingdom or society, rather than to the African continent.
- States based on slavery, particularly Dahomey, grew in power and influence. The Asante (Ashanti) people who traded in gold and in slaves dominated the area known as the Gold Coast (Ghana).

Any other relevant factors.

24. *The role of William Wilberforce was the most important reason for the success of the abolitionist campaign in 1807.* How valid is this view?

Context
In March 1807 Parliament finally ended Britain's involvement in the Slave Trade. The campaign in Britain to end the trading in enslaved Africans began in 1787 with the founding of the Society for the Abolition of the Slave Trade and was led in Parliament by the politician and spokesperson for the Society, William Wilberforce.

The role of Wilberforce
- Wilberforce put forward the arguments of the Society for the Abolition of the Slave Trade in Parliament for eighteen years.
- Wilberforce's speeches in Parliament against the slave trade were graphic and appealing and were influential in persuading many others to support the abolitionist cause.
- Wilberforce's personal qualities earned him the trust and respect of his fellow MPs.
- Wilberforce's Christian faith had led him to become interested in social reform and link the issues of factory reform in Britain and the need to abolish slavery and the slave trade within the British Empire.
- Wilberforce was prepared to work with other abolitionists to achieve his aims, including the Quakers, Thomas Clarkson and Olaudah Equiano.
- Despite campaigning inside Parliament over the course of two decades, his attempts to introduce bills against the slave trade were unsuccessful due to powerful opposition to abolition in Parliament.
- It has also been argued that other abolitionists such as Thomas Clarkson and Granville Sharp deserve as much credit for their equally tireless efforts over many years.

Other factors

The decline in the economic importance of slavery
- Effects of wars with France — slave trade declined by two-thirds as it was seen as harming the national interest in time of war.
- The slave trade had become less important in economic terms — there was no longer a need for large numbers of slaves to be imported to the British colonies. Profits made by plantation owners varied. On the other hand the use of slave labour continued after 1807 until it became illegal.
- There was a world over-supply of sugar and British merchants had difficulties re-exporting it.
- Sugar could be sourced at a lower cost and without the use of slavery from Britain's other colonies eg India.
- Industrial Revolution: technological advances and improvements in agriculture were benefiting the British economy.

Effects of slave resistance
- Successful slave rebellion in Saint-Domingue led to an exaggerated, general fear of slave revolts. It was argued that Britain began to plan for an exit from the slave trade as a result of this revolt which shook the whole system to its foundations. Already on Jamaica a substantial number of runaways lived outside the control of the authorities.
- There was an argument that if conditions were not ameliorated by, for example, the abolition of the slave trade, further revolts would follow.

Military factors
- Napoleon's efforts to restore slavery in the French islands meant that the abolitionist campaign would help to undermine Napoleon's plans for the Caribbean. Abolitionists were no longer regarded as being pro French and the abolitionist campaign revived as a result.
- The act banning any slave trade between British merchants and foreign colonies in 1806 was intended to attack French interests as a way to win the Napoleonic war. This act cleared the path for an end to Britain's participation in the Atlantic Slave Trade.

The religious revival
- Many of the first Christian opponents of the slave trade came from non-conformist congregations such as Quakers, Presbyterians, Methodists and Baptists.
- Many of the early leaders were Quakers (the Society of Friends), who opposed slavery on the grounds that Christianity taught that everyone was equal. When the Society for the Abolition of the Slave Trade was formed in 1787, 9 of its 12 original members were Quakers.
- The main thrust of Christian abolitionism emerged from the Evangelical Revival of the eighteenth century based on its beliefs on morality and sin.
- The Methodist founder John Wesley questioned the morality of slavery which influenced many Christian abolitionists including the former slave trader turned clergyman, John Newton.
- Evangelical Christians included Thomas Clarkson, William Wilberforce and Granville Sharp, who fought for the freedom of a young African, Jonathan Strong.
- Clergymen such as James Ramsay who had worked in the Caribbean were influential in exposing the facts of plantation slavery and in pointing out that many Africans died without hearing the Gospel.
- However, some Quakers continued to have links with the slave trade eg David and Alexander Barclay set up Barclays Bank, Francis Baring set up Barings Bank.
- The Church of England had links to the slave trade through the United Society for the Propagation of the Gospel (USPG) missionary organisations which owned slave plantations in Barbados.
- Scottish churches were amongst the key drivers in the abolitionist movement, although the Church of Scotland did not petition Parliament to end the slave trade.

Campaign of the Society for the Abolition of the Slave Trade
- Thomas Clarkson visited ports such as Bristol and Liverpool to collect evidence from sailors who worked on the slave trade. He obtained witnesses for the Parliamentary investigations which provided Wilberforce with convincing evidence for his speeches. Clarkson also collected objects associated with slavery-handcuffs, whips and branding irons to use as evidence on his tours around the country.
- Books and pamphlets were published eg eyewitness accounts from former slaves such as Olaudah Equiano, 'The Interesting Life of Olaudah Equiano'.
- Campaigns to boycott goods produced by slaves in the West Indies such as sugar and rum. Around 300 000 British people took part in sugar boycotts.
- Petitions and subscription lists, public meetings and lecture tours involving those with experience of slave trade eg John Newton whose sermons became famous. Churches and theatres used for abolitionist propaganda, artefacts and illustrations eg Wedgwood pottery.
- Lobbying of Parliament by abolitionists to extract promises from MPs that they would oppose the slave trade.

Effective moderate political and religious leadership among the abolitionists influenced major figures such as Pitt and Fox; abolitionists gave evidence to Parliamentary Commissions.

Any other relevant factors.

Part D: Britain, 1851—1951

25. *Britain became more democratic between 1851 and 1928 due to the effects of industrialisation and urbanisation.* How valid is this view?

Context
In 1851 political power was in the hands of a small number of land owning men. By 1928 this had totally changed and Britain could be described as a democratic country. This happened for a variety of reasons.

The effects of industrialisation and urbanisation
- Urbanisation and growing class identity within an industrial workforce and the spread of socialist ideas led to demands for greater voice for the working classes. Also the growth of the Labour party offered a greater choice.
- Demographic change, including rapid urbanisation, sparked demands for redistribution of seats.
- The growing economic power of middle class wealth-creators led to pressure for a greater political voice.
- Basic education, the development of new cheap, popular newspapers and the spread of railways helped to create an awareness of national issues.
- After 1860 the fear of the 'revolutionary mob' had declined. Skilled working men in cities were more educated and respectable. That was an argument for extending the vote in 1867.

Other factors

Changing political attitudes
- Political reform was no longer seen as a threat. In the USA and in Europe struggles were taking place for liberty and a greater political say for 'the people'. Britain tended to support these moves abroad, making it logical for this to happen in Britain too.
- The growing influence of the Liberal Party in challenging older vested interests. The Liberal Party opposed the power of the old land owning aristocracy eg the secret ballot to assist working class electorate to use their 'political voice' to promote social reforms.
- Politicians combined acceptance of changes which they suspected were unavoidable while ensuring that their own party political interests would be protected.
- The death of former PM Palmerston represented the changing tone of politics as the reactionary ideas of early 19th century gave way to new ideologies.
- The veto of the unelected House of Lords was removed in the 1911 Parliament Act partly as result of the 1910 elections fought on the issue of 'peers v people' and the financing of social reform to help the poor, especially in urban areas.

Party advantage
- In 1867 the Conservative Party became the government after 20 years out of power. To an extent the Reform Act could be seen as 'stealing the Liberals' clothes' to gain support.
- The Corrupt and Illegal Practices Act of 1883 limited the amount of spending on elections; the Liberals believed the advantage held by wealthier Conservative opponents would be reduced.

- By placing the reforms of 1883 and 1884 close to the next election, the Liberals hoped to gain advantage from grateful new voters in towns more fairly represented after the redistribution of seats.

Popular attempts to gain the franchise
- The Hyde Park demonstration 23rd July 1866 organised by the Reform League.
- The 1867 Reform Act was passed amongst considerable popular agitations.

Pressure groups
- The Suffragists and Suffragettes were influential in gaining the franchise for women.
- The Reform League and Reform Union were active in pushing for franchise change.

The effects of the First World War
- The war necessitated more political change. Many men still had no vote but were conscripted to fight from 1916. As further reform for males was being considered, fears of a revival of the militant women's campaign, combined with a realisation of the importance of women's war work led to the Reform Act of 1918 which gave votes to more men and some women.

The effects of examples of developments abroad
- In a number of foreign countries there was a wider franchise than in Britain; in others women could also vote. Neither development had threatened the established social order.

Any other relevant factors.

26. How important were the fears over national security as a reason why the Liberals introduced social reforms, 1906—1914?

Context
Government intervention to help the poor before 1906 was very limited. Attitudes towards the poor were characterised by beliefs in laissez-faire and self-help. However, these attitudes were changing due to a number of factors.

Fears over national security
- The government became alarmed when almost 25% of the volunteers to fight in the Boer War were rejected because they were physically unfit to serve in the armed forces. There was concern whether Britain could survive a war or protect its empire against a far stronger enemy in the future if the nation's 'fighting stock' of young men was so unhealthy.
- Link between national security concerns and national efficiency concerns; financial or economic security.

Other factors

The rise of Labour
- In 1893 Keir Hardie set up the Independent Labour Party, he was one of two MPs elected in 1902.
- By 1906 Labour had 29 MPs rising to 42 by 1910.
- By 1906 the newly formed Labour Party was competing for the same votes as the Liberal Party. It can be argued that the reforms happened for the very selfish reason of retaining working class votes.
- Lloyd George talked about stopping 'this electoral rot' as the party lost seats to Labour in the 1910 elections.

Concerns over poverty — the social surveys of Booth and Rowntree
- The reports of Charles Booth and Seebohm Rowntree demonstrated that poverty had causes such as low pay,

unemployment, sickness and old age. These were largely out with the control of the individual.

- The extent of poverty revealed in the surveys was also a shock. Booth's initial survey was confined to the East End of London, but his later volumes covering the rest of London revealed that almost one third of the capital's population lived in poverty. York was a relatively prosperous small town but even their poverty was deep-seated.
- Previous evidence of poverty had been relatively piecemeal, but Booth and Rowntree produced extensive surveys backed up by impressive data. It was difficult to argue against such evidence.

Municipal socialism

- By the end of the century some Liberal-controlled local authorities had become involved in programmes of social welfare. The shocked reaction to the reports on poverty was a pressure for further reform.
- In Birmingham particularly, but in other large industrial cities, local authorities had taken the lead in providing social welfare schemes. These served as an example for further reforms.

Foreign examples

- In Germany a system of welfare benefits and old age pensions had been set up in the 1880s. This raised the issue whether Britain was no longer a major European nation.
- Lloyd George was particularly impressed by the advances made in Germany as a result of Bismarck's social legislation and a direct link to its national strength.

National efficiency

- By the end of the 19th century Britain was facing serious competition from new industrial nations such as Germany.
- It was believed that if the health and educational standards of Britain's workers got worse then Britain's position as a strong industrial power would be threatened.

The rise of the New Liberalism

- New Liberals argued that state intervention was necessary to liberate people from social problems over which they had no control.
- New Liberal ideas were not important issues in the general election of 1905. Only when 'old liberal' Prime Minister Campbell Bannerman died in 1908 was the door opened for new 'interventionist' ideas championed by the likes of David Lloyd George and Winston Churchill.

Party advantage

- Since 1884 many more working class men had the vote and the Liberals had tended to attract many of those votes. Social reform was a means of appeasing this constituency.

Any other relevant factors.

27. To what extent did the Labour welfare reforms, 1945–1951, deal effectively with the social problems of Britain?

Context

In his report in 1942, William Beveridge identified 5 giants of poverty: Want, Disease, Ignorance, Squalor and Idleness. In the aftermath of the Second World War there was a desire to build a better Britain for all. Reforms based on Beveridge's report were passed by the new Labour government.

Want

- 1946 the first step was made: The National Insurance Act: consisted of comprehensive insurance sickness and unemployment benefits and cover for most eventualities.

- It was said to support people from the "cradle to the grave" which was significant as it meant people had protection against falling into poverty throughout their lives.
- This was very effective as it meant that if the breadwinner of the family was injured then the family was less likely to fall further into the poverty trap, as was common before. However, this act can be criticised for its failure to go far enough.
- Benefits were only granted to those who made 156 weekly contributions.
- In 1948 the National Assistance Board was set up in order to cover those for whom insurance did not do enough.
- This was important as it acted as a safety net to protect these people.
- This was vital as the problem of people not being aided by the insurance benefits was becoming a severe issue as time passed. Yet, some criticised this as many citizens still remained below subsistence level showing the problem of want had not completely been addressed.

Disease

- The establishment of the NHS in 1948 dealt effectively with the spread of disease.
- The NHS was the first comprehensive universal system of health in Britain.
- Offered vaccination and immunisation against disease, almost totally eradicating some of Britain's most deadly illnesses.
- It also offered helpful services to Britain's public, such as childcare, the introduction of prescriptions, health visiting and provision for the elderly, providing a safety net across the whole country: the fact that the public did not have to pay for their health meant that everyone, regardless of their financial situation, was entitled to equal opportunities of health care they had previously not experienced.
- NHS could be regarded as almost too successful. The demand from the public was overwhelming, as the estimated amount of patients treated by them almost doubled. Introduction of charges for prescriptions, etc.

Education

- Reform started by the wartime government: The 1944 Education Act raised the age at which people could leave school to 15 as part of a drive to create more skilled workers which Britain lacked at the time. Introduction of school milk, etc.
- Labour introduced a two-tiered secondary schooling whereby pupils were split at the age of 11 (12 in Scotland) depending on their ability. The pupils who passed the "11+ exam" went to grammar and the rest to secondary moderns.
- Those who went to grammar schools were expected to stay on past the age of 15 and this created a group of people who would take senior jobs in the country thus solving the skills shortages. Whilst this separation of ability in theory meant that children of even poor background could get equal opportunities in life, in practice the system actually created a bigger division between the poor and the rich. In many cases, the already existing inequalities between the classes was exacerbated rather than narrowed.
- Labour expanded university education: introduction of grants so all could attend in theory.

Housing

- After the war there was a great shortage of housing as the war had destroyed and damaged thousands of homes; and the slum cleaning programmes of the 1930s had done little to rectify the situation which was leading to a number of other problems for the government.

- Tackling the housing shortage and amending the disastrous results of the war fell upon Bevan's Ministry of Health.
- Labour's target for housing was to build 200,000 new homes a year. 157,000 pre-fabricated homes were built to a good standard, however this number would not suffice and the target was never met.
- Bevan encouraged the building of council houses rather than privately funded construction.
- The New Towns Act of 1946, aimed to target overcrowding in the increasingly built up older cities. By 1950, the government had designed 12 new communities.
- In an attempt to eradicate slums the Town and Country Planning Act provided local communities more power in regards to building developments and new housing.
- By the time Labour left government office in 1951 there was still a huge shortfall in British housing.

Idleness

- Unemployment was basically non-existent so the government had little to do to tackle idleness.
- The few changes they did make were effective in increasing the likelihood of being able to find work, because they increased direct government funding for the universities which led to a 60% increase in student numbers between 1945—46 and 1950—51, which helped to meet the manpower requirements of post-war society. This provided more skilled workers and allowed people from less advantaged backgrounds to pursue a higher education, aiming to keep unemployment rates down.
- Labour government also nationalised 20 percent of industry — the railways, mines, gas and electricity. This therefore meant that the government were directly involved with people employed in these huge industries which were increasing in size dramatically.
- This tackled idleness by the government having control which meant that employees were less likely to lose their job through industries going bankrupt and people were working directly to benefit society.

Any other relevant factors.

Part E: Britain and Ireland, 1900—1985

28. **How important was the British position, as seen by the results of the 1910 elections, as a reason for the growth of tension in Ireland by 1914?**

Context

Local self-government for Ireland in the late nineteenth century had created a number of politically experienced leaders. This, coupled with land reform, gave political nationalism an economic base from which to demand self-government. There was also an increasingly radical edge to this, albeit at the margins, through James Connolly and the Irish Socialist Republican Party. Tension was exacerbated by the reaction from the Protestant dominated north of Ireland.

The British position over Ireland — the results of the 1910 elections

- After 1910 the Liberals needed the help of the Irish Nationalists to run the country as they would not have a majority otherwise; they passed the third reform bill. In 1908 Campbell-Bannerman had been replaced as Prime Minister by Asquith, who in 1909 had declared that he was a supporter of Home Rule.
- With the support of John Redmond, leader of the Nationalists, a Bill was passed to reduce the power of the House of Lords, which was dominated by Conservatives, from being able to block a Bill to only being able to hold up the passing of a Bill for two years. As a result, the Home Rule Bill for Ireland, which was previously blocked by the House of Lords, could now be passed.

Other factors

The Irish cultural revival and the re-emergence of Irish Republicanism

- In 1884 the Gaelic Athletic Association was set up 'for the preservation and cultivation of our national pastimes.' Games like Gaelic football and hurling became very popular. In 1883 the Gaelic League was also set up whose aim it was to revive, and preserve the Irish language and Gaelic literature.
- Sinn Fein (Ourselves Alone) was founded by Arthur Griffith in 1904 to boycott all things British and to press for the Irish to set up their own parliament in Ireland, which Griffith thought would cause the British Government to collapse. The IRB was revived with Thomas Clarke recruiting young men in Dublin for the movement. Both these groups wanted an Ireland separate from Britain and both willing to use force.

Redmond and Home Rule

- Redmond claimed that the Home Rule Bill would lead to greater unity and strength in the Union, ending suspicion and disaffection in Ireland, and between Britain and Ireland. It would show Britain was willing to treat Ireland equally, as part of the empire. Redmond's Party was consistently strong throughout Southern Ireland, where there was strong support for Home Rule.

Differing economic and religious features of the Northern Counties

- Ulster was mainly Protestant and feared that a government led by Dublin would see the imposition of laws on Northern Ireland based on Catholic faith; this they were opposed to.
- Ulster people were worried they would lose the economic benefits they enjoyed from being part of the British Empire, such as the linen industry and the shipbuilding industry.

The Home Rule Bill — the responses of Unionists, and of Nationalists

- The roles of Carson and Craig: Sir Edward Carson's theatrical political performances caught the public imagination and brought the case of the Unionists to the nation. At the signing of the Solemn League and Covenant in Belfast at Town Hall, to the world's press, 250,000 Ulstermen pledged themselves to use 'all means necessary' to defeat Home Rule.
- Setting up of the UVF.
- Curragh Mutiny: British officers stationed in Ireland declared they would not use force against the Unionists.
- The Irish Volunteer Force (IVF) was set up as a reaction. Members from the Gaelic League, the Gaelic Athletic Association, Sinn Fein and the IRB all joined hoping to use the IVF for their own purposes. By May 1914 it had 80,000 members.
- In 1913, a third private army was set up, the Irish Citizen Army, under the leadership of James Connolly, a socialist. It had two clear aims — to gain independence for Ireland and set up a socialist republic, for working class of all religions to join up with to improve their lives.

Any other relevant points.

29. To what extent were divisions in the republican movement a reason for the outbreak of the Irish Civil War?

Context

The Civil War was a direct consequence of the Anglo-Irish Treaty which was itself the result of the Irish War of Independence. The terms of the treaty were opposed by many Irish Republicans, who objected to an oath of loyalty to the British Crown, to give one example. Disagreements within the Irish Republican movement eventually led to Civil War between pro and anti-Treaty factions.

Divisions in the Republican movement

- The treaty was hotly debated in the Dail. Collins and much of the IRA supported the treaty, as Ireland now had an elected government. De Valera opposed it and felt it should be resisted even if it meant Civil War. They represented the two wings of the Republican movement.
- Also influential were the widows and other relatives of those who had died; they were vocal in their opposition to the Treaty.
- The Treaty was particularly disappointing to left-wing republicans who had hopes of establishing a socialist republic.
- The treaty was accepted by 64 votes to 57 by the Dail Eireann on the 7th January, 1922.
- Collins and De Valera tried to reach a compromise to avoid war but none was reached. Some of the IRA units supported the treaty, whilst others opposed it. Some of the anti-treaty IRA took over some important buildings in Dublin eg Four Courts.
- This division, crystallised by the murder of Sir Henry Wilson (security adviser for the Northern Ireland Government), forced Michael Collins to call on the official IRA to suppress the 'Irregular IRA'.

Other factors

The Anglo-Irish Treaty

- Ireland was to be the 'Irish Free State', governing itself, making its own laws but remaining in the Empire. A Governor General was to represent the king: Britain was to remove its forces but keep the use of its naval bases. Trade relations were settled. Lloyd George threatened the Irish delegation with war if they did not sign.

Partition

- Government of Ireland Act, split Ireland in two, with six counties in the North and 26 in the South. In Northern Ireland, Unionists won 40 of the 52 seats available. A third of the Ulster population was Catholic and wanted to be united to the South.
- The 26 counties in the South had a separate parliament in Dublin. The Council of Ireland was set up. The IRA refused to recognise the new Parliament and kept up its violence. Sectarian violence increased in Ulster; without partition this could have been much worse. Ulster Special Constabulary, Special Powers Act, Local Government Emergency Powers Act.
- In the South, the Government of Ireland Act was ignored. Sinn Fein won 124 seats unopposed. Partition was a highly emotive issue, and it alone would have caused discord.

Dominion status

- Under this agreement Ireland became a Dominion of the British Empire, rather than being completely independent of Britain. Under Dominion status the new Irish State had three important things to adhere to:
  - The elected representatives of the people were to take an oath of allegiance to the British Crown.
  - The Crown was to be represented by a Governor General; appeals in certain legal cases could be taken to the Privy Council in London.
  - This aspect of the treaty was repugnant to many Irish people, not just Republicans.

The role of Collins

- Collins negotiated the treaty with Churchill, but was pressured to sign it under a threat of escalation of the conflict. He recognised that the war was unwinnable, both for the IRA and the UK government. Collins claimed Ireland had its own, elected government, so Britain was no longer the enemy. Collins defended the treaty as he claimed it gave Ireland 'freedom to achieve freedom'.

The role of De Valera

- De Valera refused to accept the terms of the treaty as they were in 'violent conflict with the wishes of the majority of the nation'. De Valera claimed that treaty meant partition of Ireland and abandonment of sovereignty. De Valera felt he should have been consulted before the treaty was signed.
- De Valera voted against the treaty and resigned as President, to be replaced by Griffith and Collins became Head of the Irish Free Government.

Any other relevant factors.

30. *Economic differences were the main obstacle to peace in Ireland between 1968 and 1985.* How valid is this view?

Context

The civil rights movement of the mid to late 1960s saw a backlash against it from elements of the unionist community, including the largely Protestant RUC. The Provisional IRA emerged as 'protector' of the Northern Ireland nationalist community. The two sides: Nationalist and Unionist, were increasingly polarised through the period with communities dividing, socially and politically, along sectarian lines. The deployment of British troops in Northern Ireland and imposition of Direct Rule saw the conflict widen.

Economic differences

- From 1973, the Common Agricultural Policy changed the decision making environment for food prices and farm economics, and employment in the farming sector continued to decline. Traditionally this sector had been dominated by the unionist community.
- Discrimination against Catholic applicants for employment declined steadily during this period as Catholics in the province began to enjoy the same civil rights enjoyed by the population of the rest of the UK.

Other factors

Religious and communal differences

- The Protestant majority in Northern Ireland belonged to churches that represented the full range of reformed Christianity, while the Catholic minority was united in its membership of a Church that dominated life in the Republic and much of Europe. These religious divisions made it very difficult for both communities to come together.
- These divisions further enhanced by traditions embraced by both communities, such as the 'marching season', which became a flashpoint for sectarian violence. Also differences in sport, language.

- Many Catholic political representatives refused to recognise partition and their views only heightened the nationalist community's sense of alienation and fostered unionist hostility towards the Catholic minority.
- The speeches and actions of unionist and nationalist leaders such as Reverend Ian Paisley and Gerry Adams polarised views in the province, and emphasised the divisions between both communities.

Hardening attitudes — the role of terrorism

- Paramilitary groups began to operate on both sides of the sectarian divide, while civil rights marches became increasingly prone to confrontation.
- In late 1969, the more militant 'Provisional' IRA (PIRA) broke away from the so-called 'Official' IRA. PIRA was prepared to pursue unification in defiance of Britain and would use violence to achieve its aims.
- Unionist paramilitaries also organised. The UVF was joined by the Ulster Defence Association, created in 1971.
- Examples of terrorist activity: by the end of 1972 sectarian violence had escalated to such an extent that nearly 500 lives were lost in a single year.
- PIRA prisoners protest at loss of special status prisoners leading to hunger strikes. Second hunger strike in 1981, led by Bobby Sands. Sands was put forward for a vacant Westminster seat and won. Sands and nine other hunger strikers died before the hunger strikes called off in October 1981.
- Sinn Fein won the by-election following Sands' death in June 1983. These electoral successes raised the possibility that Sinn Fein could replace the more moderate SDLP as the political voice of the Catholic minority in Northern Ireland.
- Indiscriminate terrorism meant Eire public opinion turned against PIRA.
- In 1985 the violence of Northern Ireland's paramilitary groups still had more than a decade to run and the sectarian divide remained as wide as it had ever been.

British government policies — Internment

- New Prime Minister Brian Faulkner reintroduced internment ie detention of suspects without trial, in 1971 in response to unrest. The policy was a disaster, both in its failure to capture any significant members of the PIRA and in its sectarian focus on nationalist rather than loyalist suspects. The reaction was predictable, even if the ferocity of the violence wasn't. Deaths in the final months of 1971 reached over 150.

Direct Rule

- A number of reforms had followed on from the Downing Street Declaration, i.e on allocation of council housing, investigate the recent cycle of violence and review policing, such as the disbanding of the hated 'B Specials' auxiliaries.
- The British government, now led by Prime Minister Edward Heath, decided to remove control of security from the government of Northern Ireland and appointed a secretary of state for the province which lead to the resignation of Stormont government. Direct rule imposed.
- Despite attempts to introduce some sort of self-rule, such as the Sunningdale agreement of 1973, which failed in the face of implacable unionist opposition and led to the reintroduction of direct rule. It would last for another 25 years.

The role of the British Army

- The so-called 'Battle of Bogside' in 1969 only ended with the arrival of a small force of British troops at the request of Chichester Clark. An acknowledgement that the govt. of Northern Ireland had lost its grip on the province's security.
- By 1971 policing the province was fast becoming an impossible task, and the British Army adopted increasingly aggressive policies on the ground.
- On 30 January 1972, the army deployed the Parachute Regiment to suppress rioting at a civil rights march in Derry. Thirteen demonstrators were shot and killed by troops, with another victim dying later of wounds. Appalling images of 'Bloody Sunday; led to increased recruitment by Provisional IRA.
- The British Army's various attempts to control the PIRA, such as house-to-house searches and the imposition of a limited curfew, only served to drive more recruits into the ranks of the paramilitaries.

The role of the Irish government.

- Irish government's role in The Anglo—Irish Agreement, signed in November 1985, confirmed that Northern Ireland would remain independent of the Republic as long as that was the will of the majority in the north. Also gave the Republic a say in the running of the province for the first time.
- The agreement also stated that power could not be devolved back to Northern Ireland unless it enshrined the principle of power sharing.

Any other relevant factors.

2017
SECTION 3: EUROPEAN AND WORLD

Part A: The Crusades, 1071–1204

31. How important was the Papal desire to channel the aggressive nature of feudal society as a reason for the calling of the First Crusade?

Context

In 1095 Pope Urban III called on thousands of knights to unite against the infidel. Pope Urban III's famous speech at Clermont also made detailed reference to the violence committed by Christians against fellow Christians. As a man of God, Urban III viewed a crusade as an opportunity to heal the evils of civil war in Europe and to deflect the violence onto the Muslims in the east.

Papal desire to channel the aggressive nature of feudal society

- Urban's appeal specifically targeted the nobility of France and northern Europe in an attempt to divert the violence of the warring European kingdoms. The nobility were regularly drawn into wars with their neighbours to take extra land or to settle disputes between rivals. Urban wanted to divert this violence in order to create peace within Europe.
- Pope Urban II preached a holy war and called on thousands of knights to fight in the Muslim Middle East. Due to the custom in Europe of a father's lands being shared among his sons on his death, land was divided into smaller portions. This increased both the number of knights and the likelihood of violent land disputes. By the eleventh century, knights often terrorised their own neighbourhoods in their attempts to increase their power. Even when enforcing the law, knights often imposed vicious physical punishments. While such brutality helped to make knights highly effective warriors, it was considered a sin for knights to use their skills in anger. Pope Urban had long considered how he could turn the nature of the Western knights to a less aggressive, less damaging activity.
- The Church was determined to reverse what it perceived as the breakdown of society in many parts of Western Europe. The culture of violence disturbed the entire local society: peasants became foot soldiers and farming and trade were disrupted. As a man of God, Urban II saw a crusade as an opportunity to avoid the evils of civil war in Europe.
- The Church had already successfully introduced the Peace of God movement which attempted to stop the violence. Attempts included forbidding fighting on certain days of the week and sparing churches and non-combatants in any conflict. Urban saw the Crusade as a way to channel this aggression out of Europe and into the Middle East which would be of benefit to Christianity.

Other factors:

The threat to Byzantium

- The Seljuk Turks had been threatening the Empire for decades. The Byzantines had been defeated in 1071 at the Battle of Manzikert in eastern Anatolia. Between 1077 and 1092 the Byzantines had been driven out of the eastern regions of Anatolia, and the Turks were now encroaching further west towards the Byzantine capital of Constantinople. There was fear in Europe that if Byzantium was allowed to fall then the expansion of this new aggressive Islamic group into central Europe would be inevitable.
- The Byzantine Emperor, Alexius was seen as a bulwark against this eventuality and his letter asking for help was taken very seriously.
- The threat to Byzantium was perhaps exaggerated by the Emperor Alexius who had negotiated a treaty with Kilij Arslan in 1092 and was hiring more and more mercenaries from Europe to protect the Empire.

Fear of Islamic expansion

- Founded by the Prophet Muhammad, the Islamic religion had exploded onto the world in the late seventh century, advancing across the Christians principalities of North Africa, through Spain and into southern France, where it had been halted in the eighth century and pushed back into Spain.
- Pope Urban used the fear of Islamic expansion in his famous speech at Clermont in 1095. He pointed to the successful Reconquista in Spain. El Cid had only captured Valencia from the Moors in 1094.
- He pointed to the threat of the Turks to Byzantium, a topic that was already talked about across Europe. He claimed that the loss of Anatolia had 'devastated the Kingdom of God'.
- He detailed claims of Turkish activities such as torture, human sacrifice and desecration.

The threat to Mediterranean trade

- The development of trade within the Mediterranean Sea had been in the hands of ambitious cities in Italy, notably Venice, but also Pisa and Genoa. By 1095 Venice had bound its future to Byzantium.
- Their preferential trade agreements with Constantinople for silk, spices and other luxury goods meant that they were keen to see Byzantium saved from the expansion of the Turks.

Attempts to assert Papal authority

- The new style of pope, influenced and trained at the monastery of Cluny, heralded a shift in the emphasis of Christianity. The papal reforms influenced by the Cluniac establishment demanded actual, as well as spiritual, power. No longer were popes to be subservient to the monarchs or warlords of Europe. A Cluniac reformer himself, Pope Urban II was keen to build on the reforms of previous popes.
- The papacy was anxious to re-join the two halves of the Christian church. Since the Great Schism of 1054, where the Pope of Rome and Patriarch of Constantinople excommunicated each other, it had been the goal of every pope to become head of the Greek Orthodox Church and to extend Roman influence into the eastern Mediterranean. Now the Crusade seemed to offer Pope Urban the opportunity to achieve this.

The ongoing struggle between church and state — the Investiture Contest

- Popes now actually challenged kings and demanded the right to appoint priests, bishops and cardinals as they saw fit. This led to the development of the Investiture Contest, a prolonged war between Pope Gregory VII and the German Emperor, Henry IV. A low point was reached in 1080 when Henry appointed a separate Pope and attacked Rome with his armies. This power struggle had damaged the reputation of the papacy and directly affected Urban, possibly influencing his decision.
- A crusade would increase the papacy's political status in Europe. The Pope would be seen as a great leader, above princes and emperors.
- It is believed the Investiture Contest may have delayed the calling of a crusade.

- There may have been a crusade to drive back the Seljuk as early as the mid-1070s but Gregory's struggle against the German Emperor meant he was too weak to see it through.

The emergence of a knightly class — the idea of chivalry

- The introduction of Norman feudalism across Western Europe had created a knightly class. Their dedication to learning the arts of war had created a culture based around the skills of fighting. Even the tournaments had come to be seen as an integral part of the culture and as entertainment. Urban knew that his appeal would arouse the enthusiasm of the warrior knights of France and Germany.

Any other relevant factors.

32. To what extent was the Christian states' lack of resources the main reason for the fall of Jerusalem in 1187?

Context

In July 1187, the Muslim leader, Saladin wiped out the crusader army at the Battle of Hattin, in Syria. Weeks later the Holy City of Jerusalem surrendered to the Islamic forces. Contributing to the fall of Jerusalem was a continual shortage of men and a lack of support from the West.

The lack of resources of the Christian states

- There was a lack of support from the Byzantine Empire. The crusader states had been strengthened by a closer relationship with the Byzantine Empire during the reign of Manuel I. In 1180, the Byzantine Emperor died and the new Emperor Andronicus I showed little interest in supporting the Latin rulers of the Near East. After 1184 Saladin made a treaty with Byzantium, leaving the Holy City without Byzantine support.

- European monarchs showed similar disinterest in the crusader states. In 1184 three of the most important men in the crusader states — the Patriarch of Jerusalem and the masters of the Hospitallers and Templars — were sent to Europe seeking support, but neither Philip II of France nor Henry II of England felt able to lead a new crusade to the Holy Land.

- The Crusaders had sought to redress their military inferiority by constructing powerful fortifications. Without the army to protect the kingdom even the massive fortifications could not withstand Saladin's forces.

- Even the combined armies of the Crusader States were not strong enough to successfully win a war, especially in the long run. It is arguable that it was inevitable for the Crusader States to fall to a united Islamic state.

Other reasons

The death of Baldwin IV

- Baldwin died in March 1185, taking his strategy of non-aggression towards Saladin with him. He was replaced for a short time by his nephew, Baldwin V. However, a short power struggle after the boy's death in August let Guy de Lusignan assume the throne, abetted by Sibylla. The marriage of Guy and Sibylla triggered factionalism and dissent among the nobles.

Divisions amongst the Crusaders

- Two factions had struggled for power within Baldwin IV's court, those of Guy de Lusignan and Baldwin's close advisor Raymond III of Tripoli. In 1180 Guy married Sibylla, Baldwin's sister. Guy tended to favour an aggressive policy.

- The activities of Reynald of Chatillon helped to destabilise the fragile peace treaty between Baldwin IV and Saladin.

- The Knights Templar, unlike the Hospitallers, were firmly in the camp of the hawks (warmongers). They wanted nothing more than to carry on with the crusading ideal and rid the Holy Lands of Muslims. Treaties and compromise were unacceptable to them.

The unification of Islamic states under Saladin

- In 1171 Saladin secured his control over Egypt.

- Saladin then began to establish his control over Syria through patient diplomacy. Following Nur-ad-Din's death, Saladin wrote to Nur-ad-Din's son, al-Salih, expressing his loyalty. Saladin gained further legitimacy by marrying Nur-ad-Din's widow. In the first years of Saladin's rule, he established his authority over other Muslims in the name of al-Salih.

- Saladin began to unite the Muslim Near East by occupying Damascus.

- By 1174 several of Syria's warlords had switched their support to Saladin.

- In 1183 Saladin finally brought Aleppo under his control.

- Saladin had managed to successfully unite the Muslims of Syria and Egypt behind his leadership. This effectively surrounded Jerusalem and left them with a very weak military position.

- After years of fighting Muslims as a precondition of waging jihad and after a severe illness in 1185–86, Saladin became more determined to recapture Jerusalem and successfully used the idea of a religious war against the Christians to hold the separate Islamic groups together.

- By way of balance, Saladin himself had his critics within the Muslim ranks, saying he was more interested in maintaining his position than defeating the Christians. It was seen by many that his stance on the Kingdom of Jerusalem was weak. After Guy assumed the throne and Reynald continued his attacks the pressure on Saladin to respond grew. This encouraged him to act aggressively.

The Christian defeat at Hattin

- King Guy led the armies of Jerusalem to save Count Tiberius's wife as Saladin's forces had surrounded her castle. Tiberius himself had a few worries about the safety of his wife. His fortress could have withstood a siege. Saladin's forces lacked the required siege engines to make a successful attack. Additionally, Saladin could not keep his disparate forces in the field for any length of time. Tiberius' advice to Guy was to hold his forces back to protect Jerusalem.

- However, figures such as Reynald had persuaded Guy that to leave the Countess of Tripoli besieged would be un-chivalric and that Guy would lose support if he did not ride out.

- The army could find little water to sustain them in the desert. Their only option was to make for Hattin and the oasis there. This was an obvious trap; Saladin surrounded them with burning brushwood and dry grass. Trapped on the Horns of Hattin the Christian army suffered badly from the sun and lack of water.

- Eventually they were forced to attack before they lacked the strength to do so. The Christian horses were too weak for a prolonged struggle and their infantry were surrounded by Saladin's horse archers and cut off.

- Saladin ordered the slaughter of all members of the militant orders, but Guy and many of his followers were allowed to surrender and enter captivity.

Any other relevant factors.

33. *The crusading ideal had declined by the time of the Fourth Crusade in 1204.* **How valid is this view?**

Context

At Clermont in 1095, Pope Urban II preached a holy war to recover Jerusalem from Muslim rule. However material motivations and the use of the Crusaders against Venice's political enemies in the Fourth Crusade showed just how far the ideals of the crusade and the religious zeal of the crusaders had declined by 1204.

Co-existence of Muslim and Crusading states

- There were many attempts at peace between Muslim and the Crusading States during the reign of Baldwin IV, before his death and the fall of Jerusalem.
- Other examples include the treaty of mutual protection signed between King Alric of Jerusalem and the Emir of Damascus prior to the Second Crusade.

Corruption of the crusading movement by the Church and nobles

- There are many examples of nobles using the Crusade for their own ends. Examples include Bohemond and Baldwin in the First Crusade and arguably Richard in the Third Crusade. The greed of many nobles on the Fourth Crusade was a far cry from the religious ideals of the early crusaders.
- At the end of the Fourth Crusade, the Pope accepted half of the spoils from the Crusaders despite his earlier excommunication of them.

The effects of trade

- Trade links directly into the Fourth Crusade and the influence of Venice.
- The Italian city-states (Genoa, Pisa and Venice) continued to trade with various Muslim powers throughout the crusading period.
- Pisa and Genoa both had a lot of influence in events during the Third Crusade; they both had favoured candidates for the vacant throne of Jerusalem for example and used trade rights as a bargaining chip to get what they wanted.

The Fourth Crusade

- The initial inspiration of the Fourth Crusade had a strong crusading ideology behind it. Pope Innocent III was a highly effective pope. He had managed to settle the problem of the Investiture Contest with Germany, and hoped to sort out the issue of the Holy Lands as well. Innocent believed that the inclusion of medieval monarchs had caused the previous two Crusades to fail, unlike the First Crusade that was nominally under the command of Bishop Adhemar. This Crusade would fall under the command of six papal legates. These men would hold true to the ideal of the Crusade and not be bound by earthy greed of politics.
- However, the Fourth Crusade has also been described as the low point of the crusading ideal. Hijacked by the Venetians, the Crusade instead became a tool for their growing political and economic ambitions.
- While attacking Zara, Alexius, son of the deposed emperor of Byzantium, arrived with a new proposal for the Crusaders. He asked them to reinstate his father, who had been imprisoned by his brother, and if they agreed they would be handsomely rewarded. He also promised to return control of the Byzantine Church to Rome. The Church was against such an attack on another Christian city, but the prospect of wealth and fame led the Crusade to Constantinople.

- When the Crusaders discovered that Alexius and his father could not, or would not, meet the payment as agreed, the Crusaders stormed the city. The murder, looting and rape continued for three days, after which the Crusading army had a great thanksgiving ceremony.
- The amount of booty taken from Constantinople was huge: gold, silver, works of art and holy relics were taken back to Europe, mostly to Venice. Most Crusaders returned home with their newly acquired wealth. Those that stayed dividing up the land amongst themselves, effectively creating several Latin Crusader States where Byzantium had once stood.

The role of Venice

- By 1123 the city of Venice had come to dominate maritime trade in the Middle East. They made several secret trade agreements with Egypt and North African emirs, as well as enjoying concessions and trade agreements within the Kingdom of Jerusalem. Byzantium however, remained a constant rival for this dominance of trade and in 1183 Venice was cut off from the lucrative trading centres of the empire.
- Venice's participation in the Crusade was only secured when the Pope agreed to pay huge sums of money to Venice for the use of its ships, and supplies as well as half of everything captured during the Crusade on land and sea.
- Venice's leader, the Doge Enrico Dandolo, had sold the Crusaders three times as much supplies and equipment as required for the Crusade. The Crusading leader, Boniface of Montferrat, found that he was unable to raise enough money to pay, and the Crusaders were all but imprisoned on an island near Venice. Dandolo's proposal to pay off the Crusaders' debt involved attacking Zara, a Christian city that had once belonged to Venice but was now under the control of the King of Hungary, a Christian monarch. Thus the Crusade had become a tool of the Venetians.
- The Fourth Crusade's intended target, Egypt, was totally unsuitable from a Venetian perspective. Thus when the Pope's representative approached the Venetians in 1201 they agreed to help transport the Crusaders, hoping to divert the Crusade to a more useful target for the Venetians. The final target for the Fourth Crusade was therefore determined by politics and economics.

Any other relevant factors.

Part B: The American Revolution, 1763–1787

34. **How important were the Navigation Acts as a cause of colonial resentment towards Britain by 1763?**

Context

By 1763, Britain had ruled the thirteen American colonies for over a century. The harmony with Britain which colonists had once held had become indifference during Whig Ascendancy of the mid-1700s. The ascendancy of George III in 1760 was to bring about further change in the relationship between Britain and America. When the Seven Years War ended in 1763, the King strengthened Britain's control over the colonies. Factors contributing to colonial resentment included George III, the Navigation Acts, the old colonial system, political differences between the colonists and the British, and British neglect of the colonies.

Navigation Acts

- The Navigation Acts stated that colonists in any parts of the British Empire could only sell their goods to British merchants, they could only import goods from British traders, and they could only use British shipping in the transportation of goods in and out of the colonies.

- This meant that colonist merchants were being denied access to European markets for their produce such as tobacco or whale products, reducing their potential income and creating opposition to this aspect of British rule.
- Moreover, although colonists had ignored the acts during the Whig Ascendancy, the laws were re-enforced by Prime Minister Grenville after the Seven Years War ended in 1763.
- This caused deep resentment, since the presence of the Royal Navy, patrolling the Eastern Seaboard for rogue Dutch, French or Spanish ships, restricted the trading ability of the colonists who felt their enterprising spirit was being penalised.
- It could, however, be argued that the Navigation Acts gave the colonists a guaranteed market for their goods. Generally though, the Navigation Acts were disliked by those wishing to trade freely with European merchants.

Other Factors

George III

- George III increased the number of British soldiers posted to the colonies after the Seven Year War ended in 1763.
- One function of the King's Proclamation of 1763 was to protect the colonies from future threats posed by foreign powers. However, all colonies and even some larger towns and cities within the colonies had their own militia already, and felt that the British Army in fact posed a threat to the colonists' freedom to defend themselves.
- In addition, George III ensured there was a highly visible Royal Navy attendance on the Atlantic coast, whose job it was to patrol for smugglers importing from Holland, France or Spain and ensure compliance with the Navigation Acts.
- This measure, to support the Revenue Bill proposed in Parliament 1763 was seen as equivalent to foreign invasion by many colonists who had acted in an independent spirit during Whig Ascendancy.
- On the other hand, it can be debated that George III was aiming to guarantee the protection of the colonies by maintaining British military presence and that together with Parliament he was planning a sensible economic strategy to raise money from the colonists to pay for their own security.
- However, cynics in America argued that the King was merely working to ensure continued revenue for Britain, whose national debt had grown from £75 million to £145 million between 1756 and 1763.

The old colonial system

- The thirteen colonies in North America had been used by Britain for almost two centuries as a source of revenue and convenient market.
- Valuable raw materials such as timber or cotton or fur were plundered from the continent and then used to manufacture goods which were then sold in Europe and around the world. This meant that the profits from North American goods were being made by British trading companies, which was resented by those colonists whose labour produced the raw materials to make goods such as fur-trimmed hats or rifles.
- In addition, colonists in the more populated New England and Middle Colonies objected to being used as a dumping ground for British goods.
- Poverty led to minor rebellions by tenant farmers against their landlords throughout the 1740s, including the Land Riots in New Jersey and the Hudson River Valley Revolt in New York.
- Elsewhere, wealthy Southern plantation owners, who considered themselves the aristocracy of the continent,

objected to members of British government attempting to control them through trading restrictions on sugar, cotton and molasses.
- Some historians would point out that being part of the British Empire meant British Army protection for the colonists against the threat of the French and Indians; the British had fought the Seven Years War which prevented the colonies being ruled by France. Despite this advantage, colonists greatly resented the efforts of Britain to restrict their movements and economic development.

The Proclamation of 1763

- Also, the Proclamation Line drawn up by Parliament in 1763 led to Frontiersmen feeling frustrated at British attempts to prevent them from settling beyond the Appalachian Mountains.

Political differences

- The colonies were more enlightened politically than Britain, as each had its own elected Assembly which had passed local laws and raised local taxes since the 1630s.
- Britain appointed a Governor for each colony, but the Governor was paid by the colony, which ensured a slight element of control for colonists over whoever was in the post.
- Lack of representation for the colonists in the British Parliament which sought to control their lives, however, frustrated many.
- In addition, radical proposals in the colonies were rejected by the British authorities, such as the abolition of slavery, favoured by the Massachusetts Assembly led by lawyer James Otis and brewer Samuel Adams but continually vetoed in the early 1760s by the British Governor Hutchinson.
- Nevertheless, some understood that the British Empire provided an order to the existence of the colonies, and Britain acted out the role of Mother Country in a protective manner. This did not stop many colonists from wishing to have a greater say in their own daily lives.

British neglect

- During the Whig Ascendancy from 1727 to 1760, colonist Assemblies had assumed the powers which should have been exercised by Governors, such as the settlement in new territories acquired during that time including the Ohio Valley and Louisiana. Although they objected to Parliament's attempt to reverse this after the Royal Proclamation of 1763, they were politically impotent and could not prevent it.
- In addition, individual colonists and land companies expanding west into the Michigan area unwittingly violated agreements between Britain and Native American Indians such as the 1761 Treaty of Detroit.
- Therefore, quarrels arose as it appeared that the British government, and in particular Secretary of State William Pitt, was ignoring colonist aspirations to explore new regions in the continent.
- One school of thought suggests that Britain's policies highlighted the status of the colonies as lands to be fought over with imperial powers like France and Spain who viewed America as potential possessions, and that British legislation maintained colonist security under the Union Jack.
- However, colonists such as planter and lawyer Patrick Henry of Virginia believed by 1763 that, whilst the right of the King to the colonies was indisputable, the right of the British Parliament to make laws for them was highly contentious.

Any other relevant factors.

35. To what extent was the American War of Independence a conflict which was global in nature?

Context
After the Declaration of Independence in 1776, Britain and the 13 American colonies went to war for five years on land and another two at sea. British troops surrendered at Yorktown in 1781, and Britain recognised American independence in 1783.

Franco—American Alliance
- France entered the war and took the conflict to Europe.
- Britain was forced to re-assign its military resources to defend itself and the Empire.
- French contribution to the colonists' cause took many forms — men, ammunition, training, supplies, and uniforms, fighting Britain around the world.
- However, France was not persuaded until February 1778 to make its alliance with America, by which time the Continental Army was already starting to make progress in the war in the colonies.

Netherlands declaring war on Britain
- The Dutch went to war with Britain in November 1780.
- Britain's navy was stretched even further and it became increasingly difficult to focus on the war in the colonies.
- European nations were now competing for parts of Britain's empire around the world.
- Dutch forces in Ceylon attacked British interests in India.
- However, the war between Britain and the colonists on land was not directly affected by Dutch involvement.

Spanish declaring war on Britain
- Spain declared war on Britain in June 1779.
- Britain was forced to pull troops and naval forces back from the American continent.
- The Spanish Armada now threatened British shores as well as challenging the Royal Navy around the world.
- Spanish troops came from Mexico to the Mississippi area to challenge the British army.

The League of Armed Neutrality
- This grouping of Russia, Sweden and Denmark gave extra cause for concern to Britain, as they were willing to fire on any Royal Navy ships which interfered with their merchant fleets.
- However, the League was not actively involved in the war, merely endeavouring to protect its own shipping.
- Portugal, Austria, Prussia and Turkey all later joined.

Control of the sea
- The battle for control of the sea drew massively on the resources of all countries involved and significantly drained Britain's finances.
- However, the war at sea continued after the surrender at Yorktown, and the British recognised the Treaty of Versailles despite regaining control of the sea, suggesting the war on land was more significant to the outcome for the colonists.

German mercenaries
- Britain used over 7,000 of these in the colonies.
- Prussian soldiers represented the only continental European involvement in the war on Britain's side.

Canadian dimension
- Congress had made an appeal to Canada before 1776 for support through official Addresses which had met with rejection.

- Some American colonists who did not support the revolution were known as Empire Loyalists and many of these left for Canada where some joined British army led by General Burgoyne.

Any other relevant factors.

36. *The American Constitution addressed the key political issues in the new United States.* How valid is this view?

Context
The American War of Independence took place between 1776 and 1781, between Britain and its thirteen colonies of North America. For many colonists, this was a revolutionary conflict fought by people fighting for freedom against tyranny, monarchy and the threat of enslavement. The United States Constitution of 1787 was an attempt to avoid problems similar to those created by British rule.

Separation of power
- The colonists built in a separation of powers to the Constitution, providing checks and balances.
- This was driven through by Alexander Hamilton and James Madison who had disapproved of the too-powerful Continental Congress.
- The separation of powers is considered to be the most revolutionary aspect of the Constitution.
- No branch of government should ever be subordinate to any other — the Executive, Legislature and Judiciary had to remain apart.
- The President could not take a seat in Congress, Congressmen could not be part of the Supreme Court, and members of the Supreme Court could only be appointed by an agreed confirmation between President and Congress.
- The President and his Cabinet, Congressmen and Supreme Court judges could all lose their jobs if they acted improperly.
- Each strand of government acted independently of each other.

Executive
- Executive power was vested in the elected President, and his Vice-President and Cabinet.
- The first President, George Washington, was elected in February 1789, and could make all key decisions and establish policy.
- Members of the Executive, including the President, or Thomas Jefferson, who became the USA's first Secretary of State, could be removed from office by the electorate in four-yearly elections.

Legislature
- Legislative power lay in the hands of an elected Congress which was divided into two Houses, the Senate and Representatives.
- The Senate was set up with each state equally represented and the House of Representatives was set up with states represented proportionately to size and population.
- The job of Congress was to pass laws and raise taxes.
- In addition, Congress was given responsibility for international trade, war and foreign relations.

Judiciary
- The newly formed Supreme Court of Justice, consisting of nine judges, would hold judicial power in the United States.

- The Supreme Court was formed in order to prevent legal matters becoming entwined with political ones.
- The Supreme Court could be called upon to debate the legality of new laws enacted by Congress. It also acted as the highest court of appeal in the United States.
- Supreme Court judges were nominated by the President upon advice from his Cabinet and political staff. New appointments had to be ratified by Congress after a rigorous vetting process.

Bill of Rights

- The Bill of Rights was drawn up in 1791 as the first ten amendments to the Constitution, after several states refused to ratify the Constitution as it stood.
- These states' delegates at Philadelphia wanted greater protections for citizens against the federal government. Therefore, the Bill of Rights became an important document that set out the limitations of the power of Congress.
- The Bill of Rights established liberty for individual citizens in states within a federal union of all states, and set out clear lines of authority between federal government and individual states.
- Central government controlled matters of national importance, and state assemblies were to be responsible for local government and administration.
- The Bill of Rights stated that neither Congress nor the government could pass laws which established religion as a part of state institutions, for example within the education system. School prayer was, therefore, prohibited.
- The Bill of Rights protected the freedom of the press, freedom of speech, and the right to peaceable assembly. Also it set out the rights of citizens who were under investigation or being tried for criminal offences; for example, no-one could be compelled to give evidence which might incriminate them.
- Any powers which had not been written into the Constitution as being delegated to the federal government would be delegated to state governments.

Democratic ideals

- The Constitution stated that "all men are created equal" and that everyone was entitled to "life, liberty and the pursuit of happiness".
- From now on, people would be asked to ratify many of the stages within democratic processes at state and national level.
- However, women and black people were excluded from the franchise, and in reality only one-fifth of eligible voters turned out for national elections.
- The Philadelphia Convention introduced an elitist system of electors in Presidential elections voting for an electoral college. The electoral college consisted of educated men who would vote for the President, a system which still exists today.

The experience of rule by Britain

- As part of the British Empire, colonists had been ruled by King and British Parliament, who together made key policy decisions, set laws and taxes, and enforced the law. As a result, there had been no checks and balances on executive, legislative and judicial processes.
- The notion of "No Taxation without Representation" had been a source of much of the original resentment towards British colonial policy.
- During their experience of being ruled by Britain, colonists had learned to be suspicious of all forms of government,

and they feared the potentially tyrannical power of a monarch.
- They designed the Constitution to thwart any future attempts of American heads of state to act in a similar manner as George III.

Other features

- The Articles of Confederation had been written in 1776, signed in 1781, and acknowledged in 1787, to declare that states would retain individual sovereignty and provided for state representatives to Continental Congress.
- In relation to religion, the Church was separated from the State in order to ensure equality was extended to include freedom of belief for everyone.
- Regarding the question of slavery, in Northern states measures were taken for the practice, already declining, to be gradually abolished, although pro-slavery sentiment in the South intensified simultaneously.

Any other relevant factors.

Part C: The French Revolution, to 1799

37. To what extent was corruption the most important threat to the security of the Ancien Régime before 1789?

Context

Despite attempts by French monarchs to centralise the organisation of the state, France remained a patchwork of different administrative systems by 1789. The Ancien Régime was inefficient and unfair in its taxation policies and access to political power. At a time of economic change and increasing literacy and wealth amongst the middle classes the system proved inflexible to the demands for change.

Corruption

- Absolutist nature of the monarchy — Marie-Antoinette. Decadence of the court.
- Financial problems — arguably the biggest threat to the Ancien Régime. Created in part by France's involvement in wars — most recently the American War of Independence — brought France to bankruptcy.
- Failure to reform.

Other factors

Taxation

- Unfair nature of the system — privileged orders of the First and Second estate. Unfair taxation system — cumbersome administration — tax collected by the Farmers General, who had a vested interest in collecting as much as they could.

The position of the clergy

- The clergy was split into the upper and lower clergy, the latter identifying more closely with the Third Estate. The church hierarchy was resented by the lower clergy; parish priests often sided with the peasants in their locality but the upper clergy viewed peasants with contempt and merely as a source of taxation.
- The Church owned a large amount of land and paid relatively little taxation. The upper clergy were concerned to protect their privileges.

The role of the nobility

- Like the clergy, the upper nobility were concerned to protect their privileged status, particularly access to posts at court and in the army, and their exemptions from taxation. Natural supporters of the monarchy, they saw some threat from the rise of the bourgeoisie.

- There were also tensions between the traditional nobility (of the sword) and the newly ennobled nobility (of the robe) wherein the 'old' sought to hold onto their control of key positions of the State, the Army and the Church, much to the annoyance of the 'new'.

The complaints of the Third Estate:

Grievances of the bourgeoisie
- Rise in the importance of the bourgeoisie — increased wealth — wish for increased participation.
- Influence of Enlightenment ideas: Voltaire, Montesquieu, Rousseau — questioned tradition — supported freedoms — press, speech. They attacked the privileges of the Church, its beliefs and the despotic nature of Ancien Régime Government. They were critical of many aspects of the Ancien Régime but not necessarily totally opposed to it. Impact may have been limited, as only certain sections of society would read their works. Some historians argue that Enlightenment ideas were only used to justify the revolution after it happened.

Grievances of the peasantry
- The bulk of French society — range of taxation and feudal rights imposed on them.
- The peasantry was becoming increasingly discontented with the disproportionate burden of taxation which fell on them.
- Pent-up resentment at their lot became clear in the Cahiers.

The urban workers
- The urban workers endured exploitation by bourgeois masters and suffered through restrictions on trade.
- They were particularly affected by bad harvests and food shortages.

Any other relevant factors.

38. How important was the threat of counter-revolution as a reason for the Terror, 1792–1795?

Context
The Terror is associated with the Committee of Public Safety, which was set up by the National Convention to oversee the protection of the new Republic from internal and external attack. As these threats were dealt with it increasingly became the tool to attack counter-revolutionaries, or perceived enemies of the increasingly radical Revolution.

The threat of counter-revolution
- One of the Convention's major concerns at the start of 1793 was to eliminate counter-revolutionary activity which intensified, particularly in the provinces after Louis' execution. At this point the Convention was still controlled by the relatively moderate Girondins.
- The Convention sanctioned a range of counter-revolutionary legislation such as:
  - the creation of the Committee of Public Safety; The Committee of General Security
  - Revolutionary tribunals to try opponents of the Republic and impose the death penalty if required and Surveillance Committees established in local areas to identify counter-revolutionary activity.
- Thus, most agree that most of the essential institutions of the Terror were actually in place before the Jacobins and Robespierre came to power. The moderates in the Convention had set up the structure of the Terror by the spring of 1793.

Other factors

The outbreak of war
- The war put pressure on the Convention to execute the war against the Republic's émigré and foreign opponents as ruthlessly and as effectively as possible. The nation's resources were mobilised to this end. The early military reverses raised alarms about sabotage and possible treason in the new armies.

The threat of invasion
- The initial defeats suffered raised the spectre of invasion.
- External dangers France faced radicalised the revolution. It occasioned a witch hunt for enemies within. The war led to the concept of the 'nation in crisis'. This had to be enforced, violently if necessary.
- It was pressure from mass demonstrations in Paris which intimidated the Convention into adopting terror as 'the order of the day' ie a method of government control. This was more to do with the exigencies of the foreign and civil wars which were threatening the Republic at this point than with Robespierre's philosophising over the nature of the Republic and the role of terror within it.

Political rivalries
- The Jacobins were one of a number of political groupings contending for power. The struggle became increasingly bitter with time. Similarly, a number of other prominent individuals had sought to control the course of the revolution. Some had already died violently. The Terror was a legitimised means of the Jacobins eliminating their political rivals — 'a revolution always consumes its children'.

The role of Robespierre
- Robespierre believed that the 'general will' of the sovereign people both created and sanctioned policy-making within the nation. The will of the people could only prevail within a Republic. Any individual who sought to oppose this was, by implication, guilty of treason against the nation itself. In such circumstances death — the ultimate weapon of Terror — was entirely appropriate. Hence Robespierre's belief that 'terror is virtue' — that to create and maintain a 'virtuous' nation which enshrined the revolutionary principles of liberty and equality, it was necessary to violently expunge any counter-revolutionary activity.
- Robespierre became a member of the Committee of Public Safety in July 1793 and came to control its operations. Until his own execution in July 1794, the Committee became the main instrument for the application of terror in defence of Robespierre's ideal of a 'Republic of Virtue'. During this period Robespierre sanctioned the use of terror against:
  - the monarchy and émigré opponents of the Republic eg Marie Antoinette executed
  - provincial counter-revolutionaries particularly in the Vendee
  - Hebertists, whose anti-Christian stance Robespierre found both distasteful and dangerous
  - Dantonists who challenged the authority of Robespierre and who were therefore (since Robespierre's government represented the 'general will') guilty of treason.
- With the imposition of the infamous Law of 22nd Prairial (June 1794), Robespierre was given virtually unlimited powers to eliminate opponents of his Republic of Virtue and during the period of the Great Terror in June and July 1794, over 1500 were executed.
- Had Robespierre lived beyond Thermidor there is no doubt the death toll would have risen even higher. However, while Robespierre must bear responsibility for the intensification of the Terror during 1793–1794, the use of

terror as an instrument of state policy was by no means confined to Robespierre.

Religious and regional differences

- The uprising in the Vendee was supported by priests and former nobles. It also secured British support. It was brutally suppressed. Many women and children were drowned in the Loire at Nantes.
- There were also demands in the south for greater autonomy.
- Under the Civil Constitution of the Clergy, priests had to swear an oath of loyalty to the state. Many refused and became leaders of resistance.

Any other relevant factors.

39. *The peasantry gained the most from the French Revolution.* How valid is this view?

Context

The French Revolution is widely considered to be one of the most important historical events in human history. Its effects within France were profound and lasting. In particular, the impact on the French Aristocracy and Clergy was long lasting as was the enduring French liking for Republicanism.

Impact on the Third Estate

The peasantry

- In contrast to the Catholic Church and the nobility the position of the peasantry was in many ways strengthened by the Revolution. The ending of feudalism in August 1789 removed many of the legal and financial burdens which had formed the basis of peasant grievances in the Cahiers des Doleances presented to the Estates-General in 1789.
- The revolutionary land settlement, instigated by the nationalisation of church lands in November 1789, had transferred land from the nobility and the clergy to the peasantry to their obvious advantage. It should be noted, however, that not all peasants benefited equally from this. Only the well-off peasants could afford to purchase the Church lands which had been seized by the National Assembly.

The impact of the Revolution on the bourgeoisie

- The Revolution instigated a fundamental shift in political and economic power from the First and Second Estates to the bourgeoisie.
- The ending of feudalism in August 1789 heralded profound social and economic change (eg facilitating the development of capitalism) whilst the Declaration of the Rights of Man and the Citizen later in the month did the same for political life. In both cases the main beneficiaries were the bourgeoisie.
- Successive constitutions and legislative reforms throughout the 1790s favoured the bourgeoisie above all other social groups by emphasising the notion of a property-owning democracy with voting rights framed within property qualifications, whilst the ending of trade restrictions and monopolies favoured an expanding business and merchant class.
- France had moved from a position of privileged estates to one where increasingly merit was what counted. It was the educated bourgeoisie who were best placed to benefit from this profound change in French society.

The urban workers

- At key points throughout the Revolution overt demonstrations of discontent by the urban masses — particularly in Paris — impacted on key events as successive regimes framed policy with an eye to appeasing the mob. However, any modest gains by the urban poor

were short-lived. A decade of almost continuous wars in the 1790s had created shortages and inflation which hit the urban poor particularly hard.

- The passing of the Chapelier Law in May 1791, by a bourgeois-dominated National Assembly protecting the interests of industrialists, effectively banned the formation of trade unions and thereafter the Revolution brought few tangible economic or political gains for urban workers.

The impact of the Revolution on the First Estate

- The Catholic Church was a key pillar of the Ancien Régime. The Upper Clergy (usually drawn from the ranks of the traditional nobility) enjoyed considerable wealth and status based on a raft of privileges and tax exemptions. These privileges and exemptions were swept away by the Revolution and the position of the Catholic Church within France by 1799 was far less assured than it had been under the Ancien Régime.
- The Civil Constitution of the Clergy (July 1790) polarised attitudes towards the place of the Catholic Church within French society and promoted conflict between opposing factions through the rest of the period to 1799. In November 1789 Church lands were nationalised, stripping the Church of much of its wealth. The net result of all of this was that the Church never regained its primacy within the French state and can be seen to have lost far more than it gained.

The impact of the Revolution on the Second Estate

- The aristocracy had enjoyed similar privileges and tax exemptions to those of the Catholic Church under the Ancien Régime. Advancement in the key positions of the State, the Army and, indeed the Church, depended more often on birth than merit. The traditional nobility monopolised these key positions and sought at all times to defend its favoured position. Again, the Revolution swept away aristocratic privilege even more completely than that of the clergy.
- The ending of feudalism in August 1789 marked the prelude to a decade when the status of the nobility in France effectively collapsed. In 1790 outward displays of 'nobility' such as titles and coats of arms were forbidden by law and in 1797, after election results suggested a pro-royalist resurgence, the Convention imposed alien status on nobles and stripped them of French citizenship.
- The Revolution brought in a regime where careers were open to talent regardless of birth or inheritance and the traditional aristocracy simply ceased to exist. Having said that, some nobles simply transformed themselves into untitled landlords in the countryside and continued to exercise significant economic and political power.

Any other relevant factors.

Part D: Germany, 1815—1939

40. *Economic factors were the main reason for the growth of nationalism in Germany, 1815–1850.* How valid is this view?

Context

In 1815 'Germany' was not a unified state but a loose confederation made up of 39 separate states with their own rulers and systems of government. However, economic development after 1815 created a greater feeling of unity and led to a growth of nationalism.

Economic factors

- Urbanisation and industrialisation of the German states — political fragmentation — can be argued to be the most important obstacle to German economic development.

- Middle-class businessmen called for a more united market to enable them to compete with foreign countries. They complained that tax burdens were holding back economic development.
- Prussian economic expansion — drift in power away from Austria and towards Prussia as the latter began to build on rich resources such as coal and iron deposits.
- Prussia's gain of territory on the River Rhine after 1815 meant it had good reason to reach an agreement with neighbours to ensure relatively free travel of goods and people between its lands in the East and the West.
- Prussia created a large free-trade area within Prussia itself.
- Railway/road development — post-1830s the development of railways/roads ended the isolation of German states from each other. This enabled the transport and exploitation of German natural resources. Economic cooperation between German states encouraged those seeking a political solution to the issue of German unity.

Other Factors:

Cultural factors
- Main unifying force was language — 25 million Germans spoke the same language and shared the same culture and literature.
- Writers and thinkers (eg Heine, Fichte, Goethe, Brothers Grimm, Schiller and Hegel) encouraged the growth of a German consciousness.
- Post-1815 nationalist feelings first expressed in universities.
- Growth of Burschenschaften pre-1815 dedicated to driving French from German soil — zealous but lacking a clear idea of how best to accomplish the task.
- The Hambacherfest and student demonstrations — little was accomplished by the students.
- Early 19th century was a time of great change in all European states and it has been suggested that the political changes of the time can be partly explained by an understanding of the cultural developments of the time.

The Zollverein
- Zollverein — the 'mighty lever' of German unification. By 1836, 25 of the 39 German states had joined this economic free-trade area (Austria excluded). Members of the Union voluntarily restricted their sovereignty (even if only for selfish interests) to allow for economic gain through joining the Prussian-led Customs Union.
- German nationalists in the late 1830s saw it as a step towards a wider political union.

French Revolution and the Napoleonic Wars
- Ideas of the French Revolution appealed to the middle classes in the German states.
- Impact of Napoleonic wars — many Germans argued that Napoleon/France had been able to conquer German states pre-1815 due to their division as separate, autonomous territories. German princes had stirred national feeling to help raise armies to drive out the French, aiding the sense of a common German identity with common goals.

Political factors
- 1848 revolutions in Germany raised consciousness greatly even though they failed.
- Many Liberals were middle-class and were also receptive to nationalist ideas.

Military weakness
- The French Revolution led to a realisation that, individually, the German states were weak.

- French troops had marched across Germany for over 20 years, and had humiliated Prussia, the strongest 'German' state at Jena and Auerstadt. Germany had been carved up by Napoleon, the North Sea coast being incorporated into France itself, and the Confederation of the Rhine set up as a puppet state. Divided, the German states could not defend their territorial integrity.
- Germany had been used as a recruiting ground by Napoleon: Germans had died to protect France. Even the enlarged post-Vienna states would be powerless, with the exception of Prussia, to prevent this happening again.

Any other relevant factors.

41. How important was Prussian economic strength in the achievement of German unification by 1871?

Context
The growth of nationalism and Prussian dominance among the German states led to pressure for unification of Germany. Historians are divided on why unification was achieved. Many argue that unification was a natural process due to favourable economic circumstances. However, it can be argued that Otto von Bismarck's policies took advantage of these conditions to achieve unification.

Prussian economic strength
- Growth in Prussian economic power eg development of railways, transport links, roads; importance of the Rhineland and the Saarland to Prussian economic development. Able to finance and equip Prussian army.
- The Zollverein, the Prussian-dominated free-trade area; its significance to German political unification — the 'mighty lever of German unification'.
- The Zollverein drew the German states together and stimulated their economic growth, at the same time firmly establishing Prussia as the economic leader in Germany.
- The Nationalverein — aim was the creation of a united Germany; composed of intelligent and economically important section of German society — businessmen; identified Prussia as leader of a united Germany.

Other factors:

The role of Bismarck
- Bismarck's aim was to increase the power of Prussia by whatever means necessary.
- His 'realpolitik'/diplomacy in the '3 wars' against Denmark, Austria and France.
- Bismarck took the initiative, as opposed to Austria, in the war against Denmark; his 'solution' to the Schleswig-Holstein question.
- His skilful manipulation of events leading up to the war with Austria in 1866 plus his establishment of friendships with potential allies of Austria beforehand.
- Bismarck's wisdom in the Treaty of Prague, 1866.
- Bismarck's manipulation of the Ems Telegram to instigate a war with France in 1870.
- The exploitation of the weaknesses of European statesmen/rulers, eg Napoleon III; mistakes made by Bismarck's adversaries.
- Bismarck's skill in isolating his intended targets (diplomatically).

Prussian military strength
- Significance of military reforms of Moltke and Roon — creation of modern powerful army which Bismarck used.
- The Prusso-Danish War 1864 and Schleswig Holstein. The Danes were easily beaten.

- The Austro-Prussian War 1866. The war was a stunning success for the Prussians.
- The Franco-Prussian War 1870. The war followed a similar pattern to the first two. The Prussian Army was aided by soldiers from the other German States.

The attitude of other states

- Foreign concerns over the idea of a united Germany. None of the Great Powers wanted to see the creation of a strong Germany which might upset the balance of power.
- Attitudes changed after 1850: Britain was increasingly pre-occupied with her Empire, particularly India (mutiny, 1857).

The decline of Austria

- The decline in Austrian power and influence — economically and militarily — during the 1850s particularly.
- Distraction of Austria due to commitments in Italy.

The actions of Napoleon III

- Napoleon III wanted France to remain Europe's greatest power. He was however no match for Bismarck. His hopes of territorial gain as a result of French neutrality in the Austro-Prussian War were dashed by Prussia's swift victory. The outcome of the Luxembourg question also deprived France of territorial gain.
- Napoleon overreacted over the Hohenzollern candidature. Viewing Leopold's candidature as totally unacceptable, Napoleon instructed the French ambassador in Berlin, to go to the spa town at Ems, to put the French case that Leopold's candidacy was a danger to France and to advise William I to stop Leopold leaving for Spain if he wanted to avoid war. Despite the fact that the affair appeared to have been settled in France's favour, Napoleon overplayed his hand by demanding an official renunciation from William I on behalf of Leopold, which gave Bismarck the opportunity to doctor the Ems Telegram and provoke war.
- Napoleon III's military leadership in the Franco-Prussian War was poor and fatal mistakes were made. He allowed himself to be surrounded and captured at Sedan, effectively ending the war.

Political factors

- Influence of Napoleon Bonaparte — reduction of number of German states; growth of a national consciousness.
- The 1848 revolutions in German states — importance of Frankfurt Parliament/decisions taken regarding a unified Germany; Prussia was a potential leader; Austria was excluded from Germany ('kleindeutschland').

Cultural factors

- Growth of German cultural nationalism/Romantic Movement — Burschenschaften, eg writers, music, leading to an increased German national consciousness among the educated classes.

Any other relevant factors.

42. To what extent was propaganda the main reason why the Nazis were able to stay in power 1933–1939?

Context

The Nazis used a variety of methods to stay in power. These ranged from economic policies that pleased the German people to the development of State terror.

Propaganda

- Nazi propaganda was important in maintaining control, spreading Nazi beliefs and in persuading people to support the regime.

- A Ministry of Propaganda headed by Josef Goebbels, an expert in propaganda, was created and took complete control of all aspects of the media.
- Newspapers were censored and used to spread Nazi government news.
- Radio became one of the most important tools for indoctrination and was used to broadcast Hitler's key speeches. The sale of cheap radios to the German population encouraged this.
- Mass rallies, for example the spectacular Nuremburg Rallies, strengthened commitment to the Nazi regime and created feelings of wishing to belong to the Nazi movement.
- Newsreels were used as propaganda in cinemas and films, such as Triumph of the Will were made to encourage involvement in the regime although most films were pure entertainment to maintain support for the Nazi regime by diverting people's attention away from unpopular policies.
- Goebbels and the Ministry of Propaganda developed the Hitler Myth in which Hitler was portrayed as Germany's all powerful Fuhrer which contributed to Hitler's personal popularity.

Other factors

Economic policies

- The immediate aims of Nazi economic policy were to tackle the Depression and to restore Germany to full employment. The other priority was to prepare Germany for war.
- Under Hjalmar Schacht as Minister of Economics, the Nazi government increased government spending and invested in a massive programme of public works which included the construction of the motorway network, the Autobahnen. Increased employment and a small rise in living conditions helped to gain the support of workers.
- Despite economic recovery being underway in 1932, Hitler was given the credit for drastically reducing unemployment which helped to win popular support.
- To maintain workers' loyalty, the Nazis set up organisations such as Strength through Joy (designed to reward loyal workers with rewards such as cruises and vacations at Nazi holiday camps) and Beauty of Work (designed to persuade employers to improve working conditions).
- From 1936 rearmament and conscription helped to create almost full employment which was popular with the army and big business.
- Hitler attempted to maintain the support of the Mittelstand (shop keepers and skilled craftsmen) by banning the opening of new department stores.
- As part of the Nazi belief in 'Blood and Soil' a number of measures were introduced to help farmers. The Nazis increased tariffs on imported food and attempts were made to cancel farmers' debts. The Reich Entailed Farm Law prohibited the sale of small farms. The Reich Food Estate was created to run the rural economy, fix wages and prices, establishing food quotas.
- Goering's Four Year Plan (1936) stressed autarky (self-sufficiency) and rearmament, which created tension between the demand for guns or butter. By 1936 workers were becoming increasingly discontented and in addition the promises to lower middle class groups remained unfulfilled.

Establishment of a totalitarian state

- Following the Reichstag Fire, the Decree of the Reich President for the Protection of the Nation and the State (28th February 1933) suspended constitutional civil rights.

- The Enabling Act (24th March 1933) passed under pressure by the Reichstag gave Hitler dictatorial powers for four years.
- The Law for the Reconstruction of the State (30th January 1934) abolished state (local) governments and Nazi Gauleiters (leaders of local branches of the Nazi Party) were appointed to run states.
- When Hindenburg died (2nd August 1934) Hitler combined the posts of Chancellor and President which secured Hitler's grip on power.
- Within eighteen months of being appointed Chancellor, Hitler had established a legal dictatorship.

The crushing of opposition
- Hitler's first actions were against opposition political parties and organisations. Communists, Social Democrats and trade unionists were imprisoned in the weeks after the Reichstag Fire.
- Trade Unions were abolished (2nd May 1933) and replaced by the German Workers' Front (DAF).
- The SPD were banned (22nd June 1933) and the other political parties dissolved themselves soon after.
- Under the *Law Against the Formation of New Parties* (14th July 1933) Germany became a one-party state.
- Hitler avoided potential opposition from the churches by reaching a Concordat with the Catholic Church (20th July 1933) and the creation of a Reich Church to co-ordinate all Protestant churches.
- The Night of the Long Knives (30th June 1934) removed internal opposition from the SA, and earned the gratitude of the Army.
- The army took an oath of personal loyalty to Hitler in August 1934 which resulted in opponents within the army being torn between their consciences and their loyalty.
- Opposition was not strong enough to pose a real threat to the Nazi regime eg the lack of cooperation between the Social Democrat or SPD and the Communist underground opposition which remained bitterly divided.

Fear and state terrorism
- Violence and terror was crucial in Hitler's rise to power and continued throughout the time of the Nazi regime and played a vital role in strengthening the Nazi dictatorship.
- The SS, the state's internal security service and the Gestapo, the Secret State Police, expanded in power and their brutal acts of repression ensured there was an atmosphere of fear that the Nazis used to control the people.
- The SS defended the Nazi dictatorship from enemies of the state and took over responsibility for running the concentration camps.
- The Gestapo, the Secret State Police, were feared due to their reputation for the use of torture to gain confessions from suspects. The use of informants was vital to maintain fear.

Social controls
- The 'Law for the Re-establishment of the Professional Civil Service' allowed for the dismissal of anti-Nazi members.
- Anti-Nazi judges were dismissed and replaced with those favourable to the Nazis. Cases involving treason were to be heard by a People's Court led by Nazi judges.
- The passing of the all-embracing law 'Acts Hostile to the National Community' (1935) allowed the Nazis to persecute opponents in a 'legal' way.

Successful foreign policy
- Much of Hitler's popularity after he came to power rested on his achievements in foreign policy, especially when he appeared to be reversing the humiliations of the Treaty of Versailles.
- A series of major foreign policy successes: the remilitarisation of the Rhineland (1936), the Anschluss with Austria (1938) and the takeover of the Sudetenland of Czechoslovakia, were hugely popular and increased support for the regime.

Social policies
- The Nazis attempted to create a *Volksgemeinschaft* (national community) in which the German people would act together and support the Nazi regime.
- The Nazis' vision of a Volksgemeinschaft also involved the exclusion of 'outsiders'. Nazi propaganda won people over to the persecution of Jews and other minority groups viewed by the Nazis as a threat to the regime.
- To indoctrinate the young, Nazi youth organisations were set up, for example the Hitler Youth to prepare boys for military service and the League of German Girls to prepare young women for motherhood.
- Also with the aim of controlling Germany's youth, the Nazis made changes to the education system. Anti-Nazi teachers were removed and the school curriculum was redesigned with stress put on physical exercise and subjects such as History and Biology used to promote nationalism and racism. New Nazi schools, NAPOLOAS, to train future leaders were set up and run by the SS.
- The Nazi view of women could be summed up in the slogan Kinder, Kirche, Kuche (Children, Church, Kitchen). Nazi policies towards women including marriage loans, increased welfare services and the setting up of women's organisations were viewed positively by many women.
- Although many Germans were not committed Nazis, they accepted the Nazi regime as for many, life was better than under the Weimar Republic.

Any other relevant factors.

Part E: Italy, 1815–1939

43. *The secret societies played the most important role in the growth of nationalism in Italy, 1815–1850. How valid is this view?*

Context
The origins of Italian nationalism can be traced back to the Renaissance and the writings of Machiavelli who urged Italians to seize Italy from the 'barbarians'. However, the ideas of Mazzini and his anti-Austrian views led to the development of a more political nationalism in the 19th century.

Secret societies
- By the time of the French invasions, secret societies, dedicated to freeing Italy from foreign rule, were already in existence. After 1815 their chief enemy was Austria.
- The growth of secret societies, particularly the Carbonari (the Charcoal Burners), led to revolts in 1820, 1821, 1831. Also 'Young Italy' and their revolts in the 1830s.
- They had support throughout Italy, mostly drawn from the middle classes — doctors, teachers, lawyers, etc. along with a few army officers.
- These groups were patriotic idealists rather than practical politicians: men prepared to risk their lives for their cause. Some wanted an Italian Republic while others looked for constitutional reforms.

Other factors

Cultural factors

- The Risorgimento was inspired by Italy's past. Poets such as Leopardi glorified and exaggerated past achievements kindling nationalist desires. Poets and novelists like Pellico inspired anti-Austrian feelings amongst intellectuals as did operas such as Verdi's 'Nabucco' and Rossini's 'William Tell'.
- There was no national 'Italian' language-regional dialects were like separate languages. Alfieri inspired 'Italian' language based on Tuscan. The poet and novelist Manzoni wrote in 'Italian'. Philosophers spread ideas of nationalism in their books and periodicals.
- Moderate nationalists such as Gioberti and Balbo advocated the creation of a federal state with the individual rulers remaining but joining together under a president for foreign affairs and trade. Gioberti's 'On the moral and civil primacy of the Italians' advocated the Pope as president whilst Balbo, in his book 'On the hopes of Italy', saw the King of Piedmont/Sardinia in the role.

Economic factors

- Economic factors were not important directly. Wealth lay in land (landowners were often reactionary) and trade (where the educated bourgeoisie were more receptive to ideas of liberalism and nationalism).
- The election of a new, seemingly reformist Pope, Pius IX, in 1846 inspired feelings of nationalism particularly amongst businessmen and traders as he wished to form a customs union.

Military weakness

- The French Revolution led to a realisation that, individually, the Italian states were weak.
- The fragmentation of Italy in the Vienna Settlement restored Italy's vulnerability to foreign invasion.

Effects of French revolution and Napoleonic wars

- 'Italian' intellectuals had initially been inspired by the French Revolution with its national flag, national song, national language, national holiday and emphasis on citizenship.
- Napoleon Bonaparte's conquest inspired feelings of nationalism — he reduced the number of states to three; revived the name 'Italy'; brought in single system of weights and measures; improved communications; helped trade, inspiring desire for at least a customs union. Napoleon's occupation was hated — conscription, taxes, looting of art.

Resentment of Austria

- After the Vienna Settlement in 1815, hatred of foreign control centred on Austria. The Hapsburg Emperor directly controlled Lombardy and Venetia; his relatives controlled Parma, Modena, Tuscany. Austria had strong ties to the Papacy and had alliances with other rulers. Conscription, censorship, the use of spies and the policy of promotion in the police, civil service and army only for German speakers was resented.
- Austrian army presence within towns like Milan and the heavily garrisoned Quadrilateral fortresses ensured that 'Italians' could never forget that they were under foreign control and this inspired growing desire for the creation of a national state.

Role of Mazzini

- Radical nationalist Mazzini not only inspired dreams of a united, democratic Italian republic through his written works, but also formed an activist movement 'Young Italy' whose aim was to make these dreams a reality.

Any other relevant factors.

44. To what extent was the decline of Austria the main reason why unification was achieved in Italy, by 1870?

Context

The nationalist reaction to the rule of Napoleon across Europe unleashed forces which eventually led to the unification of Italy. In Italy this process was dominated by the state of Piedmont, although the role of individuals like Garibaldi and the declining power of Austria also need to be taken into account.

Decline of Austria

- Austria's position was in decline in economic and military terms, particularly in regard to Prussia. Italy's relative weakness was redressed by her alliance with Prussia.
- Austria's exclusion from the Prussian-led Zollverein meant she did not share in the same economic growth as other Germanic states.
- Austria's diplomatic position also declined in the 1850s, and she was increasingly isolated. Partly this was self-inflicted. Russia never forgave Austria for her lack of support during the Crimean War.
- Austria's army failed to modernise compared to other main European states.

Other factors

The rise of Piedmont

- Piedmont was the most powerful of the independent Italian states. She was the natural leader of the unification movement.
- Piedmont was also the most economically advanced of the Italian states. Industry developed around Turin and a railway network was built.
- The army of Piedmont was advanced by Italian standards.

Role of Cavour

- He played a vital role — modernisation of Piedmont; diplomacy before War of Liberation.
- Cavour made a secret agreement to help Prussia in the war against Austria 1866.
- Prussian war against France gave the Italians the chance to take Rome.
- Provocation of Austria; encouragement of National Society especially in Duchies/Romagna and his handling of the plebiscites.
- The war of 1859 inspired rebellions in Tuscany, Parma, Modena, Romagna and demands for union with Piedmont. Napoleon III was not happy, but was persuaded to accept by British diplomacy and Cavour's renewed offer of Nice and Savoy.
- Cavour's diplomacy and manoeuvring over Garibaldi's expedition; the invasion of Papal States forced unification on Piedmontese terms.

Role of Garibaldi

- He was a committed nationalist; he fought in the War of Liberation for Victor Emmanuel. His role was crucial in forcing north/south unification — the role of 'the thousand'; military success in Sicily and Naples; handing his 'conquests' to Victor Emmanuel at Teano. He tried but failed to take Rome.

Role of Victor Emmanuel II

- The King was supportive of Cavour. Victor Emmanuel of Piedmont/Cavour realised foreign help needed to drive Austrians from Italy.
- The King 'managed' Garibaldi very well in 1866, preventing a diplomatic crisis.

Attitudes and actions of Napoleon III

- Crimean War/Paris Peace provided opportunity for Cavour to remind Britain and France of Italy's 'unhappy' state. Following the Orsini Plot, Napoleon III held a secret meeting at Plombieres, July 1858 with Cavour. The result was a formal treaty in January 1859. Napoleon III promised 200,000 men to fight for Piedmont if Austria attacked. This would prove crucial.
- Napoleon did not intervene over Garibaldi's expedition. He made a secret agreement accepting Cavour's proposed invasion of the Papal States to stop Garibaldi reaching Rome. This allowed the Piedmontese to defeat the Papal Army, taking The Marches and Umbria. In 1866 Austria handed Venetia to France who gave it to Italy.
- The Italians took Rome after the defeat of Napoleon in 1870.

The importance of foreign intervention

- War of Liberation of 1859 — the two main victories Magenta and Solferino were French. At Villafranca Austria handed Lombardy to France who gave it to Piedmont. Garibaldi acknowledged the importance of French help.
- Britain was involved in diplomacy over Duchies. British naval presence helped Garibaldi land at Marsala. Britain refused a joint naval blockade with France to stop Garibaldi crossing the Strait of Messina — crucial for Garibaldi's success.
- Britain was the first power to officially recognise Kingdom of Italy.

Any other relevant factors.

45. How important was foreign policy as a reason why the Fascists in Italy were able to stay in power, 1922–1939?

Context

Between 1922 and 1939 Mussolini was the fascist leader of Italy. Did Italians support Mussolini because of effective propaganda or did most Italians accept and even support the regime that gave them work and food and promises of a powerful Italy?

Foreign policy

- Mussolini was initially extremely popular, as evidenced by huge crowds who turned out to hear him speak.
- Foreign policy successes in the 1920s, such as the Corfu Incident, made him extremely popular. He was also able to mobilise public opinion very successfully for the invasion of Abyssinia.
- Mussolini's role in the Munich Conference of 1938 was his last great foreign policy triumph.
- As Mussolini got more closely involved with Hitler his popularity lessened. His intervention in Spain proved a huge drain on Italy's resources. The invasion of Albania was a fiasco.

Other factors

Fear and intimidation

- Mussolini favoured complete State authority with everything under his direct control. All Italians were expected to obey Mussolini and his Fascist Party.
- The squadristi were organised into the MVSN *Milizia Voluntaria per la Sicurezza Nazionale* the armed local Fascist militia (Blackshirts). They terrorised the cities and provinces causing fear with tactics such as force-feeding with toads and castor oil.
- After 1925–6 around 10,000 non-fascists/opposition leaders were jailed by special tribunals.

- The secret police, OVRA was established in 1927 and was led by Arturo Bocchini. Tactics included abduction and torture of opponents. 4000 people were arrested by the OVRA and sent to prison.
- Penal colonies were established on remote Mediterranean islands such as Ponza and Lipari. Conditions for those sentenced to these prisons were primitive with little chance of escape.
- Opponents were exiled internally or driven into exile abroad.
- The death penalty was restored under Mussolini for serious offences but by 1940 only ten people had been sentenced to death.

Establishment of the fascist state

- Nov/Dec 1922 Mussolini was given emergency powers. Nationalists merged with PNF 1923. Mussolini created MSVN (fascist militia) — gave him support if the army turned against him — and Fascist Grand Council — a rival Cabinet. These two bodies made Mussolini's position stronger and opposition within PNF weaker. The establishment of a dictatorship began:
  - 1926 — opposition parties were banned. A one party state was created.
  - 1928 — universal suffrage abolished.
  - 1929 — all Fascist Parliament elected.

Crushing of opposition

- Liberals had divided into four factions so were weakened.
- The Left had divided into three — original PSI, reformist PSU and Communists — they failed to work together against fascists.
- Pope forced Sturzo to resign and so PPI (Catholic Popular Party) was weakened and it split.
- Acerbo Law passed. 1924 elections — fascists won 66% of the vote.
- Opposition parties failed to take advantage of the Matteotti crisis. By walking out of the Chamber of Deputies (Aventine Secession) they gave up the chance to overthrow Mussolini; they remained divided — the Pope refused to sanction an alliance between PPI and the socialists. The King chose not to dismiss Mussolini.
- Communists and socialists did set up organisations in exile but did not work together. Communist cells in northern cities did produce some anti-fascist leaflets but they suffered frequent raids by OVRA.
- PPI opposition floundered with the closer relationship between Church and State (Lateran Pacts).

Social controls

- Workers were controlled through 22 corporations, set up in 1934; overseen by National Council of Corporations, chaired by Mussolini.
- Corporations provided accident, health and unemployment insurance for workers, but forbade strikes and lock-outs.
- There were some illegal strikes in 1930s and anti-fascist demonstrations in 1933 but these were limited.
- The majority of Italians got on with their own lives conforming as long as all was going well. Middle classes/elites supported fascism as it protected them from communism.
- Youth knew no alternative to fascism, were educated as fascists and this strengthened the regime. Youth movements provided sporting opportunities, competitions, rallies, camps, parades and propaganda lectures — 60% membership in the north.

Propaganda

- Press, radio and cinema were all controlled.
- Mussolini was highly promoted as a 'saviour' sent by God to help Italy — heir to Caesar, world statesman, supreme patriot, a great thinker who worked 20 hours a day, a man of action, incorruptible.

Relations with the Papacy

- Lateran treaties/Concordat with Papacy enabled acceptance of regime by the Catholic majority.
- Many Catholics supported Mussolini's promotion of 'family values'.

Economic and social policies.

- Fascists tried to develop the Italian economy in a series of propaganda-backed initiatives eg the 'Battle for Grain'. While superficially successful, they did tend to divert resources from other areas.
- Development of transport infrastructure, with building of autostrade and redevelopment of major railway terminals eg Milan.
- One major success was the crushing of organized crime. Most Mafia leaders were in prison by 1939.
- Dopolavoro had 3.8 million members by 1939. Gave education and skills training; sports provision, day-trips, holidays, financial assistance and cheap rail fares. This diverted attention from social/economic problems and was the fascist state's most popular institution.

Any other relevant factors.

Part F: Russia, 1881—1921

46. *The authority of the Tsarist state was never seriously challenged in the years before 1905.* **How valid is this view?**

Context

The Tsarist state was never seriously challenged before 1905. The main reasons for making this possible were the 'Pillars of Autocracy'. Each of these 'Pillars' strengthened the Tsar's position, and made it almost impossible for opposition groups to challenge the state.

'Pillars of Autocracy'

- **The Fundamental Law** stated 'To the emperor of all Russia belongs the supreme and unlimited power. God himself commands that his supreme power be obeyed out of conscience as well as out of fear'. This was the basis of the Tsarist state.
- **The army** was controlled by the officers who were mainly upper-class, conservative and loyal to the Tsar. They ensured that the population, and the peasantry in particular, was loyal to the Tsar. They crushed any insurgence and were used to enforce order in the country and loyalty to the Tsar.
- **The secret police (Okhrana)** was set up to ensure loyalty to the Tsar and weed out opposition to the Tsar. They did this by spying on all people of society irrespective of class. Those showing any sign of opposition to the Tsar were imprisoned or sent into exile. Large numbers were exiled.
- **The civil service** mainly employed middle-class people, therefore ensuring the loyalty of that class. The civil service was responsible for enforcing laws on censorship and corruption and controlling meetings which made it very difficult for the revolutionaries to communicate.
- **The Church** helped to ensure that the people, particularly the peasants, remained loyal to the Tsar. They preached to the peasants that the Tsar had been appointed by God

and that they should therefore obey the Tsar. Ensured the peasants were aware of the Fundamental Law.

Opposition groups

- Opposition groups, eg Social Democrats (supported by industrial workers) and Liberals (who wanted a British-style parliament), were fairly weak. However, these groups were not powerful or popular enough to effect change.
- There were various revolutionary groups like the Social Revolutionaries (supported by peasants seeking land reform). Moreover, these groups were further weakened by the fact they were divided and disorganised.
- The leaders were often in prison or in exile.

Censorship

- This controlled what people could read, what university lecturers could say, access to schools, and limited the number and type of books available in libraries.

Russification

- This was the policy of restricting the rights of the national minorities in the Russian Empire by insisting that Russian was the first language. As a result, law and government were conducted throughout the Russian Empire in the Russian language. This maintained the dominance of the Russian culture over that of the minorities. State intervention in religion and education. Treated subjects as potential enemies and inferior to Russians.

Zubatov unions

- Organised by the police, these were used to divert the attention of the workers away from political change by concentrating on wages and conditions in the factories, thus reducing the chances of the workers being influenced by the revolutionary groups. Unions in 1903 became involved in strikes and so were disbanded due to pressure from employers.

Any other relevant factors.

47. How important were military defeats in the First World War in bringing about the February Revolution, 1917?

Context

Previous limited reform was not enough to save Tsarist rule from the stresses of fighting in World War 1, highlighted by their early defeats. The war further exposed the weaknesses of the Tsarist rule and undermined loyalty to the Tsar.

The First World War — military defeat

- The war did not go well for the Russian armed forces and they suffered many defeats. Russia also lost control of Poland in 1915, which was a severe blow to Russian pride.
- The Russian army lacked vital resources, including adequate medical care, and this led to high fatality and casualty rates. There were claims of defeats caused by incompetent officers who refused to co-operate with each other, as well as communication difficulties. This led to low morale and desertions; the Tsar began to lose control and the support of the armed forces. The Generals forced his abdication at Pskov.

Other factors:

Social and economic problems — bourgeoisie, working and peasant class

- The war put a tremendous strain on the already fragile Russian economy. There was long-term discontent among both peasants and industrial workers. The inadequate transport system was unable to cope with the supply demands of the military as well as the needs of the

Russian economy and society. There was a lack of food, made worse by the transport problems and the scorched earth policy; as a result there were long queues and bread riots in the cities, culminating in the International Women's Day protest in Petrograd.

- The war was costing 17 million roubles a day and Russia had to get loans from Britain and France. Economic problems such as heavy taxes, high inflation and price rises meant that many were living in poverty.
- The people had expected the war to be won by Christmas 1914 so they were war-weary by 1917 and suffering from grief, anxiety and low morale. They wanted the war to end but they knew the Tsar would not agree to that and they became so unhappy and frustrated they protested and went on strike which led to the February Revolution as the army sympathised with them and consequently sided with them against the Tsarist system.

Tsar Nicholas II

- The Tsar was seen as a weak ruler as he was so easily influenced by the Tsarina, Rasputin and his ministers. At times the Tsar appeared to be more interested in his family than in the issues facing Russia. He was stubborn as he ignored advice and warnings from Rodzyanko and he failed to understand the severity of events in February 1917.
- In September 1915 the Tsar took personal control of the armed forces, which left him personally responsible for any defeats. This also meant that he left the Tsarina in charge, which was not welcomed in Russia as she was German and her relationship with Rasputin was viewed with suspicion.
- By February 1917 the Tsar had lost control of the armed forces as well as the support and loyalty of the Russian people, which contributed to the February 1917 revolution.

Political problems — autocracy

- There had been long-term discontent with the Tsar's autocratic rule as he seemed unwilling to share his power despite promises (October Manifesto and Fundamental Laws). The Dumas had limited power and the Tsar dissolved it and changed the franchise.
- War exacerbated existing problems with the Tsar leaving the Tsarina to run the country in his absence. Frustration grew at the incompetence of the Tsar and his ministers, Rasputin's influence and not having a say in how the country was being run and this led to protests and ultimately to the February Revolution.

Any other relevant factors.

48. To what extent was disunity among the Whites the main reason for the victory of the Reds in the Civil War?

Context

In order to secure power, the Bolsheviks had to fight a vicious Civil War with their opponents. That they won was due to the weaknesses of their White opponents, as well as the role of Trotsky.

Disunity among the Whites

- The Whites were an uncoordinated series of groups whose morale was low.
- The Whites had a collection of different political beliefs who all wanted different things and often fought amongst themselves due to differences. All of the Whites shared a hatred of Communism but other than this they lacked a common purpose.

- No White leader of any measure emerged to unite and lead the White forces eg. Yudenich, Wrangel, Kolchak and Denikin. Whereas the Reds had Trotsky and Lenin.

Other factors

Unity of the Reds

- Unified political leadership.
- Unity of land controlled.
- Co-ordinated military action.

The role of Trotsky

- Trotsky had a completely free hand in military matters.
- HQ was a heavily armed train, which he used to travel around the country.
- He supervised the formation of the Red Army, which became an army of three million men.
- He recruited ex Tsarist army officers and used political commissars to watch over them, thus ensuring experienced officers but no political recalcitrance.
- He used conscription to gain troops, and ordered deserters to be shot.
- Trotsky helped provide an army with great belief in what it was fighting for, which the Whites did not have.

The organisation of the Red Army

- The Red Army was better organised than the White armies and better equipped and therefore able to crush any opposition from the White forces.
- Use of ex-officers from old Imperial Army.
- Reintroduction of rank and discipline.
- Role of Commissars.

Superior Red resources

- Once the Reds had established defence of their lines they were able to repel and exhaust the attacks by the Whites until they scattered or surrendered.
- By having all of their land together it was easier for the Reds to defend. With the major industrial centres in their land (Moscow and Petrograd) the Reds had access to factories to supply weapons etc. and to move due to their control of the railways.
- Control of the railways meant they could transport troops and supplies quickly and efficiently and in large numbers to the critical areas of defence or attack.
- The decisive battles between the Reds and Whites were near railheads.
- The Reds were in control of a concentrated area of western Russia, which they could successfully defend due to the maintenance of their communication and supply lines.
- Having the two major cities of Moscow and Petrograd in their possession meant that the Reds held the industrial centres of Russia as well as the administrative centres.
- Having the two major cities gave the Reds munitions and supplies that the Whites were never able to access.

Use of Terror (Cheka)

- The Cheka was set up to eradicate any opposition to the Reds.
- There was no need for proof of guilt for punishment to be exacted.
- Persecution of individual people who opposed the Reds as well as whole groups of people, which helped to reduce opposition due to fear, or simply eradicate opposition.
- The Cheka carried out severe repression.
- Some of the first victims of the Cheka were leaders of other political parties.

Effects of foreign intervention

- The Bolsheviks were able to claim that the foreign "invaders" were imperialists who were trying to overthrow the revolution.
- The Reds were able to stand as champions of the Russian nation from foreign invasion.
- The help received by the Whites from foreign powers was not as great as was hoped for.
- The foreign powers did not provide many men due to the First World War just finishing and their help was restricted to money and arms.

Propaganda

- Whites were unable to take advantage of the brutality of the Reds to win support as they often carried out similar atrocities.
- The Whites were unable to present themselves as a better alternative to the Reds due to their brutality.
- The Reds kept pointing out that all of the land that the peasants had seized in the 1917 Revolution would be lost if the Whites won. This fear prevented the peasants from supporting the Whites.

Leadership of Lenin

- Introduction of War Communism.
- By forcing the peasants to sell their grain to the Reds for a fixed price the Reds were able to ensure that their troops were well supplied and well fed.
- The White armies were not as well supplied and fed as the Red army.
- Skilled delegation and ruthlessness.

Any other relevant factors.

Part G: USA, 1918–1968

49. How important was prejudice and racism as a reason for changing attitudes towards immigration in the 1920s?

Context

In the 1920s the attitudes of Americans towards immigration began to change. Rather than celebrating America's open door policy, many Americans became increasingly concerned about the millions of 'new' immigrants arriving from eastern and central Europe. Contributing to such changes in attitudes was prejudice and racism.

Prejudice and racism

- Attitudes towards immigration changed due to fears concerning the changing nature of immigration. Up until the 1880s most immigrants to the USA came from northern and western Europe from, for example, Britain, Germany and Scandinavia. After 1880 the majority of immigrants came from southern and eastern Europe, from countries such as Russia, Poland and Italy. Descendants of the more established immigrants, known as WASPs (White, Anglo-Saxon Protestants) were concerned there would be a flood of new immigrants from southern and eastern Europe which they believed would threaten their way of life. Some new immigrants continued to wear traditional dress which was not viewed as being 'American'.
- Many new immigrants were Catholic or Jewish which led to the belief that the arrival of new immigrants would threaten the Protestant religion.
- Many new immigrants were unfamiliar with democracy. This was viewed as a threat to the American constitution.
- 'Nativists' who believed immigrants brought new and threatening ideas into the USA, were most prevalent in the mid-western and southern states.

Other factors

Isolationism

- Attitudes towards immigration in the 1920s were in some respects a development of existing attitudes towards immigration apparent in the 19th century. Before the 1920s, the USA's 'open door' policy did not apply to everyone. Before 1900 the USA had reduced Asian immigration. The first significant law to restrict immigration into the USA was the Chinese Exclusion Act of 1882 which banned Chinese immigration.
- The first general Federal Immigration Law in 1882 imposed a head tax of 50 cents on each immigrant admitted and denied entrance into the USA of "any convict, lunatic, idiot, or any person unable to take care of himself or herself without becoming a public charge".
- The Immigration Restriction League was founded in 1894 to oppose 'undesirable immigrants' from southern and eastern Europe who, it was believed, threatened the American way of life.
- The 1913 Alien Land Law prohibited "aliens ineligible for citizenship" from owning agricultural land or possessing long term leases. This particularly affected Chinese, Indian, Japanese and Korean immigrant farmers.
- At the beginning of the First World War, American public opinion was firmly on the side of neutrality and wanted to keep out of foreign problems and concentrate solely on America. When the war ended, most Americans were even more in favour of a return to the USA's traditional policy of isolationism.
- Despite Woodrow Wilson's support of a League of Nations to sort out future disputes between countries, in November 1919 and March 1920 the US Senate voted against US membership of the League of Nations, and refused to accept the terms of the League of Nations covenant. The USA was determined not to be involved in Europe's problems or become dragged into another European war. The USA was now firmly committed to a policy of isolationism.

Fear of revolution

- Attitudes towards immigration changed due to the 'red scare' which increased suspicion of immigrants. The Russian Revolution in 1917 had established the first Communist state in Russia which was committed to spreading revolution and destroying capitalism. As many immigrants to the USA came from Russia and eastern Europe, it was feared that these immigrants would bring communist ideas into the USA.
- In 1919 there was a wave of strikes in the USA. Many of the strikers were unskilled and semi-skilled workers and recent immigrants from southern and eastern Europe. People opposed to the strikes linked the strikes with communism as it was believed that revolution was imminent.
- The American public's fear of red revolution appeared to be confirmed when the US Attorney General Mitchell Palmer's house in Washington, DC, was blown up and letter bombs were sent to government officials. The red scare reached a peak of hysteria in January 1920 when, one night, Palmer ordered the arrest of 4000 alleged communists in 33 cities in what became known as the Palmer Raids.

Social fears

- Attitudes towards immigration changed due to fears that immigration would lead to competition for housing and jobs. White working class Americans experienced rising rents due to the high demand for housing.

- The majority of new immigrants settled in cities in the north-east of the USA and often congregated with people from their own culture in ghettos. Some Americans felt this was a threat to their way of life.
- There were also fears that immigrants would increase the already high crime rates in cities. Such fears were heightened by the existence of organised crime gangs such as the Mafia with its Italian roots. Nicola Sacco and Bartolomeo Vanzetti were two Italian immigrant anarchists who were convicted of robbery and murder. Their trial linked crime, immigration and 'un-American' political revolutionary ideas in the minds of many Americans.
- The activities of Al Capone, the son of Italian immigrants, also reinforced the stereotype that all Italian immigrants were in some way linked to crime.

Economic fears
- Attitudes towards immigration changed due to increased fears that the jobs of 'Americans' would be threatened. Due to new production methods employers realised they could make huge profits by employing immigrants and paying them low wages. Trade unions believed that anything they did to improve conditions or wages was wrecked by Italian or Polish workers who were prepared to work longer hours for lower wages.
- New immigrants were also used as 'strike breakers' as long hours and low wages in the USA were often better than what they were used to. There was huge resentment towards immigrant strike breakers which led to an increase in the desire to stop immigrants coming into the country.

The effects of the First World War
- Many immigrants during the First World War had sympathies for their mother country which led to resentment within the USA.
- A large part of the US immigrant population was of German or Austrian origin. Many of these immigrants had supported the German side in the war and society was split when the USA joined the war against Germany. Anti-German propaganda containing stories of German atrocities increased dislike and suspicion of immigrants from Germany and the old Austrian Empire.
- Irish Americans were suspected of being anti-British.
- Many citizens felt hostile to anything foreign. During the war, many Americans resented having to become involved in Europe's problems. After the First World War the USA was even more in favour of an isolationist policy. By 1918 the USA wanted to leave Europe behind especially after the November armistice, when ships began to bring the wounded back to the United States from the European Western Front. Many Americans therefore did not want new waves of immigrants bringing 'European' problems to the USA.

Any other relevant factors.

50. To what extent was the New Deal effective in solving America's problems in the 1930s?

Context
As the Depression continued to deepen, the new President of the United States Franklin Delano Roosevelt promised to give the American people a 'New Deal'. The New Deal introduced a series of acts and new government agencies to increase the role of government in an attempt to end the Depression and bring recovery to America.

The First New Deal 1933–34
- A number of new government departments or agencies, nicknamed the 'Alphabet Agencies' were set up to tackle

the Depression. The aims of the Alphabet Agencies were to provide both immediate and longer term help to people suffering in the Depression. During the first 100 days of Roosevelt's presidency, agencies providing relief and work included the Federal Emergency Relief Administration (FERA) which aimed to help the very poor by setting up soup kitchens and providing money for clothes and school costs, the Tennessee Valley Authority (TVA) which aimed to build dams and power plants to provide electric power to rural areas along the Tennessee River in seven states, in addition to giving work to thousands of unemployed construction workers, and the Public Works Administration (PWA) which also provided work through the building of hospitals, dams, bridges and schools.
- The Economy Act cut wages of state employees by 15 per cent. It also cut the budgets of government departments by 25 per cent, in order to balance the budget.
- Economic prudence was shown by spending the savings on relief programmes.
- The unpopular prohibition was ended to raise revenue and to boost grain production.

The Second New Deal 1935–1937
- The Second New Deal introduced reforms to improve living and working conditions for many Americans through legislation.
- The National Labour Relations Act ('Wagner Act') (1935) protected the rights of workers to collectively bargain with employers. Employers were prevented from discriminating against workers who joined trade unions.
- The Banking Act (1935) established the Federal Bank Deposit Insurance Corporation that insured deposits up to $5,000, and later, $10,000.
- The WPA (Works Progress Administration) (1935) launched a programme of public works across America. By 1938 it provided employment for three million men and some women, building roads, schools and tunnels, for example.
- The Rural Electrification Act (1936) provided loans to provide electricity to rural areas of America.
- The Social Security Act (1935) provided a state pension scheme for old people and widows, as well as help for the disabled and poor children.

The role of Roosevelt and 'confidence-building'
- A number of confidence-building measures were introduced. The Emergency Banking Act (1933) allowed the closing and checking of banks to ensure they were well-run and credit-worthy. Only 'sound' banks were allowed to reopen. It was hoped these measures would restore public confidence in the banks and stop people from withdrawing all their savings.
- By the end of 1933, many small banks had closed or were merged.
- Most depositors regained much of their money.
- Roosevelt also gave 'fireside chats': over 30 from March 1933.
- Roosevelt declared that 'the only thing we have to fear is fear itself' and his fireside chats on the radio, a great novelty, did a great deal to help restore the nation's confidence.

The role of the Federal government
- The New Deal increased the role of the federal government in American society and, in particular, the economy.
- The Federal government played a role in strengthening the power of organised labour.

- The Federal government also played a role as regulator between business, labour and agriculture.
- There were however challenges in the Supreme Court to the Federal government's increased intervention.
- There was also opposition from State governments, especially in the South who believed the Federal government was becoming too powerful and was taking away individual states' rights to run their own affairs. Employers groups who formed the Liberty League opposed the New Deal. Some groups believed the New Deal was 'un-American'.

The economic effects of the New Deal

- The economic effects in terms of relief and recovery have been debated. The New Deal certainly helped in terms of providing basic relief.
- Roosevelt's first term in office saw one of the fastest periods of GDP growth in US history. However, a downturn in 1937–38 raised questions about just how successful the policies were.
- Although it never reached the heights of before the Depression, the New Deal did see a couple of positive results economically. From 1933 to 1939, GDP increased by 60 per cent from $55 billion to $85 billion. The amount of consumer products bought increased by 40 per cent while private investment in industry increased five times in just six years.
- However, unemployment continued to be a problem, never running at less than 14 per cent of the working population.
- The importance of re-armament in reducing unemployment and revitalising the American economy was considerable, particularly after the mini-slump of 1937.

Any other relevant factors.

51. *The Civil Rights movement was effective in meeting the needs of black Americans, up to 1968.* **How valid is this view?**

Context

With the passing of the Civil Rights Act in 1964 followed by a Voting Rights Act a year later it appeared that the Civil Rights Movement had achieved its aims. However, for many black Americans forced to live in the ghetto areas in the cities of the north and west, social and economic hardships and inequalities remained.

Aims of the Civil Rights Movement

- The aims were mainly pacifist and intended to bring Civil Rights and equality in law to all black Americans.
- The Black Radical Movements had more radical segregationist aims.

Roles of NAACP

- NAACP (National Association for the Advancement of Coloured People) were involved in the court case 'Brown v Topeka Board of Education',1954 which decided that segregated schools were unequal and that schools should be desegregated.
- NAACP was also involved in the Montgomery Bus Boycott, 1955 which successfully pressured the bus company into desegregating the buses.

Roles of CORE

- CORE (Congress of Racial Equality) organised sit-ins and during 1961 members of CORE organised the Freedom Rides, which aimed to ensure that segregation really had ended on interstate highways.
- CORE helped organise the March on Washington in August 1963.

- CORE helped established Freedom Schools, temporary free schools for black Americans, in towns throughout Mississippi.

Roles of SCLC and Martin Luther King

- Martin Luther King rose to prominence during the Montgomery Bus Boycott. In 1957, King was instrumental in forming the SCLC (Southern Christian Leadership Conference) which supported Martin Luther King's beliefs in peaceful, non-violent protest.
- Martin Luther King's involvement in the events at Little Rock, Arkansas. The national publicity influenced the introduction of the Civil Rights Act in 1957.
- Martin Luther King believed in peaceful, non-violent protest as exemplified by the Sit-ins and Freedom Rides.
- In 1963 Martin Luther King and the SCLC staged a huge demonstration in Birmingham, Alabama. The demonstrators, including children and students, were subjected to extreme police violence. The police chief, 'Bull' Connor used water cannons and dogs to attack the peaceful protesters. The bad publicity and hostility from white Americans forced Kennedy to order an end to segregation in Birmingham.
- Martin Luther King with other civil rights leaders organised a march on Washington, to gain publicity and support for a new Civil Rights Law. Martin Luther King gave his now famous 'I Have a Dream' speech.
- Martin Luther King believed that the Civil Rights Act of 1964 'gave Negroes some part of their rightful dignity, but without the vote it was dignity without strength'. King believed that it was vital that black Americans were also able to vote freely.
- In March 1965, King led a march from Selma to Montgomery to publicise the way in which the authorities made it difficult for black Americans to vote easily. Once more, scenes of police attacking marchers shocked TV audiences across the USA. In August 1965, Congress passed the Voting Rights Act, which removed a number of barriers to voting.

Changes in Federal Policy

- Truman used Executive Orders to make black appointments and order equality of treatment in the armed services. Kennedy signed the 1962 Executive Order outlawing racial discrimination in public housing.
- Eisenhower sent in federal troops and National Guardsmen to protect nine African-American students enrolled in Central High School, Little Rock. Kennedy sent troops to Oxford, Mississippi to protect black student James Meredith.
- The 1964 Civil Rights Act passed during Johnson's presidency made racial discrimination and segregation illegal. The Voting Rights Act of 1965 made it easier for black Americans to vote. By end of 1965 over 250,000 Black Americans newly registered to vote.

Social, economic and political changes

- The Civil Rights Act of 1964 and the Voting Rights Act of 1965 resulted in big changes in the South but were mostly irrelevant to the cities of the North where segregation and discrimination had never been the main problems. The Civil Rights Movement split due to disagreements regarding the movement's next steps. The main goals to end segregation and discrimination in the South had been met. Some black Americans no longer supported Martin Luther King's methods and aims and became disillusioned by the failure of the southern-based Civil Rights campaign to improve conditions in the cities of the North.

- Economic issues, unemployment, poor housing, high rents and poverty, were more important in the North.
- The problems facing black Americans in urban ghettos resulted in violent riots in Watts, Los Angeles in 1964. Other race related riots across urban America.
- Martin Luther King attempted to help with the problems of Chicago. In 1966 King and the SCLC proposed the Chicago Plan, a non-violent action plan to improve the Chicago area. Martin Luther King's failure to prevent the riots, which broke out, however suggested that his methods were irrelevant to black Americans in the late 1960s.
- Martin Luther King was criticised by many people due to the failure of his campaign to make any real difference to life in the ghettos in the main cites of the North and West. Urban poverty and de facto segregation were still common.

The resultant rise of black radical movements

- In 1966 a new leader emerged within the SNCC — Stokely Carmichael who called for a campaign to achieve Black Power as an alternative to King's non-violent protest methods. According to Stokely Carmichael 'Black Power' involved black Americans taking control of their political and economic future without relying on white support to 'give' black Americans their civil rights.
- Another radical group who rejected white help were the Black Panthers who supported the anti-White, Black separatist ideas of Stokely Carmichael and Malcolm X. The Panthers gained a reputation for violence due to supporting the use of guns and gunfights with the police.
- The Black Panthers were involved in self-help projects in the ghettos to help black communities out of poverty.
- Malcolm X, a leader of the Nation of Islam, also known as the Black Muslims, publicised the increasing urban problems within the ghettos of America.
- In 1968, Johnson set up an investigation into the urban riots called the Kerner Commission. Its findings that US society remained divided with one white society and one black society — one rich and one poor, shocked people across the USA.

Any other relevant factors.

Part H: Appeasement and the Road to War, to 1939

52. To what extent does the British policy of appeasement explain the aggressive nature of the foreign policies of Germany and Italy in the 1930s?

Context
Fascist belief was founded on the idea of national unity. It totally opposed the idea of internal class division. In the cases of Italy and Germany it was also expansionist in outlook. Mussolini looked to create a new Roman Empire while Hitler sought living space for the 'excess' German population. A number of factors led to this.

The British policy of appeasement.
- Appeasement was intended to solve genuine foreign policy grievances that had arisen from the 1919 peace treaties, through negotiation.
- British public opinion broadly supported the policy of appeasement, though there were voices raised in dissent. Many felt that Germany had genuine grievances which deserved to be settled.
- British appeasement to an extent encouraged both Germany and Italy to increase their demands and do so increasingly forcefully. They certainly reinforced fascist belief in the weakness of democracies.

- British attempts to keep Mussolini away from Hitler's influence during the Abyssinian crisis resulted in the Hoare-Laval Pact, which produced a popular outcry when the terms were leaked. Mussolini saw that Britain and France were not opposed in principle to gains for Italy in East Africa and he was able to defy sanctions and keep Abyssinia.
- Hitler knew of British reservations about some terms of the Versailles Treaty and was able to play on these, increasingly realising that he would not be stopped eg rearmament, the reoccupation of the Rhineland and then the Anschluss.

Other factors

The Peace Settlement of 1919
- Determination to revise/overturn Paris Peace Settlement — German resentment of Article 231 which made Germany accept guilt for starting the war, hatred of the reparations bill of £6,600,000,000, disarmament clauses were also a cause of resentment as the German army was reduced to 100,000 men and was not allowed heavy weaponry, lost territory, in particular in the east to Poland was bitterly resented.
- German desire to get revenge for defeat in WWI. Hitler called the treaty a Diktat; a dictated treaty forced on a helpless Germany.
- Italy came into the war on the side of the Allies in 1915. She suffered during the war, but hoped to gain land at the expense of Austria-Hungary, in particular the Dalmatian coast. In fact, Italian territorial gains were small scale. It was felt that the Italians had suffered and gained little.
- Mussolini in Italy promised to make Italy great again and wipe out the embarrassment of the peace treaties when he gained power in 1922.

Fascist ideology
- Fascism was nationalistic in nature; emphasising the importance of loyalty to country [and superiority over others].
- Fascism is often defined by what it dislikes. One fundamental belief was a pathological hatred of communism which led to an anti-Soviet crusade as well as contempt for the 'weak' democracies.
- Fascism as seen through Nazism was racist. This belief in the superiority of the 'German/Aryan' people, through a crude Social Darwinism, allowed Nazis to perpetuate the idea of a racial mission to conquer the world and cleanse it of 'weaker' races.
- Fascism was militaristic in nature — Fascist glorification of war; Prussian/German military traditions/harking back to the glories of the Roman Empire in Italy.
- Fascist foreign policies were driven by Hitler's and Mussolini's own belief, but also their personalities and charismatic leadership.
- Irredentism or the intention to reclaim and reoccupy lost territory, eg Hitler's commitment to incorporation of all Germans within the Reich.
- Fascism between the wars was expansionist. Mussolini's 'Roman' ambitions in the Mediterranean and Africa; Hitler's ambitions for lebensraum or living space in Eastern Europe and Russia.

Economic difficulties after 1929
- In 1929 the US economy crashed leading the world into economic recession. This had a particularly dramatic effect on Germany as unemployment soared to 6 million.

- By 1929 Italy's Fascist economic policy was failing; an aggressive foreign policy was useful in distracting the people at home.
- An aggressive foreign policy was also useful in gaining resources for the Fascist powers eg Italian invasion of Abyssinia and Hitler's obsession with lebensraum.
- Germany also developed policies to use their economic and political power to make the countries of Southern Europe and the Balkans dependent on Germany. Germany would exploit their raw materials and export manufactured goods to them. It was not a big step to invasion.

Weakness of the League of Nations

- Purpose of the League was to ensure world peace through collective security and disarmament. The League conspicuously failed to do this, allowing Fascism to grow unchecked.
- The League was divided politically. Its main supporters had their own domestic audiences which dictated their policies, which led to confusion and inconsistency in the international response to aggression.
- British policy of appeasement and concerns over their Empire.
- French political divisions between the Left and Right.
- The USA retreated into isolationism.
- There was suspicion of Communist Soviet Russia from the democracies.
- The peace treaties created many small states in Eastern Europe which were difficult to defend.
- Determined aggression worked as the League failed to stop the Italian invasion of Abyssinia. Even when the League did act, by putting mild sanctions on Italy they were too little, too late.

Any other relevant factors.

53. *British foreign policy was successful in containing fascist aggression between 1935 and March 1938. How valid is this view?*

Context

Britain was keenly aware of a domestic context that was not fully prepared for war. Therefore, Britain's foremost aim was the maintenance of peace in Europe. Up to March 1938 (and later), this was achieved.

British Foreign Policy Aims

- The maintenance of peace was Britain's foremost aim, and up to March 1938 (and later), this was largely achieved.
- Conflicts that did occur (Abyssinia, Spain) were on the periphery of Europe/the Mediterranean.

Relations with Italy: Abyssinia

- Mussolini's plans for a new Roman Empire in the Adriatic, the Mediterranean and North Africa were a blow to British foreign policy in hoping to convert Mussolini into an ally.
- Stresa Front (1935) initially seemed successful in binding Mussolini to the democracies.
- Italian invasion of Abyssinia [modern-day Ethiopia] in 1935.
- Mussolini's Italy had broken the rules of the League of Nations by using aggression and invading one of the only independent African nations and deserved to be punished under League rules.
- However, the British and French wanted to keep Mussolini friendly so attempted to contain Italy by offering concessions and land in Africa.
- The British Foreign Secretary Sir Samuel Hoare and French Foreign Minister, Pierre Laval, came up with a plan to effectively try to buy off the Italians by offering them some of Abyssinia's land from the south of the country [Abyssinia was not consulted]
- Public revulsion to Franco-British connivance at Italian aggression led to Hoare's resignation.
- The imposition of limited economic sanctions on Italy alienated Mussolini, thereby driving him closer to Hitler, yet failing to save Abyssinia.

Relations with Germany: Naval Agreement

- The Anglo German Naval Agreement (1935) successfully limited German naval strength to 35% of British, however, it also allowed for the construction of submarines, up to British strength.
- Rearmament: Hitler was successful in reintroducing conscription and rearming from 1935, but there were significant economic restraints and by the late 1930s Germany's potential enemies were rearming at a faster rate. However, by 1939, Germany had significant military assets, even if they were over exaggerated by the Germans and over estimated by the British and French.

The Rhineland

- The Rhineland had been demilitarised as part of the Treaty of Versailles. No military installations were permitted there.
- 22,000 German troops marched into the Rhineland on 7 March, 1936.
- Remilitarisation broke the Peace Treaty of 1919, yet no action was taken by Britain or France due to differing attitudes towards Hitler's actions. France was polarised politically and would not act without British support. Britain denounced the action, but there was also considerable sympathy for Hitler's actions. The Rhineland was part of Germany and why should she not have armed forces there?
- No war occurred as a result of the Rhineland crisis, but the lesson Hitler learned was that the democracies were divided. He took this to mean weakness.

The Spanish Civil War: non-intervention

- The Spanish Civil War took place between 1936 and 1939 between forces that defended the democratically elected Republic and forces that opposed it called Nationalists.
- The policy of non-intervention was sponsored by Britain and France through the Non-Intervention Committee; it also guaranteed that Britain would be on good terms with the victors.
- The policy was openly breached by Germany and Italy who sent significant military aid to Franco's Nationalist forces, and to a lesser extent the Soviet Union who sent help to the Republic.
- There was also intervention by volunteers of the International Brigades who fought for the Republic, but withdrew towards the end of 1938.
- Attacks on non-Spanish shipping ended after the British and French navies were ordered to destroy attacking foreign submarines and aircraft.
- The Spanish Civil War did not turn into a wider European conflict. In this the policy of non-intervention was successful, but at some cost as the dictators tested the weaponry and tactics that would be so successful in WWII.

Austria: The Anschluss of March 1938

- The joining together of German speaking Austria and Germany was banned by the Treaty of Versailles.
- Anschluss: failure of attempted Nazi coup in 1934 due to Italian opposition, but there was growing German influence over Austria from 1936 when they agreed to consult each other over foreign policy.

- The Austrian Chancellor Schuschnigg met with Hitler in 1938. Hitler seized the opportunity demanding jobs for Austrian Nazis in the Government.
- When Schuschnigg proposed putting this to a vote of the Austrian people Hitler acted, demanding his resignation and replacement with the Austrian Nazi, Seyss-Inquart.
- German troops and tanks then rolled into Austria on 12 March, 1938.
- The invasion itself was chaotic and inefficient from military point of view.
- War did not break out as a result of the Anschluss. Britain was sympathetic to German actions to a large extent and the enthusiastic welcome given to the German troops by the Austrians seemed to confirm it was a genuinely popular action.
- Hitler gained resources and again had got away with aggressive actions. He now turned his attention to Czechoslovakia.

Any other relevant factors.

54. How important was the invasion of Poland in causing the outbreak of war in 1939?

Context
The Nazi occupation of the Sudetenland could be justified in the eyes of Appeasers as Hitler was absorbing fellow Germans into Greater Germany. However, subsequent actions by the Nazis could not be supported in this way and any illusion of justified grievances evaporated as Hitler made demands on powers such as Poland.

The invasion of Poland
- On 1 September 1939, Hitler and the Nazis faked a Polish attack on a minor German radio station in order to justify a German invasion of Poland. An hour later Hitler declared war on Poland stating one of his reasons for the invasion was because of "the attack by regular Polish troops on the Gleiwitz transmitter."
- France and Britain had a defensive pact with Poland. This forced France and Britain to declare war on Germany, which they did on September 3.

Other factors:

The occupation of Bohemia and the collapse of Czechoslovakia
- British and French realisation, after Hitler's breaking of Munich Agreement and invasion of Czechoslovakia in March 1939, that Hitler's word was worthless and that his aims went beyond the incorporation of ex-German territories and ethnic Germans within the Reich.
- Promises of support to Poland and Rumania.
- British public acceptance that all attempts to maintain peace had been exhausted.
- Prime Minister Chamberlain felt betrayed by the Nazi seizure of Czechoslovakia, realised his policy of appeasement towards Hitler had failed, and began to take a much harder line against the Nazis.

Changing British attitudes towards appeasement
- Czechoslovakia did not concern most people until the middle of September 1938, when they began to object to a small democratic state being bullied. However, most press and population went along with it, although level of popular opposition often underestimated.
- The anti-appeasement movement gained more support as Hitler's intentions became clearer.
- Events in Bohemia and Moravia consolidated growing concerns in Britain.

- German annexation of Memel [largely German population, but in Lithuania] further showed Hitler's bad faith.
- Actions convinced British government of growing German threat in south-eastern Europe.
- Guarantees to Poland and promised action in the event of threats to Polish independence.

Importance of Nazi-Soviet Pact
- Pact — diplomatic, economic, military co-operation; division of Poland.
- Unexpected — Hitler and Stalin's motives.
- Put an end to British-French talks with Russia on guarantees to Poland.
- Hitler was freed from the threat of Soviet intervention and war on two fronts.
- Hitler's belief that Britain and France would not go to war over Poland without Russian assistance.
- Hitler now felt free to attack Poland.
- But, given Hitler's consistent, long-term foreign policy aims on the destruction of the Versailles Settlement and Lebensraum in the east, the Nazi-Soviet Pact could be seen more as a factor influencing the timing of the outbreak of war rather than as one of its underlying causes.
- Hitler's long-term aims for destruction of the Soviet state and conquest of Russian resources — Lebensraum.
- Hitler's need for new territory and resources to sustain Germany's militarised economy.
- Hitler's belief that British and French were 'worms' who would not turn from previous policy of appeasement and avoidance of war at all costs.
- Hitler's belief that the longer war was delayed the more the balance of military and economic advantage would shift against Germany.

British diplomacy and relations with the Soviet Union
- Stalin knew that Hitler's ultimate aim was to attack Russia.
- Lord Halifax, the British Foreign Secretary was invited by Stalin to go to Russia to discuss an alliance against Germany.
- Britain refused as they feared Russian Communism, and they believed that the Russian army was too weak to be of any use against Hitler.
- In August 1939, with war in Poland looming, the British and French eventually sent a military mission to discuss an alliance with Russia. Owing to travel difficulties it took five days to reach Leningrad.
- The Russians asked if they could send troops into Poland if Hitler invaded. The British refused, knowing that the Poles would not want this. The talks broke down.
- This merely confirmed Stalin's suspicions regarding the British. He felt they could not be trusted, especially after the Munich agreement, and they would leave Russia to fight Germany alone. This led directly to opening talks with the Nazis who seemed to be taking the Germans seriously by sending Foreign Minister von Ribbentrop and offering peace and land.

The position of France_
- France had signed an agreement with Czechoslovakia offering support if the country was attacked. However, Hitler could all but guarantee that in 1938, French would do nothing as their foreign policy was closely tied to the British.
- French military, and particularly their airforce, allowed to decline in years after 1919.
- After Munich, French more aggressive towards dictators and in events of 1939 were keen on a military alliance

with the Soviet Union, however despite different emphasis on tactics were tied to the British and their actions.

The developing crisis over Poland
- Hitler's long-term aims for the destruction of Versailles, including regaining of Danzig and Polish Corridor.
- British and French decision to stick to their guarantees to Poland.

Any other relevant factors.

Part I: The Cold War, 1945—1989

55. To what extent were ideological differences the main reason for the emergence of the Cold War, up to 1955?

Context
The wartime alliance had always been one of convenience owing to the common enemy of Nazism. America had not recognised the Soviet Communist government's legitimacy until 1933. As the Second World War came to an end the inherent tensions between a Capitalist America and her allies and Communist Russia became all too clear.

Ideological differences
- Impact of 1917 Bolshevik revolution in Russia on relations with the Western powers: Soviet withdrawal from WWI, involvement of West with anti-Bolshevik Whites: ideological differences between Communism and Capitalism.
- Fears in the West that Communism was on the march led President Truman to the policy of containment as well as the Marshall Plan: British power was in retreat: WWII had been expensive so the British aimed to reduce their world commitments, specifically in Greece where civil war raged between Communists and Royalists. Fear of similar problems in Italy when allied troops left; activities of Mao in China.
- Truman acknowledged world dividing into two hostile blocs in his speech to support free peoples and proposals to oppose totalitarian regimes — exemplified by the Marshall Plan. Fulton speech by Churchill talked of an Iron Curtain splitting Europe.
- Creation of competing military alliances: NATO and Warsaw Pact further polarised the world. The Soviet Union rejected the Western economic model and set up its own economic bloc: Comecon.

Other factors

Tensions within the wartime alliance
- WWII: suspicion of USSR by Britain and the USA because of Nazi-Soviet Pact of 1939.
- USSR suspicion of British because of policy of appeasement and also with USA over failure to open up a second front against Germany until 1944.
- Tensions within the wartime alliance as the defeat of Nazism became clear. Soviet Union felt they had done the bulk of the land fighting and wanted security for the USSR.
- Yalta conference: Stalin determined to hang on to land gained by the Red Army in the east so he created a series of sympathetic regimes in Eastern Europe.
- The USA wanted to create a free trade area composed of democratic states. Soviet actions in Poland, Romania, Bulgaria, etc. in creating pro-Communist regimes and Allied actions in Western Europe, Greece further increased tensions. Soviet actions were interpreted as aggressive acts by the Western Allies.
- Replacement of Roosevelt on his death with President Truman, who was anti-Communist, led to a much stronger US line with USSR in the wartime conferences.

The US decision to use the atom bomb
- President Truman hoped that one aim of the use of atom bombs on Hiroshima and Nagasaki would be to impress the USSR and make them ready to make concessions in Eastern Europe or at least restrain their 'aggression'.
- In fact, Stalin knew about the Manhattan project and refused to be intimidated and the fact it had been developed in secret made him even more suspicious of the USA.

The arms race
- Stalin was determined to make the Soviet Union a nuclear power as soon as possible; this led to the development of the arms race, which was symbolically important in showing the success of the rival economic and political systems.
- British and French were also developing their independent nuclear deterrents — which, realistically, were only aimed at the USSR.
- Development of technologies to deliver nuclear weapons.

Disagreements over the future of Germany
- The Potsdam Conference and policy over Germany whereby the allied sectors remained free as compared to Soviet sector which was stripped of assets as reparations.
- The economic status of Germany: creation of Bizonia in West. Contrast between the developing capitalist west and centrally controlled east: introduction of Deutsche mark in West led to the Berlin Blockade in 1949.

The crisis over Korea
- Stalin encouraged Communist North Korea to invade Capitalist South. This led to American-led UN intervention on behalf of the South, and resultant Chinese intervention.
- Soviet and American pilots fought each other across Korea. Stalemate along 38th parallel. The Cold War had been sealed with a Hot War.

Any other relevant factors.

56. *The Americans lost the war in Vietnam due to the relative strengths of North and South Vietnam. How valid is this view?*

Context
The French withdrawal from their Indo-Chinese colonies in 1954 led to America stepping in as the main foreign power in the region. The Domino Theory was used by American Presidents, starting with Eisenhower to justify American intervention to help the South of Vietnam in their struggles against the Communist North.

Relative strengths of North and South Vietnam
- North Vietnam: a hard peasant life bred determined soldiers. Viet Cong enlisted for years unlike American troops who signed up for a year. Belief in their cause of Communism also a factor. Great determination: eg the Ho Chi Minh trail was kept open despite American bombers continually bombing it.
- Viet Cong knew the jungle, survived in atrocious conditions, developed effective tactics and were more effective in winning the 'hearts and minds' of civilians than the Americans. Military objectives were realistic: General Giap aimed to break the will of the American Government. Support of Chinese and Soviet aid from 1965 of importance.
- Corruption and decay of South Vietnamese government, especially in Saigon. A Catholic elite controlled a largely Buddhist population. Lack of political and social cohesion in South Vietnam led to divisions and turmoil which filtered through to their armed forces.

- Strengths of the North in terms of leadership that commanded the support of the population: Ho Chi Minh.
- Strengths of the North in terms of military commitment and leadership: General Giap.
- Strengths of the North in terms of aid from Soviets and Chinese: for example, developed a sophisticated air defence system.
- Weaknesses of South in terms of leadership that was corrupt and favoured the Catholic population.
- Weakness of South in military terms. Army commanders tended to operate as private warlords.

Other factors

Difficulties faced by US military

- Terrain did not suit US military strengths of airpower and firepower.
- Difficulties dealing with the conditions and knowing which Vietnamese were the enemy led to stress and confusion. Many Americans addicted to drugs.
- Short commissions for officers and rotation of troops led to loss of expertise in the field.
- Soldiers brave, but a minority did not believe in the war. Many were also reluctant conscripts.

Failure of military methods

- Mass bombing had no real effect according to the Jason Study by MIT in 1966, owing to the agricultural nature of North Vietnam and the widespread jungle cover.
- Tactics on the ground — US technological superiority in heavy weapons negated by the terrain.
- Widespread use of helicopter gunships — inflicted heavy casualties, but were a blunt weapon. Many civilian deaths which did not help win 'hearts and minds'.
- Use of defoliants like Agent Orange: US (and their South Vietnamese allies) lost the battle for hearts and minds, despite inflicting 2,000,000 casualties for the loss of one tenth of those.

Changing public opinion in the USA

- Public opposition supported by the press was probably the main reason for withdrawal. Vietnam a media war, images showed the public the brutality of war eg South Viet police chief executing a Viet Cong in Saigon during the Tet Offensive of '68, Mai Lai massacre. Such images damaged American claims to be the 'good guys'.
- Extent of the opposition is debated. Probably a minority in '65, growing by the time of crucial Tet offensive in '68. Oct 1969 largest anti-war protest in US history. Protestors in every major city in America. Opposition of Black Power groups. Protest could be violent: May 1970 protest at Kent State University, Ohio led to four students being shot.
- Unpopularity of the draft.
- USA was a democracy: public pressure and perception mattered. Nixon noted extent of opposition: withdrawal of 60,000 troops in 1969, policy of Vietnamisation. Economic cost of the war: US deficit of $1.6 billion in 1965 increased to $25.3 billion in 1968. Tax increases unpopular. Congress only got involved in limiting money and action in late 60s and early 70s.
- Divisions within administrations: eg LBJ had Rusk advising to continue the struggle in South-East Asia, compared to Senator Fulbright arguing for de-escalation.

International isolation of the USA.

- The media war turned international opinion against the US.
- Major US allies had had misgivings about US military intervention; Harold Wilson's major achievement in keeping UK out of the war, despite dependence on US support for the British economy.
- Feeling that Vietnam was handing huge propaganda bonuses to the enemies and rivals of the US.

Any other relevant factors.

57. How important was Western economic strength in explaining the end of the Cold War?

Context

When Mikhail Gorbachev became General Secretary in 1985 he was the first leader of the Soviet Union who had not directly experienced the Second World War. He was also aware of the economic stagnation in the USSR. He sought reform at home which led to engagement with the West. An initially sceptical West eventually warmed to his initiatives leading to extensive Arms Control agreements. Gorbachev's attempts to reform Communism, however, unleashed forces that he could not control.

Western economic strength

- The Western powers were economically more developed and sophisticated than the Soviet Union. During the years of Détente, the Soviets had borrowed from the Western powers and even relied on them for food imports.
- The economic power of the West allowed America to embark on the Star Wars weapons programme.
- Perception of the affluent West through television and consumer goods undermined Communist claims of the superiority of their economic system.

Other factors

The role of President Mikhail Gorbachev

- Gorbachev saw that the USSR could not afford a new arms race.
- Gorbachev implemented policies of Perestroika and Glasnost which aimed to reform the Soviet economy and liberalise its political system. However, these attempts to control and reform the Communist system were overwhelmed by popular pressure in the satellite states and even within Russia.
- Gorbachev worked to improve relations with the USA. He took ideology out of his foreign policy, as exemplified by arms agreements to allow the USSR to concentrate on internal matters: Intermediate Nuclear Forces Treaty, Dec 1987, Nuclear Weapons Reduction Treaty, 1989.
- Gorbachev told leaders of the satellite East European states in March 1989 that the Soviet army would no longer help them to stay in power.

The role of President Ronald Reagan

- Unlike many in the US administration Reagan actively sought to challenge Soviet weakness and strengthen the West in order to defeat Communism. In 1983 he denounced the Soviet Union as an 'Evil Empire'.
- Programme of improving US armed forces, including nuclear weapons and he proposed a Star Wars missile shield to challenge the belief in MAD (SDI). He was very charming when he met Gorbachev and visited Soviet Union.

The defeat of the Soviet Union in Afghanistan

- Symptom of the problems of Soviet Union.
- Intervention in Dec 1979: conflict with the Mujaheddi'n. Russian army morale crumbled when over 20,000 Soviet soldiers died, as did support at home.
- The conflict showed the weaknesses of the Soviet economy. War led to a slump in living standards for ordinary Russians.

- Russians began to question the actions of their own government. Gorbachev withdrew troops in 1988.

Soviet economic weakness

- The Soviet economy was at breaking point by the late 1980s.
- Commitments to the arms race meant the Soviet economy was hugely unbalanced.
- Propping up allied regimes was also causing a drain on resources.
- Consumer goods and housing were neglected as a result.

The failure of Communism in Eastern Europe

- Strong Polish identity and history of hostility with Russia. By 1970s, Poland was in an economic slump. Emergence of opposition around Gdansk in 1980: industrial workers strike led by Lech Walesa, who argued for the creation of an independent trade union. Solidarity grew to nine million members in a matter of months. Movement suppressed in 1981 by General Jaruzelski's government.
- Multiparty elections in Poland, after Soviet troops left, victory for Solidarity.
- Czechoslovakia, political prisoners released in November 1989 and by the end of the month, the communist government had gone. No Soviet intervention.
- Opening of the Berlin Wall: division of Germany finally came to an end.
- Soviet domination ended.
- Perestroika and Glasnost and end of Communist rule in USSR.

Any other relevant factors.

Acknowledgements

Permission has been sought from all relevant copyright holders and Hodder Gibson is grateful for the use of the following:

An extract from 'The Wars of Scotland 1214–1371' by Michael Brown, published by Edinburgh University Press, 2004 (2015 page 4);

An extract from 'Under the Hammer: Edward I and Scotland, 1286–1307' by Fiona Watson, published by Tuckwell Press/Birlinn Ltd. 1998 (2015 page 4);

An extract from 'Edward I' by Michael Prestwich, published by University of California Press. Copyright © 1988 Michael Prestwich (2015 page 4);

An extract from 'Scotland: A New History' by Michael Lynch, published by Pimlico 1992 © The Random House Group Ltd (2015 page 6);

An extract from 'The life and impact of Scottish Reformer John Knox' by T. Booher, 2012, taken from http://tulipdrivenlife.blogspot.co.uk/2012/02/church-history-life-and-impact-of.html (2015 page 6);

An extract from 'Scotland Re-formed 1488–1587' (New Edinburgh History of Scotland, Volume 6) by J.E.A. Dawson, published by Edinburgh University Press, 2009 (2015 page 6);

An extract from 'The History Today Companion to British History' by Juliet Gardiner and Neil Wenborn, published by Collins & Brown 1995 (2015 page 8);

An extract from 'Last of the Free: A History of the Highlands and Islands of Scotland: A Millennial History of the Highlands and Islands of Scotland' by James Hunter, published by Mainstream 1999 © The Random House Group Ltd (2015 page 10);

An extract from 'The Mineworkers' by Robert Duncan, published by Birlinn Ltd., 2005 (2015 page 10);

An extract from 'The Flowers of the Forest: Scotland and the First World War' by Trevor Royle, published by Birlinn Ltd., 2006 (2015 page 12);

An extract from the Glasgow Herald, 1st February 1919 © Herald & Times Group (2015 page 13);

An extract from 'The Wars of Scotland 1214–1371' by Michael Brown, published by Edinburgh University Press, 2004 (2016 page 4);

An extract from 'Kingship and Unity, Scotland 1000–1306' by G.W.S. Barrow, published by Edinburgh University Press, 1981 (2016 page 4);

An extract from 'Scotland from Prehistory to the Present' by Fiona Watson, published by Tempus Publishing/The History Press Ltd, 2001 (2016 page 5);

An extract reproduced with permission of the Marie Stuart Society website (http://www.marie-stuart.co.uk/James%20VI.htm) (2016 page 6);

An extract from 'James VI and the General Assembly' by Alan MacDonald taken from 'The Reign of James VI' by Goodare and Lynch, published by John Donald/Birlinn Ltd., 2010 (2016 page 6);

An extract from 'The Story of the Scottish Reformation' by A.M. Renwick, published by Christian Focus, 2006 (2016 page 7);

An extract from 'A History of Britain: The British Wars 1603–1776' by Simon Schama, published by Miramax, 2001 (2016 page 8);

Two extracts from 'The Union of 1707, Why and How' by Paul Henderson Scott, published by Birlinn Ltd., 2006 (2016 pages 8 & 9);

An extract from 'The Scots in Australia' by Malcolm Prentis, published by UNSW Press, 2008 (2016 page 10);

An extract from 'The Scots Overseas' by Gordon Donaldson, published by Robert Hale Ltd, 1966 (2016 page 10);

An extract from 'To the Ends of the Earth: Scotland's Global Diaspora, 1750–2010' by T.M. Devine, published by Allen Lane/The Penguin Group, 2012 (2016 page 11);

An extract from the diary of Private MacPherson, 9th Royal Scots, 21st July 1916, published by the trustees of the Highland Division (Ross Bequest) Fund (2016 page 12);

An extract from 'Fit for Heroes? Land Settlement in Scotland after World War I' by Leah Leneman, published by Aberdeen University Press, 1989 (2016 page 12);

An extract from 'Fighting and Bleeding for the Land: the Scottish Highlands and the Great War' by Ewan A. Cameron and Iain J.M. Robertson, taken from 'Scotland and the Great War' edited by Catriona M.M. Macdonald & E.W. McFarland, published by Tuckwell Press/Birlinn 1999. Reproduced with permission of Birlinn Limited via PLSclear (2016 page 12);

An extract from 'A History of Scotland' by Neil Oliver, published by Weidenfeld and Nicholson, 2010 (2016 page 13);

An extract from 'Robert Bruce and the Community of The Realm of Scotland' by G.W.S. Barrow, published by Edinburgh University Press, 1988 (2017 page 4);

An extract from 'The Scottish Civil War: The Bruces & the Balliols & the War for Control of Scotland, 1286–1356' by Michael Penman, published by The History Press, 2002 (2017 page 4);

An extract from 'Robert the Bruce' by Caroline Bingham, published by Constable, 1999 (2017 page 4);